Yellowstone
& Grand Teton
NATIONAL PARKS

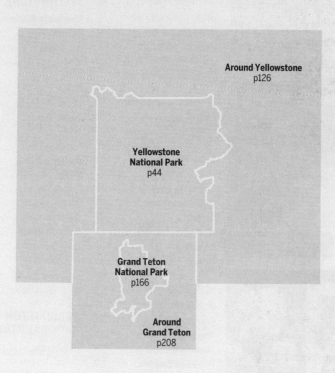

Around Yellowstone
p126

Yellowstone
National Park
p44

Grand Teton
National Park
p166

Around
Grand Teton
p208

THIS EDITION WRITTEN AND RESEARCHED BY

Bradley Mayhew, Carolyn McCarthy

GRAND TETON P189

KAREN DESJARDIN / GETTY IMAGES ©

GENERAL STORE,
GARDINER P148

MATT MUNRO / GETTY IMAGES ©

Contents

UNDERSTAND

SURVIVAL GUIDE

SPECIAL FEATURES

Welcome to Yellowstone & Grand Teton

With its raging geysers and howling wolf packs, Yellowstone stands as one last pocket of a wild, primeval America.

Wild Yellowstone

Yellowstone National Park is the wild, free-flowing, beating heart of the Greater Yellowstone Ecosystem. Its real show-stoppers are the geysers and hot springs – nature's crowd-pleasers – but at every turn this land of fire and brimstone breathes, belches and bubbles like a giant kettle on the boil. The park's highways traverse these geysers, through meadows and forests, past roadside herds of bison and campsites aromatic with pine needles and family campfires. In between lies the country's largest collection of elk, the continent's oldest, largest wild bison herds and a pristine wilderness roamed by wolves, grizzlies, moose and antelope. Yep, it's awesome.

The Tetons' Alpine Splendor

South of Yellowstone is Grand Teton National Park, home to probably the most iconic mountain range in the United States. These showy peaks, reflected in a string of easily accessed glacial lakes, come close to most people's picture-postcard image of alpine splendor and will send a shiver of excitement down the spine of even the least vertically inclined. Buckle up and climb a Teton peak, backpack the Teton Crest and then recover with the sophisticated charms of Jackson Hole. Rarely are the delights of the front- and backcountry so close together.

Beyond the Parks

The natural wonders don't stop at the parks' boundaries. The two parks and their surrounding protected areas form an interconnected area six times the size of Yellowstone and with a fraction of the crowds. Here you'll find blue-ribbon trout streams, fabulous hiking trails (without pesky permits) and a scattering of charming Wild West towns with their gaze set firmly on the great outdoors. Budget some time to get a taste of the West in Cody, try Montana's biggest skiing in Big Sky and drive America's most scenic highway across the Beartooth Plateau.

The Great Outdoors

Mountain bikers, skiers, backpackers, boaters, kayakers and snowmobilers will all find a million adventures waiting in Greater Yellowstone. Inside the parks you'll have to share space with three million visitors a year, but even in summer it's not hard to shake the crowds if you're prepared to get active. Whatever your interests, some experiences are destined to become shared memories – the taste of s'mores over a campfire, wrinkled noses at the smell of sulfurous steam and the electrifying thrill of hearing your first wolf howl. A journey to Yellowstone is not only a great vacation, but also a modern pilgrimage to two of the US' most admirable and enduring national landmarks.

Why I Love Yellowstone & Grand Teton

By Bradley Mayhew, Writer

It is the wildness of Yellowstone that amazes me; the notion that large parts of the park remain unaffected by human interaction. My most profound Yellowstone moment was in this backcountry, transfixed for hours as I watched a pack of wolves try to take down a bull elk. Occasionally the wolves would glance at me as if to suggest that perhaps I would be an easier meal. Only then did I truly realize that I was miles from the trailhead, alone in the wild. That there are places like Yellowstone that still allow for such moments is cause for celebration.

For more about our writers, see p288.

Above: Grand Prismatic Spring (p112)

Yellowstone & Grand Teton National Parks

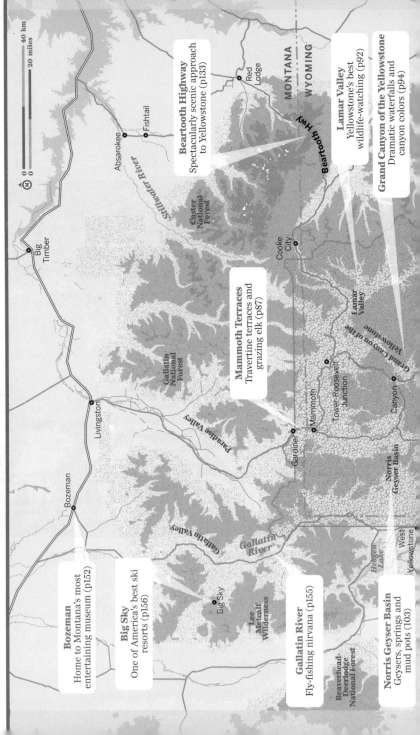

Beartooth Highway
Spectacularly scenic approach to Yellowstone (p133)

Lamar Valley
Yellowstone's best wildlife-watching (p92)

Grand Canyon of the Yellowstone
Dramatic waterfalls and canyon colors (p94)

Mammoth Terraces
Travertine terraces and grazing elk (p87)

Bozeman
Home to Montana's most entertaining museum (p152)

Big Sky
One of America's best ski resorts (p156)

Gallatin River
Fly-fishing nirvana (p155)

Norris Geyser Basin
Geysers, springs and mud pots (103)

MONTANA
WYOMING

Red Lodge

Fishtail

Absarokee

Big Timber

Stillwater River

Custer National Forest

Beartooth Hwy

Cooke City

Gallatin National Forest

Lamar Valley

Grand Canyon of the Yellowstone

Livingston

Paradise Valley

Mammoth

Gardiner

Tower-Roosevelt Junction

Canyon

Bozeman

Gallatin Valley

Norris Geyser Basin

Gallatin River

Big Sky

Lee Metcalf Wilderness

Heben Lake

West Yellowstone

Beaverhead-Deerlodge National Forest

0   20 miles
0   40 km

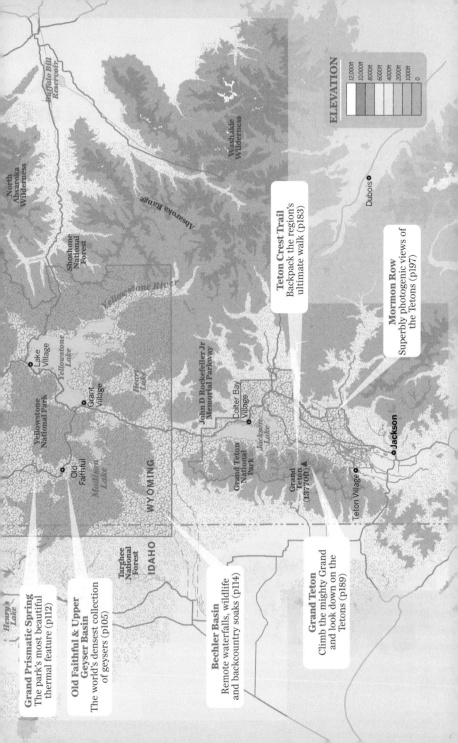

Grand Prismatic Spring
The park's most beautiful thermal feature (p112)

Old Faithful & Upper Geyser Basin
The world's densest collection of geysers (p105)

Bechler Basin
Remote waterfalls, wildlife and backcountry soaks (p114)

Grand Teton
Climb the mighty Grand and look down on the Tetons (p189)

Teton Crest Trail
Backpack the region's ultimate walk (p183)

Mormon Row
Superbly photogenic views of the Tetons (p197)

ELEVATION

12,000ft
10,000ft
8000ft
6000ft
4000ft
2000ft
1000ft
0

Henry's Lake

Buffalo Bill Reservoir

North Absaroka Wilderness

Shoshone National Forest

Absaroka Range

Washakie Wilderness

Dubois

Yellowstone River

Yellowstone National Park

Lake Village

Yellowstone Lake

Grant Village

Heart Lake

Old Faithful

Madison Lake

WYOMING

Targhee National Forest

IDAHO

John D Rockefeller Jr Memorial Parkway

Colter Bay Village

Jackson Lake

Grand Teton National Park

Grand Teton (13,770ft)▲

Jackson

Teton Village

Yellowstone & Grand Teton's
Top 20

1

Wildlife-Spotting in the Lamar Valley

1 Known as the 'Serengeti of North America,' the lush Lamar Valley (p91) is home to the densest collection of big animals in Yellowstone. A dozen pullouts offer superb views over grazing herds of bison and elk, but search the tree lines closely with a spotting scope and you'll likely also see a lone grizzly on the prowl or a pack of wolves on the hunt. Come at dawn or dusk or in the company of a biologist guide, and be prepared to stand transfixed as nature plays itself out before your eyes. Below left: grazing bison

Old Faithful & Upper Geyser Basin

2 The world's most famous geyser (p107) erupts every 90 minutes or so, so you have plenty of time to view it from several angles – from the main boardwalk, from the balcony of the Old Faithful Inn and from Observation Hill. The surrounding geyser basin offers dozens of other spectacular spouters; some that erupt dramatically just once a day, others that thrash continually in a violent rage. Check the visitor center for predicted eruption times and bring a book if you want to catch a biggie such as Beehive or Grand, as it may take a while. Below: Old Faithful geyser (p107)

RALPH LEE HOPKINS / GETTY IMAGES ©

MARC SHANDRO / GETTY IMAGES ©

JEFF DIENER / GETTY IMAGES ©

Paddling the Teton's Alpine Lakes

3 Whether soloing in a kayak or bundling the family into a canoe, paddling (p196) is a great way to glide into nature at your own pace. When your arms tire, shore up on empty beaches for a picnic or a swim. With a permit you can also backcountry camp. Jackson Lake is the Teton's biggest lake; families might prefer the smaller scale of Leigh and String Lakes. For an adventurous multiday alternative in Yellowstone, try gorgeous Shoshone Lake, the region's largest backcountry lake. Above left: Jackson Lake (p190)

Grand Canyon of the Yellowstone

4 The sublime canyon colors and dramatic 308ft drop of the Lower Falls are the big draws of Yellowstone's very own grand canyon (p94). There are several different ways to view the canyon: get close to the drop-off at the Brink of the Lower Falls, take in the big picture at Artist Point or descend steps to feel the spray on your face at Uncle Tom's. Best of all, take the rim's hiking trails to appreciate the views away from the car and the crowds.

Climbing Grand Teton

5 Buck the trend and look down on the Tetons on a guided ascent. The birthplace of American mountaineering, the chiseled and weathered Grand (p189) continues to be among America's premier climbing destinations. The two-day affair starts with a steep 7-mile approach past wildflower fields and waterfalls. Rest up, because a 3am wake-up call heralds summit day, with views of the sprawling wilderness of three states. Climbers need some prior instruction, but it can be gained locally before the climb.

Museum of the Rockies, Bozeman

6 Greater Yellowstone's most entertaining museum (p152) is the perfect combination of fun and learning. Its jaw-dropping dinosaur collection is what really catches the imagination, from the exhibits of sea monsters and fossilized dinosaur nests to the reconstructed Montanoceratops and the world's largest T. rex skull. There's a fine planetarium and the Yellowstone for Kids interactive displays are the perfect place to start or end a park vacation. Budget at least half a day.

GLENN VAN DER KNIJFF / GETTY IMAGES ©

Grand Prismatic Spring

7 Yellowstone's most beautiful thermal feature is this swimming-pool-size hot spring (p112), 10 miles north of Old Faithful. The shimmering waters are impressive enough but it's the surrounding multicolored rings of algae that push it out of this world. As the water temperature changes, so do the colors of the thermophiles, creating a rainbow of oranges, yellows and greens. From above, the spring looks like a giant eye weeping exquisite multicolored tears. For the best overviews, climb the hill behind the springs from the Fairy Falls hike.

Backpacking the Tetons

8 Don't expect any breaks; from the trailhead it's all uphill. But the payback? Rolling glades that are alight with wildflowers, snow-lipped ridges and clear alpine lakes – some of the most luscious, life-affirming scenery in the Tetons lies a day's hike in (p182). And once there, who wants to hurry home? Backpackers can spend a week on the popular Teton Crest Trail, rambling over the lofty spine of the Tetons. The shorter, but still challenging, Alaska Basin has fistfuls of summer blooms and Dall sheep as your companions.

Family Hiking

9 Nature trails, hikes to beaches, lookout points, lakes and geysers... adventure just comes naturally to kids (p39), who will be thrilled by their first sighting of a backcountry bison or belching mud pots. Junior Rangers can earn badges and nature know-how, while Yellowstone's Young Scientist Program ups the ante by helping kids explore the park with a specialized tool kit in hand. Before heading out, know the endurance level of your kids and choose your trail wisely.

Moose Watching

10 Majestic, massive and gawky as overgrown teenagers, moose are a sight to behold. Bulls can weigh twice as much as a Harley-Davidson motorcycle, with massive, cupped antlers, each weighing up to 50lb, which are shed after the fall rut. You'll find moose wherever willows grow, since it's their food of choice. They can also be spotted around lakes and marshes. In the Tetons they're common around Willow Flats and Cottonwood Creek; in Yellowstone look for them in the Bechler region and the Gallatin River drainages.

Skiing Jackson Hole or Big Sky

11 Winter is the perfect time to combine a park visit with some serious mountain fun. The region's downhill action centers on Jackson Hole (p219) in Wyoming and Big Sky (p156) in Montana, two of the continent's best resorts. Jackson Hole offers great runs near Jackson town and airport, whereas Big Sky boasts over 5500 acres of runs and one of the country's best cross-country resorts. Don't limit yourself to skiing, there are dinner sleigh rides and dogsledding in Big Sky, and backcountry yurts and even heli-skiing options in Jackson Hole. Above: Jackson Hole (p219)

Wildflowers

12 Break out the hiking boots in June and you'll discover that the hillsides across the region have quietly exploded with a mosaic of wildflowers. Golden yellow balsamroots, mauve lupines, fire-red paintbrush and pink monkey flowers are just a few of the spectacular blooms competing for your attention in meadows from the Gallatins to the Tetons. Know your blooms and you might spot more wildlife – grizzlies love beargrass, while hummingbirds are drawn to Indian paintbrush. Head to higher elevations in July for even more blooms.

Bechler Basin Waterfalls

13 Hidden in the remote southwest corner of Yellowstone, close to nowhere and accessed by a single bone-crunching dirt road, Bechler (p76) hides the park's most spectacular collection of waterfalls. Union, Dunanda, Colonnade and Cave Falls are the better-known destinations but there are dozens of other thundering falls, feathery cascades and hidden hot springs that entice hardy backpackers and day hikers to brave the fearsome mosquitoes and boggy trails. Come in August and September for the best conditions. Above: Cave Falls (p115)

Mormon Row

14 A favorite of photographers, this gravel strip of old homesteads and wind-thrashed barns backed by the Teton's jagged panorama lies just east of Hwy 191. Sure, you could drive it, but the ultra-scenic and pancake-flat loop makes for one nice bike ride (p186). In the 1890s, early settlers were drawn to this landscape of lush sagebrush for homesteading. The flats are also popular with bison and pronghorn, and the latter have used this corridor for seasonal migrations to the Yukon for over 6000 years.

Mammoth Terraces

15 Northern Yellowstone's major thermal feature is a graceful collection of travertine terraces and cascading hot pools (p87). Some terraces are bone dry, while others sparkle with hundreds of minuscule pools, coral-like formations and a fabulous palette of colors that could come from an impressionist painting. The miniature mountain of thermal action is in constant flux. Get bonus views of several terraces by taking the little-trod Howard Eaton Trail, or ski it in winter, when you'll likely share the terraces with elk.

JIM WEST / ALAMY STOCK PHOTO ©

Backpacking Yellowstone

16 Perhaps the best way to appreciate the park is to pack up your tent and join the mere 1% of visitors who experience the scale and silence of Yellowstone's backcountry (p70). Only when you wander on foot through wolf and grizzly country do you truly sense the primeval wildness of Yellowstone's remoter reaches. Traverse the Gallatin range in the park's northwest, backpack out to Heart Lake or take an adventurous trek through the remote southeastern Thorofare, as far from a road as you can get in the lower 48. Above left: Backpackers on the Heart Lake trail (p72)

Beartooth Highway

17 Depending on who's talking, the Beartooth Hwy (p133) is either the best way to get to Yellowstone, the most exciting motorbike ride in the West or the most scenic highway in the USA. We'd say it is all three. The head-spinning tarmac snakes up the mountainside to deposit you in a different world, high above the tree line, onto a rolling plateau of mountain tundra, alpine lakes and Rocky Mountain goats. The views are superb, the fishing awesome and the hiking literally breathtaking. Top right: View from Beartooth Hwy near Red Lodge (p130)

Yellowstone in Winter

18 Winter is perhaps Yellowstone's most magical season, but come prepared for the serious cold. Geysers turn nearby trees into frozen ice sculptures and the wildlife is easier to spot in the whiteness, including frosty-bearded bison warming themselves by steaming hot springs. Take a snowcoach trip to Canyon, ski past exploding geysers or snowshoe out through the muffled silence to a frozen waterfall, then finish the day sipping hot chocolate in front of a roaring fire at the Old Faithful Snow Lodge.

Norris Geyser Basin

19 Yellowstone's hottest and most active geyser basin and its tallest geyser (in fact the world's tallest, at 400ft) are not at Old Faithful but further north in Norris Geyser Basin (p103). Boardwalks lead around the bone-white plain, past hissing fumaroles, jet-blue pools, colorful runoffs and rare acidic geysers. The Yellowstone hot spot is so close to the surface here that the land actually pulsates. Stay at the nearby campground and you can stroll over from your campsite at sunset while looking out for elk along the Gibbon River.

Fly-Fishing the Gallatin River

20 Montana is sacred ground for fly-fishing enthusiasts, and the region's blue-ribbon streams don't get much better than the Gallatin River (p157), immortalized by Robert Redford in his film *A River Runs Through It*. The region's dozen or so fly-fishing shops are well stocked with lovingly crafted caddis flies and woolly buggers and can fill you in on current best fishing spots, including the nearby Madison, Yellowstone or Firehole Rivers. Most places offer guided trips and some offer casting clinics.

Need to Know

For more information, see Survival Guide (p253)

Entrance Fees
It's $30/25 per vehicle/
motorcycle per park for
seven days, or $50/40
for both parks.

Number of Visitors
Yellowstone: 3.5 million
(2014); Grand Teton: 2.8
million (2014)

Year Founded
Yellowstone: 1872 (the
world's first national
park); Grand Teton: 1929

Money
ATMs at park accom-
modations and general
stores. Cash only for
some campgrounds.

Cell Phones
Coverage good in Grand
Teton, except the can-
yons. Patchy coverage in
Yellowstone outside of
the main junctions; Veri-
zon is the best option.

Driving
Speed limit 45mph,
dropping to 25mph at
junctions. Be particularly
cautious at bearjams.
Parking at popular trail-
heads fills up by 11am in
July and August.

When to Go

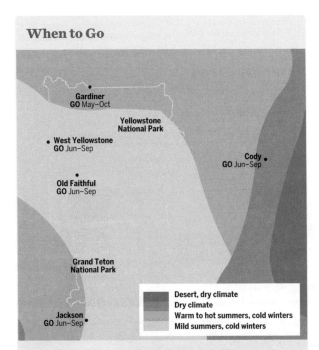

Gardiner
GO May–Oct

Yellowstone National Park

West Yellowstone
GO Jun–Sep

Cody
GO Jun–Sep

Old Faithful
GO Jun–Sep

Grand Teton National Park

Desert, dry climate
Dry climate
Warm to hot summers, cold winters
Mild summers, cold winters

Jackson
GO Jun–Sep

High Season
(Jun–Aug)

➡ Cool nights and
hot days (very hot on
the plains).

➡ Over half the
parks' visitors arrive.
Hotel rates peak
at gateway towns,
park campgrounds
fill by lunchtime and
reservations are
essential.

Shoulder
(May, mid-Sep–Oct)

➡ Cooler months
bring fewer crowds
(and more discounts)
but unpredictable
weather. September
is generally excellent.

➡ Some activities
and campgrounds
close.

➡ Some roads don't
open until the end
of May.

Low Season
(late Dec–Mar)

➡ Only 5% of visitors
see Yellowstone in
winter.

➡ Campgrounds
are closed and
transport is limited
to snowcoaches or
guided snowmobiles
inside Yellowstone,
except for the
northern Mammoth–
Cooke City road.

Useful Websites

Yellowstone National Park (www.nps.gov/yell) Official website.

Grand Teton National Park (www.nps.gov/grte) Official website.

Lonely Planet (www.lonely planet.com) Destination information, hotel bookings, traveler forums and more.

Xanterra (www.yellowstone nationalparklodges.com) Yellowstone lodges, campgrounds and activities.

Grand Teton Lodge Company (www.gtlc.com) Campsites, dining and activities.

Wyoming Tourism (www.wyo mingtourism.org, www.state. wy.us)

Montana Tourism (www.visitmt. com, www.wintermt.com)

Important Numbers

Yellowstone National Park	☑ 307-344-7381
Old Faithful Visitor Center	☑ 307-344-2751
Grand Teton National Park	☑ 307-739-3300
Xanterra reservations	☑ 307-344-7311
Grand Teton Lodge Company	☑ 307-543-3100

Exchange Rates

Australia	A$1	US$0.75
Canada	C$1	US$0.79
euro zone	€1	US$1.10
Japan	¥100	US$0.82
New Zealand	NZ$1	US$0.67
UK	£1	US$1.53

For current exchange rates see www.xe.com.

Daily Costs

Budget: less than $70

➡ Campgrounds: $15–30 per carload, RVs $40–55

➡ Budget hotel outside the park: $90

➡ Backcountry permit: $3 per person per night in Yellowstone

Midrange: $70–170

➡ Rooms in Yellowstone: $100–200, cabins from $85

➡ Restaurant meal: $20–30

➡ Rafting/Wild West cookout for a family of four: $180–210

Top end: over $170

➡ Splurge in Jackson and Jenny Lake

➡ Guided fly-fishing trip per day in a group of two: $250

➡ Winter tour in Yellowstone: per person per day from $300

Opening Dates

Yellowstone National Park

The north entrance at Gardiner is open year-round, as is the northern Gardiner to Cooke City road via Mammoth and Roosevelt. Park roads open in May on a staggered schedule, closing again in early November. Most campgrounds, park services and visitor centers close October to May. See also p124.

Grand Teton National Park

Open year-round, though most of Teton Park Rd is closed to vehicles in winter. Most campgrounds and visitor centers close October to May.

Park Policies & Regulations

Permits Required for all backcountry trips and activities such as boating and fishing.

Swimming Prohibited in waters of purely thermal origin.

Wildlife Keep a minimum of 30yd from bison and elk and 100yd from bears and wolves.

Secure food storage Required in campgrounds and backcountry areas.

Pets Not allowed on boardwalks, backcountry trails or 100ft from a road and must be leashed at all times.

Coping with the Crowds

➡ Get out of the car – you'll lose 95% of tourists simply by walking a mile from the road.

➡ Get your cues from the park animals: get up early, rest at lunchtime and stay out late. Be at the trailhead at 8am for the best light, fewer tourists and more parking spaces.

➡ Get active during the hour just before sunset, when others are rushing back to set up their campsites and the wildlife is back out again. Then eat dinner at 9pm when restaurant tables are wide open.

➡ Roads and geyser basins are busiest between 11am and 3pm.

➡ Head out of the park. While 'the Gallatin National Forest' may not have the same sexy ring as 'Yellowstone National Park,' the hikes are just as superb and you'll have the trails to yourself.

If You Like...

Wildlife

To spot a grizzly, wolf or bighorn sheep you need to know the terrain, the season and the workings of an animal's brain. Then again, you'll probably see bison, elk or even a bear without having to undo your seatbelt.

Lamar and Hayden Valleys Big herds of bison, wolf packs and the occasional grizzly make these Yellowstone's prime animal hangouts. (p92 and p97)

Grizzly & Wolf Discovery Center Didn't see a grizzly or wolf in the park? Don't despair – you're guaranteed an up-close sighting in this nonprofit educational center. (p161)

Guided tour A course with the Yellowstone Institute or a tour with a professional naturalist will really add to your understanding of Yellowstone's complex ecosystem. (p33)

Mustang tour For something a bit different try this day trip to spot wild mustangs cavorting on the high Wyoming desert. (p140)

Thermal Features

For many, Yellowstone's biggest draw is its otherworldly collection of spouters, gushers, bubblers and burpers, which together constitute over three quarters of the world's weirdest thermal features.

Old Faithful The iconic old geyser isn't the biggest or the most beautiful in Yellowstone, but it is impressive and dependable. Try to view it from various angles, including Observation Hill. (p107)

Grand Prismatic Spring Simply put, the park's most beautiful thermal feature, a swimming-pool-size spring ringed by an incredible array of rainbow colors. (p112)

A backcountry geyser There's something really special about watching a geyser away from the crowds of Old Faithful. Hike out to Lone Star or another backcountry geyser for your own private show. (p113)

Mammoth Hot Springs The graceful tiered terraces and colorful coral-like formations have a subtle beauty. (p87)

Steamboat Geyser Check to see what's happening at the world's tallest active geyser, in Norris Geyser Basin. (p103)

Scenic Drives

There's hardly a mile in Yellowstone country that isn't pull-off-the-road, drop-dead gorgeous. These are the ones that make us happy to pay park prices for our gas.

Beartooth Highway An astounding drive above the tree line from Red Lodge to Cooke City, known as the most scenic road in America. (p133)

Gallatin Valley Blending scenes from Robert Redford's *A River Runs Through It* with twin mountain ranges and some lovely ranchlands. (p155)

Paradise Valley Rolling ranchlands and snowy peaks create the perfect approach from Livingston to Yellowstone's north entrance. It's not called Paradise for nothin'. (p146)

Signal Mountain Summit Road Dramatic panoramas over the Snake River to the Tetons, from 800ft above Jackson Hole's valley floor. (p196)

Highway 191 & Teton Park Road More fantastic views of the Tetons from the flats of Jackson Hole Valley, with the chance of spotting pronghorn, deer or moose. (p188)

Backcountry Trips

Yellowstone's wildest corners are as far from a road as you can get in the lower 48. A certain know-how is essential here: you need to know what you are doing if you want to bed down with the grizzlies.

Teton Crest Trail Superlative mountain scenery on this four-day trek along the high spine of the Tetons. (p183)

Gallatin Skyline Yellowstone's northeast corner offers superb backpacking trips over mountain passes to lakes and snowcapped peaks. (p78)

Beartooth Plateau With more than a thousand lakes dotted around this alpine tundra, the Beartooth offers routes from overnighters to a fantastic full traverse. (p134)

Shoshone Lake Yellowstone's largest backcountry lake offers golden lakeshore campsites for a great multiday trek or (even better) paddle. (p73)

Heart Lake Thermal features, a peak ascent and more lakeshore campsites, just a day's walk from the road. (p72)

PLAN YOUR TRIP IF YOU LIKE...

The Good Life

Just because you're in the Wild West doesn't mean you have to rough it all the time. Take a break with the following indulgences.

Couloir Linger over a four-course dinner with wine pairings and gape at the views from Jackson Hole's only mountaintop restaurant, which also offers in-kitchen dining with special pampering from the chef. (p221)

Spring Creek Ranch Resort Snuggle by the fireplace of a luxurious cabin, sink into the spa or order sunset cocktails with screaming Teton views at the Granary restaurant. (p214)

Rainbow Ranch Lodge Share one of the lodge's 5000 bottles of wine in the romantic outdoor Jacuzzi before retiring to the gourmet restaurant or one of the ultra-stylish pondside luxury rooms. (p158)

Top: White-water rafting on the Gallatin River (p157)
Bottom: A grizzly bear at the Grizzly & Wolf Discovery Center (p161)

Chico Hot Springs Go horse riding, get a massage, then soak poolside with a microbrew at this historic resort in the Paradise Valley. (p146)

Winter

Only a fraction of Yellowstone's visitors see the park during its most alluring season. Many repeat visitors rank winter as their favorite season, despite some logistical complications (snowcoaches and skinny skis are the main ways of getting around).

Old Faithful Ski out past frozen ghost trees to frozen waterfalls and exploding geysers, before returning to the Snow Lodge for hot chocolate. (p107)

Big Sky & Jackson Hole Mountain Resort The region's premier downhill runs also offer excellent Nordic trails and dinner sleigh rides. (p219)

West Yellowstone The region's Nordic skiing and snowmobiling capital, West is also the kick-off point for snowcoach tours into Yellowstone Park. (p160)

Canyon yurt camp Take a snowcoach to your own private backcountry yurt and spend a couple of days skiing around the wildlife-rich backcountry. (p86)

Mammoth Take advantage of scheduled ski drops to glide past thermal areas or drive the park's only open road for some winter wolf-watching. (p87)

Learning

The more you learn about the Yellowstone ecosystem, the more interesting it becomes. With courses from wolf-watching to the inner workings of a supervolcano, you'll never look at the land in the same way again.

Yellowstone Institute & Teton Science School Offers a fantastic range of year-round day and weekend courses, from photography to backpacking 101, led by real experts. (p261)

Junior rangers Kids will love earning their ranger badge through parkwide projects and activities. (p40)

Fly-fishing course The photogenic streams of the Yellowstone, Gallatin and Madison are the ideal place to perfect your cast, with a private guide or in a group. (p157)

Kayaking course Several rafting companies in Gardiner and Jackson offer fun kayaking courses on the Yellowstone and Snake Rivers. (p211)

Ranger talks Both Yellowstone and Grand Teton offer excellent free talks, at visitor centers, campgrounds or on ranger hikes. (p45)

The Wild West

Montana and Wyoming still carry the ghosts of the American West. It's the proud home to cowboys, ranches, rodeos and Native American powwows.

Cody Investigate the cabins of Butch and Sundance at Old Trail Town, then saddle up to the bar of Buffalo Bill's Irma Hotel, before dancing up a storm to honkytonk tunes at Cassie's. (p138)

Stay at a dude ranch From sunset trail rides to recuperative spa treatments, nothing creates more memories than staying at a ranch. The best are in the Wapiti and Gallatin Valleys and Jackson Hole. (p260)

Roosevelt Country Ride the rumbleseat on a stagecoach before tucking into steak and beans at the park's favorite cowboy cookout. (p91)

Jackson Rhinestone cowboys, staged shootouts and gourmet chow make Jackson the poster child for Wyoming's New West. (p209)

An Adrenaline Rush

Aside from an unexpected brush with a grizzly, there are plenty of ways to get the pulse racing in the Yellowstone region. Bring a spare pair of underpants.

Climbing Grand Teton A two-day guided climb takes you to the best views in the West and gives you a real sense of achievement. (p182)

White-water rafting From wild rides on the Gallatin and Snake Rivers to family floats on the Yellowstone, these are trips the kids will love. (p211)

Paragliding Jackson Hole Get unrivaled Teton views on a tandem flight from Jackson Hole Mountain Resort. (p219)

Big Sky Ziplines, trampoline bungees and chairlift-assisted mountain-bike runs mean summer now rivals winter at this ski resort. (p156)

Month by Month

March

Mid-March marks the end of the park's winter season, and the snowplows start to clear Yellowstone's roads. Yellowstone's wildlife has the park pretty much to itself.

🏃 Spring Cycling

From the second Monday in March to the third Thursday in April most of Yellowstone's roads are closed to motor traffic, but West Yellowstone to Mammoth road is open to cyclists. There are no facilities and there might be snow, but it's a wonderful opportunity to cycle traffic-free.

April

As Yellowstone starts to shake off winter, the park's roads begin to open, starting with the West Entrance and western sections of the Grand Loop Rd.

🏃 Backcountry Reservations

On April 1 reservations are taken for Yellowstone's backcountry campsites, so if you have a specific time planned for a popular route, make sure your reservations are in by this day.

May

Rain and snowmelt create high rivers and full waterfalls, with snow at higher elevations. Wildlife-viewing is good, with baby elk and bison finding their feet, but many hiking trails are boggy.

🎊 Elkfest Antler Auction

Head to Jackson to kit out your cabin in Rocky Mountain style. In a weekend of activities (www.elkfest.org) a week before Memorial Day, boy scouts collect and sell shed antlers to raise money to buy winter feed for the National Elk Refuge.

🎊 Memorial Day

The last Sunday in May marks the beginning of high season. Park entrances, roads and access routes are now mostly open. The last to open is the road between Tower and Canyon over Dunraven Pass (8859ft) and the Beartooth Hwy, which can be delayed for a week or more by heavy snow.

June

Summer arrives at last, as average highs hit 70°F and wildflowers start to bloom at lower elevations. The last of the park accommodations open by mid-June. Mosquitoes can be bothersome until mid-August.

🎊 Plains Indian Powwow

The region's Native American culture is celebrated in mid-June at Cody's Buffalo Bill Historical Center: dancers, drummers and artisans gather in a colorful celebration of Shoshone and other traditions.

🎊 Rodeo!

Rodeo is the major cultural event of the Yellowstone year. Cody's nightly summer rodeo kicks off June 1, as does Jackson's biweekly version, with more rodeos pulling into Gardiner and West Yellowstone mid-month.

✯ Custer's Last Stand Reenactment

Hundreds of historical re-enactors head to the Battle of Little Bighorn from June 24 to 26 for the anniversary of Custer's Last Stand. Admission to the battlefield is free on the 25th.

July

Temperatures reach 80°F in lower elevations, with Cody and Billings around 10°F (or more) hotter. Afternoon thunderstorms are common but the high country is snow-free, allowing high-altitude wildflowers to bloom. One million people visit Yellowstone Park in July.

✯ Cody Stampede

The July 4 weekend brings crowds to the park and rodeo to the park's gate-ways. The Cody Stampede (www.codystampederodeo. com) is the region's biggest bash but there are also rodeos in Livingston and Red Lodge.

☆ Music Festivals

July is the month for live music. The Grand Teton Music Festival adds some classical class to Teton Vil-lage, the Yellowstone Jazz Festival funks up Cody, while Targhee Fest brings alt-country to Idaho's Teton Valley mid-month.

August

As visitor numbers peak, moose and elk retreat into the backcountry.

August is a prime hiking month, when wildflowers bloom at higher altitudes and huckleberries and chokecherries ripen.

✯ Christmas in August

Stumble into Yellowstone's Old Faithful Inn on August 25 and face the surreal sight of Christmas decora-tions and carol singers. The tradition dates back to the turn of the last century, when a freak August snow-storm stranded a group of visitors in the Upper Geyser Basin.

✯ Smoking Waters Mountain Man Rendezvous

West Yellowstone's moun-tain man rendezvous is a 10-day reenactment of an 1859 gathering and in-cludes tomahawk-throwing competitions, cowboy poetry and black-powder sharpshooting. Red Lodge has a smaller rendezvous at the end of July, as does Jackson in May.

✯ Crow Fair

More than 1000 tepees of the Apsaalooke Nation are erected in the Crow Agency, west of Billings, on the third weekend in August, for the annual Crow Fair (www. crow-nsn.gov). Highlights include dramatic Native American dances, rodeo and plenty of fried tacos.

September

Fall colors, the sounds of bugling elk, lack of mosquitoes and off-

season discounts make September a great month to visit, despite chilly nights. Ranger programs peter out after Labor Day, as park accommodations start to close.

✯ Running of the Sheep

Tiny Reed Point, Montana, hosts the annual 'Running of the Sheep,' an admirably dorky, far less exciting ver-sion of Pamplona's Running of the Bulls. A parade and evening street dance ramp up the Labor Day weekend action.

November

All Yellowstone park roads close on the first Monday in November, except for the Gardiner–Cooke City road. In Grand Teton US 26/89/191 remains open all winter to Flagg Ranch but parts of Teton Park Rd and the Moose–Wilson road close, as does Grassy Lake Rd.

🏃 Yellowstone Ski Festival

Thanksgiving week her-alds the Yellowstone Ski Festival (www.yellow stoneskifestival.com) at West Yellowstone, a great time for ski buffs and newcomers to the sport. Highlights include ski clinics (for kids, too) and gear demos. Nordic skiing kicks off around this time.

Itineraries

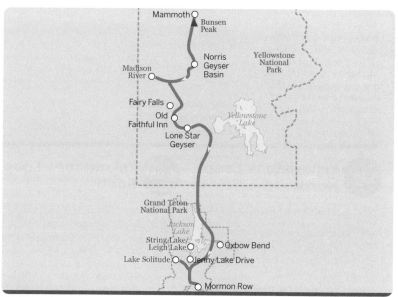

Yellowstone & Grand Teton Overview

Start in **Mammoth**, taking the morning to climb Bunsen Peak for the fantastic views, before paying a brief visit to Mammoth Hot Springs and driving to **Norris Geyser Basin**. Continue to your reserved campsite at Madison for some early evening elk- and bison-spotting or fly-fishing on the **Madison River**.

Spend the next two days in Geyser Country, hiking to either **Fairy Falls** or Sentinel Meadows for backcountry geysers and bison. Stay the night at historic **Old Faithful Inn** to experience the Upper Geyser Basin and the next day cycle out to **Lone Star Geyser** to catch a backcountry eruption.

Drive south into Grand Teton and search for trumpeter swans at **Oxbow Bend**. **Jenny Lake Drive** is worth a linger for its awesome views of the Central Tetons. Enjoy a family trip to forested **String** and **Leigh Lakes** or join the crowds for Grand Teton's most popular day hike up Cascade Canyon to **Lake Solitude**. Finally, cycle around **Mormon Row** for iconic views of barns and bison before heading south to **Jackson** for some R&R.

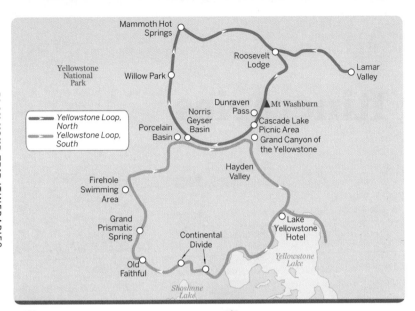

1 DAY Yellowstone Loop, North

This route through the north of the park takes in some premier wildlife-watching, views of the Grand Canyon of the Yellowstone and a sampler of geysers and hot springs. You'll need to start early and stay out late to fit it all in.

Head straight to the **Lamar Valley** around dawn to look for wolves, bears and bison. Grab a 'hiker's breakfast' at **Roosevelt Lodge** then drive up to **Dunraven Pass** to make the three- to four-hour return hike up Mt Washburn for the park's best views. Picnic amid the pines at shady **Cascade Lake** picnic area or grab lunch on the go at Canyon.

Gawp at the thundering falls and rusted colors of the **Grand Canyon of the Yellowstone** from Uncle Tom's Trail and Artist Point on the southern rim, before driving to the geysers and hot springs of **Norris Geyser Basin**. Then swing north toward Mammoth, stopping en route to watch for moose at **Willow Park**. Stroll the boardwalks at dusk to admire surreal Palette Springs and Canary Springs at **Mammoth Hot Springs**, before collapsing in the bar back at Roosevelt Lodge for a well-deserved Old Faithful Ale.

1 DAY Yellowstone Loop, South

The southern loop takes in epic Yellowstone Lake, the park's greatest geysers and a dip in the Firehole River. Starting in West Yellowstone adds 28 miles.

Start the day with a scenic drive around **Yellowstone Lake** and then branch west from West Thumb over the **Continental Divide** into Geyser Country. Check predicted eruption times at the visitor center to catch **Old Faithful** and others of the Upper Geyser Basin spouters. Head north to Midway Geyser Basin and admire **Grand Prismatic Spring**, then blow off steam with the kids in the thermally heated **Firehole Swimming Area** further north.

Continue north to the **Porcelain Basin** hot springs at Norris, grabbing a quick lunch at peaceful Norris Meadows picnic area, before turning east for views of the **Grand Canyon of the Yellowstone** from Uncle Tom's Trail and Artist Point. Swing south through **Hayden Valley** for some prime sunset wildlife-watching before enjoying the park's best food at **Lake Yellowstone Hotel's** dining room.

Above: Schwabacher's Landing (p197)

Right: Boiling River (p90), Mammoth Country

MATT MUNRO / LONELY PLANET ©

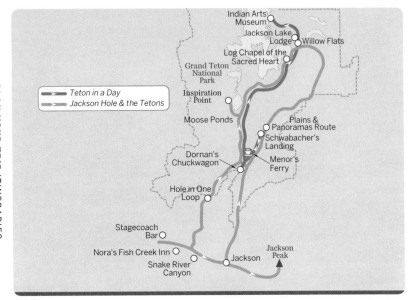

 Teton in a Day
Jackson Hole & the Tetons

Indian Arts Museum
Jackson Lake Lodge
Willow Flats
Log Chapel of the Sacred Heart
Grand Teton National Park
Inspiration Point
Moose Ponds
Plains & Panoramas Route
Schwabacher's Landing
Dornan's Chuckwagon
Menor's Ferry
Hole in One Loop
Stagecoach Bar
Nora's Fish Creek Inn
Snake River Canyon
Jackson
Jackson Peak

1 DAY Teton in a Day

Start with a hearty breakfast in Moose at **Dornan's Chuckwagon**, a pioneer-style camp serving flapjacks alfresco with great Teton views. Then glimpse the area's fascinating homesteading history at **Menor's Ferry**; audio tours are available for mobile phones. For excellent photographs, **Schwabacher's Landing** offers the best panoramas of the Teton's toothy Cathedral group.

Get off the road and into the wilderness with a short hike to the glacial moraines cupping Taggart and Bradley Lakes. Bring swimsuits and take a dip from Taggart's eastern edge if it's warm enough. Afterwards, take the short drive to the **Log Chapel of the Sacred Heart** and spread your blanket for a picnic at the edge of the pines.

Nearby, there's incredible Native American beadwork at the **Indian Arts Museum**. End your outing watching wildlife at **Willow Flats**; there's usually a moose munching in the dusky light. Finally, cap your day at **Jackson Lake Lodge** and down a huckleberry margarita at the Blue Heron.

4 DAYS Jackson Hole & the Tetons

Fuel up with a classic breakfast of pan-fried trout at Wilson's **Nora's Fish Creek Inn**, then saddle your road bike to ride the Hole in One loop – extra points for starting from Wilson. Post-ride, opt for a brew at the award-winning Snake River Brewing Co, in **Jackson**.

On day two, hike out to scenic views at **Inspiration Point** and take the ferry back for an easy return. Detour to **Moose Ponds** to snag a glimpse of its namesake ungulates. For sunset views, rumble your pickup along the dirt roads of the **Plains & Panoramas route**.

On day three, take a white-water rafting trip down the **Snake River Canyon**. Later, treat yourself to a pan-roasted elk chop at Snake River Grill and take in some culture at the modern Center for the Arts, both in Jackson.

On your final day, join the locals powering up **Jackson Peak** for valley views of the Tetons. Make your last night count at the **Stagecoach Bar**, the liveliest roadhouse around.

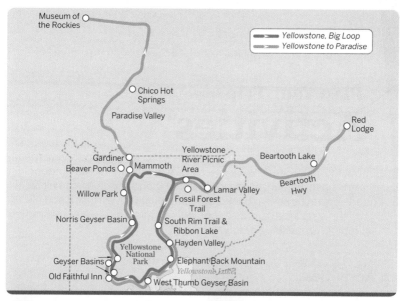

Legend:
- Yellowstone, Big Loop
- Yellowstone to Paradise

Museum of the Rockies · Chico Hot Springs · Paradise Valley · Red Lodge · Gardiner · Beaver Ponds · Mammoth · Yellowstone River Picnic Area · Beartooth Lake · Willow Park · Lamar Valley · Beartooth Hwy · Fossil Forest Trail · Norris Geyser Basin · South Rim Trail & Ribbon Lake · Yellowstone National Park · Hayden Valley · Geyser Basins · Elephant Back Mountain · Yellowstone Lake · Old Faithful Inn · West Thumb Geyser Basin

4 DAYS Yellowstone, Big Loop

From Mammoth head to some early morning wildlife viewing in the **Lamar Valley** before enjoying the crowd-free views of the Narrows on the **Yellowstone River Picnic Area** hike. Continue south to Canyon to take the **South Rim Trail & Ribbon Lake** hike before overnighting in Canyon Village.

The next day try some more early morning wildlife-watching in **Hayden Valley** before continuing south to hike **Elephant Back Mountain** for great views of Yellowstone Lake. After a lakeshore picnic on the sand bars around Gull Point, continue south to the hot springs of **West Thumb Geyser Basin** before heading west across the Continental Divide to overnight at **Old Faithful Inn**.

Spend day three visiting the geyser basins, and the next day drive to Mammoth via **Norris Geyser Basin**, arriving at lunchtime to stroll the travertine terraces at **Mammoth**. Either take a guided walk through historical Fort Yellowstone or a dusk hike to spot wildlife on the **Beaver Ponds** trail.

1 WEEK Yellowstone to Paradise

Add this three-day scenic drive onto the Yellowstone, Big Loop itinerary and you'll get a fantastic week of scenic drives, park highlights and even a trip through Paradise.

From Red Lodge, budget half a day to drive the Beartooth Hwy, stopping to stretch your legs at **Beartooth Lake**. Overnight in Cooke City, then enter the park for some early wildlife-watching in **Lamar Valley** and a hunt for petrified trees on the **Fossil Forest Trail**, before joining the Yellowstone, Big Loop itinerary at Canyon for two days' excursions to **Mammoth**.

Heading north from Mammoth on day six, squeeze in a morning rafting trip or horseback ride from **Gardiner** before continuing north through the lovely **Paradise Valley** to relax with a hot soak and gourmet dinner at **Chico Hot Springs**. Continue to Bozeman on your last day to spend a few hours at the **Museum of the Rockies** and do some last-minute shopping.

Alternatively, spend all your time in the park and throw in some more hiking, preferably the Sepulcher Mountain hike, an overnight hike to Heart Lake or even a three-day canoe trip around Shoshone Lake.

Plan Your Trip
Activities

Ranging from the Tetons' ragged spires to Yellowstone's vast meadows, the Yellowstone wilderness is a playground for the outdoor enthusiast. Fishing, hiking, backpacking and canoeing can all be done against a scenic backdrop containing wolves, bison and elk, and thrill-seekers can raise their pulse while white-water rafting, climbing, paragliding or kayaking.

Top Activities

Hiking
Grand Teton packs mountain drama, while Yellowstone brings hot springs and wildlife. And don't forget the Beartooth Plateau.

Canoeing
Paddle the backcountry waters of Shoshone or Jackson Lakes.

Fishing
Perfect the art of fly-fishing while wading in one of Yellowstone's famous rivers.

Horseback Riding
Cross Yellowstone's sagebrush country as it was meant to be done; on a backcountry horse trip.

Skiing & Snowboarding
World-class resorts at Big Sky and Jackson Hole.

Cross-Country Skiing
Glide through a winter landscape of frozen bison and ghost trees.

Mountain Biking
Downhill thrills and flowy rides at Big Sky or Jackson Hole.

Nature Walks
Stroll with a ranger to score the inside scoop on wildlife.

Summer

Every animal that burrows and snoozes the long winter away snaps to life at the prospect of a Yellowstone summer, and we should be no exception. It's well worth setting aside a night or two in the backcountry; camping equipment is readily available throughout the region. When your hiking legs get tired, saddle up, stargaze or try the region's water sports.

Hiking & Backpacking

A pair of hiking boots opens up Yellowstone, allowing you to escape the crowds, join the wildlife and enjoy abundant alpine vistas, cascading waterfalls and hidden thermal features. Yellowstone National Park boasts over 900 miles of maintained trails, and Grand Teton National Park offers another 200 miles, yet less than 1% of visitors sleep out in the backcountry. Still, popular backcountry campsites fill fast, especially in late summer, so reserve in advance or keep your itinerary flexible. See p70 and p186 for details of backcountry reservations.

Closures & Seasonal Conditions

In Yellowstone, fire outbreaks or bear activity can close trails without warning at any time and there are seasonal restrictions on some trails in early summer. Higher elevation trails may be snow-covered until late July. August and September are the driest months, and May and June are the wettest. Ticks proliferate on low-elevation trails between mid-March and mid-July, so wear insect repellent and long pants. Mosquitoes are most intense in June and July, petering out by mid-August. September is the golden month for hiking.

In Grand Teton National Park, higher elevations often remain snow-covered until late July, and high passes such as Paintbrush Divide and Hurricane Pass remain under snow as late as mid-August. Become familiar with using an ice tool; it may be necessary in early summer.

Permits

Backcountry permits are required for overnight trips in Yellowstone and Grand Teton. These can be acquired at ranger stations and cost $25 per trip in Grand Teton and $3 per night per person in Yellowstone. In Yellowstone, backcountry campers must watch a bear-safety video. Permits can be reserved in early spring, though around 30% are kept for walk-in applications.

Hike Ratings

There are hikes for every ability in Greater Yellowstone. The duration that we list for hikes refers to walking time only and doesn't include breaks. Our trail descriptions follow these guidelines:

Easy Manageable for nearly all walkers, an easy hike is under 4 miles, with fairly even, possibly paved terrain, and no significant elevation gain or loss.

Moderate Fine for fit hikers and active, capable children; moderate hikes have a modest elevation gain.

Difficult For fit and experienced hikers only. Trails might be strenuous, long and even indistinct in places. Expect significant elevation gain, and scrambling may be necessary.

Day Hikes

Almost every part of the Greater Yellowstone region offers outstanding hiking. Don't overlook the longer trails – you can fashion short day hikes by following the first couple of miles of a longer trail.

Park trails are well marked and well maintained, often with restroom facilities at the trailhead. In some forested areas these trails may be marked by a series of blazed trees; in Yellowstone trees bear orange metal tags; on rocky moraines look for cairns. For day hikes in Yellowstone see p48; for Grand Teton see p170.

Overnight Hikes

The wonders and solitude of the remote backcountry make it well worth hauling in overnight gear. Both parks offer backpacking trips for all fitness levels, taking you to remote meadows, mountain crests or backcountry fishing spots.

If you're not used to hiking with a pack, start with one of the easier options (p118). Backcountry campsites, such as those found at Yellowstone's Ribbon Lake or Grand Teton's Leigh and Bearpaw Lakes, are less than a two-hour hike from the trailhead.

Outside the parks, the best backpacking destinations are the Beartooth Plateau (p133) south of Red Lodge, and the Spanish Peaks area (p157) near Bozeman.

Other areas such as the wild Absaroka Range and Yellowstone's remote Thorofare region are untrammeled wilderness adventures best suited to the experienced and well prepared. These remote regions are favored by horse packers, because the distances are large, the terrain rugged and the trails seldom used.

Hunters frequent many areas outside the parks in late September and early

THE CONTINENTAL DIVIDE TRAIL

Extending from New Mexico to Canada, this 3100-mile through trail (CDT; www.cdtrail.org) bisects beautiful sections of the Teton Wilderness and Yellowstone National Park. This section is a great option for hearty hikers who think big, but there are some logistical problems.

Due to snow, this portion of the trail usually opens around July 1. Obtaining backcountry permits for the Yellowstone section can be tricky, as hikers must know their dates and pick up the permit in advance, but rangers are generally understanding. Old Faithful post office will hold resupply boxes for two weeks if they are mailed there with 'CDT' marked on the package. Mail to: 1000 Old Faithful, Yellowstone WY 82190.

If you're thinking of tackling the trail get the *Continental Divide Trail Guidebook Vol 3*, available from the Continental Divide Trail Society (www.cdtsociety.org).

October, so during this time wear orange clothes and expect camping sites to fill up.

Backcountry Safety

Hikers and campers must reckon with Yellowstone's unpredictable weather – you may go to bed under a clear sky and wake up under a foot of snow, even in August. Afternoon weather is particularly volatile in the Tetons, so check the weather forecast and get an early start. By knowing your limitations and the route you plan to take, you can pace yourself accordingly.

Don't rely on your cell phone for emergency contact, because coverage is spotty in the backcountry. However long your trip is, it's important to prepare well, pack bear spray and understand safe backcountry food storage.

The most cautious safety measures suggest never hiking alone. Regardless, always let someone know where you are going and how long you plan to be gone. Use sign-in boards at trailheads or ranger stations where available.

Rock Climbing & Mountaineering

American mountaineering was born in the Tetons when Paul Petzoldt built the country's first guiding school here in 1929. These huge granite faces continue to be among the US's premier climbing destinations. Excellent short routes abound, as well as the classic longer summits like Grand Teton, Mt Moran and Mt Owen, and famous routes such as the Upper Exum Ridge and Owen-Spalding route. The best season for climbing is mid-July through August.

You can get a sense of what it's like climbing the Tetons through the park's new online feature eClimb (www.nps.gov/features/grte/grandteton/eClimb.html).

A prime resource for climbers in the Tetons during summer is the American Alpine Club's Climbers' Ranch (p204). In

---

RESPONSIBLE BACKCOUNTRY USE

Backcountry environments are fragile and cannot support careless activity, especially in the wake of heavy visitation. We recommend following the Leave No Trace principles (www.lnt.org/learn/7-principles).

Hiking

➡ To prevent erosion, always stay on the trail and don't create shortcuts. Staying on muddy trails will prevent damage to the surrounding terrain.

Campsites

➡ Use old campsites instead of clearing new ones.

➡ Camp at least 200ft from the nearest lake, river or stream.

Campfires

➡ If there is already a fire ring, use it. Burn only dead and downed wood.

➡ Build fires at least 9ft from flammable material (including grass and wood).

➡ Watch fires at all times and extinguish them completely.

Water & Toilets

➡ Where no toilet exists, bury human waste in a 6in-deep 'cat hole' at least 300ft from the nearest lake or watercourse.

➡ Pack out toilet paper in a sealed plastic bag.

➡ Avoid soaps and detergents – sand or a kitchen scouring pad clean pots remarkably well. In high-altitude lakes even biodegradable soap may not degrade.

➡ Disperse dishwater far from streams and separate food residue with a small basin or strainer. Put these residuals in the trash – leaving it or dirty dishes might attract bears.

Access

➡ Please do not camp (or collect firewood) on private land without permission, and leave stock gates as you find them.

addition to serving as a hostel for climbers and hikers, the organization's extensive library and knowledgeable staff are excellent resources.

The best ice climbing in the region is found at Hyalite Canyon south of Bozeman and at the South Fork of the Shoshone River, 40 miles southwest of Cody. The season runs from November to April, with the coldest weather offering the best conditions. The Bozeman Ice Festival (www. bozemanicefest.com) in December has climbing clinics for novices.

Recommended Guide Services

The following companies offer guided climbs and courses. For a guided ascent of Grand Teton figure on $750 to $1500, depending on the amount of training and number of days.

Beartooth Mountain Guides (☑406-446-1407; www.beartoothguides.com; 513 N Cooper Ave, Red Lodge) Courses and climbs focused on ice climbing, ski touring and mountaineering, including ascents of Granite Peak, Montana's highest point.

Exum Mountain Guides (p190) The region's oldest climbing school, with guided Teton climbs.

Jackson Hole Mountain Guides (p209) An ideal center for instruction or guided climbs, with kids' programs. A branch office in Cody offers climbing and ice-climbing courses.

Montana Alpine Guides (☑406-586-8430; www.mtalpine.com; Bozeman) Offers rock- and ice-climbing courses, plus guided climbs.

Montana Mountaineering Association (www.montanamountaineering.org; Bozeman) Courses on ice climbing in Hyalite Canyon, plus backcountry skiing and mountaineering.

Cycling
Road Cycling

Road biking is possible from late April to October, when the parks' roads, topping out at 8860ft, are free of snow. Cyclists will find discounted campsites reserved for hikers and cyclists at almost all campgrounds in Yellowstone National Park. Riding can be more diverse and less stressful outside the park, away from the RV parades. Most park roads are rough and narrow and do not have shoulders; expect careless drivers with one eye on a bison and another on a map.

In spring, Yellowstone National Park opens its roads exclusively to cyclists; it's a great time to pedal the park. Still, snowbanks cover many roadsides through till June, making cycling more challenging. Bicycle repairs and parts are not available inside the park; it's typically 20 to 30 miles between services.

In Grand Teton National Park, implementation has begun of a multi-use pathway totaling 41 miles along Teton Park Rd. The section between Moose and Jenny Lake (7.6 miles) has been completed and should soon connect with Jackson.

Cycling Tours

Old Faithful Cycle Tour (p162) This annual trip in fall, organized by the Chamber of Commerce in West Yellowstone, offers a van-supported ride to Old Faithful.

Teton Mountain Bike Tours (☑307-733-0712; www.tetonmtbike.com; Jackson) Family-friendly guided mountain-bike tours of Grand Teton and Yellowstone. Half-day tours cost around $70 and include transportation, bike hire and helmet.

Mountain Biking

The best bike trip inside the parks is the climb to the summit of Mt Washburn in Yellowstone. Outside the parks Bozeman and Jackson are the main mountain bike hubs and nearby ski resorts offer lift-serviced downhill trails for the experienced. West Yellowstone's Rendezvous Ski Trails (p163) become a great summer ride for all abilities.

There is also good single track in the Gallatin Range, accessible from near Big Sky. Beartooth Publishing's *Bozeman, Big Sky, West Yellowstone* map details 14 mountain bike routes in the region. Be sure to yield to hikers and horses on shared trails.

Regulations

In the national parks, cyclists may ride on all public roads and a few designated service roads but aren't allowed on any trails or in backcountry areas. Bikes are restricted from entering designated wilderness areas, but may otherwise ride on national forest trails and roads. Trail etiquette requires that cyclists yield to other users.

Wildlife Tours

These worthwhile outings can provide much insight into the inner workings of the parks and their inhabitants. Start with naturalist-guided trips and courses from the Yellowstone Institute (p261) or

Teton Science School (☎888-945-3567, 307-733-2623; www.wildlifeexpeditions.org; Jackson).

There are a number of outstanding smaller outfits.

Grub Steak Expeditions (www.tourtoyellowstone.com) Cody-based company established by a former park ranger.

Safari Yellowstone (☎800-723-2747; www.safariyellowstone.com) Private tours, based in Livingston.

Wild Side (☎406-223-2152; www.wolftracker.com) Biologist-led guided wolf-watching and supported spring and fall treks, based in Gardiner.

Yellowstone Safari Company (☎866-586-1155; www.yellowstonesafari.com) Biologist-led trips and llama treks, based in Bozeman.

Horseback Riding & Pack Trips

Yellowstone's sagebrush country was built to be crossed on horseback. If you're eager to break in your Wranglers on a saddle, you'll find a wide range of options available throughout the region, from two-hour rides to multiday pack adventures. Guest ranches in the Wapiti, Gallatin and Paradise Valleys offer the most authentic rides and most are open to nonguests.

In Yellowstone Park there are corrals at Roosevelt and Canyon Junction. Grand Teton has rides from Jackson Lake Lodge and Colter Bay.

Check out the Dude Ranchers' Association (www.duderanch.org) for helpful information and links.

Rafting

Cold water, adrenaline and stunning scenery make rafting a prime summer draw. It's a great group activity; teens in particular will be ever grateful for trading in the minivan for a splashier ride. Commercial outfitters throughout the region offer options ranging from inexpensive half-day trips to overnight and multiday expeditions, plus combos featuring other activities.

Paddlers can choose from large rafts for 12 or more people, or smaller rafts for six; pick the latter if you prefer paddling, otherwise your full-time job will be 'holding on.' Half-day trips run around $40 per person and many operations offer activity combos that include horse riding or ziplining.

White-water trips are not without risk. It's not unusual for participants to fall out of the raft in rough water, although serious injuries are rare and the vast majority of trips are without incident. All trip participants are required to wear life jackets, and even nonswimmers are welcome. All guides are trained in lifesaving techniques.

River classifications vary over the course of the year, depending on the water level. Higher water levels, usually associated with spring runoff, make a river trip more challenging until late June.

Best Rafting Destinations

➡ Yellowstone River: the USA's longest free-flowing river flows through Yankee Jim Canyon and the Paradise Valley from Gardiner.

➡ Gallatin River: exciting trips through the 'Mad Mile' start near Big Sky.

➡ Snake River: has white-water trips south of Jackson.

➡ Wildlife-watching: float trips go down the Snake through Grand Teton National Park.

➡ Shoshone River: west of Cody, it flows through the scenic Absaroka Range.

Canoeing & Kayaking

Exploring the wilderness on water shows the breadth of beauty and solitude beyond the roads. Yellowstone offers exciting opportunities for paddlers: families can take a load off little legs and cool off, while romantics can paddle up to hidden camps on remote beaches.

One stunning destination is the pine-rimmed Shoshone Lake, the largest backcountry lake in the lower 48. It's popular with boaters who arrive via the Lewis River Channel and are headed for the remote Shoshone Geyser Basin. Vast Yellowstone Lake offers access to the most remote reaches of the park but is a serious endeavor; Bridge Bay Marina offers boat shuttles to get you started. For an easier paddle consider a sea kayak tour of West Thumb Geyser Basin from Grant Village.

Grand Teton's Jackson Lake offers scenic backcountry paddling, with several islands to explore and hiking in the little-visited northwest corner. Novice and family paddlers favor String and Leigh Lakes, and Lewis Lake in Yellowstone. The wildlife-watching is superlative on Two Ocean Lake.

Above: Horseback riding in Grand Teton National Park (p189)

Right: Snowmobiling in West Yellowstone (p163)

PER BREIEHAGEN / GETTY IMAGES ©

At Colter Bay in Grand Teton you can rent canoes, but they can't go far because trips are limited to the bay. For a longer trip, it's best to rent from an outdoor shop such as Adventure Sports (p257) at Moose.

Kayakers can paddle the Snake River, with sections appropriate for a range of abilities and top-notch wildlife-watching. Kayak rentals and instruction are available in Jackson and Colter Bay in the Tetons, as well as in Gardiner, Cody and Big Sky.

Fishing

Boasting some of the country's best rivers, Greater Yellowstone has elevated fly-fishing to more of a religion than a sport, particularly in Montana, where Robert Redford's *A River Runs Through It* was filmed.

Yellowstone offers more than 400 fishable waters with cutthroat, rainbow, brown, brook and lake (Mackinaw) trout; Arctic grayling; and mountain whitefish. Fishing season runs from Memorial Day weekend to the first Sunday in November, except on Yellowstone Lake, which opens June 15. Catch and release is standard in many areas.

The park's best fishing streams are the Gibbon, Madison and Yellowstone Rivers, though you can't really go wrong anywhere. Slough Creek has gained a reputation as angling heaven. The Madison, Gibbon and Firehole Rivers in Yellowstone are fly-fishing only.

In Grand Teton National Park, Leigh and Jenny Lakes are stocked with lake, brown, brook and Snake River cutthroat trout. One of the best fishing spots is on the Snake River just below the Jackson Lake dam (with parking on both sides of the river). Ice fishing is growing in popularity, although spring and fall offer the best fishing.

Outside the parks, the Gallatin, Yellowstone and Snake Rivers all offer stellar fishing and all gateway towns have expert fishing shops that offer equipment and guided trips to the region's prime fishing areas. Hit them up for tips on where to fish and what flies to pack.

If you are keen to learn a bit more about fly-fishing consider a half- or full-day class at Bozeman Angler (p152), in Bozeman, or Yellowstone Fly Fishing School (p145) in Livingston.

Newbies can also check out the free casting clinics at Jacklins Fly Shop (p162) in West Yellowstone every summer Sunday evening.

Fishing Licenses

A Yellowstone National Park fishing permit is required to fish in the park. Anglers 16 years and older must purchase a $18 three-day permit, a $20 seven-day permit or a $40 season permit. To fish in Grand Teton National Park, only a Wyoming fishing license is required (with a $12.50 conservation stamp for all but one-day licenses).

Outside of the two parks, Wyoming generally offers fishing all year round. Fishing licenses are purchased according to whether you want them for daily (nonresident/resident $14/6) or yearly (nonresident/resident $92/24) use. For details and to buy online contact the **Wyoming Game & Fish Department** (☑307-777-4600; http://gf.state.wy.us).

In Montana, anglers must have a conservation license (nonresident/resident $10/8) in addition to a fishing license. A seasonal license (nonresident/resident $60/18) is good for one year; a two/10-day stamp costs $15/43.50 for nonresidents. For information and an online application visit **Montana Fish, Wildlife & Parks** (☑406-994-4042; http://fwp.mt.gov/fishing).

Winter

While Yellowstone's bears snore away in hibernation and bison huddle in frosted masses, the skiing, snowshoeing and wildlife-watching options are excellent. Though it's an increasingly popular season, winter still only attracts a fraction of summer's visitor numbers, giving you lots of space to spread out in. Winter sports are a goer from the end of November to April, though February and March generally offer the best snow conditions. In Yellowstone and Grand Teton National Parks, winter activities include cross-country skiing, backcountry skiing, skate skiing (with short skis on groomed hardpack trails), snowshoeing and snowmobiling. One useful resource is the Montana Winter Guide (www.wintermt.com). For details on Yellowstone's winter facilities, see p86.

Downhill Skiing & Snowboarding

Impressive snowfalls and wild and lovely terrain make the northern Rockies a premier downhill destination. Most resorts offer a range of winter activities from snowshoeing to sleigh dinner rides, as well as top-notch ski and snowboard instruction. Cheaper packages are offered in the more precarious early season between November and early December, or the late season from March to April, when the skiing is usually quite good.

The region's premier resorts:

Jackson Hole Mountain Resort (p219) Offers world-class terrain and heart-thumping views.

Big Sky (p156) Boasting vast terrain, Montana's premier resort.

Grand Targhee (p223) Family friendly and famed for deep champagne powder.

Snow King Resort (p211) A mini-resort with tubing and night skiing in downtown Jackson.

Red Lodge Mountain (p131) Thoroughly local, but with expanding terrain, a snowboard park and no lift queues.

Cross-Country & Backcountry Skiing

Nothing approximates heaven more than gliding through snow-covered wilderness under a sharp, blue sky. Nordic (or cross-country) skiing offers a great workout in stunning settings, and saves bucks on lift tickets. The national park and forest services maintain summer hiking trails as cross-country trails during winter, offering terrific solitude and wildlife-watching opportunities.

In late November, the West Yellowstone Ski Festival brings Nordic skiers from around the world and offers demos and clinics. Many resorts offer free trail passes and rentals on Winter Trails Day (www.wintertrails.org) in January. Lone Mountain Ranch (p156) at Big Sky offers rentals and lessons for just $5 on that day.

Backcountry skiing takes skiers to more difficult terrain than regular Nordic gear can handle. The equipment – either telemark (single-camber skis with edges and free-heel bindings) or rondonee (an alpine hybrid system allowing for free-heeled ascents), fitted with climbing skins for ascents – allows skiers to travel cross-country and down steep slopes, though telemark is much better suited to cross-country terrain. Newcomers to the sport should take a lesson (available at most ski resorts) and get in some resort runs before tackling the backcountry. In addition,

backcountry skiers must be well versed in avalanche safety.

Experienced backcountry skiers will want to check out Hellroaring Ski Adventures (p163) in West Yellowstone, Teton Backcountry Guides (p192) in the Tetons, and Beartooth Powder Guides (p137) in Cooke City.

Dedicated Trails

In Yellowstone, shuttles offer ski drops in Mammoth and Old Faithful. Stay off the groomed roads meant for motorized travel. Otherwise, skiers will find ungroomed backcountry trails with orange markers.

Grand Teton National Park grooms 14 scenic miles of track between Taggart-Bradley Lakes parking area and Signal Mountain. Trails are usually marked with orange flags. Backcountry skiers must take more precautions: avalanches are a major hazard in the canyons and upper areas of the Tetons.

For details of trails in Yellowstone see p85; for Grand Teton see p192.

The Best Nordic Trails

➡ The Rendezvous Trail System (p163) in West Yellowstone (the winter training ground for the US Nordic team).

➡ A snowcoach takes you to the Old Faithful Snow Lodge for skiing around the geyser basins, or around the Grand Canyon of the Yellowstone.

➡ Near West Yellowstone, the Fawn and Bighorn Pass Trails connect to form a loop of around 10 miles through elk wintering areas.

➡ Lone Mountain Ranch (p156) at Big Sky has almost 50 miles of privately groomed trails.

➡ Red Lodge Nordic Center (p131) has 9 miles of trails.

➡ Trails around Indian Creek or along the Northern Range of the Mammoth–Cooke City Rd.

Snowshoeing

In Yellowstone and elsewhere you can generally snowshoe anywhere – the problem is getting to the trailhead. Try not to mark groomed cross-country trails with your snowshoes, though; stay a few paces from any groomed areas. You can access trails from the Mammoth–Cooke City road all winter, and ski shuttles run to snowbound parts of the park from Mammoth and Old Faithful. Most hotels and gateway towns rent snowshoes. Rangers lead snowshoe hikes from West Yellowstone's Riverside trail (BYO snowshoes) and Grand Teton's Discovery Center (snowshoes provided). Lone Mountain Ranch at Big Sky has exclusive snowshoe trails.

Snowmobiling

The park service enforces a daily cap of snowmobiles in Yellowstone National Park, and they must be accompanied by a guide. In Grand Teton, snowmobiling is allowed only on the frozen surface of Jackson Lake. A good alternative is found in the surrounding national forests, which offer hundreds of miles of trails.

Snowmobile policies are under constant revision; check with the parks for updates. Yellowstone's snowmobile travel season runs from late December to early March. Book trips a week or two in advance because spaces are limited. All roads except for the North Entrance through to the Northeast Entrance (open only to wheeled vehicles) are groomed for oversnow vehicles. The road from the West Entrance to Madison to Old Faithful is shared with cross-country skiers; ride with caution.

All snowmobiles in both parks must meet best available technology (BAT) standards. Speed limits are generally 45mph. Snowmobiles are not allowed in any wilderness areas. If you are new to snowmobiling, bear in mind that it's much more comfortable to ride solo than to double up. When renting, check the cost of clothing rental and insurance, and whether the first tank of gas is free. Backrests and heated handgrips are desirable extras.

Outside the Parks

West Yellowstone is the 'snowmobile capital of the world.' Here you can legally drive snowmobiles in town and attend March's World Snowmobile Expo (www.snowmobileexpo.com). There are over 1000 miles of snowmobile trails between West Yellowstone and Idaho's Targhee National Forest. One is the popular 34-mile Two Top Mountain Loop, the country's first National Recreational Snowmobile Trail.

Flagg Ranch Resort is the southern snowmobiling gateway to Yellowstone (for commercial tours only).

Cooke City is another regional hub for snowmobiling activity, either in the backcountry or along the Beartooth Hwy.

Snowcoach Tours

Converted vans on snow tracks, snowcoaches provide transportation in and around the park in winter, also providing a useful service for skiers. Snowcoach tours depart daily from West Yellowstone, Flagg Ranch Resort and Mammoth; most stop at Old Faithful and all stop for wildlife-watching opportunities. Xanterra (p82) operates park-based tours.

Dogsledding

If you have always wanted to travel by paw power, you can try the several companies that offer day and half-day trips in national forest areas.

Absaroka Dogsled Treks (p146) Day trips and a musher's school at Chico Hot Springs.

Continental Divide Dogsled Adventures (p211) Jackson-based operation that runs day trips or overnight trips in yurts (Central Asian–style circular tents).

Spirit of the North (☏406-682-7994; www.huskypower.com) Half-day adventures around Big Sky.

Travel with Children

If Yellowstone's wonderland of spurting geysers, gurgling mud pots and baby bison turns adults into kids, then imagine its impact on young ones. Just sharing these moments will create priceless family memories. Plus, for your kids, a visit to the parks may just kick-start a lifelong love of nature and the outdoors.

Yellowstone & Grand Teton for Kids

The national parks are as kid-friendly as a destination gets, but the wilderness must be treated with respect. The National Park Service (NPS) looks after its young visitors well, with fun outings, education programs and kid-focused presentations. Children under 12 years stay free in park accommodations and most restaurants offer kid menus. Activities ranging from horseback riding to white-water rafting offer a shared thrill for all the family.

On the Trail

Consider the following before heading out on a hike:

➡ Pick a route that offers an easy out. Just in case.

➡ A cool destination, such as a lake or falls, offers extra incentive.

➡ Choosing a shorter route gives kids a chance to slow down and explore. Let kids set the pace.

➡ A scavenger hunt list, made from features described in hike descriptions, can help keep their attention.

➡ Outfitting kids with a mini backpack, a small hiking stick or camera helps them feel part of the expedition.

Best Regions

Almost every part of Greater Yellowstone has something to offer families. A visit here is a US rite of passage.

Yellowstone National Park

The main attractions: bison spotting, ranger programs, campfires and ice cream, plus belching mud pots. (p44)

Grand Teton National Park

Paddling and beaches at String Lake, bike rides, ranger programs and a chuckwagon at Dornan's. (p166)

Jackson

Lots of teenage adrenaline fun, with alpine rides, rafting trips, climbing walls, kayak courses, and a staged shootout for the younger ones. (p209)

West Yellowstone

A high ropes course for the rambunctious; guaranteed grizzly spotting and family-orientated slapstick at the Playmill Theater. (p160)

Cody

A Wild-West flavor, with kids calf-roping at the night rodeo, a museum for all the family and an afternoon shootout at the Irma. (p138)

National Parks Programs

Take advantage of Yellowstone's ranger-led activities, many of which are aimed at families. Several campgrounds run family-oriented campfire programs with lectures or live music in the early evenings and there are hikes to family-friendly destinations including Storm Point and Wraith Falls. See the park newspapers for details. Grand Teton's campfire program is based in Colter Bay.

Kids can earn a very cool badge through the **Junior Ranger Program** (www.nps.gov/yell/forkids/beajuniorranger.htm; booklet $3; ⊙Jun-Labor Day), an iconic and worthwhile program. Tasks include completing an activity book with questions and games, attending a ranger talk and doing a hike. The program can be completed in two days and is aimed at five- to 12-year-olds (although adults can enjoy it too). Madison's Junior Ranger Station offers kid-related activities all day.

Grand Teton's Grand Adventure Program (www.nps.gov/grte/forkids/index.htm; donation $1) also trains Junior Rangers; inquire about it at any visitor center.

Junior Rangers and their families can participate in Yellowstone Wildlife Olympics, a field day with physical challenges that pit your abilities against those of notable wildlife (no pronghorn are injured in the making of this game). This three-hour activity is held at different visitor centers three times a week at noon; see the park newspaper for details.

Yellowstone also operates the Young Scientist Program (www.nps.gov/yell/forteachers/youngscientist.htm; booklet $5), which lets kids investigate the mysteries of the park with a special toolkit in hand, completing tasks for a coveted patch or keychain. It's for ages five and up.

At the in-depth program Expedition: Yellowstone! (lodging/instruction per day $35/60) kids learn about preservation, the park's natural and cultural history and current issues affecting the Greater Yellowstone Ecosystem. It includes hikes, field investigations, discussions, creative dramatics and journal writing. This four- to five-day curriculum-based residential program is for students in grades four to eight. Badger your teachers to arrange a visit; parents can come along as chaperones. It's based at Lamar's Buffalo Ranch or Mammoth.

Private Programs

Inside the parks, concessionaires and nonprofits run a range of family-friendly activities. Two-hour stagecoach rides from Roosevelt Lodge travel the sagebrush flats. Trips go several times per day and run from early June to August.

For more in-depth experiences, the **Yellowstone Association** (☑307-344-2289; www.yellowstoneassociation.org) offers a range of excellent year-round family programs. The most popular is Yellowstone for Families, where a qualified naturalist takes families (with children aged from eight to 12 years) animal tracking, exploring and wildlife-watching in the park. Other fun stuff includes painting at Artist Point and taking wildlife photos.

PLAY, LEARN & PLAN ONLINE

If your kids really won't be pried away from their iPads, then get them in the mood for the parks with these online games and interactive activities.

➡ Test sleuthing skills and try park puzzles at www.nps.gov/webrangers.

➡ Teens can travel on award-winning electronic field trips at www.windowsintowonderland.org.

➡ Scavenge for clues about Yellowstone's explosive past or play with jackelopes at the official Yellowstone site: www.nps.gov/yell/forkids/index.htm.

➡ Find the mystery animal or take the first steps toward the Junior Ranger badge at the official Grand Teton site: www.nps.gov/grte/forkids/index.htm.

➡ Identify animal tracks and make electronic field trips at www.nps.gov/grte/learn/kidsyouth/parkfun.htm.

➡ Explore more Junior Ranger fun at www.discovergrandteton.org/junior-rangers.

KEEPING IT SAFE

➡ Use a checklist for hiking supplies, including water, sunscreen and first aid.

➡ Kids should carry a flashlight and whistle, and know what to do if they get lost.

➡ Keep children within sight on the trail.

➡ Be especially careful roadside when everyone's eyes are on the bison, not the traffic.

➡ Scenic overlooks with sheer drops require extra attention, especially at the Grand Canyon of the Yellowstone.

➡ Caution kids about thermal areas before visiting them.

➡ A pre-trip practice outing helps kids know what to bring and expect.

➡ Let kids know the proper way to handle an animal encounter.

➡ Introduce them to Leave No Trace ethics (see also p32).

Children's Highlights
Adventure

Fishing (p152) Cast for cutthroat trout in a pristine mountain lake or river, or take a class.

Grazing elk, Mammoth (p87) Families of elk chew nonchalantly on park lawns every day.

Rafting (p211) White water or scenic floats on the Snake, Yellowstone or Gallatin Rivers.

Horseback riding (p260) Mosey through the open range at a dude ranch (kids eight years old and up).

Paddling, String Lake (p196) Rent a canoe or kayak in Grand Teton National Park.

Snow King Resort (p211) Ziplines, alpine slides and a new coaster ride in summer or tubing and boarding in winter.

Multi-use path, Jackson Hole (p186) Cycle a paved pathway through Grand Teton National Park.

Wilderness Adventures (☑307-733-2122; www.wildernessadventures.com) Operates multisport trips for teens.

High ropes (p162) Tarzan swings and ziplines at ropes courses in Jackson, Gardiner or West Yellowstone.

Yellowstone Hikes

Most kids will enjoy the following hikes (and rides) for little legs; all are within 2 miles of a road. Rangers lead hikes on several of these routes.

Wraith Falls (p89) A 79ft cascade on the Mammoth to Tower–Roosevelt road.

Trout Lake (p91) Easy fishing destination in the park's northeast corner.

Pelican Creek Bridge (p101) A fantastic nature trail to a beach on Yellowstone Lake.

Natural Bridge Trail (p80) Pedal an old stage-coach road to a 50ft rock bridge.

Mystic Falls (p65) Geysers and hot springs to explore in Biscuit Basin.

Artist Paint Pots (p104) Belching and farting mud pots near Norris Junction.

Storm Point Trail (p102) Bison, moose and marmots north of Lake Yellowstone.

Entertainment

Night rodeo, Cody (p143) Kids love the calf-roping and staged gunfights. Also in Jackson.

Museum of the Rockies (p152) Huge dinosaur skeletons and an interactive Yellowstone for Kids exhibit.

National Museum of Wildlife Art (p209) Make your own art at this studio.

Grizzly & Wolf Discovery Center (p161) Try out zookeeper duties and help feed the grizzlies.

Chico Hot Springs (p146) Splash about in a spring-fed pool, or go alfresco at Yellowstone Park's Boiling and Firehole Rivers.

Dining

Chuckwagon dinners Oversize grills and steaming cast-iron cauldrons.

Camping Toasting marshmallows under a canopy of stars.

Picnics Yellowstone has great picnic areas, many of them riverside or lakeshore.

Red Box Car (p132) Burgers and shakes from a defunct train car.

Running Bear Pancake House (p165) Short stack pancakes.

Pioneer Grill (p205) Hot fudge sundaes at a classic diner.

Montana Candy Emporium (p132) Sweet-tooth heaven.

Rainy Day Refuges

Climbing walls Indoor fun in Jackson, Bozeman and Cody.

Buffalo Bill Center of the West (p139) Kids' workshops and interactive exhibits.

Yellowstone Giant Screen Theater (p165) Yellowstone IMAX-size.

Old Faithful Visitor Center (p265) Aimed at kids.

Coolest Camps

Most ski resorts also offer daycare or camp outings.

Field Learning (www.tetonscience.org) Runs GPS scavenger hunts and ecology expeditions. The Teton Science School offers outstanding programs for small fries, high schoolers and families.

Mini Mountaineers (www.jhmg.com/school/kids/index.php) The Kids Rock program offers kids six to 10 years old a chance to get vertical (with parents in tow) in a safe and fun outing run by mountain pros. Teens can choose programs that expand on climbing technique and teamwork. Most kids' fave? Tramping through snowfields in summer.

Rock Star Treatment (www.jhrocknrollcamp.com) Rock & Roll camp means jamming in day or over-night programs under the tutelage of a professional musician. Budding Claptons and the like must have a year's instrument instruction under their belts. The camp culminates in a live performance.

Playmill Theater (p165) Offers a four-day summer theater camp for children aged 14 to 18.

Planning

What to Pack

Kids should have comfortable outdoor clothing, a bathing suit, sunhat, a shell jacket and warm clothing for chilly days and nights. If you are picky about your bug spray, it's best to bring it from home. Before your trip, make sure everyone has adequate hiking shoes – this could be any-thing from sneakers to waterproof boots, depending on the range of terrain you'll cover; just make sure they are broken in. Sandals or Crocs can also be useful for around camp. A cheap digital camera or pair of binoculars can provide lots of enter-tainment since there's so much wildlife to

watch. Bring your own marshmallows and toasting sticks.

Most car-rental agencies can add a child's car seat for a nominal fee. Strollers may be harder to come by, so it is best to take yours with you. Baby backpacks are especially handy for getting beyond the boardwalk and onto the trails.

Most bike rental places offer children's bikes and even trailers or tandem bikes.

Before You Go

Keep the kids in mind as you plan your itinerary or include them in the trip plan-ning from the get-go. If they have a stake in the plan, they will be more interested when they arrive, or so the theory goes. Lonely Planet's *Travel with Children,* by Cathy Lanigan, provides good information, advice and anecdotes.

If you decide to book a Yellowstone As-sociation program or popular park activity like a Yellowstone stagecoach ride be sure to do so months in advance. A few ranger programs only admit limited numbers, so it's always a good idea to show up early.

Catering to Teens

The Tetons and Yellowstone offer tons of things for teens to do. If your teens do not have much outdoor experience, it may be wise to enroll them in a course. Bike rent-als are available in all gateway towns and Old Faithful. Climbing gyms usually have short beginner courses appropriate for teens, ski resorts often have mountain bik-ing or alpine slide options, and a few places have day-long kayaking courses. Readers suggest white-water rafting and swimming as perfect activities – there are plenty of alpine lakes that become divine retreats when the temperatures soar. Teens of every skill level can have a blast exploring ski and snowboard runs at area resorts. Most hikes are appropriate for fit teens.

At Yellowstone National Park, the Youth Conservation Corps (www.nps.gov/yell/parkmgmt/yccjobs.htm) offers teens month-long summer jobs in the park, with training in conservation and trail rehabili-tation. Weekend activities include hiking, rafting, fishing and assisting scientists or field rangers. The program offers a couple of month-long sessions in a residential setting for young people between the ages of 15 and 18 years. Only 60 spots are avail-able, chosen from a random draw. Enroll-ment is six months prior to summer.

On the Road

Yellowstone National Park

Best Hikes

➜ Mt Washburn (p61)

➜ Bunsen Peak (p50)

➜ Yellowstone River Picnic Area Trail (p55)

➜ Beaver Ponds Trail (p49)

➜ Sepulcher Mountain (p53)

Best Places to Stay & Eat

➜ Old Faithful Inn (p120)

➜ Lake Yellowstone Hotel (p119)

➜ Backcountry campsites (p70)

➜ Mammoth Hot Springs Dining Room (p121)

➜ Lake Yellowstone Hotel Dining Room (p123)

Why Go?

Yellowstone National Park is the crown jewel of the Greater Yellowstone Ecosystem. From the steaming geysers and sublime lakes of the south to the golden canyons and wildlife-rich valleys of the north, the park has several distinct regions and you need to visit several to get a sense of the park's complex diversity.

Yellowstone's roadside sights are the crowd-pleasers, but the park's real joys only reveal themselves at the end of a backcountry hiking or fishing trail, so try to fit in at least a couple of our hikes. From golden lakeshore sunsets to dawn mists rising over a steaming geyser basin, Yellowstone's beauty is both spectacular and subtle.

Our advice is not to try to pack everything into one visit. The crowds and traffic seem twice as bad if you're in a rush, and you'll appreciate some extra time if you have a surprise encounter with a moose or bison.

Road Distances (miles)

	Mammoth	Old Faithful	Grant Village	Canyon Village
Old Faithful	50			
Grant Village	70	20		
Canyon Village	30	40	35	
Lake Village	50	35	20	20

Note: Distances are approximate

Entrances

Park entrances are open to vehicles 24 hours a day during open months (p124). The North Entrance station is at Gardiner, Montana, and the Northeast Entrance is near Cooke City; both are open year-round. The East Entrance is on US 14/16/20, from Cody, and the South Entrance is on US 89/191/287, north of Grand Teton National Park; both are open early May to early November. The West Entrance is on US 20/191/287 near West Yellowstone, Montana, and is open mid-to-late April to early November.

DON'T MISS

One of the best free services offered by the park service is its series of **ranger-led activities**. From boardwalk strolls explaining the interior plumbing of a geyser, to guided wildlife-watching at dawn and short, guided hikes, the commentary given by the park's affable rangers will really add to your understanding of the park. Check times in the park newspaper, *Yellowstone Today,* and time your itinerary around a couple of these presentations. At the very least, catch the nightly campfire talks given at most park campgrounds, some of which are aimed specifically at young families.

If you're nervous about hiking by yourself and would prefer to hike in a group, rangers also lead **guided walks** to several places in the park. Destinations vary year to year, but currently include short hikes to Mystic Falls, Beaver Ponds, Lake Overlook, Storm Point, the southern rim of the Grand Canyon of the Yellowstone and around the Upper Geyser Basin. Walks are limited to a couple of hours, are free and include some of the most interesting strolls in the park.

When You Arrive

➡ A seven-day pass to either Yellowstone or Grand Teton National Park costs $30/25 per vehicle/motorcyclist, or $15 for cyclists or hikers on foot. Credit cards are accepted. An annual pass to either park costs $60.

➡ Visitors receive a free map and the *Yellowstone Today* newspaper, which has a schedule of ranger-led activities, park facilities, road closures and opening hours.

➡ Notice boards at entrances indicate which campgrounds are full or closed.

SAFETY

Stay 30yd from bison and elk; 100yd from bears and wolves.
    Keep on boardwalks at thermal areas.
    Carry bear spray in the backcountry.

Fast Facts

➡ Area: 3472 sq miles

➡ Highest elevation: 11,358ft (Eagle Peak)

➡ Lowest elevation: 5282ft (Reese Creek)

Reservations

Reserve six months in advance for in-park accommodations and Western cookouts, and a couple of weeks in advance for Xanterra (p115) campgrounds. Reservations open May 1 for the following year.
    Reservations are not accepted for park-service campgrounds.

Resources

➡ **National Park Service** (www.nps.gov/yell) Official park site.

➡ **Xanterra** (www.yellowstone nationalparklodges.com)

➡ **Yellowstone.net** (www. yellowstone.net)

➡ **General Yellowstone Information** (www.yellow stonenationalpark.com)

➡ **National Park Trips** (www.yellowstonepark.com)

Yellowstone National Park

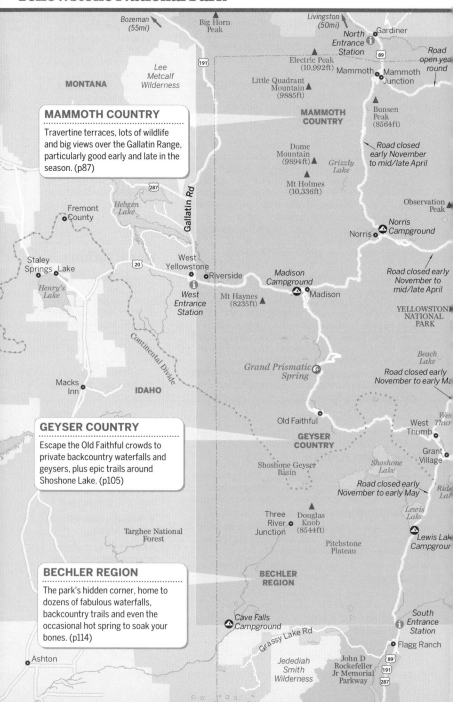

Bozeman
(55mi)

Big Horn
Peak

Livingston
(50mi)

North
Entrance
Station

Gardiner

Road
open year
round

Lee
Metcalf
Wilderness

Electric Peak
(10,992ft)

Mammoth

Mammoth
Junction

MONTANA

Little Quadrant
Mountain ▲
(9885ft)

MAMMOTH
COUNTRY

Bunsen
Peak
(8564ft)

MAMMOTH COUNTRY

Travertine terraces, lots of wildlife
and big views over the Gallatin Range,
particularly good early and late in the
season. (p87)

Dome
Mountain
(9894ft) ▲

Grizzly
Lake

Road closed
early November
to mid/late April

Mt Holmes
(10,336ft)

Observation
Peak ▲

Fremont
County

Hebgen
Lake

Norris
Campground

Norris

Staley
Springs ● Lake

West
Yellowstone

Henry's
Lake

Riverside

Madison
Campground

Road closed early
November to
mid/late April

West
Entrance
Station

Mt Haynes
(8235ft) ▲

Madison

YELLOWSTONE
NATIONAL
PARK

Macks
Inn

IDAHO

Grand Prismatic
Spring

Beach
Lake

Road closed early
November to early Ma

GEYSER COUNTRY

Escape the Old Faithful crowds to
private backcountry waterfalls and
geysers, plus epic trails around
Shoshone Lake. (p105)

Old Faithful

GEYSER
COUNTRY

Shoshone Geyser
Basin

Wes
Thur

West
Thumb

Shoshone
Lake

Grant
Village

Road closed early
November to early May

Ride
La

Three
River
Junction

Douglas
Knob
(8544ft) ▲

Lewis
Lake

Pitchstone
Plateau

Lewis Lak
Campgrour

Targhee National
Forest

BECHLER REGION

The park's hidden corner, home to
dozens of fabulous waterfalls,
backcountry trails and even the
occasional hot spring to soak your
bones. (p114)

BECHLER
REGION

Cave Falls
Campground

South
Entrance
Station

Ashton

Grassy Lake Rd

Jedediah
Smith
Wilderness

John D
Rockefeller
Jr Memorial
Parkway

Flagg Ranch

Continental Divide

Gallatin Rd

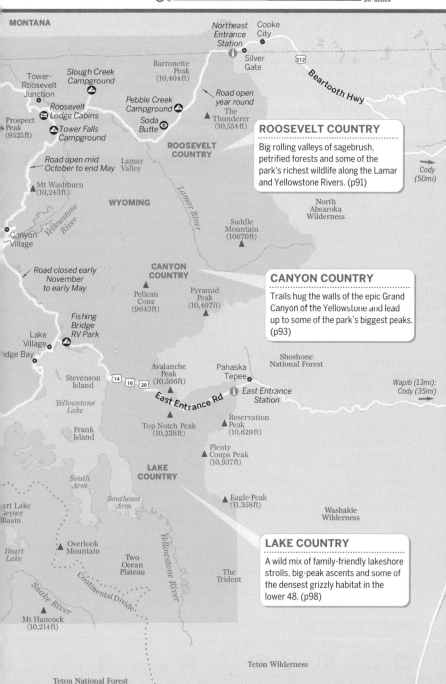

MONTANA

0 — 40 km
0 — 20 miles
Ⓝ

Northeast Entrance Station
Cooke City
Silver Gate
212
Beartooth Hwy

Barronette Peak (10,404ft)
Slough Creek Campground
Road open year round
Tower-Roosevelt Junction
Roosevelt Lodge Cabins
Pebble Creek Campground
The Thunderer (10,554ft)
Prospect Peak (9525ft)
Tower Falls Campground
Soda Butte

ROOSEVELT COUNTRY

Big rolling valleys of sagebrush, petrified forests and some of the park's richest wildlife along the Lamar and Yellowstone Rivers. (p91)

Road open mid October to end May
Lamar Valley
Cody (50mi)

Mt Washburn (10,243ft)

WYOMING

ROOSEVELT COUNTRY

North Absaroka Wilderness

Saddle Mountain (10670ft)

Canyon Village

Road closed early November to early May

CANYON COUNTRY

Pelican Cone (9643ft)
Pyramid Peak (10,497ft)

CANYON COUNTRY

Trails hug the walls of the epic Grand Canyon of the Yellowstone and lead up to some of the park's biggest peaks. (p93)

Fishing Bridge RV Park

Lake Village
idge Bay

Shoshone National Forest

Stevenson Island
14 16 20
Avalanche Peak (10,566ft)
Pahaska Tepee
East Entrance Station
Wapiti (13mi); Cody (35mi)

East Entrance Rd

Yellowstone Lake

Frank Island

Top Notch Peak (10,238ft)
Reservation Peak (10,629ft)

Plenty Coups Peak (10,937ft)

LAKE COUNTRY

South Arm
Southeast Arm

Eagle Peak (11,358ft)

Washakie Wilderness

art Lake Geyser Basin
Overlook Mountain
Two Ocean Plateau

LAKE COUNTRY

A wild mix of family-friendly lakeshore strolls, big-peak ascents and some of the densest grizzly habitat in the lower 48. (p98)

Heart Lake

Continental Divide

The Trident

Snake River

Mt Hancock (10,214ft)

Teton Wilderness

Teton National Forest

🚶 DAY HIKES

Even if you drive every road in Yellowstone you'll still see only 2% of the park. Easily the best way to get a close-up taste of Yellowstone's unique combination of rolling landscape, wildlife and thermal activity is on foot, along the 900-plus miles of maintained trails.

Hiking is also the best way to escape the summer crowds. Only 10% of visitors step off the road or boardwalks, only half of those venture further than a mile and a paltry 1% overnight in the backcountry. It's one thing to photograph a bison from your car, it's quite another to hike gingerly past a snorting herd out on their turf. So pick up a map, pack some granola bars and work at least a couple of great hikes into your Yellowstone itinerary.

Note that the park uses a three-character code (eg 2K7) to identify both trailheads and specific backcountry campsites, and we have included these wherever useful.

Trail Guides Yellowstone   HIKING
(☎ 406-595-1823; www.trailguidesyellowstone.com)
This Bozeman-based company offers guided day hikes and backpacking trips. The website offers great detail on the range of hikes available in Yellowstone.

Mammoth Country

Hikes in the relatively low-elevation area around the park's North Entrance highlight scenic canyons, panoramic peaks and numerous lakes, streams and waterfalls, all under the backdrop of the Gallatin Range. This is one of the park's hottest regions in summer and is one of the first areas to be snow-free in spring. Consider hiking early or late in the season, or outside of midday.

YELLOWSTONE NATIONAL PARKS HIKES

NAME	REGION	DESCRIPTION
Bechler Meadows & Falls (p69)	Bechler Region	A solitary walk through lush forest, with big falls and wildlife-watching opportunities
Bechler River Trail (p76)	Bechler Region	A wild backcountry adventure filled with rivers, cascades, hot springs and prolific wildlife
South Rim Trail & Ribbon Lake (p60)	Canyon Country	Fine family hike or a first overnighter to moose habitat and views of the Grand Canyon of the Yellowstone
Mt Washburn (p61)	Canyon Country	The park's most popular trail, offering epic views of Yellowstone caldera, and a mountain-bike route option
Cascade Lake & Observation Peak (p62)	Canyon Country	Wet hike through meadows and past grazing bison, then up the side of a mountain for expansive views
Mt Washburn & Sevenmile Hole (p70)	Canyon Country	Shuttle hike from mountain peak to canyon floor through the heart of grizzly country
Lone Star Geyser (p67)	Geyser Country	Bike or stroll along an old service road to a fine backcountry geyser that erupts every three hours
Sentinel Meadows & Queen's Laundry Geyser (p66)	Geyser Country	Loop hike past bison and hot springs to a historic backcountry geyser, with some off-trail sections
Fairy Falls & Twin Buttes (p68)	Geyser Country	Flat stroll through lodgepole forest to a 197ft waterfall and a little-visited geyser
Mystic Falls & Biscuit Basin (p65)	Geyser Country	Loop hike from a colorful geyser basin to a pretty waterfall, with a more challenging return option
North Shoshone Lake & Shoshone Geyser Basin (p73)	Geyser Country	Part of the Continental Divide Trail to a remote geyser basin and stunningly silent backcountry lake

  Wildlife-Watching   View   Great for Families   Waterfalls   Thermal Features

🚶 Beaver Ponds Trail

Duration 2½ hours

Distance 5 miles

Difficulty Easy–moderate

Elevation Change 350ft

Start/Finish Sepulcher Mountain/Beaver Ponds trailhead (1K1)

Nearest Town/Junction Mammoth

Summary An enjoyable loop hike, perfect if you're overnighting at Mammoth, that climbs to five ponds and offers a good chance of spotting moose and waterfowl.

This loop, with gentle climbs and lots of early morning and evening wildlife, begins between Liberty Cap and a park residence next to the bus parking lot at Mammoth. The trail ascends through the fir and spruce forests along **Clematis Creek** and in miles reaches a series of five ponds amid meadows, where beavers and moose emerge in the mornings and evenings. Black bears are also a distinct possibility. Most families will be able to tackle this walk, as long as you bring mosquito repellent.

Before you get started, it's worth pausing at trailside **Hymen Terrace**, named after the Greek god of marriage and one of the prettiest of Mammoth's many hot-spring terraces.

The route is clearly signposted and follows the Sepulcher Mountain Trail for the first 0.7 miles, taking a right at the first junction over a wooden bridge. Follow the trail as it starts to switchback up the hill and about 20 minutes into the hike you reach the signed junction, marking the end of the main elevation gain. Turn right for the **Beaver Ponds Loop** (left for the Sepulcher Mountain Trail).

DIFFICULTY	DURATION	DISTANCE	ELEVATION CHANGE	FEATURES	FACILITIES
easy-moderate	3½hr	8 miles	negligible		
moderate	4 days	33.3 miles	1100ft		
easy	4hr	6 miles	negligible		
moderate	4hr	6.4 miles	1400ft		
moderate	4-5hr	10.4 miles	1400ft		
moderate-difficult	2 days	15.6 miles	2800ft		
easy	1½-2½hr	4.8 miles	negligible		
easy	2hr	3.2 miles	negligible		
easy	3-4hr	6-7 miles	negligible		
easy-moderate	1½-2hr	4 miles	800ft		
moderate	2 days	19.2 miles	600ft		

  Restrooms
  Ranger Station
 Backcountry Campsite
 Picnic Sites
 Grocery Store Nearby

YELLOWSTONE NATIONAL PARK DAY HIKES

	REGION	DESCRIPTION
Elephant Back Mountain (p62)	Lake Country	This easy ascent follows a well-trodden path to fine lake views
Avalanche Peak (p64)	Lake Country	Relentlessly steep ascent above the tree line, offering unparalleled views of the Absarokas and Yellowstone Lake
Pelican Valley (p63)	Lake Country	Bird-watchers favor this rolling stroll through meadows and sagebrush in the heart of bear country
Heart Lake & Mt Sheridan (p72)	Lake Country	Solitude at this backcountry lake near thermal features; challenge-seekers can climb Mt Sheridan (3145ft)
Beaver Ponds Trail (p49)	Mammoth Country	Rolling hike from Mammoth Junction through sagebrush and wildflowers to five secluded ponds
Bunsen Peak (& Osprey Falls; p50)	Mammoth Country	Short uphill climb to mountaintop views, with an optional canyon descent to up-close views of a little-visited waterfall
Sepulcher Mountain (p53)	Mammoth Country	A varied and scenic loop with superb views and a secret peek at Mammoth's hidden thermal features
Monument Geyser Basin (p65)	Norris	A steep but rewarding climb to a little-visited thermal feature, with fine views
Yellowstone River Picnic Area Trail (p55)	Roosevelt Country	Crowd-free views of the lower Grand Canyon of the Yellowstone; a must for amateur geologists
Lost Lake (p56)	Roosevelt Country	A peaceful hike to a secluded lake and a petrified tree – perfect for anyone staying at Roosevelt Lodge Cabins
Fossil Forest Trail (p56)	Roosevelt Country	Steep, unmaintained trail to several 50-million-year-old petrified trees and fine views

 Wildlife-Watching   View   Great for Families   Waterfalls   Thermal Features

As the path flattens, it passes through patches of moody Douglas fir forest and open meadows of wildflowers before a side trail reveals fine views over Mammoth and the sediment strata of Everts Ridge. Ten minutes later the trail crosses a 4WD service track leading up to a hilltop radio transmitter, before passing a patch of quaking aspens and descending through forest to the first of several beaver-dammed ponds (1¼ hours from the trailhead). The fifth and final pond offers fine views of Sepulcher Mountain in the background and is a good place to spot moose, elk and pronghorn. Cross the outlet at the far end of the lake and ascend to a small ridge.

From here, the trail continues across an open sagebrush plateau, offering views down on Gardiner town and both the modern and former stagecoach roads to the park, until you reach a ridge with fine views over the orderly buildings and manicured green lawns and white thermal terraces of Mammoth. Continue right along the ridge for more views, or descend to the employee parking lot and the 4WD road to Gardiner that leads off behind the Mammoth Hot Springs Hotel. Grab a well-deserved ice cream at the general store before returning to your vehicle.

Bunsen Peak (& Osprey Falls)

Duration 2½ hours (6–7 hours with side trip)

Distance 4.2-mile round-trip (10.2 miles with side trip)

Difficulty Moderate (difficult with side trip)

Elevation Change 1300ft (2100ft with side trip)

Start/Finish Bunsen Peak trailhead (1K4)

Nearest Town/Junction Mammoth

Summary A short but steep hike up the

DIFFICULTY	DURATION	DISTANCE	ELEVATION CHANGE	FEATURES	FACILITIES
moderate	2–2½hr	3.5 miles	800ft		
moderate-difficult	3½hr	4 miles	2100ft		
moderate-difficult	6–8hr	16 miles	negligible		
moderate-difficult	2–3 days	16 miles	345ft (3145ft with side trip)		
easy-moderate	2½hr	5 miles	350ft		
moderate (difficult with extension)	2½hr (6–7hr)	4.2 miles (10.2 miles)	1300ft (2100ft)		
difficult	7hr	11.5 miles	3400ft		
moderate	2hr	2 miles	800ft		
easy	1½–2hr	4 miles	350ft		
easy	2hr	3.3 miles	600ft		
moderate-difficult	2½–3½hr	3.5 miles	800ft		

Restrooms   Ranger Station   Backcountry Campsite   Picnic Sites   Grocery Store Nearby

side of an ancient lava plug for superb views, with the option of descending to an impressive canyon waterfall.

Bunsen Peak (8564ft) is a popular half-day hike, and you can extend it to a more demanding day hike by continuing down the mountain's gentler eastern slope to the Bunsen Peak Rd and then *waaay* down (800ft) to the base of seldom-visited Osprey Falls. It's also possible to bike 'n' hike out to Osprey Falls and not visit Bunsen Peak.

The initial Bunsen Peak Trail climbs east out of Gardner's Hole to the exposed summit of Bunsen Peak, offering outstanding panoramas of Mammoth, the Gallatin Range, Swan Lake Flat and the Blacktail Deer Plateau. Even if you just make it halfway up the hill you'll be rewarded with superb views.

Bunsen Peak's trails (especially along the south slope) are free of snow much earlier than those on most other peaks in the park

and thus can be negotiated as early as May with some mild glissading. Be prepared for frequent afternoon thunderstorms, which bring fierce winds and lightning year-round.

Bunsen Peak was named by the 1872 Hayden Survey for German scientist Robert Wilhelm Eberhard von Bunsen (after whom the Bunsen burner was also named), whose pioneering theories about the inner workings of Icelandic geysers influenced early Yellowstone hydrothermal research. The mountain is actually an ancient lava plug, the surrounding volcanic walls of which have partially eroded away. So, yes, you are effectively climbing up the inside of a former volcano!

From the Mammoth Visitor Center, drive 4.5 miles south on Grand Loop Rd, cross the **Golden Gate Bridge** and turn left into the unpaved parking area on the east side of the road, just beyond the Rustic Falls turnout. The parking lot is small and fills up quickly, so get here early or try the overflow a little further on at Swan Lake Flats.

From 7250ft, the well-trodden singletrack dirt trail begins just beyond a barricade on the left (north) side of unpaved **Bunsen Peak Road**. The trail climbs immediately through sagebrush interspersed with wildflowers, then enters a young Douglas fir and lodgepole pine mosaic. You'll get early views of the Golden Gate below and to the left, and the ash-colored jumble of the hoodoos to the north. About half an hour from the trailhead a series of meadows offer views southwest to Swan Lake Flat, Antler Peak (10,023ft), Mt Holmes (10,336ft), Terraced Mountain and Electric Peak (10,992ft). Five minutes later, at one of the many switchbacks, you'll gain a great view of the eroded sandstone cliffs and spire of Cathedral Rock, with views down to the red roofs and bleached travertine mounds of Mammoth. The layered sandstone-and-shale mountain of Mt Everts (7841ft), to the north, offers proof that the area was underwater 70 to 140 million years ago. Beyond the Cathedral Rock outcrop, the switchbacks get steeper on the north side of the mountain and the exposed dome-shaped peak comes into view. Keep your eyes peeled for bighorn sheep.

The trail passes under electricity wires before communications equipment marks

the first of three small summits, 2.1 miles from the trailhead. Continue east along the loose talus ridge to the exposed easternmost summit for the best southern panoramas. Electric Peak, one of the highest in the Gallatin Range, looms largest to the northwest, marking the park's northern boundary, with the Absaroka Range to the northeast.

Either retrace your steps down the west slope or wind around the peak to descend the east slope to the Osprey Falls Trail.

SIDE TRIP: OSPREY FALLS & SHEEPEATER CANYON
3–4 HOURS / 6 MILES / 800FT ASCENT

From the south side of the third summit, the trail descends east through the burnt forest and volcanic talus of Bunsen Peak's eastern flank. It's 1.9 miles (one hour) downhill to Bunsen Peak Rd. After about 45 minutes, just after you catch sight of Bunsen Peak Rd, look for the orange marker that points you left along a subtrail to the **Osprey Falls trailhead**.

From the marked trailhead, the 1.4-mile Osprey Falls Trail wanders along the cliffs for 10 minutes before dropping like a stone into **Sheepeater Canyon**, losing 800ft in a bit less than a mile on a series of narrow, rocky switchbacks. Finally the trail levels out by the Gardner River to reach the base of the impressive, little-seen, 150ft **Osprey Falls**,

Mammoth Country – Day Hikes

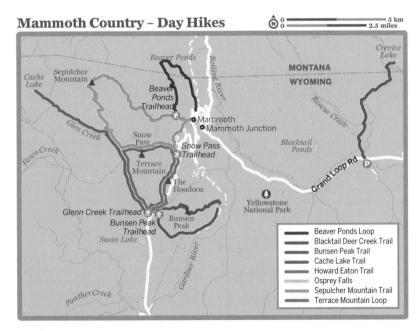

ORIENTATION

Seven distinct regions make up the 3472-sq-mile park (starting clockwise from the north): Mammoth, Roosevelt, Canyon, Lake and Geyser Countries, the Norris area and remote Bechler region in the extreme southwest corner.

Conceived by Lt Daniel C Kingman in 1886, the 142-mile, figure-eight Grand Loop Rd passes most of the park's major attractions. The 12-mile Norris–Canyon road divides the Grand Loop Rd into two shorter loops: the 96-mile Lower (South) Loop and the 70-mile Upper (North) Loop.

A clockwise drive from the North Entrance begins at Mammoth Hot Springs in the dry, low-elevation northwest corner of the park. East of here is the sagebrush country of Tower-Roosevelt Junction, a center for Wild West cookouts and trail rides. Further east is Roosevelt Country, the wildest part of the park accessible by road and home to wolves and bison in the Lamar Valley. From Tower-Roosevelt Junction the mountain highway climbs south past Mt Washburn (10,243ft) and over Dunraven Pass (8859ft) to Canyon Junction, where the views of the 1200ft-deep canyon and the central location make it a popular logistical base.

Continue south along the Yellowstone River through wildlife-rich Hayden Valley and the hot springs of Mud Volcano to Fishing Bridge Junction. This is Lake Country, beloved by springtime grizzlies and dominated by the watery wilderness of Yellowstone Lake. Here you'll find lakeshore accommodations and a marina at nearby Bridge Bay.

The Grand Loop Rd skirts the lake's northwest shore to West Thumb Junction, then heads west over the Continental Divide to Old Faithful in the heart of Geyser Country, home to the park's richest collection of geothermal features.

Turning north from Old Faithful, the Grand Loop Rd follows the Firehole River past several beautiful geyser basins to Madison Junction (6806ft) and the popular fly-fishing stretches of the Madison and Gibbon Rivers. From here a road leads west out of the park to the gateway town of West Yellowstone. The Grand Loop Rd continues northeast up the Gibbon River canyon to Norris Junction, home to the park's second-most-impressive collection of geysers. From here the road heads north past views of the snowcapped Gallatin Range to the west back to Mammoth Hot Springs.

The Bechler region, in the far southwest, is only accessible by road from Ashton, Idaho, from the John D Rockefeller Jr Memorial Parkway to the south of Yellowstone, or by a four-day hike from the Old Faithful region.

set below an impressive basalt cliff and spire. You're more likely to see marmots or water ouzels in the canyon than the namesake bighorn sheep or osprey, which now prefer to nest along the Yellowstone River. The falls are a refreshing spot to linger over a packed lunch and contemplate the relentless chaos and synergy of the park's natural forces.

Retrace your steps back out of the canyon and haul yourself back up 45 minutes to Bunsen Peak Rd, from where it's a fairly dull 3.2-mile (1¼-hour) trudge along the abandoned dirt road back to the Bunsen Peak trailhead. After 20 minutes look for a pair of antlers by the side of the trail, shortly before views of the upper Gardner River. In the early morning and evening, hikers often spot wildlife (elk, bison, waterfowl and otters) in the meadows and ponds of **Gardner's Hole**, near the parking area. Look for muskrats in the roadside pond.

🥾 Sepulcher Mountain

Duration 7 hours

Distance 11.5 miles

Difficulty Difficult

Elevation Change 3400ft

Start/Finish Beaver Ponds/Sepulcher Mountain trailhead (1K1)

Nearest Town/Junction Mammoth

Summary A long but varied and incredibly scenic loop hike that offers superb views over half the park and gives a secret peek at hidden thermal features of the Mammoth terraces.

The first half of this day hike is a cardio workout, gaining almost 3500ft before descending through meadows and forest in a long but leisurely stroll back. It's a relentless climb but it's well graded, offering plenty of interest en route. The hike starts at the same trailhead as the Beaver Ponds hike, so you can park anywhere in the Mammoth area. Trails Illustrated's 1:63,360 map No 303 *Mammoth Hot Springs* covers the route.

After 20 minutes the Sepulcher Mountain trail branches left away from the Beaver Ponds Trail, then 25 minutes later continues straight at a junction with the Clagett Butte/Snow Pass Trail. Continue up through burnt meadows, past an easily missed pond on your right, before ascending steeply up onto a ridge where you'll get your first views of Sepulcher Mountain and the impressive Gallatin Range to the west. The trail winds below the ridgeline through patches of forest and sagebrush to a viewpoint overlooking Gardiner and the lower Paradise Valley, north of the park boundary. As you continue the ascent, look for a **cairn** marking the path along the ridgeline to the tomb-like rocky outcrops that give Sepulcher Mountain its name. At a second cairn junction take the right branch for one minute to awesome views of the Paradise Valley and a well-deserved lunch spot. The main trail and actual **summit** (9646ft) are to the left of the cairn junction, past fine views of Electric Peak (10,992ft) and Cache Lake below.

The trail then descends to open meadows and an equally awesome panorama over Gardner's Hole, stretching from Bunsen Peak to Fawn Pass, with views across half the park as far as the Tetons. Descend the hillside on wide ribbonlike switchbacks before reentering a patch of forest and the junction with the Cache Lake/Glen Creek/Sportsman Lake Trail; take a left here.

After 15 minutes along Glen Creek you enter an open valley and branch left (east) to cross tiny Snow Pass (follow the electricity poles). Descend past a trail junction, ignoring the left branch signed for the Sepulcher Mountain Trail. As you descend here look for white chunks of travertine beside the forested trail – proof that you're skirting the Mammoth-like destroyed former hot springs of **Pinyon Terrace**.

At the trail junction by the signboard, take the left branch on the **Howard Eaton Trail**. The final 1.3 miles take you around the back of the upper **Mammoth terraces** – take care if you decide to explore the side trails that lead to extinct cones, sinkholes and caves (emitting deadly carbon dioxide). Past Orange Mound Spring are views of some beautiful hidden white terraces (not visible from Mammoth's Upper Terraces)

and Narrow Gauge Terrace, before descending past views over Mammoth to where you started, six or seven long, but highly enjoyable, hours ago.

🏃 Other Mammoth Country Hikes

One enjoyable loop hike is the three-hour **Terrace Mountain Loop**. Starting at Snow Pass trailhead, just south of Mammoth's Upper Terraces, the trail meanders through the interesting Hoodoos, climbing high above the road to views of Rustic Falls, Mt Holmes and Swan Lake Flat, before swinging right through the open sagebrush of Glen Creek and then taking a right turn, following the electricity lines over Snow Pass and downhill past Pinyon Terrace (the last section of the Sepulcher Mountain hike). An alternative is to start at Glen Creek trailhead.

If you can arrange a vehicle shuttle, one excellent, easy and little-seen route (all downhill!) is to follow the **Howard Eaton Trail** from Glen Creek trailhead down past views of Rustic Falls and the Hoodoos, past the junction to Snow Pass and down along the back side of Mammoth terraces to Beaver Ponds trailhead (3.8 miles). The last section is described in the Sepulcher Mountain hike.

Cache Lake is a satisfying 11.2-mile, three-quarter-day hike that is long enough to give you a workout, but not hard enough to wipe you out. From Bunsen Peak/Glen Creek trailhead (1K3), 4.5 miles south of Mammoth, the trail crosses open sagebrush country, passing turnoffs to Fawn Pass and the Sepulcher Mountain Trails, along the Sportsman Lake Trail. Keep an eye out for moose grazing in the lush meandering valley of Glen Creek. Turn right at the final junction with the Sportsman Lake Trail and climb to the lovely lake, ringed by golden meadows and thick forest, with impressive 10,992ft Electric Peak looming to the right. It's about 2½ hours to the lake from the trailhead. Budget some time to savor the lake before retracing your steps. For an ambitious overnighter, continue on to backcountry sites 1G3 or 1G4 and then climb (not technical) to the summit of Electric Peak the next morning.

An appealing shorter hike is the 8-mile-return **Blacktail Deer Creek Trail**, 7 miles east of Mammoth. It descends 1100ft from the trailhead north into the Black Canyon of the Yellowstone to join the river near Crevice Lake. The return is all uphill.

Roosevelt Country

Hikes in this region are among the first in the park to be clear of snow and are accessible by road year-round.

🥾 Yellowstone River Picnic Area Trail

Duration 1½–2 hours

Distance 4-mile round-trip or loop

Difficulty Easy

Elevation Change 350ft

Start/Finish Yellowstone River picnic area (2K7)

Nearest Town/Junction Tower-Roosevelt

Summary A lovely stroll that offers crowd-free vistas over the Narrows, with much historical and geological interest.

Popular with picnickers, this scenic stroll offers fantastic views into the eroded towers and basalt formations of the Narrows and Calcite Springs sections of the Yellowstone Valley, and possible glimpses of osprey and bighorn sheep: bring your binoculars. It's a good family hike but you'll need to watch the little ones because there are lots of sheer drop-offs and no guardrails.

To get to the trailhead, take the Northeast Entrance Rd across the bridge from Tower-Roosevelt to the picnic area parking lot, 1.5 miles east of the junction. Park in the lot just west of the picnic area, not in the picnic area itself.

Several unofficial dirt trails climb the slopes behind the picnic area but the official (signed) trail leads off from the picnic site left of the vault toilets to ascend a couple of hundred feet and deposit you puffing on the rim of the Grand Canyon of the Yellowstone. En route the trail passes several large erratic boulders, deposited in the valley over 10,000 years ago from the Beartooth Mountains by slow-moving glaciers. Notice how many of the Douglas firs have prospered in the moist, protective shade of these huge boulders. The hike traces the canyon's north rim for a couple of miles, providing unobscured views down past the crooked canyon walls to the Yellowstone River and north and east beyond rolling ridges to the peaks of the Absaroka Range.

The trail stays in open country on the ridgeline, 800ft above the canyon floor, for the whole route. About 20 minutes from the trailhead you may smell sulfur, a sign that you are about to pass 180-degree views of the Calcite Springs thermal area across the canyon. Ten minutes further come fine views of the breccia spires of the Narrows.

YELLOWSTONE NATIONAL PARK DAY HIKES

Roosevelt Country – Day Hikes

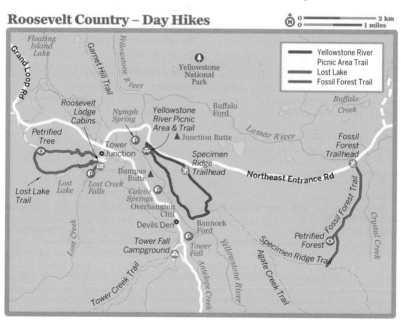

Look out for bighorn sheep below the basalt columns at **Overhanging Cliff**.

The trail ends abruptly at a bald **hilltop lookout** that offers views down on the site of the Bannock Indian ford, used by the Bannock to cross the Yellowstone River during their annual hunting trips across the park. You can also see the Tower Fall region (but not the falls themselves) to the right and the fire tower atop Mt Washburn in the distance.

From here you can retrace your steps to investigate the views of the canyon for a second time, or alternatively take the trail left (northeast) for a few minutes to the three-way junction with the **Specimen Ridge Trail**. Take a left at this junction to return downhill back to the road and picnic area. (If you have some excess energy, you could ascend partway up Specimen Ridge along the Specimen Ridge Trail for fabulous views over the Lamar Valley.)

Just before reaching the road, branch left at the trail register and cut cross-country back to the trailhead, paralleling the road to a large erratic boulder. Otherwise you'll have to hike along the road, an unpleasant end to a lovely hike.

🥾 Lost Lake

Duration 2 hours

Distance 3.3-mile loop

Difficulty Easy

Elevation Change 600ft

Start/Finish Roosevelt Lodge

Nearest Town/Junction Tower-Roosevelt

Summary A peaceful early-morning hike to a secluded lake and a petrified tree – perfect for families and anyone staying or dining at Roosevelt Lodge.

The Lost Lake loop trail begins directly behind Roosevelt Lodge (take the right fork), climbing about 300ft past Lost Lake to a petrified tree, from where the trail climbs onto a plateau and then descends to the Tower Ranger Station. Before you even start the hike, warm up with a quick 10-minute detour left at the trailhead to the small but pretty **Lost Creek Falls**.

From the trailhead the trail switchbacks surprisingly steeply for the first 10 minutes onto the ridge. Look out for mule deer here in the early morning. Take a right at the junction (left leads to Tower Fall Campground, 2.9 miles away) and you'll come to the meadows surrounding **Lost Lake**, about 30 minutes from the trailhead. The trail traverses the length of the lake, past lily pads and dragonflies, to a good potential picnic spot at the end of the lake. If you're lucky, you might spot moose here.

From here the trail descends through meadows thick with spring wildflowers to reach the parking lot for the **petrified tree**. Take a couple of minutes to appreciate the 50-million-year-old stone redwood (there used to be three such trees here, but early tourists chipped away the other two!). If you started the hike early, you'll have the place to yourself; later in the day the parking lot will be jammed with reversing SUVs.

The trail back to Roosevelt Lodge follows orange markers up the hill from the edge of the parking lot and ascends to an open sagebrush plateau, offering fine views ahead to Junction Butte, Specimen Ridge and the Absaroka Range to the east. The trail then descends to the **Tower Ranger Station**. You'll likely see mule deer grazing in the meadows here; at the very least you'll see a John Deere parked by the ranger station. Follow the orange trail markers and in two minutes you'll be back at the cabins of Roosevelt Lodge, where breakfast will be waiting.

🥾 Fossil Forest Trail

Duration 2½–3½ hours

Distance 3.5 miles

Difficulty Moderate–difficult

Elevation Change 800ft

Start/Finish Unmarked trailhead

Nearest Town/Junction Tower-Roosevelt

Summary A must for amateur geologists, this unmaintained trail climbs steeply to several petrified trees and offers fine views. Listen for howling wolves in the early morning.

This hike leads to a couple of isolated patches of petrified forest scattered along Specimen Ridge, thought to hold the word's largest collection of petrified trees. The forests were buried suddenly in ash around 50 million years ago, or turned to stone by a vengeful Crow medicine man, depending on your beliefs. Paleodendrochronologists (scientists who date fossilized trees, something of a niche profession!) have identified dozens of different species of tree here, including tropical avocado and breadfruit, with dozens of ancient petrified forests stacked atop even older petrified forests. Some of the trees were buried where they grew, but others were probably deposited by a mudflow caused by volcanic eruptions about 50 million years ago.

Please don't pocket any of the petrified wood here or elsewhere in the park. If you are desperate for a petrified-wood souvenir, head to Tom Miner Basin (p147) in the Paradise Valley.

This trailhead isn't easy to find, so be sure not to confuse it with the Specimen Ridge Trail a couple of miles further west. The parking area is marked 'Trailhead' and is just a few hundred yards west of the Lamar Canyon bridge, 5 miles east of Tower-Roosevelt Junction and about 1 mile southwest of the turnoff to Slough Creek Campground. Look for the information board on wolves.

The trail is not formally maintained by the park service, so it isn't as easy to follow as most other trails in the park, though visitor centers do have a handout on the hike if you ask nicely. There is no water along the trail. Keep an eye out for the weather; the exposed ridge is definitely not the place to be during a storm.

From the unmarked trailhead the fairly clear path starts off following a dirt double track (a former service road to the nearby Crystal Valley) and then veers right after 100yd to head up the hillside for 45 minutes, through meadows of July wildflowers and past buffalo trails to a small patch of forest. Branch right along the steeper path and, after 10 minutes' uphill climb, you'll reach your first petrified tree stump by a bend in the trail. Five minutes later comes the second stump, with a third piece lying by the side of the trail. Most of the side trails lead to more stumps. From here it's more uphill, past a volcanic outcrop enclosing another fossilized tree and into ridgeline meadows.

The main trail continues up the ridge and, after a couple of minutes, branches right on a subtrail, skirting and then traversing a small patch of forest to the stump of a petrified giant redwood. This fabulous tree would once have topped out at 200ft in height! Below the huge stump are two thinner but taller upright trees and views back up towards the redwood's petrified roots. The views over the Lamar and Yellowstone Valleys are superb.

The subtrail continues up the hillside to join the main trail just before a small cairn. Continue for 20 minutes uphill along the ridge to the summit of Specimen Ridge, marked by a cairn. There are wonderful views from here of bison herds in the valley below, birds of prey riding the thermals, and Mt Washburn in the distance. Return the way you came for about an hour – the views west are stunning.

🏃 Other Roosevelt Country Hikes

From the stagecoach road just north of Tower-Roosevelt Junction, the 7.5-mile Garnet Hill Trail is an easy three-hour loop north of the Grand Loop Rd. The trail heads northwest along Elk Creek and then loops around Garnet Hill to return to Roosevelt Lodge. For an extension, take a left at the Garnet Hill junction, then a right to cross the suspension bridge over the Yellowstone River, and drop down to Hellroaring Creek, where there are several backcountry campsites (add 2.5 miles). You can also reach the trail from Hellroaring trailhead, 3.5 miles west of Tower-Roosevelt Junction.

For a good day hike with fine fishing, try the first part of the Slough Creek Trail. Head uphill past the patrol cabin to where the trail rejoins the river at the first meadow (a 4-mile round-trip), or continue to the second meadow or nearby McBride Lake (cross Slough Creek) for a 6-mile round-trip hike. Be sure to take the right branch at the junction with the trail that continues up to the Buffalo Plateau. There's also nice hiking along the fishing trails that head up Slough Creek from the campground.

Pebble Creek Trail to Warm Creek trailhead (3K4) is a scenic 12-mile hike that requires a vehicle shuttle. The trail heads up Pebble Creek for 10 miles through burns and lovely wildflowers, crosses a pass, then drops down to the Warm Creek trailhead and a nearby picnic area on the Northeast Entrance Rd. The hike includes several river crossings that can prove tricky in early summer.

Specimen Ridge Trail is a popular but long 19-mile hike up and along the ridge, past Amethyst Mountain, then down into the Lamar Valley. Check with rangers beforehand that the Lamar River ford is passable. You'll need to arrange a shuttle.

Canyon Country

Though the surrounding backcountry draws far less attention than the Grand Canyon of the Yellowstone, it is every bit as interesting. Abundant wildlife, good camping, mesmerizing cascades and great vistas await. You can also consider the Seven Mile Hole Trail as an 11-mile day hike.

MATT MUNRO / LONELY PLANET ©

1. Mammoth Hot Springs (p87)
Mammoth Country's renowned geothermal area makes a scenic picnic spot.

2. Wildlife watching (p242)
Be on the lookout for black bears in montane and subalpine forests throughout Greater Yellowstone.

3. Yellowstone River (p55)
The USA's longest free-flowing river is a popular destination for white-water rafting and fishing.

4. Black Pool (p99)
Rising water temperatures contributed to this hot spring's spectacular color change from black to blue.

🚶 South Rim Trail & Ribbon Lake

Duration 4 hours

Distance 6 miles

Difficulty Easy

Elevation Change Negligible

Start/Finish Uncle Tom's parking lot

Nearest Town/Junction Canyon Village

Summary An incredibly varied hike that combines awesome views of the Grand Canyon of the Yellowstone with a couple of lakes and even a backcountry thermal area.

Southeast of the Grand Canyon of the Yellowstone's South Rim, a network of trails meanders through meadows and forests and past several small lakes. This loop links several of these and makes a nice antidote to seeing canyon views framed by the wind-shield of your car. Come early in the morning and the canyon is all yours.

Park at Uncle Tom's parking area on the Canyon's South Rim Dr and, after checking out the views of the Upper Falls and the Lower Falls from Uncle Tom's Trail, take the South Rim Trail east from Uncle Tom's Trail, along the rim of the canyon to Artist Point for some of the finest canyon views available.

From Artist Point take the trail east toward Point Sublime, taking in the superb views halfway along the trail, then retrace your steps to the junction where you branch right past Lily Pad Lake for 0.3 miles to another junction. Branch left here and descend for 1.2 miles to Ribbon Lake, actually two conjoined ponds, with a good chance of spotting moose. For a close-up view of Silver Cord Cascade, continue on the path to the canyon rim, then head left along the canyon wall to the small falls. A faint path connects to the main trail at a small footbridge. This is the furthest point of the hike, 3.4 miles from the start.

Canyon Country – Day Hikes

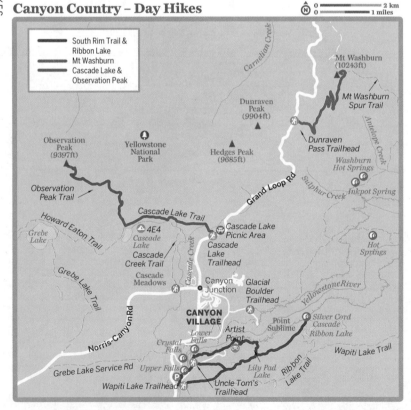

Two secluded backcountry sites by the lake make for an easy overnighter less than 2 miles from the trailhead (4R1 is right on the lake; 4R2 is on the main trail and less private). Mosquitoes can be a problem here before mid-August, so pack some spray.

From Ribbon Lake head back to the junction with Lily Pad Lake and instead of returning the way you came, continue straight, past several minor fumaroles and hot springs to the acidic, spring-fed waters of Clear Lake, 1.5 miles from Ribbon Lake. Continue along the Clear Lake Trail and, at the next unsigned junction, take the right branch for the final 0.7 miles back to Uncle Tom's parking area.

Alternatively, the left branch continues across open grassland (good wildlife spotting) for just over a mile to the Wapiti Lake trailhead, where you can link up with the South Rim Trail by Chittenden Bridge and return through forest to Uncle Tom's, passing fine views of the Upper Falls en route. This longer loop adds 1 mile to the hike but is a worthwhile option if you have the time.

🚶 Mt Washburn

Duration 4 hours

Distance 6.4 miles return

Difficulty Moderate

Elevation Change 1400ft

Start/Finish Dunraven Pass trailhead (4K9)

Nearest Town/Junction Canyon Village

Summary Yellowstone's most popular day hike offers unsurpassed 360-degree mountaintop views, with the chance of spotting bighorn sheep and black bears.

This popular return hike climbs gradually to the fire lookout tower on the summit of 10,243ft Mt Washburn for some of the park's best views. Over 10,000 hikers do this trail annually, so leave early to get trailhead parking. Older teenagers should be able to do the hike.

Mt Washburn is all that remains of a volcano that erupted around 640,000 years ago, forming the vast Yellowstone caldera. Interpretive displays in the lookout tower point out the caldera extents, making this a memorable place to get a sense of the awesome scale of the Yellowstone super-volcano. The peak is named after Montana surveyor general Henry Washburn, who rode up the peak to see the view during the Washburn, Langford and Doane expedition of 1870.

The suggested route starts from Dunraven Pass (8859ft) on the Grand Loop Rd, 4.8 miles north of Canyon and 14.2 miles south of Tower. An alternative route begins from the larger Chittenden parking area (5 miles north of the pass) for a marginally shorter but less interesting hike (but good bike trail) to the summit. Use Trails Illustrated's 1:63,360 map No 304 *Tower/Canyon*.

Snow often obstructs the Dunraven Pass approach through the end of June and can block the trail into July. Wildflower displays in July and August are legendary. Frequent afternoon thunderstorms bring fierce winds and lightning, so pack a windbreaker even if the weather looks clear, and be ready to make a quick descent if a storm rolls in. Keep in mind that grizzlies flock to Mt Washburn's east slopes in large numbers during August and September in search of ripening whitebark pine nuts.

The wide trail follows a rough, disused road (dating from 1905) and so makes for a comfortable, steady ascent, following a series of long ribbon-like loops through a forest of subalpine firs. After 20 minutes the views start to open up. The fire tower appears dauntingly distant, but the climb really isn't as painful as it looks. Continue northeast up broad switchbacks, then follow a narrow ridge past a few stunted whitebark pines (look out for bears) to the gravel Chittenden Road at the Mt Washburn Trail junction. At the junction the road left leads up to the three-story fire-lookout tower, about two hours from the trailhead. The side trail right at the junction leads down the Washburn Spur Trail to Canyon Junction.

The viewing platform and ground-level public observation room has restrooms (but no water), a public 20x Zeiss telescope, displays on the Yellowstone caldera and graphics to help you identify the surrounding peaks and valleys. The fire tower was built in the 1930s and is one of three in the park still staffed from June to October. The majestic panoramas (when the weather is clear) stretch over three-quarters of the park, across the Yellowstone caldera south to Yellowstone Lake, Canyon and the Hayden Valley and north to the Beartooth and Absaroka Ranges. Below you are the smoking Washburn Hot Springs. Keep your eyes peeled for bighorn sheep basking near the summit. If the crowds get too much, you can always head five minutes down the Washburn Spur Trail for some peace and quiet. From the summit, return the way you came.

ALTERNATIVE ROUTE: MT WASHBURN SPUR TRAIL TO CANYON

6 HOURS / 11.2 MILES / 2340FT DESCENT

If you can arrange a shuttle, or hitch a lift to Dunraven Pass, consider hiking from Mt Washburn along the 5.4-mile Mt Washburn Spur Trail to the junction with the Seven-mile Hole Trail (p70) and on to the Glacial Boulder trailhead in Canyon, a total 11.2-mile hike through the heart of grizzly country. This hike can be done in reverse, but this adds 850ft of ascent.

🏃 Cascade Lake & Observation Peak

Duration 4–5 hours

Distance 10.4 miles

Difficulty Moderate

Elevation Change 1400ft

Start/Finish Cascade Lake trailhead (4K5)

Nearest Town/Junction Canyon Village

Summary There's plenty of flexibility here for all levels, mixing an easy hike to Cascade Lake with fine views atop Observation Peak.

There's something for everyone on this trail, which starts just a couple of minutes' drive north of Canyon Village. The full hike climbs 1400ft to Observation Peak (9397ft), but the turnaround at Cascade Lake gives an easy, level hike of only 4.4 miles return (2½ hours). You can also add on a 4-mile return side trip to Grebe Lake, should you want.

Start the hike at the Cascade Lake trailhead, 1.5 miles north of Canyon Junction, or the nearby picnic area of the same name. July is a great time for wildflowers along this route, but the trail can be wet early in the season.

The path quickly joins the trail from the picnic area and continues past the trailhead board to enter an open valley frequented by bison. The double-wide track crosses several creeks before swinging into forest to follow a meandering creek. One mile into the hike you'll hit the Cascade Creek Trail that leads here from the Canyon–Norris road, offering a different, dryer early-season approach if you can arrange a car shuttle. Take the right branch to Cascade Lake.

Ten minutes from the junction, the path leads into a wide valley, past backcountry site 4E4 on the left to the trail junction at the west end of the lake, less than an hour from the trailhead. The right branch leads to backcountry site 4E3 and Observation Peak; straight ahead takes you to the eastern part of the lake and on to Grebe Lake 2 miles away. The first time we did this hike we stood transfixed here for over two hours as a pack of six wolves attempted to take down a bull elk by the edge of the forest.

The lake itself opens to meadows on the west and backs on to the Solfatara Plateau and its ghost forest of burnt snags. The lake is worth exploring for its wildfowl and occasional moose. Bison often graze the meadows to the east. The lake's waters drain down Cascade Creek, eventually to plunge into the Yellowstone River over Crystal Falls.

The hike up to Observation Peak, part of the Washburn Range, takes about 1¼ hours and gains 1400ft in 3 miles. After 30 minutes the trail crests a saddle and curves to the left, opening up views of the peak ahead. It loops further to a ridgeline, giving you time to catch your breath before the final 20-minute climb to 4P1, one of the park's most unusual backcountry campsites, in a forested hollow just below the main peak. The site makes a fine place to enjoy dusk and dawn views, but there's no water here, so you'll have to haul up everything you need.

The views from the peak are superb: Cascade and Grebe Lakes sit below you, smoking Norris Geyser Basin is to the west and the Hayden Valley yawns to the south. To the north is the Washburn Bear Management Area, classic grizzly country, so keep your eyes peeled. The ranger hut at the summit is normally closed. The descent back to Cascade Lake takes about one hour, from where you return to the trailhead the way you came.

Lake Country

Lake Country is best known for its boating opportunities, but its great hikes are also worth getting to know. Bear activity in the river inlets to Yellowstone Lake delays the hiking season here (the Pelican Valley, Natural Bridge and Heart Lake trails are closed until July), making it a limited early-season option. Check with a visitor center if you are coming in early summer and always hike with others.

🏃 Elephant Back Mountain

Duration 2–2½ hours

Distance 3.5-mile loop

Difficulty Moderate

Elevation Change 800ft

Start/Finish Elephant Back trailhead

Nearest Town/Junction Lake Village

Summary This relatively easy ascent follows a well-trodden path and rewards you with fine lake views near the top.

This hike is a great short-but-sweet picnic option, suitable for families with teenagers. The trailhead is 1 mile south of Fishing Bridge Junction and 0.5 miles north of the Lake Village turnoff on the Grand Loop Rd. From Lake Yellowstone Hotel an alternative side trail cuts 0.25 miles through the woods past Section J of the hotel's cabins to access the trail. Use Trails Illustrated's 1:83,333 map No 305 *Yellowstone Lake*.

The start of this lollipop loop trail parallels the Grand Loop Rd for 100yd, then abruptly ducks into the forest. A few minutes from the road it passes the old water pipes of Lake Village, then crosses beneath a power line and begins a steady climb. The forest floor here is thick with wildflowers, wild berries and fungi. Watch for deer and moose. After passing through 1 mile of lodgepole pines, the trail reaches a junction.

Both trails lead to the **panoramic overlook** (8600ft). The trail to the left (0.8 miles) is steeper than the trail to the right (0.9 miles). Hike clockwise up the steep one and

down the easier one for an easy-on-the-knees loop. You can picnic with a view at the wooden bench at the top. Looking out, Pelican Valley's meadows lie to the left, Stevenson Island sits in the lake ahead, and the Absaroka Range outlines the horizon in the distance.

🥾 Pelican Valley

Duration 6–8 hours

Distance 16-mile loop

Difficulty Moderate–difficult

Elevation Change Negligible

Start/Finish Pelican Valley trailhead (5K3)

Nearest Town/Junction Fishing Bridge

Summary Bird- and wildlife-watchers favor this rolling stroll through remote meadows and sagebrush in the heart of bear country.

Rangers recommend a minimum party of four hikers for this lollipop loop, through some of the most concentrated grizzly country in the lower 48 states. Backcountry camping is not allowed anywhere in the valley. Bring plenty to drink and a hat, since there's no shade along the trail. Hiking in the morning or late afternoon on overcast, rainy or even snowy days offers the best chance to catch a glimpse of wildlife.

Lake Country – Day Hikes

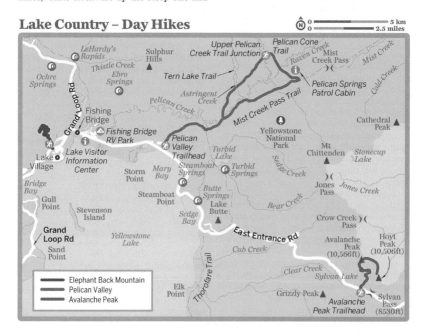

Pelican Valley (including the nearby Turbid Lake Trail) is closed for bear activity from April 1 to July 3 and is open for day use only (9am to 7pm) from July 4 to November 10. The July 4 opening is typically the busiest day in the valley. Off-trail travel is prohibited on the first 2.5 miles of the trail.

The trailhead sits at a gravel parking lot on the east end of an old service road. It is off the north side of the East Entrance Rd, 3.5 miles east of Fishing Bridge and 23.5 miles west of the East Entrance. The lot is across the road from the trailhead for Storm Point and Indian Pond. Use Trails Illustrated's 1:63,360 map No 305 *Lake Yellowstone*.

The **Pelican Valley Trail** follows the abandoned Turbid Lake service road due east for a few minutes, then veers north along the forest edge to an overlook, which provides the first sight of the Pelican Creek drainage, a couple of miles away. Look for pelicans at the mouth of the creek. The trail descends through open meadow to the valley floor, passing through boggy sections. Near the poorly marked Turbid Lake Trail junction, scan the forest edge (and trail) for signs of coyotes, bison, elk and grizzlies.

A mile further on the trail passes the rickety remains of the **Pelican Creek Bridge**. Make the easy ford and climb a terrace for 1.5 miles to the bridge over **Astringent Creek**, just before another junction. The marshy area around a group of thermal springs just south of the trail offers good wildlife-watching. Continue east along the forest edge, scanning the clover patches for bear scat.

Follow the old service road northeast for 1.5 miles to another easy ford of Pelican Creek and the Upper Pelican Creek Trail junction. Stay in the meadows to the right for 0.3 miles to the Pelican Cone Trail junction, where a small stream provides the valley's best drinking water. The ill-defined trail cuts south away from the valley edge, crossing meadows to ford **Raven Creek**. There are plenty of waist-deep swimming holes here.

Beyond Raven Creek the poorly defined trail heads southeast through sagebrush-interspersed meadows. The trail passes through a dormant thermal area fragrant with sulfur. After a patch of unburned forest, follow through rolling sagebrush hills to the **Pelican Springs Patrol Cabin** and the Mist Creek Pass Trail junction. From here, it's a well-defined, undulating 5 miles back to the Pelican Bridge junction along the forested south edge of the valley.

🏃 Avalanche Peak

Duration 3½ hours

Distance 4-mile loop

Difficulty Moderate–difficult

Elevation Change 2100ft

Start/Finish Avalanche Peak trailhead (5N2)

Nearest Town/Junction Fishing Bridge

Summary Relentlessly steep, this challenging peak ascent offers unparalleled views of the Absaroka Range and Yellowstone Lake.

This thigh-burner starts off steeply, gets steeper and then continues uphill (steeply) for the entire duration. You can't say we didn't warn you... Check for closures; in early fall the trail is frequented by grizzlies foraging whitebark pine nuts.

During the late-spring snowmelt, subalpine wildflowers peak, leading in midsummer to a profusion of high-alpine butterflies. From midsummer on get an early start since afternoon lightning storms are common. Regardless of the season, pack your hiking poles and a shell jacket for protection against gusty winds and afternoon thundershowers. Snowfields persist above the tree line through mid-July, even on the trail's south-facing slopes. July to September are the most reliable months for this hike.

The trailhead sits off the East Entrance Rd, 0.5 miles west of Sylvan Pass, 19 miles east of Fishing Bridge Junction and 8 miles west of the park's East Entrance. Park in the small paved lot on the south side of the road by Eleanor Lake's west side picnic area (no toilet). Use Trails Illustrated's 1:63,360 map No 305 *Yellowstone Lake*.

From the signed **trailhead** (8466ft) across the road, the trail climbs steeply through lush forests of spruce and fir along a small unnamed stream. Thirty minutes from the road the trail traverses west across an old avalanche chute, then east again into mature whitebark pine forest.

A little over a mile from the road the trail levels out and emerges at the base of a huge amphitheater-like bowl. At a prominent cairn the main trail veers steeply to the left, climbing along open talus slopes to arrive at the mountain's south ridge. Two trails climb the final section, meeting at a rock shelter, so you can take one route up and the other down.

Above the glacial cirques and well above the tree line, panoramic views extend north to the Beartooths and south to the Tetons.

Thousands of acres just west of the peak were burned in the summer of 2003 after a lightning strike. The true summit (10,566ft) sits to the northeast, along the narrow ridge, by a series of talus wind shelters. After a summit picnic, retrace your steps.

An alternative for the sure-footed is to follow the steep, unstable talus trail down the east arm of the peak toward the saddle shared with jagged Hoyt Peak (10,506ft), at the Shoshone National Forest boundary. A side trail climbs to a minor peak, from where you can see the hidden lakes below Hoyt Peak. If you're not comfortable scree surfing down the steep slope, head back the way you came to take the lower path that circles round the back of the peak, offering an easier descent. Descend through a series of sparsely forested rolling hills to rejoin the main trail at the foot of the bowl.

🥾 Other Lake Country Hikes

South of Grant Village the 5-mile round-trip Riddle Lake Trail traverses the Continental Divide and drops down to the lake and its marshy meadows, a favorite of moose. The trailhead is off the South Entrance Rd, 3 miles south of Grant Village. Bear activity closes the trail from April 30 to July 15.

Shoshone/Dogshead trailhead offers two ways of getting to lovely Shoshone Lake, the largest backcountry lake in the lower 48. Popular with anglers, the 6.5-mile Shoshone Lake (Lewis River Channel) Trail follows the north shore of Lewis Lake, along the Lewis River Channel, to Shoshone Lake. Return the same way or via the shorter (4.7 miles), forested Dogshead Trail.

Norris

In addition to the hike listed here don't forget the 2 miles of trails that lead around Norris Geyser Basin (p103).

🥾 Monument Geyser Basin

Duration 2 hours
Distance 2 miles
Difficulty Moderate
Elevation Change 800ft
Start/Finish Monument Geyser trailhead
Nearest Town/Junction Norris
Summary A steep but rewarding climb to a little-visited thermal feature, with fine views over Gibbon Meadows.

Norris – Day Hike

The semidormant chimney-like cones of Monument Geyser Basin are among the park's tallest. There's limited thermal action here these days (no geysers or spouters), but you'll likely have them all to yourself.

The short but steep hike follows the Gibbon River for 0.5 miles, then heads steeply uphill for another 0.5 miles, offering fine views of Gibbon Meadows and Mt Holmes en route. The most prominent feature in the bleached basin is Monument Geyser (also known as Thermos Bottle Geyser), which still lets off steam, unlike the other cones, which have sealed themselves up over the centuries. To get back to your car return the same way. Budget around 45 minutes up, half an hour down and 30 minutes to explore the minor springs and fumaroles.

Geyser Country

Even the short hikes described here will get you away from the crowds at Old Faithful to some spectacular waterfalls and geysers.

🥾 Mystic Falls & Biscuit Basin

Duration 1½–2 hours
Distance 4-mile loop
Difficulty Easy–moderate
Elevation Change 800ft
Start/Finish Biscuit Basin (OK4)
Nearest Town/Junction Old Faithful
Summary A short, family-friendly stroll from an interesting thermal basin to a 70ft waterfall, with the option for a longer moderate loop hike.

The shorter, out-and-back option to the base of the falls is relatively flat and thus popular with families. Due to a lack of shade, the longer loop hike to the overlook is best done in the morning or late afternoon. The trail is closed from the end of the winter season until the last Saturday of May due to the presence of bears.

The Biscuit Basin turnoff is 2 miles north of the Old Faithful overpass and 14 miles south of Madison Junction, on the west side of Grand Loop Rd. Use Trails Illustrated's 1:63,360 map No 302 *Old Faithful*.

From the parking area, head west across the Firehole River bridge. Follow the Biscuit Basin boardwalk loop 0.3 miles around to the left, past several notable geysers and hot springs. Just west of Avoca Spring, the wide, sandy Mystic Falls Trail (blazed but unsigned) ducks into burned lodgepole forest dotted with wildflowers.

The undulating trail parallels, but does not cross, the Little Firehole River. Soon you'll reach the signed Summit Lake/Little Firehole Meadows junction. From here it's 0.7 miles to the left on the most direct route to the falls, saving the longer overlook loop – visible on a cliff to the right – for the return trip. Heading upstream into the canyon, the path can be muddy where seeps cross the trail. After 10 to 15 minutes the trail arrives at the bottom of the 70ft Mystic Falls, 1.2 miles

from Biscuit Basin, where orange hot-spring bacterial seeps are in abundance. A series of switchbacks lead to the top of the falls.

Retrace your steps to complete the 2.4 mile family-friendly version. If you're fit, or traveling without children, you can choose instead to complete the loop (which adds a sweaty 500ft elevation gain) by continuing 0.5 miles through more burned lodgepoles to the Fairy Creek/Little Firehole Meadows Trail junction. Turn right and descend to the Biscuit Basin Overlook for an expansive bird's-eye view of the Upper Geyser Basin. Follow the switchbacks downhill to rejoin the Mystic Falls Trail, then retrace your steps to Biscuit Basin.

🏃 Sentinel Meadows & Queen's Laundry Geyser

Duration 2 hours

Distance 3.2 miles return

Difficulty Easy

Elevation Change Negligible

Start/Finish Freight Rd trailhead (OK6), Fountain Flat Dr

Nearest Town/Junction Madison Junction

Summary Some off-trail exploring to a little-visited geyser basin, with a good chance of spotting bison.

Geyser Country – Day Hikes

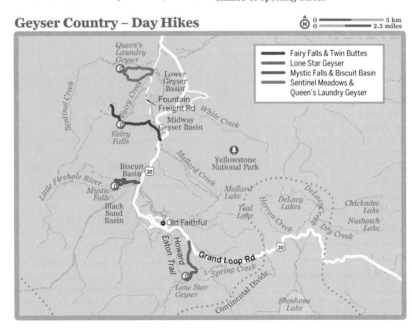

This trail is a good choice if you fancy a bit of simple off-route trail finding. It's flat and easy but requires some basic navigation skills. Bring waterpoof boots before July. Park at the end of Fountain Flat Drive, just off the main Grand Loop Rd, 6 miles south of Madison Junction and 13 miles north of Old Faithful.

From the parking lot it's 0.3 miles along the dirt road to the Ojo Caliente (p113) spring and the bridge over the Firehole River, which is where the Sentinel Meadows Trail branches west off the gravel road. You can cycle this first section and chain your bike to the bridge for your return.

Turning onto the Sentinel Meadows Trail, the route swings away from the Firehole River, passing beneath telephone lines. The soil quickly turns to white, hinting at the thermal features lying ahead. Twenty-five minutes into the hike you pass backcountry campsite OG1. The trail climbs a small hill to offer views of the valley, its four smoking thermal features and a probable scattering of bison. Mound Spring is the closest and most expansive of the springs, Steep Cone is the tallest, and Flat Cone is the furthest, across the creek. The trail ascends a second small hill, before skirting around a patch of new-growth forest, 1.7 miles from the trailhead.

This is where things get tricky. As the main trail bends to the left to hook around the forested hill, look to the right to see the steam of Queen's Laundry Geyser – this is your destination. Two faint trails lead here; one directly from the main trail, the other further south (a post in the ground makes a rough marker), which swings northwest, skirting the forest. Both are wet and boggy early in the season so you'll just have to scout out the driest path. In general trace an arc counter-clockwise to the right of the bog, staying on dry ground to get to the far northern side of the geyser, by a ruined wooden cabin.

The historic cabin is a former bathhouse, built in 1881 by park superintendent Norris as the first national-park building designed solely for public use. The geyser gets its name from the bathing costumes that used to hang to dry on strings beside the bath-house. The deep blue geyser (really more of a pool) drains past the bathhouse into a wide cascade. Don't get too close to the geyser – act as if the normal boardwalks and warning signs were in place.

Back at the junction you can return the way you came. Alternatively, continue on the main trail as it curves east, past a pond, across a bridge, over a small rise and then along the edge of Imperial Meadows, beside an open plain favored by bison. After 20 minutes you'll see an orange arrow pointing across the boggy plain. Ignore this and continue straight (east) along the forest edge until you see a cliff-like butte straight ahead. As the trail peters out, continue straight (east) across the plain toward the right side of the hill. Take a minute to investigate Boulder Spring, a perpetual spouter that looks as if it's coming straight out of the hill. Several creek pools offer potential soaking sites here.

Head straight under the telephone poles to rejoin Fountain Freight Rd. The trailhead is a five-minute walk to the left and the parking lot is 10 minutes further. If you fancy some more exploration, check out the off-trail geysers of Pocket Basin (p113), accessed from two unmarked trails on either side of the Firehole Bridge.

🧍 Lone Star Geyser

Duration 1½–2½ hours

Distance 4.8-mile return

Difficulty Easy

Elevation Change Negligible

Start/Finish Lone Star trailhead (OK1)

Nearest Town/Junction Old Faithful

Summary An easy, level riverside stroll along a former service road to one of the park's largest backcountry geysers. Even better, do it as an easy 20-minute bike ride.

This paved and pine-lined hike is popular with both day hikers and cyclists, yet is quite a contrast to the chaotic scene around Old Faithful. Isolated Lone Star erupts every three hours for between two and 30 minutes and reaches 30ft to 45ft in height. The Old Faithful Visitor Center no longer offers predicted eruption times so you'll just have to bring a book or a packed lunch for the wait. If the parking lot at Lone Star trailhead is full, park at the neighboring Kepler Cascades turnout.

From Lone Star trailhead, above Kepler Cascades (where the Firehole River speeds through a spectacular gorge), take the old paved road (closed to cars) past a tiny weir that diverts water to Old Faithful village.

The road crosses the Firehole River bridge and follows the upper Firehole River, heading upstream past the Spring Creek Trail junction (1.6 miles) to end at the steep-sided, 9ft-tall Lone Star Geyser after an easy 2.4 miles. Check the NPS logbook (in the wooden information box in front of the geyser) to gauge exactly when the next eruption might occur; if you catch an eruption, fill in the log for future visitors. If you have time to kill, consider following the Shoshone Lake Trail for 20 minutes to check out the two minor thermal areas along the Firehole River.

To completely avoid the crowds, consider taking the quieter but hillier Howard Eaton Trail (OK2) from 1 mile south of the Old Faithful overpass as an alternative 5.8-mile return route. The trail joins the Shoshone Lake Trail 0.3 miles beyond Lone Star Geyser. You could take one route in and the other out if you can arrange a vehicle shuttle.

To guarantee an eruption to yourself, camp overnight at backcountry campsite OA1 or OA2, 10 minutes' and 20 minutes' walk away respectively.

🏃 Fairy Falls & Twin Buttes

Duration 3–4 hours

Distance 6–7 miles return

Difficulty Easy

Elevation Change Negligible

Start/Finish Fairy Falls trailhead (OK5)

Nearest Town/Junction Old Faithful

Summary A short jaunt to one of the most accessible backcountry cascades, with views over the park's most beautiful thermal feature and one of the largest backcountry geysers.

Tucked away in the northwest corner of the Midway Geyser Basin, 197ft Fairy Falls is a popular hike, largely because it's only a short trip from Old Faithful. Beyond Fairy Falls the trail continues to a hidden thermal area at the base of the Twin Buttes, two conspicuous bald hills severely charred in the 1988 fires. The geysers are undeveloped and you're likely to have them to yourself – in stark contrast to the throngs around Grand Prismatic Spring.

The Fairy Falls (Steel Bridge) trailhead is just west of the Grand Loop Rd, 1 mile south of the Midway Geyser Basin turnoff and 4.5 miles north of the Old Faithful overpass. The parking lot fills up early in the day (often before 11am) so get here early. Use Trails Illustrated's 1:63,360 map No 302 *Old Faithful*. The trail is closed until Memorial Day weekend due to the presence of bears.

Cross the Firehole River on the silver trestle bridge, then head northwest along Fountain Flat Dr, which is a wide gravel cycling and hiking path. After 1 mile you'll notice multicolored steam rising from Grand Prismatic Spring on the right. You can't reach the boardwalk from this trail, but you can scramble up the unofficial trails to your left for one of the park's greatest secrets – an astonishing bird's-eye view of Yellowstone's most beautiful thermal feature. The park service plans to build a formal trail here if funds allow.

Continue 0.3 miles to a trail junction and turn left onto the narrower Fairy Creek Trail. If you are cycling this first section (an excellent idea), lock your bike at the rack here. The trail winds 1.6 miles past backcountry campsite OD1 through lodgepole forest burned in the 1988 fires.

At 197ft, Fairy Falls is the park's seventh-highest waterfall, but the wispy volume of water is hardly on a par with the falls on the Yellowstone River. Still, patterned streaks of white water blanket the dark lower rocks, and clumps of raspberries and fireweed flourish around a pretty pool, which makes for a fine swimming hole on a hot and sticky summer day.

After crossing a footbridge, the trail continues 0.7 miles northwest toward the prominent Twin Buttes and several conspicuous plumes of rising steam. Cross several marshy patches with the aid of log bridges and then take the right branch to the closest plume emanating from Spray Geyser, erupting frequently to a height of 6ft to 8ft.

Continue west, following the outlet from Imperial Geyser, which is lined with orange algae. Imperial plays almost perpetually, projecting blasts of water up to 20ft into its large rainbow pool. If you care to climb onto the buttes, head across the open slopes behind Imperial Geyser for fine views. After discovering the collection of lily-choked ponds hidden in a hollow between the two summits, you can continue to either summit without much difficulty. Views to the east encompass the Lower and Midway Geyser Basins, while to the west the trail-free Madison Plateau stretches off toward the park boundary. Retrace your steps to the Fairy Falls trailhead.

🏃 Other Hikes in Geyser Country

The best way to get to the shores of Shoshone Lake on a day hike is the three-hour (6-mile) return hike along the DeLacy Creek Trail. The meadows en route are good habitat for moose, elk, mule deer, coyote and sandhill cranes, but bring bug repellent before August. The trailhead is east of Craig Pass, near the DeLacy Creek picnic area, halfway between Old Faithful and West Thumb Junction. Bring a picnic.

Bechler Region

Bechler boasts the highest concentration of waterfalls in Yellowstone and some of the best backcountry hot-spring soaks anywhere. Its forests also escaped the worst of the 1988 fires. The area's remoteness means it's best suited to experienced hikers taking long backcountry trips, but some rewarding shorter hikes are possible. In early summer trails are knee-deep in water, so aim to hike here from August onwards. Inquire about conditions at another ranger station before driving all the way out here.

🚶 Bechler Meadows & Falls

Duration 3½ hours
Distance 8-mile loop
Difficulty Easy–moderate
Elevation Change Negligible
Start/Finish Bechler Ranger Station (9K1)
Nearest Town/Junction Driggs, Idaho
Summary A solitary walk through lush forest, with big falls and wildlife-watching opportunities.

Bechler Meadows' extensive wetlands are a wildlife magnet. Grizzlies and black bears, as well as rare waterfowl such as gray owls and great blue herons, are often spotted. Add substantial cascades to an already spectacular mix by starting from the Cave Falls trailhead, or by taking the Bechler Falls side trip.

This route avoids all fords, so there's no need to inquire about river levels before departing. Use Trails Illustrated's 1:63,360 map No 302 *Old Faithful*. From Bechler Ranger Station, follow the Bechler Meadows Trail 3 miles northeast past the Boundary Creek Trail junction through lodgepole pine forest to the Bechler River/Rocky Ford cutoff junction.

If it's not too buggy, hike an extra 0.5 miles north to Bechler Meadows. You will cross a wooden suspension bridge over Boundary Creek past campsite 9B1. It's an ideal spot to look for sandhill cranes and moose, or angle the waters for rainbow trout.

Retrace your steps 0.5 miles back to the junction and then continue southeast 0.7 miles past campsite 9C1 to the wide Rocky Ford at the Bechler River Trail junction. Instead of fording the river, trace the river's west bank south for 2 miles to the next junction, where a cutoff leads west 1.6 miles through forest back to the ranger station. The east branch leads to Bechler Falls.

Bechler Region – Day Hikes

SIDE TRIP: BECHLER FALLS & CAVE FALLS
1½–2 HOURS / 3 MILES / ELEVATION CHANGE NEGLIGIBLE

Finish your hike with a 3-mile side trip to Bechler Falls and Cave Falls. The worthwhile detour heads 0.5 miles downstream from the Bechler River/Ranger Station cutoff junction to Bechler Falls, one of Bechler's widest and most voluminous waterfalls. Continue east on the riverbank trail 0.5 miles to the broad-spanning Cave Falls (20ft) and its refreshing swimming hole.

From here you can get picked up, hike back the way you came to Bechler Ranger Station, or even cycle 5 miles on the road to the ranger station (leave a bike here en route to the Bechler Ranger Station).

🚶 Other Bechler Region Hikes

At the west end of Grassy Reservoir, by the dam, trailhead 9K5 is the start of the 15.5-mile round-trip hike to Union Falls, one of the most spectacular in the national park. After a mile the trail branches right, fords Cascade Creek and then branches left (right leads to the Pitchstone Plateau Trail). After another 4 miles the trail fords Proposition Creek and then a mile later branches right onto the Union Falls Trail for another 2 miles. At 250ft, feathery Union Falls are the second-highest falls in Yellowstone National Park. If that seems too ambitious, a shorter 3.6-mile return hike leads from the same trailhead to a series of cascades known as Terraced Falls.

At the east end of Grassy Reservoir a pullout marks the trailhead for the 6-mile round-trip hike northeast to Beula Lake, with its two backcountry campsites. The trail crosses the South Boundary Trail en route.

All hikes are accessed from Grassy Lake Rd, south of the park.

🏃 OVERNIGHT HIKES

There's no better way to experience the raw wildness of Yellowstone than on an overnight backpacking trip. Some experience of backcountry camping is important before heading out into the wild, particularly with bear awareness and hanging food. That said, there's a huge range of challenges available, from easy strolls, to backcountry campsites an hour from the road, to multiday expedition-style traverses of the Thorofare corner or Gallatin Range through some of the remotest terrain south of Alaska. Choose the right trip at the right time of year and arrive prepared, and there's no better way to experience the park.

If you don't fancy organizing a multiday trek yourself, consider a company like Trail Guides Yellowstone (p48) or Wildland Trekking Company (☎ 800-715-4453; www.wildlandtrekking.com), with backpacking trips that cost $260 per day, including meals, guide and transportation from Bozeman.

For easy backcountry camping options less than 2 miles from the road, see p118.

Backcountry Permits

A backcountry-use permit, available at visitor centers and ranger stations, is required for all overnight backcountry trips (day hikes don't require permits). There is a $3 per person per night charge for backcountry use between Memorial Day and Labor Day weekends. If you are camping for more than eight nights you can opt for a $25 season pass.

About half the backcountry sites can be reserved by mail; a $25 reservation fee applies regardless of the number of nights. Booking starts on April 1, when all existing reservations are dealt with at random, and continues up to 48 hours before your start date. Reservations can be made in person at a ranger center, by fax to 307-344-2166 or through the mail to Backcountry Office, PO Box 168, Yellowstone National Park, WY 82190. Applications must be on a Trip Planner Worksheet, available at the park website, and you must give two itinerary alternatives.

The downloadable Backcountry Trip Planner (www.nps.gov/yell/planyourvisit) is an essential guide to the park's backcountry sites. To see which sites are available contact the central backcountry office (☎ 307-344-2160; YELL_Backcountry_Office@nps.gov) in Mammoth. Outside of summer call ☎ 307-344-7381.

Once you've ascertained by phone that the sites and dates you want are available, send the nonrefundable cash, check or money order with booking. You will receive a confirmation notice, which must be taken to a backcountry office to exchange for a permit not more than 48 hours before your trip but before 10am on the day of your trip departure.

Around 20% of backcountry-use permits are issued no more than 48 hours (effectively three nights) in advance on a first-come, first-served, walk-in basis (no $25 fee). This means you can leave your planning to the last minute, as long as you are flexible with your itinerary. (You may, for example, have to walk further one day than you had planned if your desired site is already booked.)

The most popular areas are the Hellroaring region of the Black Canyon of the Yellowstone in spring, Slough Creek in early summer, Shoshone Lake in August, Bechler region in August/September and Heart Lake throughout summer. You should include a back-up itinerary if applying for a popular region or trail in peak season.

There are backcountry offices (⊙ 8am-4:30pm) at Canyon Visitor Center, Mammoth Visitor Center, Grant Village Visitor Center, Bridge Bay Marina, Bechler Ranger Station, Tower Ranger Station, Old Faithful Ranger Station, West Yellowstone Visitor Center and South Entrance Ranger Station.

Get to the office at least half an hour before closing because you have to watch an 18-minute video on backcountry safety before you can get your permit. The backcountry-use permit is site and date specific and states the campsite where you must overnight. Part of your permit goes on the dashboard of your car; the main permit stays with you on your pack.

Canyon Country

🏃 Mt Washburn & Sevenmile Hole

Duration 2 days

Distance 15.6 miles

Difficulty Moderate–difficult

Elevation Change 2800ft

Start Dunraven Pass trailhead (4K9)

Finish Glacial Boulder trailhead (4K6)

Nearest Town/Junction Canyon Village

Summary Fabulous views, a backcountry thermal feature and a descent into the Grand Canyon of the Yellowstone that feels like it's '5 miles in and 7 miles out.'

Mt Washburn & Sevenmile Hole

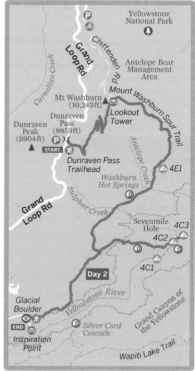

This excellent overnight shuttle hike takes you to the top of one of the park's highest peaks and then down, down, down to Sevenmile Hole, a minor hydrothermal area at the bottom of the Grand Canyon of the Yellowstone. It's not a particularly long hike, but it does involve a lot of elevation change (most of it downhill). When the insect hatch is on, the backcountry sites at Sevenmile Hole are very popular, so book your spot well in advance.

DAY 1: MT WASHBURN & SEVENMILE HOLE

6–7 HOURS / 10.7 MILES / 1400FT ASCENT / 3500FT DESCENT

The popular hike up to Mt Washburn (p61) makes up the first couple of hours of this hike.

From the four-way junction just below Mt Washburn, the Mt Washburn Spur Trail drops southeast along an undulating ridge past alpine wildflower meadows. After dipping through a saddle to another little gap at the tree line, bear right and descend 2.6 miles from the summit through small clearings to Washburn Meadow and campsite 4E1 (campfires allowed).

Keep your wits about you – this is prime grizzly habitat. The Antelope Bear Management Area, east of the trail on the mountain's east slope, is closed annually from August 1 to November 10 and open May 10 to July 31 only by special permit, so avoid wandering off-trail.

The trail descends southwest through boggy grassland grazed by elk and deer to Washburn Hot Springs, a small field of inky black mud pots, pools and hissing fumaroles. Proceed past more small thermal areas to the Sevenmile Hole Trail junction, 3 miles from campsite 4E1.

The steep trail switchbacks down 1400ft through Douglas firs, passing a 10ft-high geyser cone before arriving at a more active thermal area. Continue down past the easily missed turnoff to campsite 4C1, then cross a small thermal stream for the final walk to campsite 4C2 beside the Yellowstone River. This entire area is known as Sevenmile Hole. Large springs emerge from the reddish chalky cliffs on the river's east bank. To reach campsite 4C3, ford narrow Sulphur Creek (can be tricky early in the season), then follow the riverbank past a tiny hot pool. Stock animals and wood fires are not allowed at any of the campsites. Unattended food must be out of reach of bears – if you are day-tripping down here, hang (don't dump) your pack at the junction.

DAY 2: SEVENMILE HOLE TO GLACIAL BOULDER TRAILHEAD

4 HOURS / 4.9 MILES / 1400FT ASCENT

Back at the junction after the hard ascent, heading southwest, the trail is broader and leads along the north rim of the 1200ft-deep Grand Canyon of the Yellowstone for the final 2.7 miles, passing through lodgepole forest carpeted with fragrant, low-lying grouseberry shrubs. The views are increasingly spectacular as you pass the unsigned overlook of long, thin Silver Cord Cascade, which drops nearly 1000ft to the canyon floor. The amazing technicolor columns of the canyon's eroding sides stretch another 1 mile to the Glacial Boulder trailhead. Canyon Village is 1.5 miles west along paved Inspiration Point road.

ALTERNATIVE ROUTE: GLACIER BOULDER TO SEVENMILE HOLE

6–7 HOURS / 11 MILES / 1400FT ASCENT/DESCENT

An alternative route for hiking to Sevenmile Hole starts at the Glacial Boulder trailhead just before Inspiration Point. This out-and-back route is an 11-mile hike and drops 1400ft in 1.5 miles; as always, the hard part is the return trip. It's a decent day hike or a relaxed overnighter.

Lake Country

🏃 Heart Lake & Mt Sheridan

Duration 2–3 days

Distance 16-mile round-trip

Difficulty Moderate–difficult

Elevation Change 345ft (3145ft with side trip)

Start/Finish Heart Lake trailhead (8N1)

Nearest Town/Junction Grant Village

Summary A backcountry geyser and thermals, the opportunity to peak-bag or fish the lake bestow myriad options onto this straightforward hike. July to October are the best months.

While the shores of Heart Lake suffered damage in the 1988 fires, it remains a beautiful, rewarding and popular destination. An extensive thermal field extends from the northwest shore of the 2160-acre lake, showcasing boiling hot pots and a large geyser. Heart Lake provides rich habitat for waterfowl, and there are plentiful stocks of cutthroat and elusive, but record-setting, lake (Mackinaw) trout.

The highest summit in the Red Mountains, Mt Sheridan (10,308ft), rises high above Heart Lake's west shore, providing terrific panoramas. While the extremely fit can knock off Heart Lake in a long day hike, it's worth spending a night (or two) along the lakeshore to relax, watch the bald eagles and osprey, and explore.

The Heart Lake Trail is closed from April 1 to June 30 due to bear activity – reconfirm the opening date with a backcountry office. Elk carcasses from winter hardship tend to pile up here, leading to an early-season grizzly fiesta.

All west-shore campsites have a two-night limit from July 1 to September 1. Snow persists along the trail up to Mt Sheridan until mid-July.

Use Trails Illustrated's 1:63,360 map No 305 *Yellowstone Lake*. Two 1:24,000 USGS maps also cover the route: *Heart Lake* and *Mount Sheridan*. The trailhead is 5.3 miles south of Grant Village and 16.7 miles north of the South Entrance, off South Entrance Rd. There's a toilet at the trailhead.

DAY 1: HEART LAKE TRAILHEAD TO HEART LAKE

3–5 HOURS / 8 MILES / 345FT ASCENT

Follow the sandy, mostly single-track trail southeast through strewn trunks and new-growth lodgepole forest. After a few miles, the trail rises slightly over a minor watershed to the first group of smoking fumaroles at the north foot of bald-topped Factory Hill (9607ft), 1½ to two hours from the trailhead. Heart Lake, 2 miles downhill, comes into view.

Wind your way down into the intensely active Heart Lake Geyser Basin. Numerous spurting springs and boiling pools sit a short way off to the right. The trail crosses warm Witch Creek several times to reach the Heart Lake patrol cabin, just off the lake's north shore (7450ft). Witch Creek is a prime spot for bathing near thermal spots. You can inquire about this and current fishing conditions at the log-cabin ranger station (which is staffed in summer).

Trail Creek Trail departs left (east) around the lake's northeast shore; it's a popular jumping-off point for stock users bound for the Thorofare region.

Heart Lake Trail continues right, first following the gray-sand beach to cross the Witch Creek inlet on a log bridge and then tracing the lake's west shore to reach campsite 8H6. This is the first of five sites alongside firs and spruces fringing the shoreline.

Follow the steam along an often-overgrown trail at the tree line behind 8H6 to another fascinating thermal area. Here you will spot the azure Columbia Pool. Rustic Geyser spouts up to 50ft at irregular intervals, while other springs bubble up into large calcified bathtubs.

The main trail continues past campsite 8H5 to the junction with the Mt Sheridan Trail then proceeds about another mile south past campsites 8H4 and 8H3 to 8H2; only 8H2 and 8H3 allow campfires. The secluded lakeshore campsite 8J1, which boasts views of Mt Sheridan, is the most coveted.

There are good views across the 180ft-deep lake east to Overlook Mountain (9321ft) and southeast to flat-topped Mt Hancock (10,214ft). In the evenings, pairs of grebes often dive and court each other with mellow, lilting voices.

Heart Lake & Mt Sheridan

There are six additional campsites around Heart Lake: 8J1 (two-night limit) and 8J2 (two-night limit, stock parties only) on its northeast side, 8J4 and 8J6 on the southeast shore, 8J3 nearby along Surprise Creek and 8H1 at the lake's southwest corner. All sites except 8H1 allow campfires.

SIDE TRIP: MT SHERIDAN
4–6 HOURS / 6 MILES / 2800FT ASCENT

The **Mt Sheridan Trail** crosses open meadows briefly before starting its spiraling ascent along a steep spur largely covered in whitebark pines. Bring plenty of water; there is none available on the trail.

You will come to a saddle flanked by wind-battered firs. Continue left (southeast) up the narrowing tundra ridge, over old snowdrifts, to reach the 10,308ft talus-covered summit. The fire lookout (staffed in summer, but otherwise locked) scans 360 degrees, taking in Pitchstone Plateau to the west, Shoshone Lake to the northwest, Yellowstone Lake to the northeast and the jagged Tetons to the south. Snowdrifts often persist through mid-July.

DAY 2: HEART LAKE TO HEART LAKE TRAILHEAD
3–5 HOURS / 8 MILES / 345FT DESCENT

Retrace your steps from day one back to the start.

Geyser Country

🚶 North Shoshone Lake & Shoshone Geyser Basin

Duration 2 days

Distance 19.2 miles

Difficulty Moderate

Elevation Change 600ft

Start Lone Star trailhead (OK1)

Finish DeLacy Creek trailhead (7K2)

Nearest Town/Junction Old Faithful

Summary Follow the Continental Divide Trail on this easy overnighter that combines a backcountry geyser basin with an unforgettable night by silent Shoshone Lake.

Shoshone Lake is one of the park's real hidden gems. Not only is it the largest backcountry lake in Yellowstone, at more than 8000 acres, but it's also the largest lake in the lower 48 states not reachable by road. There are many possible routes around the lake, including loops from three directions (Lone Star, DeLacy Creek and Lewis Lake). Much of the first half of this route follows the Continental Divide Trail, which continues along the southern shore of the lake to the Dogshead trailhead.

The route described here traces the northern shore of the lake and requires a short shuttle or hitch along the Grand Loop Rd. Note that Kepler Cascades turnout is a slightly more secure overnight parking spot than the Lone Star trailhead, since it sees much more traffic.

Between Lone Star and Shoshone Lake, the trail crosses gentle Grants Pass, which normally isn't clear of snow until late June. The lake is normally frozen until early June and some backcountry campsites are flooded into July, making mid-July the earliest reliable start date for this trip. Mosquitoes can be an irritant until August.

Use Trails Illustrated's 1:63,360 map No 302 *Old Faithful*. Two USGS quads also cover the route: *Old Faithful* and *Shoshone Geyser Basin*.

Shoshone Lake is a popular backcountry destination (about one-third of the entire park's backcountry use is concentrated along the shores of the lake), so it's worth reserving sites well in advance. Campsite 8R5 in particular gets booked early because of its proximity to the Shoshone Geyser Basin. Sites open to hikers along the northern shore include 8T1, 8R5, 8R3, 8R2, 8S3 and 8S2. The latter two sites make a good short overnight trip from DeLacy Creek, but are too far north to be convenient for your first night on this trip. Sites 8R2 and 8S2 are mixed hiker- and boat-accessible campsites. All of the lakeshore sites are no-wood-fire areas.

DAY 1: LONE STAR TRAILHEAD TO SHOSHONE LAKE
6 HOURS / 11.6 MILES / 400FT ASCENT

Take the first 2.4 miles as part of the Lone Star Geyser hike (p67). Proceed past the geyser and turn left after 0.3 miles at the junction with the Howard Eaton Trail to head southwest. The trail passes the least-desirable campsite, OA1 (campfires allowed), to cross the Firehole River on a footbridge. From here you follow the Shoshone Lake Trail 5.8

North Shoshone Lake & Shoshone Geyser Basin

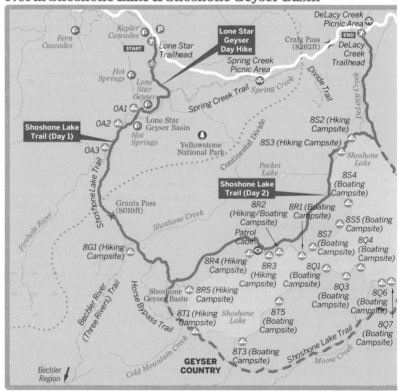

miles south to the Shoshone Geyser Basin. The trail soon passes a small thermal field of scalding hot pools and hissing steam vents (so no, that growling isn't a grizzly bear!). Past OA1 you'll pass the most attractive off-trail campsite, OA2 (campfires OK), in 0.4 miles, and finally the best option for through hikers, campsite OA3, in another 0.8 miles. If you got a late start and plan a leisurely three-day hike, break the first day here.

Climb south over the broad rolling ridge to cross the unsigned Grants Pass (8010ft), which marks the almost imperceptible Continental Divide. The sandy trail heads down through superb stands of tall, old-growth Engelmann spruce and whitebark pine to reach the Bechler River (Three Rivers) Trail junction, which is about one hour from OA3 and 1½ hours from the trailhead.

Inviting campsite 8G1 (no campfires) is a short way down the Shoshone Lake Trail, on a rise above the meadows framing Shoshone Creek, 2 miles short of the impressive Shoshone Geyser Basin.

The trail descends through the prime moose and bear habitat of Shoshone Creek meadows, occasionally crossing the creek on log bridges. One mile from the Bechler Junction a stock trail branches right over the creek to avoid the marshy geyser basin.

At the North Shoshone Trail junction (8.5 miles from the trailhead, 8.4 miles to DeLacy Creek) it's worth detouring for an hour to explore the geyser basin. Cross the marshy area on wooden logs and take the left branch to dump your pack in one of the bear-proof lockers. Just past here is a small beach, which offers a fine place for a snack.

Continue straight into the geyser basin for around 0.5 miles. The surrounding meadows are fine places to spot moose and other animals at dusk. Shoshone Geyser Basin is home to over 80 thermal features and was visited in 1839 by trapper Osborne Russell. The main ones include Little Great Geyser, the Minute Man group, Little Bulger and the Orion group further south; its Union Geyser used to erupt to heights of 100ft. T Scott Bryan's encyclopedic *The Geysers of Yellowstone* details 40 of the basin's geysers, none of which are marked on-site.

Back at the North Shoshone Trail junction, you'll branch off the Continental Divide Trail after following it for 6 miles (just 3094 miles left...). Head northeast along the trail through forest to the backcountry site along the northern shore that you've reserved. Site 8R5 appears after five minutes, while 8R3 and 8R2 are a further hour away. Just before reaching 8R3 you pass an unmarked trail that leads to a ranger patrol cabin.

DAY 2: SHOSHONE LAKE TO DELACY TRAILHEAD
4 HOURS / 7.6 MILES / 200FT ASCENT

From sites 8R3 and 8R2 it's another hour's walk through undulating forest to the northern shoreline. The trail parallels the lovely shore for half an hour before dipping back into forest to pass site 8S3. Five minutes further on a lovely little spit offers a superb place to stop and soak up the silence.

Ten minutes later the trail hits site 8S2 and the northern point of the lake as the beach curves to the right in front of large meadows. Follow the beach, looking for the occasional orange metal markers.

Fifteen minutes later the trail cuts inland to join a trail junction at the northeastern point of the lake. From here it's 3 miles along the lily ponds and meadows of De-Lacy Creek to the end of the hike, about 1¼ hours away. The right-hand branch leads 4.2 miles to Dogshead Channel and Lewis Lake.

ALTERNATIVE ROUTES: DELACY CREEK LOOP & DOGSHEAD LOOP

3 & 4 DAYS / 27 & 32 MILES / ELEVATION CHANGE NEGLIGIBLE

There are plenty of other route options, including the 27-mile, three-day lollipop loop of the lake from DeLacy Creek trailhead, or the 32-mile loop of the lake from Dogshead trailhead near Lewis Lake. Thirteen exclusively boat-in sites along both the north and south shores offer those with floating transportation the option of spending weeks here.

Bechler Region

🚶 Bechler River Trail

Duration 4 days

Distance 33.3 miles

Difficulty Moderate

Elevation Change 1100ft

Start/Finish Bechler Ranger Station (9K1)

Bechler River

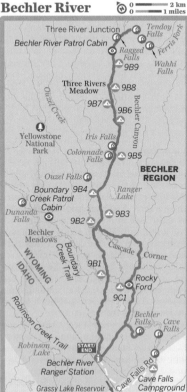

Nearest Town/Junction Driggs, Idaho

Summary Traverses wild backcountry filled with rivers, cascades, wildlife and even some hot-spring soaks.

Near the head of Bechler Canyon, your destination here is the Ferris Fork side stream, home to several hidden waterfalls and an outstanding hot-springs soak. Sandals and hiking poles are extremely useful for river crossings. Always bring rain gear – Bechler gets three times as much rain as the park's northern range.

Popular with horse-pack trips, backpackers and anglers, Bechler sees fierce competition for backcountry campsites in the prime months of August and September. Campsites may only be reserved for dates after July 15. In-person permits may be granted before this, weather permitting. Ask rangers about river-ford and trail conditions – high water and swarms of bugs typically persist along this route through mid to late July. All of the campsites mentioned here (except 9B9) limit stays to one night.

Waterfall obsessives should pick up *Yellowstone Waterfalls and their Discovery* by Paul Reubenstein, Lee Whittlesey and Mike Stevens, for photos, maps and coordinates of over 250 waterfalls, many of them in the Bechler region.

Use Trails Illustrated's 1:63,360 map No 302 *Old Faithful*. Three USGS 1:24,000 quads also cover the route: *Trischman Knob, Cave Falls* and *Bechler Falls*.

DAY 1: BECHLER RANGER STATION TO CAMPSITE 9B4

3–4 HOURS / 9.1 MILES / ELEVATION CHANGE NEGLIGIBLE

Take the Bechler River (Cutoff) Trail from Bechler Ranger Station to Rocky Ford, with the option of a 1.5-mile return side trip to Bechler Falls (p69). The extremely wide crossing of the Bechler River at Rocky Ford is tricky even in low water (from mid-July) and may be completely impassable after heavy rain.

The less interesting, slightly shorter alternative is Bechler Meadows Trail, which requires a shorter, knee- to thigh-high ford near campsite 9B2 (no campfires) and treading some boggy terrain.

Beyond the ford, the Bechler River Trail heads east past the Mountain Ash Creek Trail junction. It then cuts north through forested patches and open grassy plains beside the meandering river to campsite 9B3, at the edge of a broad clearing 8 miles from the trailhead. For the first night's stay, the semi-private, hiker-only campsite 9B4 (no campfires), located 0.5 miles further, at the mouth of Bechler River Canyon, is recommended.

DAY 2: CAMPSITE 9B4 TO THREE RIVER JUNCTION
3½–4½ HOURS / 6.7 MILES / 600FT ASCENT

The trail continues to parallel the river, climbing through fir and spruce forests, birch trees and boulder fields bordering meadows thick with raspberries, thimbleberries and huckleberries. After 1.8 miles a marked side trail descends yards to a scenic overlook of Colonnade Falls, where the Bechler River plunges 85ft in two stages. The trail steepens, passing damp campsite 9B5 to reach the spectacular Iris Falls, a 40ft curtain of water spraying thick rainbow-filled mist.

The trail ascends through more old fir and spruce forest past gliding cataracts with picturesque islets and riverside campsite 9B6 to another major ford (a 50ft-wide, waist-deep wade). Upstream, the trail sees many muddy moments as it crosses several cold minor side streams before trailside campsite 9B7. A mile upstream, just before campsite 9B8 (and a pit toilet), is the last, less-serious ford, below a patch of burned forest.

Another mile on, the trail passes several algae-rich thermal areas fringing Three Rivers Meadow then passes inviting campsite 9B9 (no campfires and a two-night limit), with a hiker-only site tucked away on the east side of the canyon near the base of thundering Albright Falls, which descends from towering Batchelder Column. The 9B9 stock campsite and an NPS patrol cabin lie across a bridge on the opposite riverbank.

It's worth the steep extra mile of slog up out of the lovely river flats to the canyon's wild upper valley, where hidden campsite 9D1 (no campfires, sometimes not open until August) awaits beyond a footbridge over the Bechler's Ferris Fork. It doesn't get any lovelier than this: camp perched on a peninsula near Three River Junction, overlooking the Gregg, Ferris and Phillips Forks' tumbling confluence.

DAY 3: CAMPSITE 9D1 TO FERRIS FORK HOT SPRINGS
3–4 HOURS / 4.8 MILES / 500FT ASCENT

Having made it all this way, you will be giddy if you have booked an extra night in the 9B group of campsites, allowing you a day to explore.

Beyond 9D1, the trail switches back uphill half a mile past 45ft Ragged Falls to an unsigned (but well-trodden) turnoff on the east side of the trail for Ferris Fork Hot Springs.

The springs' submerged thermal source emanates from the middle of a 40ft-wide, waist-deep pool, where it mixes with chilly water from the stream's main channel, creating a royal, five-star soak often nicknamed 'Mr Bubbles'.

After checking out the surrounding thermal features, you might choose to hike another 0.5 to 1.5 miles upstream along the Ferris Fork to explore a quintuplet of seldom-seen waterfalls: 33ft Tendoy Falls, 20ft Gwinna Falls, 35ft Sluiceway Falls and 28ft Wahhi Falls.

Retrace your steps down into Bechler Canyon to your chosen 9B series campsite. If you are unable to reserve a campsite for the final night, it's a lengthy but manageable 13.5-mile descent back to the ranger station.

DAY 4: BECHLER RIVER CANYON TO BECHLER RANGER STATION
4–5 HOURS / 12.7 MILES / 800FT DESCENT

Retrace your steps down the canyon to the Bechler Ranger Station, taking a slightly different and more direct route back via the Bechler Meadows Trail.

Other Overnight Hikes

🎒 Mammoth Country

One of northern Yellowstone's most popular backpacking trips is the 18.5-mile Black Canyon of the Yellowstone from the Hellroaring trailhead past the fine fishing waters of the Yellowstone River. This part of the park is said to have one wolf, mountain lion or bear every 2 sq miles. There are 18 backcountry sites along the trail (site 1Y7 is a good halfway spot). You'll need to arrange a shuttle. The final section of trail into Gardiner was recently rerouted to the Eagle Creek forestry service campground to avoid a dispute with a private landowner.

The 19-mile trail to Mt Holmes (10,336ft) begins south of Indian Creek at Willow Flats picnic area and heads west to the summit. Make camp at 1C4 or 1C5 for the first night and tackle the peak the next morning. Radial hikes to Trilobite Lake look tempting, but the trail is unmaintained, with lots of downed trees in the way.

Three longer east–west backpacking routes begin west of Mammoth and lead to US 191 in Montana: the 19.5-mile Bighorn Pass Trail begins from Indian Creek Campground, and the 21-mile Fawn Pass Trail and 23-mile Sportsman Lake Trail to its north both begin at Glen Creek trailhead, south of Mammoth. Link two of them together for a rewarding loop. Off-trail travel is prohibited in this bear management area.

One exciting high-altitude option is the weeklong, 40-mile Gallatin Skyline route that crosses the Gallatin Range from west to east, from Dailey Creek in the far northwest to Mammoth, sticking to the high ridges along the Sky Rim Trail via Big Horn Peak, Shelf Lake, High Lake, Sportsman Lake and Electric Peak. Another great but slightly shorter variant (30 miles) is to hike the Sky Rim Trail as far as High Lake and then swing back to Specimen Creek trailhead for a fantastic four-day trip.

🚶 Roosevelt Country

The Bliss Pass hike, which begins half a mile before Slough Creek Campground, is a pleasant overnight shuttle hike along a popular fishing stream. Head east up Elk Tongue Creek, cross Bliss Pass (8 miles from the trailhead) and descend Pebble Creek to the namesake campground for a total hike of 21 miles. Bliss Pass may be snowbound until mid-July, and fording Pebble Creek can be tricky early in the season. This is a popular horse trail. The first part of the hike follows a historic wagon trail still used by the Silver Tip Ranch – though it lies just outside the north boundary, the trail is only accessible from the park and enjoys a historic right of access. Backcountry sites along Slough Creek are limited to a maximum stay of three nights between mid-June and mid-September.

🚗 DRIVING

There's hardly a single mile on Yellowstone's 142-mile Grand Loop Rd that can't be described as scenic. The views are always fantastic, whether it's the panoramic scenes from Dunraven Pass, shore views across Yel-

lowstone Lake or open valley views across meandering rivers and lodgepole forests.

Geyser Trail

Duration Half-day

Distance 25 miles

Start Madison

Finish Old Faithful

Nearest Town West Yellowstone

Speed Limit 45mph, sometimes dropping to 35mph; 25mph approaching Old Faithful area

Summary The drive south from Madison Campground links several geyser basins and wildlife-watching spots with opportunities to hike, cycle and even swim.

The northern approach to Old Faithful through the heart of Geyser Country offers lots of possible stops, so don't expect to cruise this route in one hit. The drive parallels the Firehole River and there are dozens of potential fly-fishing spots along the route.

Drive south from Madison Junction, past the junior ranger station, and after 2 miles take Firehole Canyon Dr to the right. This 2-mile side road takes you past rhyolite cliffs and rapids, Firehole Falls and the popular Firehole swimming area.

Back on the main road it's another 3 miles south to Fountain Flat Dr, which branches right to give access to the pleasant Nez Percé picnic area, the Sentinel Meadows hike (p66), Pocket Basin (p113) backcountry geyser area and the cycleable Fountain Freight Rd (p81).

Back on the main road, 1 mile south, the road crosses Chief Joseph Creek, where an interesting pullout details the flight of the Nez Percé (pronounced 'Nez Purse') tribe, who crossed this creek in August 1877 fleeing the US Army.

TRUMAN EVERTS

Everts Ridge, northwest of Mammoth, is named after Truman Everts, a member of the 1870 Washburn-Langford-Doane expedition and a notable early tourist-disaster story.

Separated from his group on the southern shores of Yellowstone Lake in September 1870, the 54-year-old tax inspector soon lost his bearings and promptly broke his glasses. His horse then bolted, taking all Everts' equipment with it, save for a penknife and a pair of opera glasses (not quite as useless as they sound – they helped him make fire!). He kept warm at night by cuddling up to hot springs near Heart Lake, until he ended up badly burning himself. At one point he spent the night in a tree, as a pacing mountain lion stalked him from below.

After 37 days lost in the wilderness, Everts was finally discovered, shoeless, frostbitten, emaciated, delirious and raving like a madman...but alive.

YELLOW STONE

The name Yellowstone was not inspired by the technicolor walls of the Grand Canyon as many people think, but rather the yellowish-tan bluffs near the confluence of the Yellowstone and Missouri Rivers in western North Dakota (though some sources also suggest the bluffs near Billings). In 1798 British fur trader David Thompson anglicized the phrase 'R des roches jaunes,' which means 'Yellow Rock (or Stone) River,' and which was used on a French map to describe the area near the Mandan villages of the upper Missouri. The French had, for their part, simply translated the Minetaree Native American name for the river, Mi tsi a da zi (Rock Yellow River).

In the region of the upper Yellowstone, near what is now the park, the Crow people knew the river as the Elk, but Elk National Park just doesn't have the same ring to it...

From here on you'll get your first views of the amazing thermal features ahead. A pullout 1 mile ahead offers a fine view of the smoking geysers and pools of Midway Geyser Basin to the right and Firehole Lake Basin on the left, as well as the meandering Firehole Valley and some of the park's largest bison herds – a classic Yellowstone vista.

Just 1 mile further, take a right into Fountain Paint Pot (p113). Another 1.5 miles south take the left on Firehole Lake Dr and make the leisurely 3-mile drive past Great Fountain Geyser and Firehole Lake to see what's on the boil. Next up is Midway Geyser Basin (p112), which is worth a stop. As you continue south, you'll see the colorful runoffs from Excelsior Pool flowing into the Firehole River.

Two miles further is busy Fairy Falls trailhead, a popular starting point for hikes to Fairy Falls, views over Grand Prismatic Spring (p112) and bike rides along the gravel Fountain Freight Rd. You'll also likely see bison and fly-fishers in this vicinity.

It's a further 2 miles to the minor thermal sites of Biscuit Basin (p111) and Black Sand Basin (p111), from where cyclists can get out and ride to Old Faithful, 1.5 miles away.

ᛂᛈ CYCLING

Cycling on Yellowstone's roads requires precautions. The roads are narrow and the RVs wide: in essence, you can't underestimate the threat of a rear-view mirror. For this reason, it is best to cycle on the main loops between dawn and 9am, before the traffic starts to snarl. Entering the park in the evening or leaving in the morning has you traveling against the flow of traffic.

Another alternative is to cycle early or late season, before the crowds of late June and after their departure in early September. From mid-March to the third Thursday in April, park roads between West Yellowstone and

Mammoth are open only to nonmotorized travel, creating a vehicle-free playground for cyclists and in-line skaters. For other roads, check the park for spring plowing information. Yellowstone has very few trails on which mountain biking is allowed. Among them are the service roads to Lone Star Geyser, Natural Bridge and the Bunsen Peak Rd double-track. In general bicycles are more useful for getting around campgrounds and riding on short family-friendly paved roads, rather than adventurous downhill trips.

Mammoth Country

The Old Gardiner Road between Mammoth and Gardiner offers a traffic-free ride along the late-19th-century stagecoach route into the park. After an initial uphill the dirt road then descends 1000ft in 5 miles. It's not a stunning ride, but does offer a rare opportunity to cycle in peace inside the park. You'll have to arrange a car shuttle or face a long uphill back. From May to October the road is open to motorized traffic (no RVs or trailers) one way to Gardiner; bikes can travel in either direction. From Gardiner you can continue along dirt roads to Corwin Springs, Yankee Jim Canyon and further into the Paradise Valley.

Unpaved Blacktail Plateau Dr offers a potential ride, though there can be a fair amount of vehicle traffic.

ᛂᛈ Bunsen Peak Road & Osprey Falls

Duration 1 hour (plus a 1½-hour strenuous hike to Osprey Falls)

Distance 6.8 miles return

Difficulty Easy

Elevation Change Negligible (800ft descent on hike to Osprey Falls)

Start/Finish Bunsen Peak trailhead (1K4)

Nearest Town/Junction Mammoth

Summary An easy ride on a former service road, best combined with the strenuous hike down to Osprey Falls.

Now closed to motor vehicles, 6-mile Bunsen Peak Rd is a largely flat dirt road popular among family cyclists. For active adults the best option is to combine the bike ride with a hike to Osprey Falls. To do this, lock your bike at a rack by the Osprey Falls trailhead, 3.4 miles into the ride. Return the way you came.

From the Osprey Falls junction a shuttle option is to continue downhill to a service road and vehicle-maintenance depot just above Mammoth, from where you can descend along the main road and then a walking trail beside the corral to Mammoth Junction. You'd have to arrange a car shuttle for this. Cycling back up the Grand Loop Rd isn't recommended due to the gradient, traffic and lack of a bicycle lane.

Canyon Country

As well as the easy bike rides around Canyon's north and south rim roads, the Canyon region offers the park's main uphill mountain-bike challenge.

₰ Mt Washburn

Duration 2 hours

Distance 5.6 miles return

Difficulty Difficult

Elevation Change 1400ft

Start/Finish Chittenden Rd trailhead (2K6)

Nearest Town/Junction Canyon Village

Summary The park's toughest mountain-bike trip, offering fabulous views from the peak and a thrilling descent.

Mt Washburn is accessed by two former service roads: the southern route from Dunraven Pass is open only to hikers, but the northerly Chittenden Rd is open to hikers, cyclists and the occasional park vehicle delivering supplies to the fire tower atop Mt Washburn. This isn't an easy jaunt you can attempt on a $50 bike from Wal-Mart (as we did), but rather a serious high-elevation climb for well-conditioned cyclists who have the luxury of plenty of low gears to choose from. Even then it's a tough haul. The fire tower offers restrooms (no water), a public telescope and displays on the Yellowstone caldera.

The large trailhead is just over 1 mile off the main Grand Loop Road and has a vault toilet. The road to the trailhead is sometimes closed at the main road early in the season. In this case you face an extra couple of miles and 500ft of elevation gain.

Access the old service road by the side of the metal gate that blocks the road to cars. This road was originally open to motor vehicles, though the early Model T Fords that attempted the route had to reverse all the way up the mountain because the engines didn't yet come with fuel pumps! The only traffic you'll see today is tourists and the occasional grizzly bear. The wonderful 1400ft descent is back along the same road. Watch out for hikers and other cyclists on the tarmac-and-gravel downhill run, as there are several blind corners. This is also prime grizzly summer habitat, so keep your eyes open for bears.

Lake Country

₰ Natural Bridge

Duration 45 minutes

Distance 2.4 miles

Difficulty Easy

Elevation Change 110ft

Start/Finish Bridge Bay

Nearest Town/Junction Bridge Bay

Summary A family-friendly ride to an interesting natural feature.

An excellent family cycling trail follows an old stagecoach road that once linked West Thumb to Lake Village. The paved road starts opposite the northbound turnoff to Gull Point Dr, just south of the Bridge Bay turnoff. There is parking just to the south. It is 1.2 miles to Natural Bridge, joining en route the hiking trail from Bridge Bay Marina. The flat route leads to rhyolite cliffs forming a natural bridge 51ft above Bridge Creek. You can hike the short uphill trail to the top, but don't walk on the fragile bridge. The trail is closed from late spring to early summer due to bear activity.

Geyser Country

In the Upper Geyser Basin bikes are allowed on the road (not the boardwalk) between Old Faithful and Morning Glory Pool (1.4

miles), and between Daisy Geyser and Biscuit Basin (1.3 miles).

You can hire bikes at Bear Den Bike (Map p108; Old Faithful Snow Lodge gift shop; half-/full day $25/35, kids' bikes $15/22.50). Bike trains (a kid's bike that hooks on the back of an adult bike) and trailers are also available. Rentals come with a helmet and lock.

In addition to the Fountain Freight Rd route described here, the former service road to Lone Star Geyser makes for a fine (and flat) 5-mile, round-trip ride, though you'll have to dismount for the last few yards to the actual geyser. Take a packed lunch for the geyser wait. Park in the Lone Star Geyser lot next to Kepler Cascades.

◖ Fountain Freight Road

Duration 1 hour cycling (up to 4 hours with excursions)

Distance 7 miles return

Difficulty Easy

Elevation Change Negligible

Start/Finish Fountain Flat Dr trailhead

Nearest Town/Junction Old Faithful

Summary An easy, flat bike ride on a gravel road that allows lots of stops and detours on foot – perfect for families.

The 4-mile Fountain Freight Rd between Fountain Flat Dr and Fairy Falls trailhead offers an opportunity to combine some pedaling with a hike to Fairy Falls and exploration of the Pocket Basin backcountry thermal area.

Just a few hundred yards from the Fountain Flat Dr trailhead, park your bike at the bridge over the Firehole River and check out the Ojo Caliente (p113) hot spring on the north bank. It's also well worth making the short hike along the unmarked trail east on the north side of the river to the hot springs and geysers of little-visited Pocket Basin (p113), just 10 minutes from the bridge. The two-hour Sentinel Meadows and Queen's Laundry Geyser hike (p66) also departs from here.

Continue south, past the Imperial/Sentinel Meadows trailhead to Goose Lake, the northern shore of which makes for a good picnic spot, either now or on the way back. Pedal south for 1.2 miles to the turnoff to Fairy Falls (p68). You can't cycle this side trail, but you can park your bike at the rack and make the 3.2-mile return hike to the waterfalls.

From the Fairy Falls turnoff continue 0.5 miles and you'll see the blue blur of Grand

Prismatic Spring to the left. Park the bike here and make the short but steep hike up the volcanic hillside to the left for fantastic aerial views over the colorful spring. From here turn around and cycle the 3.5 miles back to your car.

With help of a shuttle driver you could continue 0.5 miles to the Fairy Falls trailhead parking lot, throw your bikes in the car to Biscuit Basin, 3 miles away, then pick up the 1.3-mile cycleable trail to Daisy Geyser and on 1 mile to Old Faithful, where you can buy your driver a well-deserved ice cream.

OTHER ACTIVITIES

Horseback Riding

Stagecoach rides (adult/under 11yr $13.50/7) depart from the Roosevelt Lodge corral three or four times daily and last around 45 minutes. For a treat, ask for the tallyho seat.

Old West cookouts are a fun family trip, either on horseback (one-hour trips adult/under 12 $79/69, two-hour trips $88/81) or by horse-drawn wagon (per person $60/49). Reservations are required months in advance. Trips depart daily in the afternoon and travel to the former site of Uncle John Yancey's Pleasant Valley Hotel (1884–87), one of the park's earliest accommodations, for a gut-busting, all-you-can-eat chowdown of steak and beans accompanied by

BEST PLACES IN YELLOWSTONE TO SPOT WILDLIFE

The following places offer an excellent chance to get a glimpse of some seriously charismatic megafauna. Maximize your chances by arriving at dawn or dusk and renting a spotting scope from Silver Gate or Gardiner.

Roosevelt Country The Lamar Valley is known as the 'American Serengeti' for its dense population of wolves, bison, grizzlies, pronghorn, elk and trumpeter swans. Try also Antelope Creek for grizzlies and wolves.

Mammoth Country Elk trimming the lawns at Mammoth Junction, bighorn sheep on Everett Ridge between Mammoth and the North Entrance, wildfowl at Blacktail Ponds, moose at Willow Park and bears and wolves in the backcountry Gallatin Range.

Lake Country Birdlife at Sedge Bay; bison, moose, marmots and waterfowl at Storm Point; springtime grizzlies and moose at Pelican Creek; moose around Lewis Lake; grizzlies around Fishing Bridge in spring.

Norris Elk Park for, well, elk, as well as bison.

Canyon Country Spotters crowd the pullouts of the Hayden Valley at dusk searching for bison, coyotes, wolves and grizzlies (the latter two especially in spring). Ospreys in the canyon; south of Mud Volcano for bison. Mt Washburn for bighorn sheep, black bears and grizzlies.

Geyser Country The Firehole River and Madison Valley for bison, especially in winter.

campfire music. The excursion lasts about three hours.

Corrals next to Roosevelt Lodge offer trail rides (1/2hr $45/68) three or four times a day through sagebrush country. There are similar rides at Canyon (eight times a day, late June to late August). Two-hour rides run just once a day, so reserve, preferably a month or more ahead. Children must be over eight years of age. Rides can be canceled during afternoon storms or after rain.

Private horse-packing parties must obtain a backcountry-use permit ($5 per night per person) for overnight trips. A horse-use permit is also required for day trips. Both are available at most ranger stations. The *Horse Packing in Yellowstone* pamphlet lists regulations. Pack animals include horses, burros, mules, ponies and llamas.

Some backcountry trails are closed to stock, and those that are open may be temporarily closed in spring and early summer due to wet conditions. Overnight pack trips are not allowed until July 1. Stock can only be kept at designated campsites. Hay is not permitted at the trailhead or in the backcountry.

Xanterra OUTDOORS
(307-344-7901; www.yellowstonenationalpark-lodges.com) The park concessionaire operates most activities in Yellowstone. Reservations are essential and can be made by phone or at activities booths at most hotels. All activities operate from early June to early September.

Yellowstone Wilderness Outfitters HORSEBACK RIDING
(406-223-3300; www.yellowstone.ws) One of several professional outfitters licensed to run day rides ($225) and multiday pack trips in the park.

Boating

Yellowstone has some epic options for experienced boaters, though the lakes of the Tetons offer more scenic shorter paddles. Apart from some guided kayak trips near West Thumb, and some local boat rentals at Bridge Bay, you'll have to bring your own boat or rent one in a gateway city.

Park Regulations

A boating permit is required for all vessels, including float tubes.

Permits for motorized vessels cost $10 per week, or $20 per year, and are available from Bridge Bay Ranger Station, Grant Village Backcountry Ranger Office and the South Entrance.

Permits for nonmotorized vessels cost $5 per week, or $10 per year, and are available from the same offices, as well as the West Entrance, Northeast Entrance, West Yellowstone Chamber of Commerce, Bechler Ranger Station and backcountry offices at Old Faithful, Canyon and Mammoth.

Backcountry permits are required for all overnight boating trips in the park. Get these at Bridge Bay or Grant Village backcountry offices. Other regulations:

➤ Boating is permitted May 1 to November 1, although some areas may close during the season.

➤ Motorized vessels are allowed only on Lewis Lake and parts of Yellowstone Lake.

➤ Sylvan, Eleanor and Twin Lakes, plus Beach Springs Lagoon, are closed to all boating, as are all park streams and the Yellowstone River, except on the Lewis River between Lewis and Shoshone Lakes, where hand-propelled vessels are allowed.

➤ Launching is permitted only at Bridge Bay, Grant Village (open mid-June) and Lewis Lake. Hand-carried vessels may launch at Sedge Bay.

➤ The speed limit on Yellowstone Lake is 45mph. The limit on the south arms is 5mph, while the southernmost inlets are closed to motorboats.

➤ Landing is not allowed on the thermally affected shore of Yellowstone Lake between Little Thumb Creek and the south end of the West Thumb thermal area.

➤ Boating permits from Grand Teton National Park are honored, but you need to get a free Yellowstone validation sticker.

➤ Unlike Grand Teton, waterskiing and jet skis are prohibited in Yellowstone.

➤ Personal flotation devices (PFDs) are required for all craft.

Boating regulations pamphlets are available at all visitor centers. General boating information is at www.nps.gov/yell/planyourvisit/boating.htm.

Yellowstone Lake

Vast Yellowstone Lake just begs for extended kayak, boat and sailboat exploration, but it is important to plan your outing carefully. Drowning is the leading cause of death in Yellowstone. Water temperatures are very cold, averaging only 45°F (7°C) in the summer. Moreover, sudden winds can quickly churn up 3ft to 5ft waves, capsizing small vessels, so it's preferable to paddle in the early morning or late afternoon and avoid open-water crossings. Prevailing winds come from the southwest, so if you're headed south, you'll need to set off around dawn.

One pleasant, easy trip from Grant Village is the 5-mile return paddle to West Thumb Geyser Basin and Potts Geyser Basin. There's nowhere in the park to rent a kayak, so you'll have to bring your own or rent from Cody, Gardiner or Jackson (p99). Several companies in Jackson offer guided trips.

From Grant Village, the closest campsites are at Breeze Bay (8 to 10 miles away), some of which are for first- and last-night use only. The canoe and kayak put-in at Sedge Bay (trailhead 5K4) is the closest point from which to access the lake's southeast arm (21 miles), from where you can hike to the park's remote reaches. The nearest backcountry sites start 4 miles away.

If you want to spend a few days paddling around the remote southern arms of the lake, Bridge Bay Marina operates a boat shuttle ($95 per hour, two-hour minimum) for up to six people and their kayaks to docks at Eagle Bay (7L6), Wolf Bay (7L5), Plover Point (7M4), Promontory Tip (5L8) or Columbine Creek (5E6) on the east shore of the mouth of the southeast arm. Arrange it in advance and it'll pick you up again after a few idyllic days of remote paddling. There's only one boat, so book well in advance.

Certain shorelines are off-limits due to wildlife protection:

➤ Frank Island and the south end of Stevenson Island are closed from May 15 to August 15 to protect nesting ospreys and bald eagles.

➤ A 0.5-mile closure around Molly Island protects around 2000 breeding pelicans that summer here between April and September.

➤ The south and east shorelines are off-limits May 15 to July 14 to prevent bear disturbance.

The lake also has several anchor-only sites, including two at Frank Island. Boats need to be fully out of the water at some sites, others have docks.

Grant Village
Backcountry Ranger Office   BOATING
(☑307-242-2609; ☺8am-4:30pm) An excellent resource for boaters, this office has a folder detailing Yellowstone Lake campsites, with GPS coordinates, photos and mileage from the nearest boat put-ins. Some sites have restrictions on docking, hiking etc. Grant Village also has a marina nearby. Bridge Bay also has a good backcountry office for boaters.

Bridge Bay Marina   BOATING
(☑307-242-3880, boat shuttle 307-242-3893; ☺8am-8pm mid-Jun–early Sep) Offers rowboat ($10/45 per hour/day) and outboard ($50

per hour with fuel) rentals, as well as dock slip rentals ($20 to $27 per night) and backcountry boat shuttles.

Shoshone Lake

The largest backcountry lake in the lower 48, Shoshone Lake spells paradise for canoeists and kayakers. The serene lake is closed to motorized vessels and is lined with a dozen secluded boater-only campsites. On its far western edge, Shoshone Geyser Basin's pools, thermals and mud pots comprise the largest backcountry thermal area in the park. One-third of all of Yellowstone's backcountry use takes place along its shores, which are accessible only to hikers and hand-propelled boats.

Boaters must access the lake up the channel from Lewis Lake. From mid-July to August the channel requires portage of a few hundred yards in cold water (bring appropriate footwear), though in spring you can often paddle through.

Of 20 lakeshore campsites, 13 are reserved for boaters, four for hikers and three are shared. All have pit toilets. Rangers claim the nicest campsites are 8Q4, 8R4 and 8R1. Wood fires are not allowed along the lakeshore.

Most boaters make their first camp on the south shore (campsites nearest to the channel are reserved for first- and last-night use only). If you need to cross the lake, do so early in the morning and at the half-mile-wide Narrows in the center of the lake. Prevailing winds are from the southwest and pick up after noon. The lake is icebound until mid-June, when flooding is possible at shoreline campsites. Backcountry boating campsites at Shoshone Lake cannot be reserved before July 1 or 15, depending on the site.

Fishing

Yellowstone is justly famous for its fly-fishing, and the park's gateway towns have dozens of excellent fly-fishing shops that can offer expert local advice on current flows, flies and hatches, or arrange fully guided trips. Where else can you cast your line in sight of a grazing bison, or the steam of an exploding geyser?

Cutthroat trout, grayling and mountain whitefish, among 11 species that are native to the park, are catch-and-release only. Some areas (such as the Gibbon River below Gibbon Falls) are open to fly-fishing only. Lead weights are prohibited; only nontoxic alternatives are sanctioned.

Fishing season usually runs from June 15 to the first Sunday in November, except for streams that flow into Yellowstone Lake and some tributaries of the Yellowstone River, which open July 15. Other rivers are permanently closed to fishing, including a 6-mile stretch of the Yellowstone River in the Hayden Valley; some may close during the season due to bear activity. The useful *Fishing Regulations* pamphlet details the park's complex rules and regulations.

A Yellowstone park fishing permit is required for anglers aged 16 and older (state licenses are not required). Permits cost $18/25 for three/seven days, or $35 for the season; free permits are required for unsupervised anglers aged 15 and under. Permits are available from ranger stations, visitor centers and Yellowstone general stores.

Detailed fishing information can be found at www.nps.gov/yell/planyourvisit/fishing.htm.

Yellowstone Lake

Yellowstone Lake is stocked with cutthroat trout, longnose dace, redside shiners, longnose suckers and lake chub. Popular shore or float-fishing spots include Gull Point, Sand Point picnic area, Sedge Bay, Mary Bay and Steamboat Point.

BE A HERO: GO FISHING

Lake (or Mackinaw) trout were introduced to Yellowstone Lake illegally (although the park itself had stocked Lewis and Shoshone Lakes with them earlier). Since they have no natural predators, their Pac-Man-like presence has wreaked havoc on native cutthroat trout. In a year, one lake trout can eat 41 cutthroats, sushi dinners normally destined for feeding grizzlies and bald eagles. If the trend continues, the native trout population may fall to 10% of historic highs, tipping the overall ecological balance.

With a fishing rod and free time you could help redress the situation. Regulations encourage anglers to catch lake trout. The Volunteer Fly Fishing Program (www.nps.gov/yell/naturescience/vol_fishing.htm) puts anglers on the park's 2650 miles of streams and 150 lakes to help collect biological data through catch-and-release techniques.

THE TALLEST TALES IN THE WEST

Jim Bridger is famed as a mountain man and trapper who explored the Yellowstone region in the 1830s, but he was also the West's consummate teller of tall tales. Level-headed lowlanders may have dismissed his outrageous stories with a patronizing slap on the back but, as with most enduring stories, much of the fiction was actually based in fact.

Bridger's most famous tales told of Yellowstone's petrified trees (fact, though he couldn't resist upping the ante to 'peetrified birds singing peetrified songs'); a 'mountain of glass' that acted as a giant telescope (fiction, but based on the volcanic glass of Obsidian Cliff); a river that flowed so fast that friction made it hot on the bottom (actually thermal runoff on the Firehole River); and a spot on Yellowstone Lake where you could throw out a line and reel in a cooked fish (fact, a technique proved by early tourists at Fishing Cone, with the help of an underwater geyser).

He also told of a place where fish could cross the Rocky Mountains (actually Two Ocean Plateau, just south of the park), with a stream atop the Continental Divide branching into two, one leading to the Atlantic, the other to the Pacific. (Lake Isa does the same thing between Old Faithful and Yellowstone Lake, but has no fish.)

Fishing is not allowed on Pelican Creek from its outlet to 2 miles upstream, or on the Yellowstone River from 0.25 miles upstream of Fishing Bridge to its outflow from Yellowstone Lake. Hayden Valley is closed to fishing except for two short catch-and-release stretches. All lake trout caught in Yellowstone Lake should be killed.

Bridge Bay Marina   FISHING
(☑307-344-7311; fishing trips per 2/4½hr $180/405; ☺mid-Jun–mid-Sep) The marina rents boats and offers guided Yellowstone Lake fishing trips. Prices are for up to six people, and include three rods and reels. The marina also has a tackle shop and offers good fishing information. The marina area itself is closed to fishing.

Geyser Country

The Madison and Gibbon Rivers offer some of the park's best and most scenic fly-fishing. The Firehole (between Biscuit and Midway Geyser Basins), Madison and Gibbon (downstream from Gibbon Falls) Rivers are open for fly-fishing only and lots of pullouts offer access. During hot summers the Firehole is often closed completely to fishing because of high water temperatures.

The pullout beneath Mt Haynes, on the Madison River between Madison Junction and West Yellowstone, offers a good, wheelchair-accessible, riverside fishing spot.

Roosevelt Country

Slough Creek is the sweetest fishing spot in the northeast (closely followed by Pebble Creek and Soda Butte Creek), which is one reason why the park's Slough Creek Campground is regularly the first to fill up. Ensure that you make your backcountry reservations early if you want to overnight in any of the Slough Creek backcountry campsites. Other good places include the Black Canyon of the Yellowstone and the Lamar River.

Cross-Country Skiing & Snowshoeing

All backcountry trails are denoted with orange markers, so you can theoretically ski or snowshoe most of the backcountry trails in the area.

Once in the park, skier shuttles will transport you to and from set trailheads, where you can take a trail or just ski back. Shuttles operate from Mammoth to Bunsen Peak Rd and Indian Creek ($21 round-trip, three per day, four days weekly) and to Tower Creek ($31 round-trip, three days weekly). A daily one-way shuttle also runs from Old Faithful Snow Lodge (p121) to Fairy Falls or Divide trailheads ($21 one way; you must ski back).

Combined snowcoach and ski/showshoe tours run from Old Faithful to Canyon ($185) daily.

Cross-country ski ($25 per day) and snowshoe ($22) rentals are available at Mammoth Hot Springs Hotel (p116) and the Snow Lodge at Old Faithful, as is ski instruction ($26 for two hours, $40 with equipment).

The Canyon to Washburn Hot Springs Overlook section of the Grand Loop Rd is open to Nordic skiers.

YELLOWSTONE'S WINTER WONDERLAND

Winter is a magical time to visit Yellowstone. The falls turn to frozen curtains of ice, the geysers spurt taller and steamier than normal and surrounding 'ghost trees' turn into surreal frozen steam sculptures. The warm thermal areas around Old Faithful, Norris and Mammoth become winter refuges for elk and bison, and the thermally heated (and thus still flowing) rivers attract plenty of waterfowl.

The winter season runs from late December to mid-March, and activity centers on Mammoth Hot Springs Hotel (p116) and Old Faithful Snow Lodge (p121), the only two accommodations open in the park. Independent travel is more difficult in winter and most people sign up for a lodging and activity package, which often works out cheaper than arranging things yourself. The Yellowstone Institute (Map p92; 307-344-2293; www.yellowstoneassociation.org/institute) runs some particularly good winter programs.

Accessing the park is an adventure in itself. The only road open year-round is the northern Mammoth–Cooke City road via Tower-Roosevelt Junction, plus an extension to Mammoth's Upper Terraces. During the season, Xanterra (p82) operates one-way snowcoach tours once daily between Old Faithful and Mammoth ($93.75) and Flagg Ranch ($93.75). It also operates a road shuttle between Bozeman Airport and Mammoth ($52.50). Private snowcoach companies offer only return day trips from West Yellowstone.

Trips inside the park include day snowcoach tours to Canyon ($166.50) from Old Faithful and Mammoth, half-day tours to Norris from Mammoth ($83) and half-day tours from Old Faithful to West Thumb ($72), the Madison Valley ($83) or the Firehole Basin ($62.50).

Winter Facilities

Mammoth Hot Springs Hotel and Old Faithful Snow Lodge and their restaurants are the only places open, though there is limited (and cold!) winter camping at Mammoth Campground. You can snow camp anywhere in the park, with a backcountry permit, but winter camping conditions are for specialists only.

Both hotels rent snowshoes and cross-country skis. You can ice skate in Mammoth and Old Faithful (with free skate rental). After a day on skis you'll appreciate Mammoth Hotel's hot-tub cabins or a massage at the Old Faithful Snow Lodge.

There are no public accommodations in Canyon, but Yellowstone Expeditions (800-728-9333; www.yellowstoneexpeditions.com) runs a winter yurt camp there for its cross-country ski and snowshoe tours. Four-day tours from West Yellowstone cost around $1100 per person, including transportation, heated accommodations, sauna, food and a guide.

Visitor centers at Old Faithful and Mammoth are open during the winter season. There are winter warming huts at Mammoth, Indian Creek, Old Faithful (in yurts), West Thumb, Fishing Bridge, Madison and Canyon; the latter two have fast food. Snowmobile fuel is available at Canyon, Fishing Bridge, Old Faithful and Mammoth. Mammoth Clinic is open weekdays and Old Faithful Clinic is open periodically.

Snowmobile Regulations

The park service enforces a daily cap of 'transportation events' (ie winter vehicles) into the park. Snowmobilers have to be accompanied by a commercial guide, in a maximum group size of 10, though new regulations now permit snowmobilers to take an online course and get a private permit to enter the park. These limited permits (one per day) are awarded through a lottery. See www.recreation.gov for details and to apply. Park entry fees are $25 per snowmobile for each national park ($40 for both).

Snowmobiles are banned from all the park's side roads, including the Lake Butte Overlook, Firehole Canyon Dr and a section of the Grand Loop Rd from Canyon to Tower. All other roads are groomed for over-snow travel. Snowmobile operators must carry a valid state driver's license. The speed limit between the West Entrance and Old Faithful is 35mph; elsewhere it is 45mph. Roads are only open 7am to 9pm and off-road snowmobiling is prohibited.

Mammoth & Roosevelt Country

The north of the park is logistically easier to visit in winter because the road between Mammoth and Cooke City remains open year-round. Around the Mammoth region it's possible to ski from Indian Creek Campground to Sheepeater Cliffs and then along a backcountry trail to Bunsen Peak Trail and left to the Mammoth–Norris road (5 miles) or right downhill along Bunsen Peak Rd to upper Mammoth terraces. There are also marked loops around Indian Creek (2.2 miles) and partway along the nearby Bighorn Trail (5.5 miles).

The groomed 1.5-mile Upper Terrace Loop Trail follows the Upper Terrace road and is a good place to test out your Nordic legs. A side trail from here follows an old wagon track steeply uphill to Snow Pass and then along Glen Creek back to the Bunsen Peak trailhead (4.2 miles). It's easier in the opposite direction.

In the park's northeast corner a popular ski trail (3.5 miles) parallels the Northeast Entrance Rd below Barronette Peak (10,404ft) between the Soda Butte Creek bridges. The nearby 2-mile Bannock Trail runs east out of the park from the Warm Creek picnic area along an old mining road to Silver Gate.

Around Tower-Roosevelt, the 8-mile Blacktail Plateau Trail follows the unplowed road of the same name and is a popular shuttle option. The trail climbs gradually to the Cut and then descends for 2 miles to the main Mammoth–Cooke City road.

Rangers lead free guided snowshoe walks around Mammoth Upper Terraces at 2pm on Sunday from December to the end of February (check the park newspaper).

Geyser Country

The area around Old Faithful has the most trails and facilities in winter. Xantera runs three-hour guided snowshoe tours ($30, with shoe rental $38) twice daily. Half-day guided ski tours ($55) to Lone Star Geyser leave Old Faithful on Sunday.

Upper and Midway Geyser Basins both make for some fine ski trips. You can ski or snowshoe from Old Faithful to Black Sand Basin via Daisy Geyser (4 miles), or to Biscuit Basin via Morning Glory and Atomizer Geyser (5 miles, with a possible extension to Mystic Falls). The frozen Fairy Falls hike is a popular ski day trip – get dropped off at the southern end of Fountain Freight Rd, visit the falls and ski back to Old Faithful (11 miles).

An 8-mile return trip can take you from Old Faithful Snow Lodge and the Mallard Lake trailhead along the Kepler Cascade Ski Trail, crossing the main road to join the main trail to Lone Star Geyser. The Divide ski shuttle will allow you to take the 8-mile Spring Creek Trail (a former stagecoach road) to Lone Star Geyser.

◉ SIGHTS

◉ Mammoth Country

Mammoth Country is renowned for its graceful geothermal terraces and the towering Gallatin Range to the northwest. As the lowest and driest region of the park, it's also the warmest and a good base for winter and early or late-season activities.

The region's Northern Range is an important wintering area for wildlife, including the park's largest herds of elk, pronghorn, mule deer and bighorn sheep. Around half the park's population of elk winter here, attracted by the lower temperatures and lack of snow on many south-facing slopes (due to the sun and prevailing wind). The poorly aerated and drained soil supports scant vegetation, creating 'dry desert' conditions.

For visitors (and most elk) the focal point of the Mammoth region is Mammoth Junction (6239ft), 5 miles south of the North Entrance, on a plateau above Mammoth Campground. The former park headquarters contains the region's main services, including a visitor center, backcountry office, post office, gas station, medical center and even a church and courthouse. The Mammoth Hot Springs Hotel has espresso and public showers, while the Yellowstone General Store offers groceries, souvenirs and cold beer.

Just south of the junction is Mammoth Hot Springs, the area's main thermal attraction. From here roads go south to Norris (21 miles) and east to Tower-Roosevelt Junction (18 miles).

Mammoth

Mammoth Hot Springs   HOT SPRINGS
(Map p88) The imposing Lower and Upper Terraces of Mammoth Hot Springs are the highlight of the Mammoth region. An hour's worth of boardwalks wend their way around the Lower Terraces and connect to the Upper Terraces Loop, which is also accessed by car. Surreal Palette Springs (accessed from

the lower parking lot) and sulfur-yellow Canary Springs (accessed from the upper loop) are the most beautiful sites, but thermal activity is constantly in flux, so check the current state of play at the visitor center.

The famously ornate travertine formations that characterize the lower terraces of Minerva Spring have been dry since 2002 but are still beautiful. The terraces are the product of dissolved subterranean limestone (itself originally deposited by ancient seas), which is continuously deposited as the spring waters cool on contact with air. As guidebooks love to say, the mountain is in effect turning itself inside out, depositing over a ton of travertine (limestone deposits) here every year. The colored runoff from the naturally white terraces is due to the bacteria and algae that flourish in the warm waters.

At the bottom of the terraces, by the parking area, is the phallic, dormant 36ft-high hot-spring cone called Liberty Cap, apparently named after hats worn during the French Revolution. The former spring must have had particularly high water pressure to create such a tall cone over its estimated 2500-year life span.

Across the road, Opal Spring is slowly converging on a century-old residence designed by Robert Reamer (the architect of the Old Faithful Inn and Roosevelt Arch). Park strategists have to decide which to preserve – the architecture or the spring. The rutting Rocky Mountain elk that sometimes lounge on Opal Terrace in fall are a favorite photo opportunity.

A 1.5-mile paved one-way road loops counterclockwise around the Upper Terraces; vehicles longer than 25ft will have to park on the main Grand Loop Rd. The overlook affords impressive views of the Lower Terraces and Fort Yellowstone and offers access to Canary Springs and New Blue Spring. Highlights further around the loop include the spongelike Orange Spring Mound and the perfectly named White Elephant Back Terrace. The loop joins the main road near the large Angel Terrace.

For an alternative perspective on foot, walk the Howard Eaton Trail from Orange Spring Mound (unsigned) or from the Snow Pass trailhead.

Ninety-minute ranger walks leave from the Upper Terrace daily at 9am.

Fort Yellowstone   HISTORIC SITE

(Map p88) Mammoth Hot Springs was known as Fort Yellowstone from 1886 to 1918, when the US Army managed the park from this collection of historic buildings. Elk regularly

Mammoth Country Area

graze the manicured lawns of the campus-like historic and administrative centre, bringing traffic to a standstill, and the high-pitched cries of bugling elk echo around the region in fall.

If you're particularly interested in park history, pick up the *Fort Yellowstone Historic District Tour Guide* brochure for a self-guided tour of the fort's original buildings. The tour takes in the former jail, barracks, granary and stables, most of which have been converted to employee residences. The guardhouse at the end of the row once controlled all public access into the park. If you are here on a Sunday morning, pop into the lovely English-style church (1913), where the stained-glass windows depict Old Faithful and Yellowstone Falls. (You can even get married here if you like). Other notables include the green-tiled Chinese-style roof of the chief engineer's office (nicknamed the 'pagoda') and the bear statues that guard the entrance to the historic post office.

Rangers lead hour-long history walks daily at 6pm, departing from the visitor center.

Albright Visitor Center MUSEUM
(Map p88; ☎307-344-2263; ⊙8am-7pm) Mammoth's recently revamped visitor center features displays on the park's early visitors,

alongside lots of stuffed animals. Don't miss the fine photographs of former superintendent Norris in his trademark buckskins, and mountain man Jim Bridger bearing an uncanny resemblance to country singer Willie Nelson. Rangers give talks in front of the center at 10am, 2pm and 3pm.

The visitor-center complex is named for Horace Albright, park superintendent between 1919 and 1929 and director of the National Park Service from 1929 to 1933. The center was formerly the army's bachelor quarters.

Mammoth Hot Springs Hotel HISTORIC BUILDING
The Mammoth Hot Springs Hotel is worth a visit even if you are not staying. Piano music echoes around the lobby from 5pm followed by video or slide presentations in the side Map Room, where you can also check out the huge wall map of the United States assembled from 15 types of wood from around the world. Also worth noting is the charming antique water fountain to the left of the Activities Desk.

Mammoth to Tower-Roosevelt

The 18-mile road to Tower-Roosevelt Junction heads east from Mammoth over the Gardner River Bridge, where the Gardner River meets the Yellowstone River. By the roadside, just over 2 miles from Mammoth, is pretty, three-tiered **Undine Falls**, aptly named for an alluring water nymph. Get private views of the falls from the north side of the river by hiking less than half a mile along Lava Creek Trail from the nearby Lava Creek picnic area.

The easy 1-mile round-trip walk to **Wraith Falls** is a good family hike through pretty meadows and fire-burn patches. The trail begins at the pullout east of Lava Creek picnic area, 5 miles from Mammoth, and follows Lupine Creek for 15 minutes to the base of a 79ft cascade. Rangers lead walks here twice weekly at 9am.

Just past the **Blacktail Ponds** pullout (good for spotting muskrats and waterfowl) is the Blacktail Creek trailhead, where trails lead down Rescue Creek or into the Black Canyon of the Yellowstone near Crevice Lake.

Two miles past here, the 0.5-mile **Forces of the Northern Range Self-Guiding Trail** is an accessible boardwalk that teaches children about the environmental forces of this part of the park. Kids will get a kick from placing their hand on a wolf print.

Mammoth Country Area

◉ Sights
1	Albright Visitor Center	B2
2	Back Basin	B7
3	Fort Yellowstone	B2
4	Mammoth Hot Springs	B3
5	Museum of the National Park Ranger	B6
6	Norris Museum	B7
7	Porcelain Basin	B7

☺ Activities, Courses & Tours
8	Beaver Ponds/Sepulcher Mountain Trailhead	B2

⊜ Sleeping
9	Eagle Creek Campground	B1
10	Indian Creek Campground	B4
11	Mammoth Campground	B2
12	Mammoth Hot Springs Hotel	B2
13	Norris Campground	B6

⊗ Eating
	Mammoth Hot Springs Dining Room	(see 12)
	Mammoth Terrace Grill	(see 12)

◉ Drinking & Nightlife
	Espresso Cart	(see 12)

BOILING RIVER: THE PARK'S WORST-KEPT SECRET

One of the few places where you can take a legal soak in Yellowstone is Boiling River, halfway between Gardiner and Mammoth. From the parking area by the Montana–Wyoming border a trail leads 0.5 miles along the river to a point where an underground hot spring surfaces from below a limestone overhang. There are several pools along the riverside (be aware of the potential dangers of soaking in hot springs) and these can get busy in summer.

Bring a towel and flip-flops. The only changing area is the vault toilet at the parking lot. Swimming is allowed only during daylight hours and food, pets, alcohol and nudity are prohibited. The pools are closed when river levels are high (most commonly in spring).

The turnouts north of here are good places to spot pronghorn in the summer and bighorn sheep and elk in the winter. Also to the north is a sign that marks the 45th parallel, halfway between the equator and the North Pole.

The 6-mile one-way Blacktail Plateau Drive detours off the main highway to follow part of the Bannock Trail, a hunting route taken by Bannock Indians in the mid-19th century. The trail originated in Idaho, crossed the Yellowstone Valley at the Bannock Ford and continued through the Lamar Valley to Soda Butte Creek before leaving what is now the park at its northeast corner and continuing to Bighorn Valley. Along the second half of this drive, near Crescent Hill, is the spot where Truman Everts was finally discovered after wandering lost in the park for 37 days (p78). RVs and trailers are not allowed down the rough, unpaved road, but bikes are an option if you have someone to pick you up at the other end.

Instead of taking Blacktail Plateau Dr, you can continue east on the main Grand Loop Rd. You'll pass Phantom Lake (one of three interconnected lakes that are normally dry by July) and an unsigned scenic overview of Hellroaring Mountain, Garnet Hill and the Yellowstone River and Hellroaring Creek valleys. A couple of miles further is the Hellroaring trailhead, a short drive down a dirt road and popular with horse packers headed into the Black Canyon of the Yellowstone.

Half a mile past here, Floating Island Lake is dense with vegetation, making it a good place to spot birds.

Just before you reach Tower-Roosevelt Junction is the 0.25-mile turnoff (no RVs or trailers) to the heavily visited Petrified Tree, surrounded by a fence like a priceless work of art. The tree is worth a quick look if you've never seen one before, but the parking lot can be cramped and busy. A nicer way to visit the tree is on an early-morning or evening hike from Roosevelt Lodge on the Lost Lake loop (p56).

Mammoth to Norris

The 20-mile road from Mammoth to Norris passes the Upper Terraces and enters a jumbled landscape of hoodoos, formed when the 65,000-year-old travertine deposits of nearby Terrace Mountain slipped down the hillside, breaking into boulder-like fragments. (You can get an up-close look at the hoodoos on the Terrace Mountain Loop hike, or by walking the Howard Eaton Trail from Glen Creek trailhead down to Mammoth.) The road climbs to the cantilevered road of Golden Gate, named after the light-colored welded rock formed from cooled ash flows. The sprouting knob of rock on the outside of the road was actually pulled down and then replaced when the road was widened!

Shortly afterwards a pullout offers views of tiny Rustic Falls, a natural funnel that was probably used by the Sheepeater people to trap bighorn sheep. The Sheepeaters, also known as the Tukudika, were a subtribe of the Shoshone and the park's earliest year-round inhabitants.

The peak rising to the left is Bunsen Peak (8564ft), a plug of solidified magma that formed inside a long-since-eroded volcanic cone. Hiking and cycling trails head up and around Bunsen Peak from the busy Bunsen Peak/Glen Creek trailhead. Further along on the right, delightful Swan Lake, in the middle of Gardner's Hole, offers good bird-watching (look for trumpeter swans in winter and early spring) and views of the Gallatin Range. A board helps identify various peaks.

Two miles further south, turn off for the Sheepeater Cliffs, an amazing collection of 500,000-year-old hexagonal basalt columns, stacked like building blocks. You'll find a scenic picnic area and strolls along the river to more formations (no buses, trailers or RVs allowed on this road).

The road passes a nice fishing spot and winter warming hut near Indian Creek Campground, then continues to a series of four pullouts at Willow Park and Moose Bogs, 2 miles further south and a good place to look for some of the park's 200-or-so moose. Soon after comes a pleasant picnic spot at Appolinaris Spring, once a popular stagecoach stop for parched travelers headed to Norris.

Obsidian Cliff, to the left of the road, exposes the interior of a 180,000-year-old lava flow. Rapid cooling prevented the formation of crystals and fused the lava into this form of volcanic glass. Obsidian, used for spearheads and arrowheads, was widely traded by Native Americans and was one of the major reasons early people visited the Yellowstone region. The park service was forced to remove the cliffside trails of this National Historic Landmark due to pilfering of the obsidian – leave it alone!

Just 1 mile further, the Beaver Lake picnic area offers a fine spot for a picnic and some wildlife-watching. Just past here, isolated fumaroles, hot springs and other thermal features start to appear by the side of the road, heralding the approach of the thermally active Norris region.

Roaring Mountain is a huge bleached hillside pockmarked with hissing fumaroles. During its heyday, around the turn of the last century, visitors could hear the roar of the fumaroles from over 4 miles away. The activity is much reduced today.

From here the road passes pretty North and South Twin Lakes and descends to beautiful Nymph Lake. The lake's bubbling pools, bleached white shoreline and steaming geysers lend the area a powerfully primeval air – something out of the landscapes of Tolkien or the age of the dinosaurs. Just south of here is the unsigned but superbly named Devil's Frying Pan springs. The smell of sulfur stays with you as the road quickly descends into the Norris Geyser Basin.

◉ Roosevelt Country

President Theodore Roosevelt visited this rugged mountainous area in the park's northeast corner during a two-week jaunt through the park in 1903, lending his name to the rustic Roosevelt Lodge by Tower-Roosevelt Junction that opened three years later. Fossil forests, the wildlife-rich Lamar Valley, its tributary trout streams and the dramatic and craggy peaks of the Absaroka Range are the highlights in this remote, scenic and undeveloped region. The rustic cabins, stagecoach rides and Western cookouts at the Roosevelt Lodge add a cowboy flavor to the region's frontier feel. The area is also the birthplace of the park's current bison and wolf populations and one of Yellowstone's great wildlife-viewing areas.

The 29-mile Northeast Entrance Rd passes from Cooke City through the Lamar Valley to Tower-Roosevelt Junction (6270ft) and then continues west for 18 miles to Mammoth Junction. This is the only road in the park that remains open year-round. From Tower-Roosevelt Junction the Grand Loop Rd heads south to Canyon Village, over the high Dunraven Pass.

Roosevelt Lodge has accommodations, food, showers, a small grocery store and a nearby ranger station and gas station, as well as a horse corral for trail rides and hiking trails to nearby Lost Lake.

Northeast Entrance to Tower-Roosevelt

It's 29 miles from the Northeast Entrance to Tower-Roosevelt. A couple of miles inside the Northeast Entrance the road enters Wyoming and follows Soda Butte Creek, offering fine views of the craggy ridgeline of towering Barronette Peak (10,404ft) to the west. It was Jack Baronet who rescued Truman Everts (p78) for a promised $600 reward. Not only did he not get the reward, but the park misspelled the peak it named after him! Near Pebble Creek Campground at tiny Icebox Canyon, the lovely valley warms up and opens wide. Southeast is a ridgeline known as the Thunderer (10,554ft), after the frequent storms that gather here.

Two miles past Pebble Creek is the trailhead for the short 0.5-mile walk through fir forest and summer wildflowers to scenic Trout Lake, named after the abundant cutthroats that spawn here in early summer. The 10-minute uphill hike to the pretty lake is steep enough to leave you puffing, but it's still one of the park's best short family hikes. It's popular also with anglers, who are allowed to keep their catch of rainbow (but not cutthroat) trout. Lose the crowds by following the side trail from the stream inflow for 10 minutes to Buck Lake.

Further along the road, watch (and sniff) for the whitish-yellow travertine cone of Soda Butte, the only thermal feature in this part of the park.

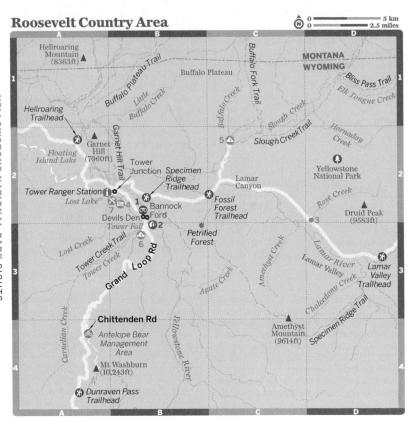

Roosevelt Country Area

The road now joins the mixed sagebrush and grasslands of the **Lamar Valley**, one of the park's premier wildlife-viewing areas. The roadside turnouts between Pebble Creek and Slough (pronounced 'slew') Creek campgrounds, particularly the stretch between Lamar River trailhead and the Lamar Canyon, are prime places to spot wolves from the Lamar Canyon pack. Elk and large herds of bison also make the broad Lamar Valley their winter range, occupying separate ecological niches alongside coyotes, pronghorns and bears.

Also here is the former **Buffalo Ranch**, which almost single-handedly raised Yellowstone's bison herds between 1907 and 1960. The buildings are now home to the excellent Yellowstone Institute (p86).

About 6 miles before Tower-Roosevelt Junction, a dirt road turns off north to Slough Creek Campground, offering fishing and hiking access. Further along the main road are several glacially formed 'kettle'

ponds, which are periodically closed to protect nesting trumpeter swans.

Just before Tower the road passes the popular Yellowstone River picnic area and hiking trail (look for wildlife here) and bridges the Yellowstone River.

Tower-Roosevelt Junction

Calcite Springs Overlook   VIEWPOINT
(Map p92) This worthwhile overlook 1.5 miles south of Tower-Roosevelt Junction offers vertiginous views of a section of the Grand Canyon of the Yellowstone known as the Narrows. A short trail leads to views north of the gorge's sulfuric yellows and smoking sides. All around are vertical basalt columns, part of a 25ft-deep lava flow that covered the area 1.3 million years ago. Below the basalt are glacial deposits; above the basalt are layers of volcanic ash.

More hexagonal basalt columns hang above the roadside a little further along the main road, though parking here is limited. You'll find dramatic (and crowd-free!) views of Calcite Springs and the Narrows from the Yellowstone River Picnic Area Trail.

Tower Fall   WATERFALL
(Map p92) Two-and-a-half miles south of Tower-Roosevelt Junction, Tower Creek plunges over 132ft Tower Fall before joining the Yellowstone River. The fall gets its name from the volcanic breccia towers around it, which are like a demonic fortress and earn it the nickname The Devil's Den. A short trail leads to a viewpoint over the falls and then continues down 200 vertical feet to the Yellowstone River.

Local storytellers claim that prominent Minaret Peak gets its name from one Minnie Rhett, the girlfriend of an early park visitor, but that sounds to us like one of Jim Bridger's tall tales (see p85). Iconic landscape painter Thomas Moran created one of his most famous paintings here.

Stop in for well-deserved ice cream at the Yellowstone General Store on the way back. Tower Fall Campground is just across the road from the parking area. The busy parking lot often fills up by the middle of the day. The potholed and narrow section of road between Tower Fall and Tower-Roosevelt Junction is one of the worst in the park.

Tower-Roosevelt to Canyon

It's 19 miles from Tower-Roosevelt to Canyon. The Grand Loop Rd starts to climb from Tower Fall on its way to **Dunraven Pass** (8859ft), the highest part of the Grand Loop Rd and named after the British earl who traveled here in 1874 (it was Dunraven's travelogue, *The Great Divide*, that popular-

ized the park in Europe). Several turnouts offer popular wildlife-watching opportunities toward Antelope Creek, a prime grizzly habitat that's closed to visitors.

Named after Hiram Chittenden, one of the park's early road engineers and historians, Chittenden Rd branches off to the left before the pass. The road is a popular hiking and mountain-biking trail to the summit of **Mt Washburn** (10,243ft). A second, hiking-only trail leads to the peak from Dunraven Pass, 5 miles further south.

Just below Dunraven Pass is the **Washburn Hot Springs Overlook**, where an interpretive sign describes the hot springs and the surrounding Yellowstone caldera, which you now enter as you continue south. This is also a good wildlife-watching area, especially for grizzlies that wander here from the surrounding Washburn and Antelope Bear Management Areas.

☉ Canyon Country

The Canyon area is the second-most heavily visited part of the park after Old Faithful, due largely to the scenic grandeur of the Grand Canyon of the Yellowstone, but also due to the junction's central location and its concentration of visitor services. The impressive canyon is the star of the show and a series of scenic overlooks and a network of trails along the canyon's rims and interior highlight its multihued beauty from a multitude of angles.

Canyon Village

Canyon Village lies just east of Canyon Junction along North Rim Dr. It's the logistical base for the central part of the park and has accommodations, three restaurants, a visitor center, backcountry office, general store, outdoor gear store and ATM. The campground area has showers, laundry and an ice machine.

Canyon Visitor Center   MUSEUM
(Map p96; ☏307-242-2550; ⊗8am-8pm late May–mid-Oct) This modern visitor center is well worth a visit for its innovative and interactive displays on Yellowstone's geology. The highlight is a room-sized relief model of the park, on which you can visualize the terrain of your upcoming hike. Twenty-minute movies play on the hour and half-hour and there are ranger talks for children (3pm) and adults (6pm). Upstairs there's a sobering map of earthquakes that happened that day in the park (an average of 2000 each year,

most of them in the Norris basin), scratchy black-and-white videos of Old Faithful through the years and a computer animation booth that details the annual bison migrations through the parks. One surprise is the artist's impression of what the park may have looked like 20,000 years ago – covered in a 4000ft-thick layer of ice.

Grand Canyon of the Yellowstone

After its placid meanderings north from Yellowstone Lake through the Hayden Valley, the Yellowstone River musters up its energy and suddenly plummets over **Upper Falls** (109ft) and then the much larger **Lower Falls** (308ft), before raging through the 1000ft-deep Grand Canyon of the Yellowstone. More than 4000ft wide at the top, the canyon snakes for 20 miles as far as the Narrows near Tower-Roosevelt Junction.

Much of the canyon's beauty comes from its subtle range of colors, from an egg white to a flamboyant salmon pink, a by-product of iron oxidization in the rock. As park publications note, the canyon is, in effect, rusting. Whiffs of steam still rise from vents in the canyon wall, hinting at the thermal activity that played a major role in the creation of the Grand Canyon of the Yellowstone (by weakening the rhyolite rock). The canyon is relatively recent in geological terms, carved out not by glacial erosion but by water supplied by ice dams that melted and flooded the region during the recent ice age.

The Lower Falls are twice the height of Niagara and are most impressive in spring, when the water volume can be up to 12 times that of fall. The eye-catching green notch indicates a patch of deeper and less turbulent water. At the base of the falls the reds and creams of the canyon walls turn to a mossy green, fed by the thundering spray of the river. Bring binoculars to spot ospreys that nest in the canyon from late April till early September. In winter, the spray freezes into a giant cone in front of the falls.

Canyon Country Area

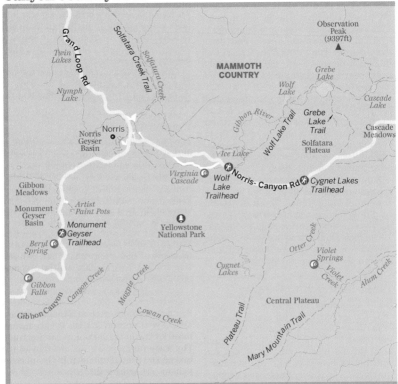

Rangers lead hikes daily at 9am from the parking lot above Uncle Tom's trailhead and give short talks four times a day (10am for kids) at Artist Point.

NORTH RIM

Four popular scenic overlooks line the one-way 2.5-mile North Rim Dr.

Brink of the Lower Falls   WATERFALL
(Map p96) The first of the North Rim view-points leads down a steep 0.75-mile trail, descending 600ft for close views of the tumbling white water as the Yellowstone River rushes over the lip of the lower falls. Heading back up isn't half as much fun as going down.

Lookout Point   VIEWPOINT
(Map p96) Popular Lookout Point offers the best views of the Lower Falls, while an adjacent 0.5-mile trail drops 500ft to Red Rock for even closer views. The average age of the crowd plummets with the elevation (it's hard on the knees). The trails here can

be very slippery so watch your step. It was around here that iconic early painter Thomas Moran made the sketches for his famous painting of the canyon, allegedly weeping over the lack of colors in his palette.

Grandview Point   VIEWPOINT
(Map p96) The one-way North Rim Dr leads to Grandview Point, which offers views north over the colorful smoking canyon walls.

Inspiration Point   VIEWPOINT
(Map p96) A side road branches off the North Rim Dr to reach busy Inspiration Point, which offers an overview of the length of the canyon and a small section of the lower falls. There are a few steps to descend – there used to be more, before the old lookout point fell (literally) victim to the canyon's relentless erosion.

Glacial Boulder   LANDMARK
(Map p96) Just before Inspiration Point is this huge granite boulder scooped up from the Beartooth Mountains, 15 miles away, by a glacier and deposited here 80,000 years ago. The **Glacier Boulder Trail** starts here for the 11-mile return hike to Sevenmile Hole. An easy, one-hour (2-mile) round-trip hike takes you along this trail, through forest and past intermittent canyon vistas to views of **Silver Cord Cascade**, the park's highest falls (or rather, series of falls).

This is a particularly fine late-afternoon hike, but keep a tight rein on the kids, as there are no barriers between them and the sheer canyon drop-offs.

UPPER FALLS VIEWPOINT

The less dramatic Upper Falls Viewpoint is also accessible by road: the turnoff is south of Canyon Junction and Cascade Creek on the main Grand Loop Rd to Fishing Bridge. A short walk to the right (south) leads to the Brink of the Upper Falls, though the best views of the falls are actually from the Uncle Tom's parking area across the gorge. A five-minute walk north along the North Rim Trail (a former stagecoach road) leads to an overview of the much smaller but graceful **Crystal Falls**, the 'Hidden' or 'Third' waterfall of the Canyon region.

SOUTH RIM

South Rim Dr passes the Chittenden Bridge and Wapiti trailhead en route to the canyon's most spectacular overlook at Artist Point. The 3.25-mile **South Rim Trail** follows the canyon rim from Chittenden Bridge to Point Sublime via Artist Point.

Uncle Tom's Trail   VIEWPOINT

(Map p96) Uncle Tom's Trail offers the best views of the Upper and Lower Falls. The trail itself is a steep route that descends 500ft down 328 metal steps to the base of the Lower Falls. The trail was constructed in 1898 by early park entrepreneur Uncle Tom Richardson, who would lead tourists down a series of trails and rope ladders for views of the falls and a picnic lunch. Sadly the rope ladders are now a thing of the past.

The park service once turned down an application to build an elevator here that would whisk tourists down to the canyon floor, though you may wish it had changed its mind as you make the tough return climb. Rangers lead a 1-mile stroll from here at 3pm, as well as a longer 3-mile walk at 9am. This is one of the region's largest parking areas.

Artist Point   VIEWPOINT

(Map p96) Artist Point is probably the most famous of the canyon's viewpoints. It was not, as many people assume, named for the spot where Thomas Moran sketched his famous landscape of the falls (a copy of which is on display in the Canyon Visitor Center). It was actually named by the park photographer FJ Haynes for its superlative scenic views.

Canyon Village

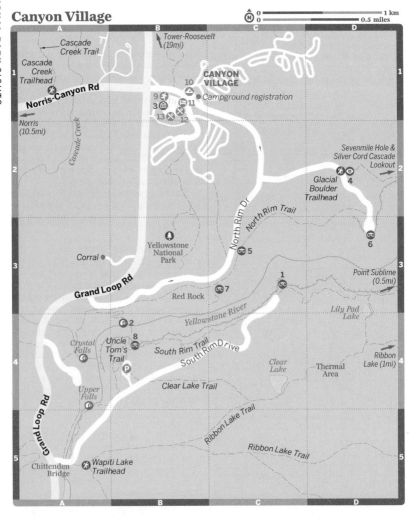

Rangers give short talks here four times a day, with the 11am talk aimed at kids.

Point Sublime VIEWPOINT
(Map p94) From Artist Point a trail leads 1 mile to this viewpoint for more fabulous views of the canyon walls. The 4-mile (two-hour) round-trip hike to Ribbon Lake (p60) branches off from here.

Canyon to Lake Village

South of Canyon Junction, the Grand Loop Rd winds 16 miles down to Lake Yellowstone via the excellent wildlife-watching opportunities of the Hayden Valley and the interesting Mud Volcano. This section of road makes for a good two-hour bike ride, though as always you'll have to watch out for the traffic.

HAYDEN VALLEY
The Yellowstone River is broad and shallow as it meanders gently through the vast grasslands of Hayden Valley, named after the expedition leader whose 1871 survey led to the establishment of the park the following year. This former lakebed was formed in the last ice age when a glacial outburst flooded the valley, turning the region into an arm of Yellowstone Lake. The fine silt-and-clay soil prevents water from percolating into the ground, making the area marshy and impenetrable to most trees. This supports the rich shrubs and grasses favored by bison.

Canyon Village

◉ **Sights**

➕ **Activities, Courses & Tours**

🛏 **Sleeping**

🍴 **Eating**

The Hayden is the largest valley in the park and one of its premier wildlife-viewing areas. With patience you're likely to see coyotes, springtime grizzlies, elk and lots of bison, plus one of the largest fall ruts. Birdwatching is equally good, including white pelicans and trumpeter swans, sandhill cranes (also at Alum Creek), ospreys, bald eagles and Canada geese. There are popular viewing areas 1 mile north of Sulfur Cauldron and 1.5 miles north of Trout Creek. Set up your spotting scope early, as the pullouts fill with cars an hour or two before dusk.

MUD VOLCANO
One of the park's most geologically volatile regions, this thermal area 10 miles south of Canyon Junction and 6 miles north of Fishing Bridge Junction contains an assortment of mud pots and other gurgling sulfurous pits. The nearby Sour Creek resurgent dome is the fuel that superheats the mud volcanoes, while the high acidity breaks down rock into mud pots rather than creating the pressurized geyser plumbing more characteristic of alkaline thermal features. During a series of earthquakes in 1979 the mud pots developed enough heat and gases to literally cook lodgepole pines and grasses on neighboring hillsides. One mud pot recently emerged from underneath the parking lot.

Mud Volcano itself has not erupted since the 1871 Langford-Washington-Doane expedition first encountered it. A crater is all that remains of the original cone. Dragon's Mouth Spring gets its name from the deep thumping and crashing that emanates from a hidden lair that looks like it guards the gateway to the underworld. In 1999 the pool cooled and its color changed from green to white and now gray.

The easiest way to see the other sights is to follow the 2.3-mile loop boardwalk (there are some steps) clockwise, past Mud Geyser and up Cooking Hillside. Halfway up, Churning Cauldron is a favorite; waves of water have created tiny beaches here. The dark colors of this and other pots are due to the presence of iron sulfides.

Black Dragon's Cauldron appeared in 1948 in a crack in the earth and has since moved south 200ft along the crack to produce an elliptical pool. The rolling motion of the water is actually due to rising gases rather than boiling water. Nearby Sour Lake looks like a nice place for a swim, but its waters are as acidic as battery acid. Further downhill, Grizzly Fumarole changes throughout the year from a fumarole to a

ℹ CANYON WITHOUT THE CROWDS

Most visitors drive between the viewpoints of the North Rim, but you can also hike the **North Rim Trail**. The trail parallels the road from Inspiration Point to Upper Falls Overlook (2.5 miles), from where you can continue 0.75 miles to Chittenden Bridge on South Rim Dr, where it links up with the South Rim Trail. The only disadvantage to this route is that it's one way, so you'll have to either retrace your steps or arrange a designated driver (thanks, dad…) to pick you up.

One option if you have a **bike** is to park at the Brink of the Lower Falls, cycle to Inspiration Point (there's a cycle lane) and then walk back along the North Rim Trail. The trail is mostly through forest, but every now and then you pop out onto the canyon rim for views that you'll have all to yourself. Figure on two hours with detours and cycling.

mud pot and even a muddy spring, according to the amount of moisture in the ground.

Sulfur Cauldron, just a few hundred yards north, by a pullout in the road, is one of the most acidic springs in the park, at pH 1.3. Other thermal areas, visible across the Yellowstone River, can only be reached by hiking the Howard Eaton Trail from Fishing Bridge.

Rangers lead two-hour walks around the site at 4pm, but sadly no longer go to the **Gumper**, a huge seething mud pot behind Sour Lake and off-limits to visitors.

◉ Lake Country

Yellowstone Lake (7733ft) is Lake Country's shimmering centerpiece – one of the world's largest alpine lakes, with the largest inland population of cutthroat trout in the US. Yellowstone River emerges from the north end of the lake and flows through Hayden Valley to the Grand Canyon of the Yellowstone. The lake's south and eastern borders flank the steep Absaroka Range, marking the border of the park's remote and pristine Thorofare region.

A 22-mile section of the Grand Loop Rd hugs Yellowstone Lake's shoreline between Fishing Bridge Junction to the north and West Thumb Junction to the west. Visitor centers and convenience stores are at Fish-

ing Bridge and Grant Village. Grant and Lake Village offer the most visitor services, including dining. Bridge Bay Marina rents outboard motorboats and rowboats and has a fishing/grocery store, dump station, ranger station and picnic area. The busy Fishing Bridge area offers showers and laundry, as well as a gas station, groceries and camping supplies at the Yellowstone General Store.

Yellowstone Lake

The largest high-altitude lake in North America, the deep-cobalt Yellowstone Lake (136 sq miles) has been a human draw for millennia; artifacts found along the lakeshore date back 12,000 years. Traditionally this was only a summering spot for native groups. The lake remains frozen almost half the year, from January to early June, though its average depth is 140ft (maximum 390ft) and parts of the lake floor boil with underwater hot springs.

In addition to excellent fishing and boating, the lake also offers prime birding and wildlife-watching. Early summer visitors shouldn't miss an amazing display of spawning cutthroat trout at Fishing Bridge and LeHardy's Rapids, 3 miles north of the bridge. As crucial food sources for grizzlies and waterfowl, some spawning areas around the lakeshore are closed during spring and early summer. Thermal activity rings the lake, and in cold weather steaming thermals blur into the water.

Rangers lead tours of Yellowstone Lake's shoreline daily from Fishing Bridge.

LeHardy's Rapids   RIVER
These rapids are named after topographer Paul LeHardy, whose raft overturned here, spilling guns, provisions and bedding but sparing his life. Rock uplift created this step-like cascade, which formally marks the end of Yellowstone Lake. Cutthroat trout are plentiful in late springtime, where they can be seen resting in the pools before hurling themselves up the rapids to spawning grounds near Fishing Bridge.

Just north of here are three picnic areas, of which the Nez Percé Ford picnic site, with riverside tables, is the nicest.

Fishing Bridge   BRIDGE
(Map p100) There has been a bridge at Fishing Bridge since 1902, but it closed to fishing in 1973 to protect spawning cutthroat trout, to the benefit of resident grizzlies. Because of heavy grizzly activity, there is continuing pressure to close the area to protect this crucial habitat.

Fishing Bridge Visitor Center MUSEUM
(Map p100; ☎307-242-2450; ☺8am-7pm late May-
late Sep) This visitor center was originally
built in 1931 as an information station for the
first automobile tourists. The center contains
displays on local birdlife (look for the great
skulls on the candelabra), alongside a stuffed
grizzly and an intriguing 3D geothermal map
of Yellowstone Lake. Ranger talks are held
here at 3pm and beside Fishing Bridge at
6pm. Most people miss the steps behind the
center that lead to a nice section of lakeshore.

Lake Yellowstone Hotel HISTORIC BUILDING
(Map p100) The buttercup-yellow Lake Yellowstone Hotel, dating from 1891, is the
park's oldest building and certainly its most
elegant. Robert Reamer (who also designed
the Old Faithful Inn) rebuilt the hotel in
1903, adding Ionic columns and false balconies. Swank and expansive, this Southern-
style mansion is the perfect setting for
pre-dinner drinks. There are also lovely sunset strolls in front of the hotel, including one
trail that goes all the way to Fishing Bridge.
Hotel tours start at 5:30pm.

LAKE VILLAGE TO WEST THUMB
You'll find several delightful spots to picnic
and/or fish between Lake Village and West
Thumb. Near Bridge Bay Marina, 2-mile
Gull Point Drive is a scenic picnic spot
and popular fishing area that also offers a
short bike ride for families staying at Bridge
Bay. Opposite the turnoff is the road for the
3-mile biking trip to Natural Bridge. An
alternative hiking trail leads to the bridge
from Bridge Bay Marina.

Other nice lakeshore spots include Sand
Point picnic area, from where trails lead
400yd down to a lagoon and black volcanic-
glass beach, and Pumice Point, a beach of
dark-black sand. There are more sand bars
and lagoons to explore 2 miles, 4.5 miles and
6.5 miles further toward West Thumb.

If you fancy getting on the water, try the
one-hour sightseeing cruises (adult/child
$17/10) from Bridge Bay Marina that travel
to Stevenson Island and the wreck of the
steamship SS *Waters* (1905). They operate
at least five times daily from mid-June to
mid-September and rangers accompany the
first three trips of the day.

WEST THUMB
Named for its location in the hand-shaped
Yellowstone Lake, West Thumb is a small
volcanic caldera spawned 150,000 years ago
inside the much larger Yellowstone caldera.
Yellowstone Lake filled the crater, creating

West Thumb Bay, a circular inlet at the lake's
west end. The geyser basin pours more than
3000 gallons of hot water into the lake daily.

West Thumb Geyser Basin GEYSER
(Map p100) Although West Thumb is not one
of Yellowstone's prime thermal sites, its 0.5-
mile shoreline boardwalk loop (with a shorter inner loop) passes more than a dozen hot
springs. At Fishing Cone, anglers once used
the infamous 'hook 'n' cook' method to prepare their catch, casting fish into the boiling
water. Fishing is now prohibited.

Fluctuating lake levels in spring and early
summer sometimes submerge Fishing Cone
and Lakeshore Geyser. You can spot the underwater features by looking for slick spots
or a slight bulge in the water. Abyss Pool is
one of the park's deepest springs. Rangers
lead talks here after lunch. Nearby Black
Pool is one of the prettiest, though it's now
completely clear after years of lower temperatures supported mats of black thermophiles. Thumb Paint Pots are struggling to
regain the energy that once catapulted boiling mud 25ft into the air.

Smaller thermal areas surrounding West
Thumb include the roadside Pumice Point
and Potts Hot Spring Basin.

West Thumb
Information Center VISITOR CENTER
(Map p100) This former ranger station, dating from 1925, serves as a summer bookstore
and winter warming hut. Rangers lead a
1½-hour 'Hot Water Wilderness' walk daily
at 10:30am and 3pm from here in summer.
Other West Thumb programs rotate, so see
the park newspaper for details.

Lake Overlook VIEWPOINT
(Map p100) If you have a spare hour, the
2-mile round-trip Lake Overlook Trail is a
good family hike that starts from the south

> **WORTH A TRIP**
>
> **KAYAKING WEST THUMB**
>
> For a different angle on the West
> Thumb Geyser Basin, OARS (www.oars.
> com/Wyoming), Snake River Kayak
> (www.snakeriverkayak.com) and Gey-
> ser Kayak Tours (www.geyserkayak.
> com) in Jackson offer half-/full-day
> sea-kayaking tours on Yellowstone Lake
> ($99/175), as well as sunset paddles
> and overnight trips. Tours meet at Grant
> Village and paddle out 2.5 miles to West
> Thumb and Potts Geyser Basins.

side of the West Thumb parking lot. The interesting loop winds past forest, elk, open grassland and even some thermal features, finally climbing 400ft to commanding views over Yellowstone Lake, Mt Sheridan to the south and the wild Absorka Range and Washakie wilderness to the east. Rangers lead hikes along the route daily at 9:30am.

A shorter 1-mile return hike also runs from the parking lot to the shores of Duck Lake.

Grant Village

Grant Village is a sterile scar of blockhouses and tourist facilities named after Ulysses

S Grant, the president who established Yellowstone National Park in 1872. Facilities include a gas station, public showers, laundry, post office, marina and backcountry office.

Grant Village
Visitor Center   VISITOR CENTER
(Map p100; ☏307-242-2650; ⊗8am-7pm late May-late Sep) The Grant Village Visitor Center offers an exhibit on fire and an hourly 20-minute video entitled *Ten Years After the Fire*, as well as wildlife talks in the morning and afternoon and a junior-ranger presentation at 11:30am. The early-evening

Lake Country Area

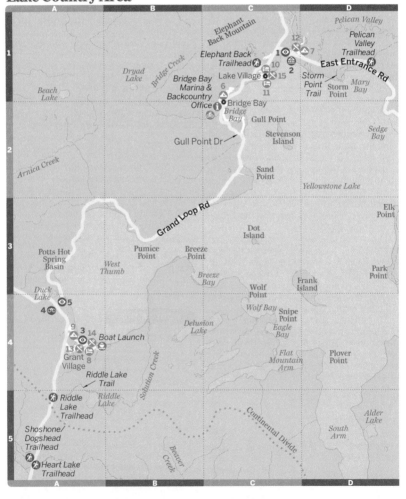

presentations at the amphitheater are geared toward families; the 9:30pm version is for grown-ups.

Grant Village to South Entrance

From Grant Village the road climbs to the Continental Divide (7988ft) and drops into a burn area, past several trailheads. Lewis Lake, the third largest in the park, comes into view here, and several lake-view pullouts offer nice picnic spots. Boaters use Lewis Lake as the gateway to remote Shoshone Lake.

When you hit traffic south of the lake, you have probably arrived at the 30ft Lewis Falls.

Walk a little way along the north side of the falls for the best views, or along the south side for the closest access. In good weather, look for a glimpse of the Tetons to the south.

To the west, the Pitchstone trailhead cuts over the remote mudstone (ash tuft) plateau to Grassy Lake Rd, one of the park's least-visited corners. Its roadside meadows are excellent places to spot moose.

A major burn area signals the start of Lewis Canyon. There are lots of pullouts along the roadside, but the southernmost offers the best views. Volcanic rock that dates from an eruption 70,000 years ago comprises the canyon walls.

Just before the South Entrance, a small pullout beside a bridge offers access to small Moose Falls and Crawfish Creek.

The entrance station is adjacent to the Snake River picnic area. From here it's 18 miles to Colter Bay and 43 miles to Moose Visitor Center, both in Grand Teton National Park.

Fishing Bridge to East Entrance

There are a couple of great family hiking trails west of Fishing Bridge. At Pelican Creek Bridge, 1 mile east of Fishing Bridge Visitor Center, an easy 1.3-mile loop nature trail winds through lodgepole forest to a

YELLOWSTONE NATIONAL PARK SIGHTS

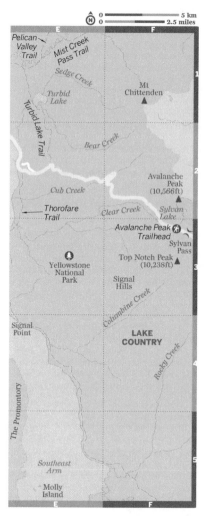

pleasant beach and lake views. Keep an eye out for moose and springtime grizzlies in the wetlands. The lakeside ponds south of the bridge offer great bird-watching.

Formed by a giant steam (not lava) explosion, Storm Point, 1.5 miles further east, juts into the north end of the lake. The 2.3-mile (one hour) Storm Point Trail loop begins near Indian Pond, strolling through diverse wildlife habitats, including meadows, shoreline and old forest. Wildlife, such as bison, moose, marmots and waterfowl, is particularly active around dusk and dawn. Rangers lead a guided hike here at 4pm. The trail closes in late spring and early summer due to bear activity and can be buggy early in summer.

Just east of Storm Point, a dirt road branches north to the Pelican Valley trailhead. The lush meandering meadows here rank among the park's prime grizzly habitats.

Like West Thumb, crater-shaped Mary Bay is the result of a thermal explosion. Both Mary Bay and neighboring Sedge Bay are peppered with underwater thermal areas, of which roiling Steamboat Point is the most obvious. Sedge Bay beach is a launching point for canoe or kayak trips south

along the lake's east shoreline and is a fine place for a picnic. Birdwatchers flock to the bay's southeast corner.

As the East Entrance Rd turns away from the lake, a mile-long paved road (no buses or trailers) branches north to the Lake Butte Overlook, which offers grand sunset views of Yellowstone Lake and the remote Thorofare corner of the park. Further east is the less impressive Yellowstone Lake Overlook.

The main road gradually climbs up the west slope of the remote Absaroka Range past lovely Sylvan Lake (with a picnic area and catch-and-release fishing), Eleanor Lake and the Avalanche Peak trailhead. The road peaks at the avalanche area of Sylvan Pass (8530ft), dominated by 10,238ft Top Notch Peak to the south. Look for the Howitzer gun mounted on the south side of the pass, employed to set off controlled avalanches during the dangerous winter months.

East of the pass the landscape becomes more rugged and impressive. The high barren walls of Mt Langford (10,774ft) and Plenty Coups Peak (10,937ft) rise to the south. Middle Creek, with several good fishing spots, parallels the south side of the road.

The East Entrance marks the boundary between Yellowstone National Park and Shoshone National Forest. From here the Buffalo Bill Scenic Byway leads to Cody via the Wapiti Valley.

◉ Norris

The Norris area was a former US Army outpost. Norris is named after Philetus W Norris, the park's second superintendent (1877–82), who is notable for constructing some of the park's first roads and for the shameless frequency with which he named park features after himself.

Norris sits at the junction of roads from Madison (14 miles), Canyon (12 miles) and Mammoth (20 miles). North of the junction is Norris Campground; west is Norris Geyser Basin, with busy bathrooms, an information station and a bookstore. A pleasant 1-mile trail (no bikes) connects the basin and the campground.

Museum of the National Park Ranger   MUSEUM
(Map p88; ☏307-344-7353; ◷9am-5pm Jun-Sep) The historic log Norris Soldier Station (1908), one of only three left from the era of the park's army control, now houses this small museum, often staffed by chatty retired NPS employees. The exhibits detail the

evolution of the ranger profession from its military origins, including a fun mock-up of an old ranger cabin. See if you can guess which future US president served as a park ranger in Canyon in 1936, before entering the oval office 38 years later.

The Gibbon River flows through meadows in front of the building, making it a pleasant place to look for wildlife. Norris Campground is right next door.

Norris Geyser Basin

North and west of Norris Junction, the Norris Geyser Basin is North America's most volatile and oldest continuously active geothermal area (in existence for around 115,000 years). It's also the site of Yellowstone's hottest recorded temperatures, where three intersecting faults underlaid by magma rise to within 2 miles of the surface. Barely 1000ft below the surface, scientific instruments have recorded temperatures as high as 459°F (237°C). Norris is also home to the majority of the world's acidic geysers, fed by the basin's abundant supplies of sulfur. In Norris the earth sighs, boils and rages like nowhere else on the planet.

Norris' geothermal features change seasonally, most commonly in August or September: clear pools transform into spouting geysers or mud pots and vice versa. Thermal activity is also affected by earthquake swarms and other mysterious disturbances, which generally last only a few days before things revert to 'normal.'

Norris Geyser Basin features two distinct areas: Porcelain Basin and Back Basin. Concentrate on Porcelain Basin if you are low on time. Overlooking Porcelain Basin is the tiny **Norris Museum** (Map p88; ☑307-344-2812; ⊙9am-6pm late May-Sep), which opened as the park's first museum in 1930. There are ranger-led walking tours of the basin at 9:30am daily and short talks at Steamboat Geyser at 2pm, 2:30pm and 3pm.

The area's only bathrooms are in the parking lot, next to the cold-drinks machines. The parking area and toilets can get crowded, so try to schedule a visit early or late in the day.

Porcelain Basin   GEYSER
(Map p88) One mile of boardwalks loop through Porcelain Basin, the park's hottest exposed basin. (The name comes from the area's milky deposits of sinter, also known as geyserite.) The bleached basin boils and bubbles like some giant laboratory experiment and the ash-white ground actually pulsates in places. Check out the overviews from **Porcelain Terrace Overlook**, near the Norris Museum – views that, in the words of Rudyard Kipling, made it look 'as though the tide of desolation had gone out.'

As you descend from the museum, veer left before the continually blowing fumarole of **Black Growler Steam Vent**, said to be the park's hottest. As with most fumaroles, this vent is higher than the basin floor and is thus without a reliable supply of water. Below here is the large but currently inactive Ledge Geyser.

Going clockwise, the boardwalk heads left past **Crackling Lake**, which bubbles like a deep-fat fryer, and the **Whale's Mouth**, a gaping blue hot spring.

The swirling waters of **Whirligig Geyser** became dramatically acidic in 2000, helping support the green cyanidium algae and yellow cyanobacteria that create many of the stunning colors in its drainage channels. The color of these bacterial mats indicates the relative temperatures of the water, from very hot blues and whites (up to 199°F, or 92°C), to cooler yellows and greens (144°F, or 62°C) and even cooler beiges and dark browns (130°F to 80°F, or 54°C to 26°C). Nearby **Constant Geyser** used to erupt every 20 minutes or so, but was much less frequent in 2015.

A side path leads past Hurricane Vent to **Congress Pool**, which appeared in 1891, the year scientists convened in Yellowstone for a geologic congress. The footpath to Norris Campground leads off beside Nuphar Lake.

Back Basin   GEYSER
(Map p88) Two miles of boardwalks and gentle trails snake through Norris' forested Back Basin. The main show here is **Steamboat Geyser**, the world's tallest active geyser, which infrequently skyrockets up to an awesome 380ft (over twice as high as Old Faithful). The geyser was dormant for half a century until 1961 and quiet again for most of the 1990s, but erupted in 2013 and 2014. At the time of research the geyser was splashing with frequent but minor bursts only.

As you exit the museum from Porcelain Basin, take the right-hand path into Back Basin. **Emerald Spring** combines reflected blue light with yellow sulfur deposits to create a striking blue-green color. For a shorter loop take the right branch just past Steamboat Geyser; otherwise, continue clockwise around the basin.

Near to Steamboat Geyser, yellow-and-green **Cistern Spring** is linked to Steamboat through underground channels and empties for a day or two following Steamboat's eruptions. The spring is slowly drowning its surroundings in geyserite deposits.

Dramatic Echinus Geyser (e-ki-nus), the park's largest acidic geyser, erupted every couple of hours until fairly recently, with spouts reaching up to 60ft and sometimes continuing for more than an hour, but these days it's pretty quiet. You can get closer to the action here than at almost any of the park's other geysers, and if you sit in the grandstand, you may well get wet during an eruption (kids love it). Furious bubbling signals an imminent eruption. Echinus is named for its spiny geyserite deposits (echinoderms include sea urchins), characteristic of acidic solutions.

After deposits sealed its tiny, 2in-wide vent, Porkchop Geyser exploded in 1989, blowing huge lumps of geyserite 200ft away (you can see a lump of Porkchop in the Old Faithful Visitor Center). Recent rises in the ground temperature forced the park service to reroute the boardwalk around the back of Porkchop Geyser for safety purposes.

Nearby Pearl Geyser is one of the park's prettiest. Punsters love the British pronunciation of Veteran Geyser – 'Veteran Geezer.' Minute Geyser is a victim of early visitor vandalism and sadly no longer erupts every 60 seconds, despite its constant bubbling.

Norris to Madison Junction

The 14-mile Norris to Madison Junction road quickly enters aptly named Elk Park, a fine place to spot elk and bison – you'll likely have to navigate a car jam here.

Just under 5 miles south of Norris Junction an easy 1-mile trail leads through burned forest to the fun mud pots and springs of Artist Paint Pots, a family favourite. The best mud pots are in the far-right-hand corner.

The road passes through Gibbon Meadows with its pleasant riverside picnic area and abundant bison herds, then passes the trailhead that leads to little-visited Monument Geyser Basin (two hours return). Next comes pretty, blue-green Beryl Spring (where the rolling action of the water comes from escaping gases rather than boiling water).

As the road and river descends off the Solfatara Plateau, you pass Gibbon Falls, one of the park's prettiest. For the best views of the 84ft falls you'll have to park and walk downhill along the road. Like so many of Yellowstone's waterfalls and cascades, the falls flow over hard rhyolite that marks the edge of the Yellowstone caldera.

Several picnic areas follow, of which Gibbon Falls is the nicest, offering views down to the river. Tuft Hill picnic area sits at the foot of a wall of rock welded together in a cloud of volcanic ash.

Five miles further west a parking area on the right gives access to Terrace Spring, a large pool with a rolling geyser in the corner. Two lovely hot springs above form the namesake terrace. You could safely miss both Terrace and Beryl Springs if you are tight on time.

From here the road drops down to Madison Junction, with its campground and junior ranger station (Map p106; ⊘9am-6pm late May-Sep). The station is a good place to stop if you have kids. There are plenty of kid-friendly activities, bear skins to stroke and talks every half-hour. Spotting scopes offer a close-up look at the elk that frequent the Madison Valley.

Norris to Canyon Village

The 12-mile Norris–Canyon road connects the two parts of the Grand Loop Rd across the burnt forest and cooled lava flows of the Solfatara Plateau. Just past the junction the pleasant Norris Meadows picnic area offers some fine bird-watching over the plain of the meandering Gibbon River.

About 2 miles into the drive a one-way side road branches off past Virginia Cascade, which, like Gibbon Falls, lies on the caldera boundary. One story goes that the superintendent wanted to name the falls after his wife, Virginia, but the NPS was against naming park features after living people, so they compromised by naming the fall after the state of (ahem...) Virginia. The narrow 2.5-mile road follows the old stagecoach road along the Norris Cutoff and is closed to buses, trailers and RVs.

Back on the main road a small boardwalk trail marks the spot where a freak tornado ripped through the plateau in 1984. This was also the spot of the fiercest of 1988's wildfires.

Ice Lake Trail leads 0.5 miles to the peaceful namesake lake, with a wheelchair-accessible backcountry site (4D3) on its southern shore. In his book Lost in My Own Backyard, Tim Cahill wrote of the lake: 'Is this a great country or what? Where else would the wilderness – or one lovely part of it – be made accessible in such a way that the disabled can spend entire sleepless nights worried about being eaten by a

REGENERATION – AFTER THE FIRE

Catastrophic wildfires swept across 1.4 million acres of the Greater Yellowstone Ecosystem in the summer of 1988 and torched one-third of Yellowstone National Park. More than 25,000 firefighters battled 51 fires during the driest summer in 112 years. The fires jumped roads, rivers and even the Grand Canyon of the Yellowstone.

Twenty-five years later, the aftermath of the fires is still very much in evidence. Yet far from marking a disaster, many observers now describe the fires as a natural event heralding a new cycle of growth.

Many plants and trees depend on high temperatures to trigger the release of their seeds (lodgepole pines require temperatures of 113°F degrees to melt the resin holding theirs in place), and surveys estimated that there were as many as one million seeds per acre on the ground during the fall of 1988. It was also found that only 390 large mammals (less than 1% of the park's total) perished in the fires, the vast majority being elk (and six bears). The year after the fires, the populations of all grazing and browsing mammals flourished thanks to succulent new vegetative growth. Birds thrived on the increased numbers of insects living on dead wood. Ten years later grasses, wildflowers and shrubs were clear winners, aided by increased sunlight and soil nutrients.

For hikers, Yellowstone's scenery has been affected to a certain degree, but not all in a bad way and certainly not to the apocalyptic degree described by the media at the time. Wildflowers are blooming, many views are now unimpeded and it's easier to see the wildlife thanks to the burns and richer grazing. Smokey the Bear would be proud.

---

bear, just like any able-bodied hiker?' Sites 4D1 and 4D2 are just a mile or so from the road and make a great first backcountry site for young families, though avoid the heavy mosquito months of June and July. Camping here feels like owning your own private lake. Trails continue northeast along the border of a major burn area to Wolf Lake (3 miles) and Grebe Lake (another 1.5 miles). There are also some longer hike options to Cascade Lake.

Further down the Norris–Canyon road, you'll pass the Cygnet Lakes and then the Grebe Lake and Cascade Creek trailheads, which offer alternative routes through burned forest to Grebe and Cascade Lakes.

◉ Geyser Country

Yellowstone's Geyser Country holds the park's most famous geothermal features (over half the world's total), concentrated in the world's densest concentration of geysers (over 200 spouters in 1.5 sq miles). It is Geyser Country that makes the Yellowstone plateau utterly and globally unique.

The majority of the geysers line the Firehole River, the aquatic backbone of the basin, whose tributaries feed 21 of the park's 110 waterfalls. Both the Firehole and Madison Rivers offer superb fly-fishing, and the meadows along them support large wildlife populations.

The most famous geysers always attract a crowd, but sometimes it's the smaller features that are the most interesting. The smaller geysers make up for their lack of size with great names, such as North Goggles, Little Squirt, Gizmo, Spanker, Spasmodic, Slurper and Bulger (aliases the seven dwarfs might adopt to form a criminal gang).

In the introduction to *A Lady's Life in the Rocky Mountains* (1960), historian Daniel Boorstin attributed Yellowstone Park's enormous appeal 'to the fact that its natural phenomena, which erupt on schedule, come closest to the artificiality of "regular" tourist performances'. So grab some popcorn and check show times at the visitor center.

Upper Geyser Basin

This heavily visited basin holds 180 of the park's 200 to 250 geysers, the most famous of which is geriatric Old Faithful. Boardwalks, footpaths and a cycling path along the Firehole River link the five distinct geyser groups, the furthest of which is only 1.5 miles from Old Faithful.

Entering the Old Faithful parking area comes as a bit of a shock after you've spent some time in the park. As well as the visitor center, the complex boasts two gas stations, three hotels and several general stores, including the original 1897 knotty-pine Hamilton Store, the oldest structure still in use in the park. The Yellowstone General Store,

Geyser Country

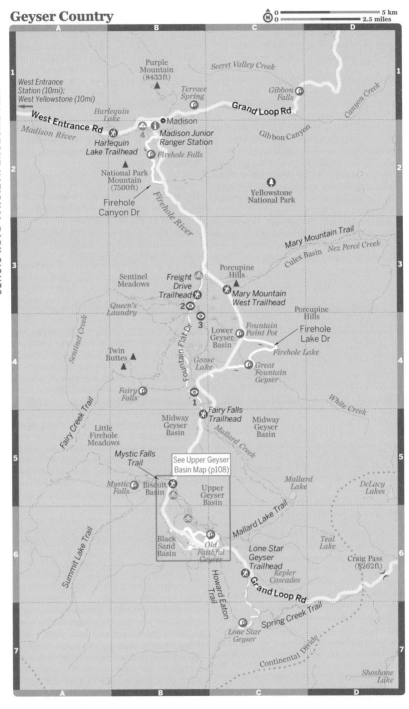

N

0 _____ 5 km
0 _____ 2.5 miles

West Entrance
Station (10mi);
West Yellowstone (10mi)

West Entrance Rd

Madison River

Harlequin
Lake

Harlequin
Lake Trailhead

National Park
Mountain
(7500ft)

Firehole
Canyon Dr

Purple
Mountain
(8433ft)

Terrace
Spring

Madison

Madison Junior
Ranger Station

Firehole Falls

Firehole River

Secret Valley Creek

Gibbon
Falls

Grand Loop Rd

Gibbon Canyon

Canyon Creek

Yellowstone
National Park

Mary Mountain Trail

Culex Basin   Nez Percé Creek

Sentinel
Meadows

Queen's
Laundry

Twin
Buttes

Fairy
Falls

Little
Firehole
Meadows

Freight
Drive
Trailhead

2

3

Fountain Flat Dr

Goose
Lake

1

Midway
Geyser
Basin

Porcupine
Hills

Mary Mountain
West Trailhead

Lower
Geyser
Basin

Fountain
Paint Pot

Great
Fountain
Geyser

Fairy Falls
Trailhead

Porcupine
Hills

Firehole
Lake Dr

Firehole Lake

Fairy Creek Trail

Sentinel Creek

Mallard Creek

Midway
Geyser
Basin

White Creek

Mallard
Lake

DeLacy
Lakes

Mystic Falls
Trail

Mystic
Falls

Biscuit
Basin

Black
Sand
Basin

See Upper Geyser
Basin Map (p108)

Upper
Geyser
Basin

Old
Faithful
Geyser

Lone Star
Geyser
Trailhead

Kepler
Cascades

Grand Loop Rd

Mallard Lake Trail

Teal
Lake

Craig Pass
(§262ft)

Summit Lake Trail

Howard Eaton Trail

Lone Star
Geyser

Spring Creek Trail

Continental Divide

Shoshone
Lake

next to the Snow Lodge, has the park's best selection of groceries and sells fishing flies, spotting scopes and fishing permits.

The combined ranger station, backcountry office and medical clinic are set back from the main parking area, across the west parking lot from the visitor center. The Old Faithful Snow Lodge gift shop offers bike rentals in the summer and snowshoe and ski rentals in winter.

Rangers give a geology talk in front of Old Faithful eight times a day and offer an evening presentation in the theater at 7pm. There's a short talk for kids at 10am. Daily 1½-hour geology walks depart at 5:30pm from Castle Geyser and at 8:30am from the visitor center, with a shorter walk around Old Faithful at 2:30pm.

Public showers (6:30am to 11pm) are available in the reception area at Old Faithful Inn. There are no campgrounds in the Old Faithful area.

Old Faithful   GEYSER

(Map p108; Old Faithful Rd, Upper Geyser Basin) FREE Though it's neither the tallest nor the most predictable geyser in the park, Old Faithful is the most frequently erupting big geyser in Yellowstone. Every 90 minutes or so the geyser spouts some 8000 gallons (150 bathtubs!) of water up to 180ft in the air. It's worth viewing the eruption from several different locations: the geyser-side seats, the upper-floor balcony of the Old Faithful Inn and, our favorite, from a distance on Observation Hill.

For over 75 years the geyser faithfully erupted every hour or so – one reason for the name the Washburn expedition gave it in 1870. The average time between shows these days is 90 minutes and getting longer, though this has historically varied between 45 and 110 minutes. The average eruption lasts around four minutes. Water temperature is normally 204°F (95°C) and the steam is about 350°F (176°C). The longer the eruption, the longer the recovery time. Rangers correctly predict eruptions to within 10

minutes about 90% of the time. And no, Old Faithful has never erupted on the hour.

After years of studying the geyser, we have our own method of calculating exactly when an eruption of Old Faithful is imminent. Just count the number of bored people seated around the geyser – the number of tourists is inversely proportional to the amount of time left until the next eruption.

If you get bored waiting for the old salt, pause a minute to consider the power of recycling – you are sitting on a boardwalk made from around three million recycled plastic water jugs.

Old Faithful Visitor Center   VISITOR CENTER

(Map p108; ☎307-545-2750; ◷8am-8pm mid-Apr–early Nov & mid-Dec–mid-Mar; ☻) This new, improved and environmentally friendly center offers a bookstore and information booth and shows films 30 minutes before and 15 minutes after an eruption of Old Faithful. Kids will enjoy the hands-on Young Scientist displays, which include a working laboratory geyser. There are ranger talks in the theater at 7pm. The center closes at 5pm or 6pm outside of summer.

Old Faithful Inn   HISTORIC BUILDING

(Map p108) Designed by Seattle architect Robert C Reamer and built in 1904, this is the only building in the park that looks like it actually belongs here. The log rafters of its seven-story lobby rise nearly 80ft, and the chimney of the central fireplace (actually eight fireplaces combined) contains more than 500 tons of rhyolite rock. It's definitely a worthwhile visit, even for nonguests.

The Crow's Nest, a top-floor balcony where musicians once played for dancers in the lobby below, is wonderful (but unused since 1959). Look also for the huge popcorn popper and fire tools at the back of the fireplace. The 2nd-floor observation deck offers the chance to enjoy fine views of Old Faithful geyser over a drink, and the lobby hosts local artists and authors. Free 45-minute Historic Inn tours depart from the fireplace at 9:30am, 11am, 2pm and 3:30pm.

Old Faithful Haynes
Photo Shop   HISTORIC BUILDING

(Map p108; ◷10am-6pm Wed-Sun) This historic building was constructed in 1927 as one of the original Haynes photo shops. The Haynes family operated 13 photo shops in Yellowstone and produced 55 million postcards and the park's earliest guidebooks, some of which are on display. The early stereoscopic photographs are fun.

Upper Geyser Basin

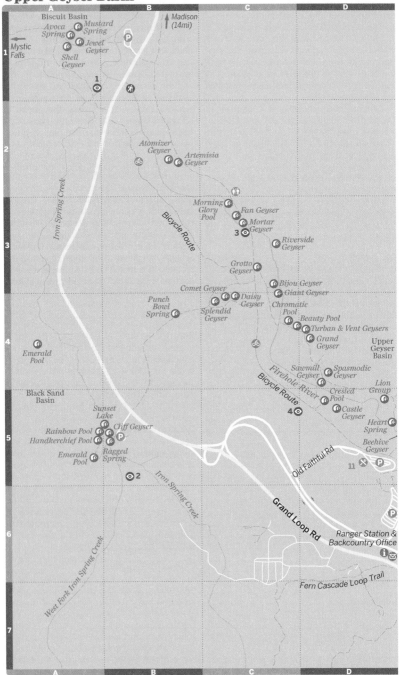

Madison
(14mi)

Biscuit Basin
Avoca Spring
Mustard Spring
Jewel Geyser
Mystic Falls
Shell Geyser

1

Atomizer Geyser
Artemisia Geyser

Bicycle Route

Morning Glory Pool
Fan Geyser
Mortar Geyser
3
Riverside Geyser

Grotto Geyser

Comet Geyser
Bijou Geyser
Giant Geyser

Punch Bowl Spring
Daisy Geyser
Splendid Geyser
Chromatic Pool
Beauty Pool
Turban & Vent Geysers
Grand Geyser

Upper Geyser Basin

Emerald Pool

Iron Spring Creek

Sawmill Geyser
Spasmodic Geyser

Firehole River

Bicycle Route

4

Crested Pool
Castle Geyser

Lion Group

Black Sand Basin

Sunset Lake
Cliff Geyser

Rainbow Pool
Handkerchief Pool
Emerald Pool
Ragged Spring

Heart Spring
Beehive Geyser

2

Iron Spring Creek

Old Faithful Rd

11

Grand Loop Rd

Ranger Station & Backcountry Office

West Fork Iron Spring Creek

Fern Cascade Loop Trail

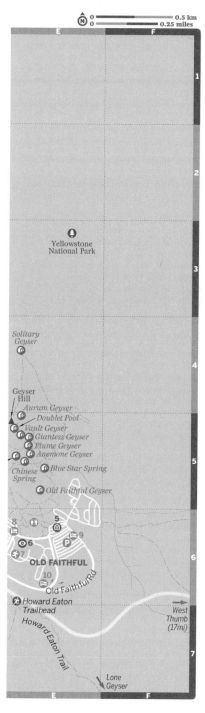

OBSERVATION HILL

For an alternative view of the Old Faithful eruption, and a pre- or post-eruption overview of the entire basin, follow a branch trail from the Firehole River up a couple of hundred vertical feet to Observation Point. From here you can descend to Solitary Geyser to rejoin the boardwalk for a 1.1-mile loop.

Solitary Geyser started off as a hot spring until it was diverted into a swimming pool in 1915 (the pool was dismantled in 1950). The lowering of the water level turned the spring into a geyser, triggering eruptions that continue to this day, even though water levels have returned to normal. Small sudden bursts occur every four to eight minutes.

GEYSER HILL

This collection of geysers closest to Old Faithful is most easily visited clockwise on the inner boardwalk loop. Not far from Old Faithful is the unmarked **Chinese Spring**, named after an Asian (actually Japanese) laundry that once operated here. Dirty clothes were put into the spring along with soap, and the owners waited for the clothes to fly out, apparently clean, in an induced eruption. Don't try a repeat performance, unless you want a citation.

Upper Geyser Basin

ⓘ GEYSER-GAZING STRATEGIES

The first thing to do when you arrive at Old Faithful is check the predicted geyser eruption times at the visitor center and then plan your itinerary around these. Predictions are made for the region's six main geysers – Old Faithful, Grand, Castle, Riverside, Daisy and the Lower Geyser Basin's Great Fountain – and these are also posted at Old Faithful Lodge, Old Faithful Inn and the Madison Junior Ranger Station. You can also get this information on the park service's 'Yellowstone Geysers' app, on the @GeyserNPS Twitter feed, or by phone at ☎307-344-2751.

Remember, though, that geysers rarely erupt on schedule, so take some snacks and sunblock for the wait. Riverside runs to within 30 minutes of predictions, but Grand is only reliable within two or three hours. Still, there's always something erupting in Upper Geyser Basin, and if you're really lucky you'll catch a biggie such as Beehive or Daisy.

Budget at least half a day to see the area around Old Faithful, and a whole day to see all the geyser basins, though you could easily spend a day or two more if you catch the geyser-gazing bug. If time is tight, concentrate on Upper and Midway Geyser Basins and skip Biscuit and Black Sand Basins.

The best loop around the Upper Geyser Basin follows the paved road one way and the boardwalk the other for a total of 3 miles. To this you can add a small hike up to Observation Point for views over the basin. There is a smaller loop around Geyser Hill, but you'll miss many of the best geysers if you limit yourself to this.

One interesting way to see the geysers is to cycle out 1.4 miles along the road to Morning Glory (where there's a bike rack), then continue on bike to Biscuit Basin via Daisy Geyser (1.3 miles). From here you can hike to Mystic Falls or cycle along the Grand Loop Rd to Black Sand Basin and get picked up there. Bikes can be rented at Bear Den Bike (p81) in the Old Faithful Snow Lodge.

Nearby, riverside **Blue Star Spring** was the site of a macabre incident in winter 1996–97, when a young bison fell into the boiling waters and died, causing the pool to smell like beef soup for days.

Consistent seepage from **Giantess Geyser** and **Vault Geyser** has created geyserite terraces that look like scaled relief maps. Giantess springs to life between two and six times a year, though when active the geyser erupts twice hourly for up to 40 hours. The surrounding area shakes from underground steam explosions just before it erupts. Vault Geyser was inactive for a decade until bursting back into life in 1998.

Doublet Pool is known for its deep-blue color, thin scalloped geyserite border and the occasional thumping that emanates from collapsing steam and gas bubbles deep underground. **Aurum Geyser** ('aurum' means gold in Latin) is thought to be connected somehow to water deposits in the meadow behind it. It erupts to 20ft every 2½ to five hours.

The **Lion Geyser** group is a gathering of four interconnected geysers (two lions and two cubs), whose eruptions are preceded by a roar, hence the name. **Heart Spring** is said to resemble the shape of a human heart.

Beehive Geyser erupts twice a day, rising up to 190ft through its 4ft-high cone-shaped nozzle, and is the second- or third-tallest regularly active geyser in the park. Beehive has an 'indicator' – a smaller vent that, when active, signals the main eruption.

Erupting every 20 minutes, **Plume Geyser** is one of the easiest geysers to catch. It's also one of basin's youngest geysers, created by a steam explosion in 1922. Interestingly, its eruptions seem to have different phases at night and day. Nearby **Anemone Geyser** erupts every 15 minutes or so.

Rangers lead 1½-hour walks of Geyser Hill daily at 8:30am.

MAIN LOOP

Along the tarmac trail in front of the Old Faithful Inn is **Castle Geyser**, whose huge cone, resembling a bleached sand castle, attests to its status as the oldest geyser in the region, somewhere between 5000 and 15,000 years old (and built atop an even older spring). Castle goes off every 13 hours or so and can be predicted to within two hours – predicted times are posted by the geyser. The water eruption is followed by a noisy 30-minute steam phase, as the heat and steam energy long outlast the water supply. Nearby, 42ft-deep **Crested Pool** is almost constantly boiling. This is one of the best places to get overviews of the basin.

The predictable **Daisy Geyser** lets loose at an angle up to 75ft every three hours or so and can be predicted to within 45 minutes, except when nearby **Splendid Geyser** erupts. Splendid is one of the largest in the region but erupts irregularly – apparently sometimes triggered by a change in atmospheric pressure, which slightly reduces the pool's boiling point. Don't confuse Daisy with the larger, constantly splashing cone of **Comet Geyser**. All three geysers are linked by underground chambers.

Grotto Geyser erupts every eight hours for anywhere between one and 10 hours. The cone takes its weird shape from trees that have been encased in the geyserite. Increased activity in Grotto generally means less activity in Giant Geyser. The picturesque **Riverside Geyser** puts on an amazing show when a 75ft column of water arcs into the Firehole River, often capped by a rainbow. Twenty-minute outpourings occur about every six hours; water spilling over the cone signals an imminent eruption.

Across the Firehole River, riverside **Fan** and **Mortar Geysers** erupt infrequently but in unison, with Fan bursting water out of 17 individual jets.

Next comes beautiful Morning Glory pool, from where hard-core geyser-gazers can follow a walking trail to several minor features such as **Artemisia Geyser**, named for its similarity to the color of sagebrush *(Artemisia)*, and **Atomizer Geyser**, named for the large amounts of steam that follow its minor eruptions.

Heading back toward Old Faithful, take the boardwalk that branches off the cycle path to **Giant Geyser**, which produces stupendous eruptions, but may be dormant for decades (it last erupted in 2010). Eruptions can last an hour, reach heights of 180ft to 250ft and expel an astonishing one million gallons of hot water with each eruption. The cessation of otherwise continuous **Bijou Geyser** nearby signals an imminent eruption of Giant Geyser.

The strikingly colorful **Chromatic Pool** and **Beauty Pool** are linked, so when one drops the other rises.

Next is **Grand Geyser**, ranking as the world's tallest predictable geyser (150ft to 180ft). It spews in bursts every eight hours or so and lasts about 12 minutes. It will often pause after nine minutes and then restart after a minute or so; the subsequent bursts are typically the most spectacular. Grand is a fountain geyser, not a cone like Old Faithful. Nearby **Turban Geyser** acts as a trigger for Grand and, along with **Vent Geyser**, continues to rage for one to two hours after Grand subsides.

Sawmill Geyser is in eruption about 30% of the time, but its extents are highly variable. Water spins violently in its crater like a circular saw. Nearby **Spasmodic Geyser** is also in eruption a third of the time and erupts from more than 20 vents.

Rangers lead 1½-hour walks of the Upper Geyser Basin daily at 5:30pm.

Black Sand Basin

Black Sand Basin GEYSER

(Map p108) This geyser basin, 1 mile northwest of Old Faithful, has a few interesting features. The eponymous black sand is derived from weathered volcanic glass (obsidian). You can access Black Sand Basin by car or, better, by foot from Daisy Geyser. Rangers lead hour-long walks here daily at 1pm.

Cliff Geyser is named for the geyserite wall that separates the geyser from Iron Spring Creek and is a frequent splasher. Nearby **Ragged Spring** frequently joins in the action with 12ft bursts. **Emerald Pool** looks like an exquisite flower with a lovely orange lip and gets its pretty color from yellow bacteria that blend with blue reflected from the sky. **Rainbow Pool** is connected to nearby Sunset Lake and is one of the more colorful in the park. The ground under the boardwalks here is literally boiling.

Unsigned **Handkerchief Pool**, just to the south of Rainbow Pool, was once one of Yellowstone's most famous features. Visitors would place a handkerchief in the pool and watch it get sucked down and then spat out 'clean' through a side vent. The pool stopped functioning in the 1920s, after one dimwit jammed logs into the opening, but it has since restored itself. Today it's illegal to throw anything into any of Yellowstone's thermal features.

Biscuit Basin

Biscuit Basin GEYSER

(Map p108) Two miles north of Black Sand Basin, Biscuit Basin is named for biscuit-like deposits that surrounded stunning **Sapphire Pool**, but these were destroyed during violent eruptions that followed the nearby 1959 Hebgen earthquake. If you're low on time, this is one basin you could safely miss.

The main features here are deep **Jewel Geyser**, which erupts every 10 minutes or so, with lovely yellow runoff, and **Shell Geyser**,

YELLOWSTONE NATIONAL PARK SIGHTS

DON'T MISS

MORNING GLORY POOL

A steamy favorite that's well worth the walk, beautiful Morning Glory Pool (Map p108) is named after its flower shape. Unfortunately, the pool is slowly changing temperature and, therefore, color, due to the tons of trash thrown into the pool by past visitors (the main access road to Old Faithful passed beside the pool until 1971). The refuse diminishes circulation and accelerates heat loss. As the pool cools, orange bacteria spreads from its sides, replacing the gorgeous blue tones.

In 1950 park staff induced an eruption to empty and clean the spring, pulling out $86.27 in pennies, 76 handkerchiefs, several towels, socks, shirts and even women's underwear!

which is shaped like a clamshell and linked underground. Mustard Spring is named for its iron-oxide-induced dark-yellow color.

A 0.5-mile hiking and cycling trail leads from across the highway to Upper Geyser Basin's Daisy Geyser, and a hiking-only path crosses the road to lead to Artemisia and Atomizer Geysers in the Upper Geyser Basin.

The Mystic Falls hiking trail (p65) starts here. There are free daily ranger-led hikes to the falls at 9am.

Midway Geyser Basin

Five miles north of Old Faithful and 2 miles south of the Firehole Lake Dr entrance is Midway Geyser Basin. The key sight here is the algae-tinged indigo water of the Grand Prismatic Spring.

Grand Prismatic Spring   SPRING
(Map p106) At 370ft wide and 121ft deep, Grand Prismatic Spring is the park's largest and deepest hot spring. It's also probably the most beautiful single thermal feature in the park. Boardwalks lead around the multicolored mist of the gorgeous pool and its spectacularly colored rainbow rings of algae. For the most dramatic photos of Grand Prismatic Spring, drive south to Fairy Falls trailhead, walk for 1 mile and then take a faint path up the side of the fire-burned ridge (itself a lava deposit from the west rim of the caldera). From above, the spring looks like a giant blue eye, weeping exquisite multicolored tears.

The spring drains into Excelsior Pool, a huge former geyser that blew itself out of existence in the 1880s with massive 300ft explosions of water. The last eruptions here were in 1985, when the pool erupted almost continuously for 46 hours, before lulling itself back into a deep sleep. The pool continually discharges an amazing 4000 gallons of boiling water a minute into the Firehole River – according to T Scott Bryan's *The Geysers of Yellowstone*, that's enough to fill 300,000 automobile gas tanks every day. More water is expelled here in a single day than Old Faithful releases in two months. You can admire the colorful yellow and orange runoff as you approach the basin over the bridge.

The features are linked by a 0.5-mile accessible boardwalk; budget about 30 minutes here.

Lower Geyser Basin

Separate roads access the three main sections of this sprawling thermal basin: the main Grand Loop Rd passes Fountain Paint Pot; the one-way Firehole Lake Dr loops off the main road to Great Fountain and other geysers; and Fountain Flat Dr offers access to hiking trails and minor thermal features. The latter two roads both offer the potential for a short bike ride.

FIREHOLE LAKE DRIVE

Firehole Lake Dr is a one-way, 3-mile road starting 2 miles north of Midway Geyser Basin and about 1 mile south of the Fountain Paint Pot parking lot. It passes several pretty pools and large geysers, including lovely Firehole Spring and then huge Great Fountain Geyser, which soars up to 200ft in a series of wide staccato bursts every 11 hours or so. Eruption times are predicted by the visitor center at Old Faithful to within a couple of hours, and you'll often find people waiting with a picnic lunch and a good book. The crater begins to overflow 1½ hours before an eruption and violent boiling signals an imminent eruption, which can last one hour.

The nearby 30ft cone of White Dome Geyser usually erupts every half-hour or so. The geyser is the symbol of the Yellowstone Association. Nearby Pink Cone Geyser gets its color from manganese dioxide deposits. A road was built right across the side of this cone in the 1930s.

Firehole Lake is a large hot spring ringed by several small geysers, including the raging waters of Artemisia Geyser and the sensuous black-and-tan smoothness of Young Hopeful.

Runoff from Firehole Lake flows into Hot Lake (also known as Black Warrior Lake) across the road, which offers more geysers and even a small cascade of boiling water. Steady Geyser is in continual eruption through one of two vents.

FOUNTAIN PAINT POT

Roughly midway between Madison Junction and Old Faithful, Fountain Paint Pot Nature Trail takes in four types of thermal features along a 0.5-mile boardwalk loop. The Fountain Hotel, one of the park's earliest lodges, was located here until 1917.

Just past pretty Silex Spring, Fountain Paint Pot is a huge bowl of plopping goop that ranks as one of the biggest in the park. The action is sloppiest in spring, with some mud pots drying up by August. The area around the thermal features is slowly being drowned in deposits, while a grassy basin beyond supports the park's largest bison herd.

The mud pots are the top-billed comedians of the show. Red Spouter is particularly interesting, since it acts like a muddy hot spring in early summer, only to become a mud pot and then a fumarole later in the year. It only appeared after the huge Hebgen Lake earthquake of 1959. Morning and Fountain Geysers are impressive but infrequent gushers; the latter drains into Spasm Geyser.

Clepsydra Geyser has erupted almost constantly since the 1959 earthquake. The geyser was named Clepsydra (Greek for 'water clock') at the time, when it used to go off every three minutes on the button. Jelly Geyser does indeed look like an upside-down bowl of Jell-O.

In 1981 Celestine Pool was the site of one of the park's most famous accidents, when a young Californian man dived headfirst into the hot spring to save his dog, which had decided to cool off in the enticing pool. Sadly, both died as a result of their burns.

For a map of Fountain Paint Pot and Firehole Lake Dr, pick up the park-service trail guide ($1). Rangers lead tours here three times a week at 9am.

FOUNTAIN FLAT DRIVE

This former freight road turns off the Grand Loop Rd at the pleasant Nez Percé picnic area (with toilets) and continues south for 1.5 miles to a hiking and cycling trailhead. From here the road is accessible to cyclists and hikers all the way to Fairy Falls trailhead, 4 miles away. The trail is wheelchair accessible for 2.2 miles to the Goose Lake (OD5) campsite, one of two wheelchair-accessible backcountry campsites in the park.

Ojo Caliente Hot Spring — SPRING

(Map p106) Just beyond the Fountain Flat Dr parking lot is this pool (Ojo Caliente means 'Hot Spring' in Spanish), which empties into the river. Just south of the bridge is the trail to Sentinel Meadows (p66) and on either side of the bridge are trails to Pocket Basin.

Pocket Basin — THERMAL AREA

(Map p106) Pocket Basin is one of the least-known and little-visited thermal basins in the valley. It's actually a miniature caldera, originally created by a hydrothermal explosion that must have been roughly on the scale of an atomic bomb. The basin isn't on the scale of the more famous thermal features further south, but this is one place you can explore away from the boardwalks and parking lots. Remember, however, to take the normal precautions when approaching any thermal feature.

The northern trail leads past the belching mud pot of Grotto Spring and inviting Baby Bathtub Spring to the River Group, a collection of geysers and hot springs that includes Cavern Spring, Bath Spring, Azure Spring, Diadem Spring and Cone Spring. Across the river is Mound Spring, which erupts every half-hour or so. The southern trail leads to two lovely pools and then continues for another couple of minutes to a collection of riverside hot springs.

BEST BACKCOUNTRY THERMAL FEATURES

It's great to see a geyser or hot spring from the boardwalk, but it's quite another thing to explore a steaming off-trail thermal basin. With a bit of leg work you'll likely have the following backcountry secrets to yourself.

Shoshone Geyser Basin (p74) Lakeshore basin best visited on a multiday backpacking or canoe trip.

Washburn Hot Springs (p71) En route from Mt Washburn to Canyon's Glacial Boulder trailhead.

Mr Bubbles (p77) The king of backcountry soaks, in Bechler.

Pocket Basin (p113) Just a few hundred yards from the Fountain Flat Dr trailhead.

Howard Eaton Trail at Mammoth (p54) Explore Mammoth's terraces and vents from the back side.

Firehole Canyon Drive

The one-way Firehole Canyon Dr leaves the Grand Loop Rd just south of Madison Junction. The road passes 40ft-high **Firehole Falls** at the foot of towering dark rhyolite cliffs, but the main attraction here is the lukewarm **Firehole Swimming Area** (no fee), one of the few locations in the park that's open for swimming. The kids will love it. There are two toilets here, but limited parking.

Madison to West Yellowstone

Madison Junction sits at the confluence of the Firehole, Madison and Gibbon Rivers. Towering above the small junior ranger station is **National Park Mountain** (7500ft), which commemorates the spot where, in 1870, the idea of preserving Yellowstone was allegedly first mentioned.

The Madison Valley is of interest mainly to anglers and wildlife-watchers, though all will appreciate the sublime afternoon light and active herds of deer, elk and bison. Due to the long snow-free season many elk live in the valley year-round, while bison migrate through the valley between their winter habitat near the park's western boundary and summer grazing in the Hayden Valley. The 14-mile road to West Yellowstone is also one of the park's busiest tourist corridors.

Two miles east of Madison, the family-friendly **Harlequin Lake Trail** leads 0.5 miles north to a pond. Rangers lead a hike here on Monday mornings. The trailhead is also a fine place to spot wildlife in the lovely valley to the south. Elk often lie in the meadows here, with only their heads poking above the long grass.

From here the road threads between volcanic bluffs, with towering Mt Haynes (8235ft) on the left and Mt Jackson on the right, and past several excellent fly-fishing spots, before the valley opens up to views of the distant Gallatin Range.

Halfway along the road the Seven Mile Bridge marks the Madison River picnic area, popular with fly-fishers, and the Gneiss Creek trailhead. The area south of the road here is closed to protect a trumpeter swan habitat. In 1988 this section of the park was engulfed in the North Fork fire, the largest of that summer's giant blazes.

Four miles further, **Riverside Drive** is a 1-mile, two-way road that's useful for fishing access and perhaps some family cycling. Three miles later the Two Ribbons Trail is a 0.75-mile, wheelchair-accessible trail that of-fers a fairly dull loop or point-to-point stroll through some fire burns.

Shortly after you enter Montana, about 2 miles before West Yellowstone, the dirt Barnes Rd to the north accesses several more fishing spots. And then suddenly, just like that, you are out of the wilderness and in the middle of bustling West Yellowstone.

Old Faithful to West Thumb

Three miles into the 17-mile drive between Old Faithful and West Thumb is **Kepler Cascades**, where a wooden platform offers fine views of the 125ft falls. Just past the cascades turnout is the parking area for the worthwhile hike or bike ride to Lone Star Geyser (p67). The road climbs past Scaup Lake, the Spring Creek picnic area (site of the park's biggest stagecoach robbery in 1908) and the Continental Divide trailhead before reaching **Craig Pass** (8262ft).

Craig Pass is an unassuming spot of deep significance. Lily-choked **Isa Lake** sits astride both the road and the **Continental Divide** and in spring it drains (or rather seeps) into both the Atlantic and Pacific drainages. The west side of the lake drains year-round into the Firehole River, which flows into the Missouri and Mississippi Rivers before finally reaching the Atlantic *to the east;* the east side (in spring only) flows into Shoshone Lake and then the Lewis, Snake and Columbia Rivers and thus the Pacific Ocean *to the west.* The lake was named after Isabelle Jelke, the first park tourist to visit the lake, and it freezes solid in winter under around 15ft of snow.

From the pass, the road descends to the **DeLacy Creek** picnic area and trailhead and shortly afterward offers a tantalizing sliver of a view toward remote Shoshone Lake. From here the road ascends back across the Continental Divide (8391ft) before finally descending to excellent views of Yellowstone Lake and the turnoff to West Thumb.

⊙ Bechler Region

Visitors must go out of their way to find the Bechler (*Beck*-ler) region. Located in the remote southwest area of the park, it cannot be reached from the main entrance points or loops. Known for its numerous waterfalls and the park's highest rainfall, the remote region, also known as Beckler Corner or Cascade Corner, is largely the preserve of hardy backpackers, outfitters and horseback riders who brave flooded streams, monster mosquitoes and boggy marshland to access beautiful backcountry with the park's largest waterfalls and outstanding thermal soaking springs. The 19,700-acre meadow is home to diverse wildlife, including sandhill cranes, moose and coyotes. Early season visits are impractical here – trails are often flooded into July and mosquitoes can be brutal along the river until the beginning of August.

Visitors en route to a hike in the region, or traveling Grassy Lake Rd, might want to detour by car or foot to the Cave Falls cascades and swimming hole.

Bechler is accessed via Bechler Ranger Station or Cave Falls trailhead, both off the mostly unpaved Cave Falls Rd via US 20, 26 miles from Ashton, Idaho, itself a two-hour drive from West Yellowstone, Montana, via ID Hwy 47 and Marysville Rd. Alternative approaches include coming from Driggs, Idaho, to the south (joining US 20), or the brutal, unpaved Grassy Lake Rd/Reclamation Rd from the turnoff just north of Flagg Ranch, part of John D Rockefeller Memorial Parkway, 2 miles south of Yellowstone's South Entrance; allow at least two hours from Flagg Ranch.

🛏 SLEEPING

Although competition for campsites and lodging may be fierce, there's nothing quite like falling asleep to the eerie sounds of bugling elk and howling wolves and waking to the sulfur smell of the earth erupting and bubbling in the area.

You can make reservations for park accommodations and five of the park's 12 campgrounds through the park concessionaire, Xanterra (☑866-439-7375, 307-344-7311; www.yellowstonenationalparklodges.com). Online bookings are now possible for both hotels and campgrounds.

Camping in the Park

Most of Yellowstone's campsites are in natural junctions, areas once frequented by Native Americans as well as early trappers, explorers and the US Army. There are around 2200 formal campsites in the park, plus well over 100 backcountry sites.

Aside from backcountry campsites (which require a hike to reach), camping inside the park is allowed only in 12 designated campgrounds and it is limited to 14 consecutive days from July 1 to Labor Day, and 30 days for the rest of the year. Check-out time is 11am.

The NPS has seven campgrounds available on a first-come, first-served basis only. Call ☑307-344-2114 for recorded NPS campsite information.

Xanterra runs five of the park's 12 campgrounds (Canyon, Madison, Fishing Bridge, Bridge Bay and Grant Village) and these are a few dollars pricier than the national-park campgrounds. They feature flush toilets, cold running water and vending machines and a couple have showers (included in the price).

A few sites are reserved for backpackers and cyclists at all campgrounds except Slough Creek and Canyon. Slough Creek fills early, due to popularity with anglers and wolf-watchers. Canyon is popular because of its central location. Boaters favor Grant Village and Bridge Bay; canoeists and anglers often base themselves at Lewis Lake. The Madison Campground is closest to Old Faithful, though Grant Village isn't far off. Fishing Bridge is always full of RVs in midsummer, and reservations are essential.

Lodging in the Park

Today's cabins and campgrounds are direct descendants of classy turn-of-the-century hotels and Wylie tent camps, the latter an affordable early option that opened up the park to budget-minded auto tours. Of the cabin options, rustic Lake Lodge is the most peaceful, and Roosevelt Lodge offers the most authentic Western experience. Lake Yellowstone Hotel and Old Faithful Inn provide the park's most atmospheric and upscale accommodations. For reservations and information call Xanterra.

Rooms are priced here at double occupancy, but most lodges have rooms that sleep up to six for an extra $16 per person. All Yellowstone hotel rooms are nonsmoking and none have televisions.

🛏 Mammoth Country

Camping

Mammoth Campground   CAMPGROUND **$**
(Map p88; sites $20; ☺year-round) The park's most exposed campground, this is a barren, sagebrush-covered area with sparse shade. On a hairpin bend in the road below Mammoth Hot Springs, it gets road noise – the inner road sites are quietest – but its relatively low elevation makes it the warmest campground and a good choice for early- or late-season visits.

Showers and other facilities are in Mammoth, just to the south, or Gardiner, 5 miles north by the North Entrance. When staffed, the registration office assigns sites, accepts credit cards and offers change. There are several wheelchair-accessible and hiker/cyclist sites, and firewood for sale between 6pm and 8:30pm. Join one of the ranger talks at the amphitheater at 9pm or 9:30pm, depending on the month.

Indian Creek Campground CAMPGROUND $

(Map p88; sites $15; ☺ mid-Jun–mid-Sep) This low-key spot is probably the park's most underused campground – most people speed by between Mammoth and Old Faithful – which is one reason we like it. Plus, it's often the last in the park to fill up. The site is 8 miles south of Mammoth Junction.

It's set in open forest on a low rise, surrounded by moose territory and there are several hiking trails nearby – to Indian Creek, along the former stagecoach road, or partway along the Bighorn Pass Trail (look for a handout detailing campground trails). Generators are not allowed, but firewood is sold.

Lodging

Mammoth Hot Springs Hotel HOTEL $$

(Map p88; cabins $93-250, r with/without bath $140/90; ☺ May–mid-Oct) A classy vibe, a good variety of accommodations and a useful location make this one of the park's most popular hotels. The main choice is between the hotel rooms in the main building or cabins out back.

YELLOWSTONE NATIONAL PARK CAMPGROUNDS

CAMPGROUND	LOCATION	DESCRIPTION	NO OF SITES	ELEVATION (FT)
Canyon (p118)	Canyon Country	A huge 11-loop site slap-bang in the center of the park	272	7734
Madison (p120)	Geyser Country	Lovely riverside location and the closest campground to Old Faithful	270	6806
Bridge Bay (p119)	Lake Country	A multiple-loop mega-complex appealing to boaters and anglers	400	7800
Fishing Bridge RV Park (p119)	Lake Country	A reservations-essential, RV-only spot, with hookups	340	7800
Grant Village (p119)	Lake Country	A spacious and shady multiloop complex with conveniences and the lake nearby	435	7800
Lewis Lake (p119)	Lake Country	A shady, quiet campground close to backcountry trails and the lake	85	7800
Indian Creek (p116)	Mammoth Country	Quiet, small, secluded and woodsy	70	7300
Mammoth (p115)	Mammoth Country	Fairly barren spot near the North Entrance, but the warmest site in spring and fall	85	6239
Norris (p120)	Norris	Quiet site with a walking trail to the nearby geyser basin	116	7484
Pebble Creek (p117)	Roosevelt Country	Fairly cramped site, popular with wolf-watchers in the nearby Lamar Valley	27	6800
Slough Creek (p118)	Roosevelt Country	A favorite with anglers, this site fills up the earliest in high season	23	6400
Tower Fall (p118)	Roosevelt Country	Small site that fills up quickly, with several hiking trails	31	6650

*Reservations possible through Xanterra (p115).

 Drinking Water
 Restrooms
 Ranger Station
 Wheelchair Accessible
 Grocery Store Nearby

The main en suite hotel rooms echo the historic feel of the hotel, with some rooms boasting antique-style bathroom fittings and claw-foot tubs. The cabins (closed in winter) are mostly duplex units, with a porch to sit on, but if you value your privacy you can request a detached cabin. Families might like the two-bedroom rustic cabins ($186) without bathroom, which can sleep up to six.

Frontier cabins ($152) come with a private bathroom, shower and two double beds. Some come with a queen bed and private outdoor hot tub, enclosed in a privacy fence, for $250. The hotel suites ($479) have a living room and bedroom, the only satellite TV in the park and can sleep four in two queen beds.

The cheaper options come with a sink and communal bathrooms, either down the hall in the hotel block or in a separate block out back by the budget cabins.

🛏 Roosevelt Country

Camping

Pebble Creek Campground CAMPGROUND $ (sites $15; ⊙ mid-Jun–late Sep) The park's remotest campground is set along the banks of a creek in grizzly habitat and surrounded on three sides by the rugged cliffs of the Absaroka Range. It's popular with hikers and wolf-watchers, even though the sites are a bit cramped. It's 10 miles from the Northeast Entrance, at the lower end of Icebox Canyon.

OPEN	RESERVATION POSSIBLE?	DAILY FEE	FEATURES & FACILITIES
late May–early Sep	yes*	$27	
early May–mid-Oct	yes*	$22.50	
late May–mid-Sep	yes*	$22.50	
early May–late Sep	yes*	$47.50	
mid-Jun–mid-Sep	yes*	$27	
mid-Jun–early Nov	no	$15	
mid-Jun–mid-Sep	no	$15	
year-round	no	$20	
mid-May–late Sep	no	$20	
mid-Jun–late Sep	no	$15	
mid-Jun–early Oct	no	$15	
mid-May–late Sep	no	$15	

 Summertime Campfire Program

 RV Dump Station

EASY BACKCOUNTRY OVERNIGHTS

Taking your kids or spouse on their first backpacking trip? The following backcountry sites are all within 2 miles of the trailhead, perfect for easy access and emergency exit.

Blacktail Creek Site 1A1, 1.8 miles from Blacktail trailhead; campfires allowed.

Lava Creek 1A3, 1.4 miles from the Lava Creek picnic area trailhead past Undine Falls.

Indian Creek 1B1, 1 mile from Indian Creek Campground/Bighorn Pass trailhead.

Ice Lake 4D1 and 4D2 are on the lakeshore; 4D3 is an accessible site five minutes' walk from the road. Buggy before July.

Cascade Lake 4E4, 1.7 miles from Cascade Lake trailhead.

Norris Campground 4F1 is 2.3 miles up Solfatara Creek.

Ribbon Lake 4R1 and 4R2, 2 miles from Artist Point trailhead in Canyon.

Lone Star Geyser OA1 is within earshot of the geyser, and you can cycle most of the way there.

Fairy Falls OD1, 2.5 miles from the trailhead and part of the hike can be done on a bike.

Sentinel Meadows OG1, 1 mile from Fountain Freight Rd.

The nearest showers and supplies are at Tower-Roosevelt Junction. The Pebble Creek hiking trail starts nearby and there's good fishing at nearby Soda Butte Creek. Generators are not allowed. Most sites are pull-through.

Slough Creek Campground   CAMPGROUND **$**
(Map p92; sites $15; ☉ mid-Jun–early Oct) This remote, peaceful site, 2.2 miles up an unpaved road, is in grizzly habitat along a prime fishing stream. A couple of walk-in sites are available and there's easy access to the Slough Creek Trail. Generators are not allowed. The campground is 10 miles northeast of Tower-Roosevelt Junction. An anglers' paradise, it fills up by 11am in high season.

Tower Fall Campground   CAMPGROUND **$**
(Map p92; sites $15; ☉ mid-May–late Sep) This small single loop of 31 sites is high above Tower Creek in an open pine forest. There are hiking trails up Tower Creek and groceries at nearby Tower Falls. It's 3 miles southeast of Tower-Roosevelt Junction. There are hiker/cyclist sites. Generators not allowed.

Lodging

Roosevelt Lodge   CABIN **$$**
(Map p92; cabins with/without bath $135/80; ☉ Jun–early Sep; ⛽ 🐾) Founded in 1906 as a tented camp, present-day Roosevelt Lodge was built in 1919 and retains an Old West feel, offering 80 rustic cabins, horseback rides and a Wild West cookout in the heart of sagebrush country. Frontier cabins come with a private bathroom, while the simpler Roughriders share communal wash blocks with hot showers and ice.

For groups, families or couples traveling together, the Roughrider cabins are a good deal as some cabins come with three beds, meaning you can shoehorn six people in here for around $20 a head! The simple but pleasant wooden cabins come with a log-burning stove, though the one-bed cabins are cramped (because it's the same price, book a larger cabin). All beds are doubles rather than queens, so can be small for couples. There are no en suite bathrooms and no running water in the room.

Frontier cabins are nicely decorated and come with private bathroom, electric heating and two or three double beds. There are two wheelchair-accessible cabins with private bathroom.

Cabins should be booked several months in advance, though you might find a Roughrider free on the off-chance. There are a limited number of outdoor grills if you want to cook your own food. There's good hiking nearby. The hike to Lost Lake (p56) starts from just behind the lodge.

🛏 Canyon Country

Camping

Canyon Campground   CAMPGROUND **$**
(Map p96; sites $27; ☉ late May–early Sep) This huge campground is the most densely forested in the park, but it's also the largest (11 loops!) and one of the most cramped, which

makes staying here feel like being churned through a Pink Floyd–style tourism meat grinder. Still, thanks to its central location as a base for day trips to other parts of park, it's very popular.

There are showers and laundry on-site (rates include two showers) and the restaurants and supplies of Canyon Village are nearby. Canyon also offers the most tent-only sites (four out of 11 loops) of any campground. Head to the amphitheater at 9pm or 9:30pm for the nightly campfire programs. Snow can linger here well into early summer.

Lodging

Canyon Lodge   LODGE **$$**
(Map p96; cabins $194, r $122-222; ⊘ Jun-Sep) This enormous complex dates from the opening of the park to mass tourism in the 1950s and 1960s – a drive around the multiple low-rise and potholed loops is like a drive back in time to a classic Middle American suburb. New lodges are currently being built to replace the aging cabins.

The modern Dunraven Lodge and Cascade Lodge both offer cozy modern hotel rooms that were built in the 1990s, some with forest views. Both have coffeemakers and some wheelchair-accessible rooms, but no telephone. Two new lodges opened in 2015, with three more due to open in 2017.

The remaining cabins are laid out barracks-style, grouped into blocks of four or six, with two queen beds, a coffeemaker, porch and tub/shower. Two hundred cabins were pulled down in 2014 and the rest are due to be phased out over the coming years.

🛏 Lake Country

Camping

Most campgrounds feature dump stations, but only Fishing Bridge has full sewer and electrical hookups.

Bridge Bay Campground   CAMPGROUND **$**
(Map p100; sites $22.50; ⊘ late May–mid-Sep) This mega-complex adjacent to the marina, 3 miles southwest of Lake Village, appeals to fishing and boating enthusiasts. Some lower sites offer lake views, but the more private ones are in the upper section. Showers and laundry facilities are 4 miles away at Fishing Bridge. There are campfire programs at 6pm and 9:30pm, the former aimed at young families.

Tent campers will appreciate the more desirable, forested, tent-only loops (I and J). Loops A, B and C are barren and exposed. Get groceries at the nearby marina general store.

Fishing Bridge RV Park   CAMPGROUND **$**
(Map p100; RV sites $47.75; ⊘ early May-late Sep) Near the north shore of Yellowstone Lake, 1 mile east of Fishing Bridge Junction, this place only allows hard-shelled RVs because of heavy bear activity. Public facilities include a pay laundry and showers. Stroll over to the nearby visitor center at 9pm or 9:30pm for a ranger talk. Rates are for up to four people and include water, sewerage hookups and two showers. All sites are back-ins, with a 40ft maximum length. Reservations are essential.

Grant Village Campground   CAMPGROUND **$**
(Map p100; sites $27; ⊘ mid-Jun–mid-Sep) On the west shore of Yellowstone Lake, 22 miles north of the South Entrance, this is the park's biggest campground, with a nearby boat launch, an RV dump station and three loops of tent-only sites. Rates include two showers and there is a laundry and groceries. You'll find lovely spots for lakeshore strolls nearby. The campground only opens when bears have stopped fishing the nearby spawning streams, which can be as late as June.

Lewis Lake Campground   CAMPGROUND **$**
(sites $15; ⊘ mid-Jun–early Nov) This forested campground is at the south end of Lewis Lake, about 10 miles north of the South Entrance. It's popular with boaters as the nearby boat launch provides easy access to Lewis Lake and the Lewis River channel. Snow often remains here through June because of its high elevation and shaded location, so it may not be the best early-season campground. Bring insect repellent. Generators not allowed.

Lodging

★ **Lake Yellowstone Hotel**   HOTEL **$$**
(Map p100; cabins $149, annex r $160, hotel r $363-405; ⊘ mid-May–early Oct; @ 🛜) Right on the lakeshore, this buttercup behemoth sets romantics aflutter. It harks back to a bygone era, though the 296 rooms that cost $4 in 1895 have appreciated somewhat. The spacious main-building rooms were upgraded in 2014, with new carpet and the park's only wired internet connections. Lakeside rooms cost extra and sell out first, but don't guarantee lake views. The comfortable Frontier cabins are boxed in neat suburban duplexes. The motel-style Sandpiper annex is dated, with pink walls and floral bedspreads, but renovations are planned.

Lake Lodge
CABIN **$$**

(Map p100; cabins $83-194) The Western cabins ($194) here are spacious, modern and ideal for families, either in forested back loops or (in the A loop) with French windows and outdoor seating. Cramped Pioneer cabins ($83) recall the 1920s, with propane heaters and rustic decor last updated when Yogi Bear last wandered into the park. The midrange Frontier cabins ($131) are a good compromise.

The best feature is the rustic main lodge with rockers creaking on the porch, roaring fires inside, a dining hall and a laundromat.

Grant Village
HOTEL **$$**

(Map p100; Grant Village; r $160-201; ☉ late May–Sep; ☎) The 300 condo-like boxes with standard hotel interiors at Grant Village were once dismissed by author Alston Chase as 'an inner-city project in the heart of primitive America, a wilderness ghetto.' They do happen to be the closest lodging to the Tetons for those getting an early start. Premium rooms ($201) are fresher, thanks to a recent renovation.

🛏 Norris

Norris Campground
CAMPGROUND **$**

(Map p88; sites $20; ☉ mid-May–late Sep) Nestled in scenic open forest on an idyllic, sunny hill overlooking the Gibbon River and bordering meadows, this is one of the park's nicest campgrounds. The few riverside sites in loop A get snapped up very quickly. Campfire talks are held at 7:30pm and firewood is sold between 7pm and 8:30pm.

There are fishing and wildlife-viewing opportunities nearby, Solfatara Creek trailhead is in the campground and there's a 1-mile trail from near the campground (just over the bridge) to Norris Geyser Basin. Bring water, as the stuff in the campground spigots is putrid.

DON'T MISS

YELLOWSTONE STARGAZING

The excellent Stars Over Yellowstone interpretive program runs for two weekends in June and July at Madison Campground's amphitheater and is a must for budding astronomers. Astronomers from Museum of the Rockies offer a guided tour of the night sky and there are all kinds of telescopes on-site to play with, courtesy of the Southwestern Montana Astronomical Society.

🛏 Geyser Country

Camping

Madison Campground
CAMPGROUND **$**

(Map p106; sites $22.50; ☉ early May–mid-Oct) The nearest campground to Old Faithful and the West Entrance occupies a sunny, open forest in a broad meadow above the banks of the Madison River. Bison herds and the park's largest elk herd frequent the meadows to its west, making for great wildlife-watching, and it's a fine base for fly-fishing the Madison.

Tent-only sites are ideally placed along the river. A junior ranger station (p104) and campground amphitheater lie just a short walk away and offer nightly ranger talks. The campground is just west of Madison Junction, 14 miles east of the West Entrance and 16 miles north of Old Faithful. Vending machines offer ice, soft drinks and newspapers, but the nearest food and showers are at Old Faithful.

Lodging

★ Old Faithful Inn
HOTEL **$$**

(Map p108; old house d with shared/private bath from $108/162, standard r $199-260; ☉ early May–early Oct) The lobby of this historic place is a bit of a zoo during the day, but the day-trippers quickly disappear with the sun. The building is full of charm, with 327 rooms, a lovely balcony, library-style desks and century-old furniture, plus a pianist and singer at lunch and dinner. A stay here is a quintessential Yellowstone experience.

The hotel has a vast variety of rooms, including some wheelchair-accessible rooms. The cheapest 'Old House' rooms pack the most atmosphere, with log walls and original wash basins, but the bathrooms are down the hall. Rooms with two queens are larger than those with one, but cost the same. Beware also that you can hear every footstep through the creaking wooden ceiling, and the radiator heat can be noisy early and late in the season. Easily the best rooms of this kind are the two- and three-bed 'dormers' off the 3rd-floor lobby.

The only rooms that have a view of Old Faithful are a couple of 'superior' east-wing rooms ($260); these get snapped up a year in advance. Even if you face Old Faithful, you'll find that the pine trees block most of the view, so get a room in the east wing and save yourself $30.

The only bum rooms in the hotel are the 'garden view' rooms that are below the ground floor. Staff refer to these affectionately as the 'dungeon rooms.' Request a higher floor when booking. Book well in advance, or you'll find there's no room at the inn.

Old Faithful Snow Lodge HOTEL $$
(Map p108; cabins $109-155, r from $240-259; ☺May–mid-Oct & late Dec-Feb; ☏) This modern lodge was built in 1999 in a 'New Western' style and offers the only winter accommodations available at Old Faithful. The main lodge has a stylish lobby decorated in bear and elk motifs and 134 comfortable, cozy and somewhat-bland modern hotel rooms, with two double beds, a hair dryer and a coffeemaker. The pine-walled Frontier cabins ($109) are fairly simple, but come with bathrooms and a coffeemaker. The modern Western cabins ($155) are more spacious, with two queens, and are warmer in winter.

Old Faithful Lodge Cabins CABIN $$
(Map p108; cabins with/without bath $140/83; ☺mid-May–early Oct) Glummer than its glamorous cousins, the 132-cabin lodge was built in 1923 and has its historical roots in Yellowstone's turn-of-the-century tent camps. It's definitely a notch down in atmosphere, though the rooms themselves are fine.

The remodeled Frontier cabins ($140) come with a private bathroom, but no telephone. Budget cabins ($83) have sinks with hot water, but the toilets and showers are in outside blocks. Most cabins are in blocks of twos or fours.

🛏 Bechler Region

Cave Falls Campground CAMPGROUND $
(☏208-524-7500; www.fs.usda.gov/caribou; sites $10; ☺Jun–mid-Sep) Situated in the Caribou-Targhee National Forest, just at the southwestern park border, by Bechler's trailheads and Cave Falls, the 23 pleasant woodsy sites line a river cliff offering a slight breeze to ward off mosquitoes. Sites feature picnic tables, fire rings and grills. Vault toilets, bear boxes and water are available.

✗ EATING & DRINKING

Food in the park is split between campfire cuisine, cafeteria food, a couple of fast-food choices and the more pleasant dining rooms of the park's historic inns. The park concessionaire, Xanterra (p115), runs most dining

options, so don't be surprised if you get a serious dose of déjà vu every time you open a menu. That said, most places are pretty good value considering the prime real estate, and there have been moves in recent years to add a range of healthy and gluten-free options. Preview park menus at the Xanterra website.

The park's cafeterias are bland but convenient, and reasonably economical for families. All places serve breakfast and most offer an all-you-can-eat buffet that can quickly wipe out even the best-laid hiking plans. Kids' menus are available almost everywhere. Almost all offer sandwiches for lunch and heavier, more interesting fare for dinner.

There's also fast food at major junctions, plus snack shops and grocery supplies in the Yellowstone General Stores. The Grant Village, Old Faithful Inn and Lake Yellowstone Hotel dining rooms all require dinner reservations (☑307-344-7311).

✗ Mammoth Country

Mammoth Terrace Grill FAST FOOD $
(Map p88; mains $4-8; ☺7am-9pm late Apr–mid-Oct; ☝) Line up for MacYellowstone-style burgers, chili cheese fries and ice cream, along with some healthier options and breakfast foods.

★Mammoth Hot Springs Dining Room AMERICAN $$
(Map p88; dinner mains $12-26; ☺6:30-10am, 11:30am-2:30pm, 5-10pm May–mid-Oct & mid-Dec–early Mar; ☏) There are a few surprises in this elegant place, including our favorite, the delicious Thai curry mussels starter. Dinner is a serious affair, with huckleberry barbecued chicken, and pistachio and parmesan-crusted trout. Try a 'Yellowstone caldera' – a warm chocolate truffle torte with a suitably molten center – for dessert. Reservations are only necessary in winter.

The attached bar has nice fireside seating in winter and serves restaurant starters if you just fancy a light dinner. Drink highlights include the draft Teton Ale and the huckleberry margaritas. The hotel lobby's **Espresso Cart** (Map p88; ☺6.30-10am & 4-9pm) will help you kick-start the day and sells beer and wine in the evening.

✗ Roosevelt Country

Limited groceries and cold beer (as well as bear spray) are available at the small **Yellowstone General Store** (Map p92; ☺7:30am-9:30pm).

Roosevelt Lodge Dining Room   AMERICAN $$
(Map p92; lunch & breakfast $10, dinner $14-27; ⊘7-10am & 11:30am-9:30pm early Jun-early Sep) Popular for its applewood-smoked Western-style ribs and Wyoming cheese steak, the meaty menu stretches to bison burgers and wild-game chili, but has glaringly little for vegetarians. Take a post-lunch or pre-dinner stroll up to the Lost Creek Falls (p56), a 10-minute walk behind the lodge. The porch rockers are a fine place for a nightcap.

Old West Cookout   BARBECUE $$$
(Roosevelt Country; Map p92; ☑866-439-7375; dinner & wagon ride adult/child $60/49; ⊘3-5pm Jun-early Sep; ◉) The Roosevelt Lodge activities center offers this fun cookout, with steak, beans and the kind of cowboy coffee you have to filter through your teeth. Kids will love it. Swap the wagon ride for a horse ride for an extra $20. Reservations are required, preferably months in advance.

✕ Canyon Country

Don't expect too much from Canyon's restaurants; a single kitchen prepares all meals – up to 5000 per day!

Canyon Lodge Cafeteria   CAFETERIA $
(Map p96; meals $7-10; ⊘6:30-10:30am & 11:30am-9:30pm late May–mid-Sep) There are no surprises at this huge and echoing cafeteria, but it's cheap and easy, serving up salads, lasagne, rice bowls and bison sloppy joes, with the same menu as the Old Faithful Lodge Cafeteria. Oatmeal and fruit salads are among the lighter options. Hours are limited in June and September.

Canyon Yellowstone General Store   DINER $
(Map p96; www.visityellowstonepark.com; mains $9-11; ⊘7:30am-8:30pm; ◉) The fun, old-fashioned soda-fountain counter here churns out burgers, chili dogs and root-beer floats, plus there's ice cream and coffee (with refills). Breakfasts include blueberry flapjacks with bacon. The grocery store has fresh fruit and is open an hour later.

Canyon Deli   SANDWICHES $
(Map p96; sandwiches $9; ⊘7:30am-9:30pm Jun-late Sep) Offers anaemic-looking prepackaged deli sandwiches, yogurt with granola, salads and very popular ice cream (try the Moose Tracks), with a couple of outdoor seats in the sun.

Canyon Lodge Dining Room   AMERICAN $$
(Map p96; dinner mains $10-17; ⊘7-10am, 11:30am-2:30pm & 5-10pm Jun-late Sep) This eatery has a

dated casino/steakhouse lounge feel – the kind of place you might spot a 1970s-era Joe Pesci in a perm and a leisure suit – but it will do. Lunch features epic burgers (including lamb or turkey), but the restaurant only truly spreads its chicken wings for dinner, with bacon-wrapped game meatloaf and a famed prime rib au jus. The $11 all-you-can-eat soup-and-salad-bar option is low-grade but refreshing if you've been living on canned food. The breakfast menu has some light options, such as yogurt with fresh fruit, as well as a full breakfast buffet ($12). The lounge bar is open 3:30pm to 11pm.

✕ Geyser Country

All of the food options in Geyser Country are clustered around Old Faithful. The espresso cart (9am to 10pm) in the Old Faithful Inn serves the best coffee in the park.

Old Faithful Yellowstone General Stores   FAST FOOD $
(Map p108; www.visityellowstonepark.com; mains $9-11; ⊘7:30am-8:30pm) Old Faithful's two general stores both serve up snacks. The original knotted-pine Hamilton's Store near Old Faithful has a '50s-style diner counter, complete with original fountain stools, that serves up burgers, malts and sandwiches. The modern store near the Snow Lodge offers individual pizzas, salads, breakfast biscuits and prepackaged sandwiches in a cafeteria-style setting.

Geyser Grill   FAST FOOD $
(Map p108; sandwiches $5-9; ⊘8am-9pm mid-Apr–early Nov & mid-Dec–mid-Mar; ◉) Attached to the Snow Lodge, this is a fast-food place with burgers, breakfasts, fish and chips and a bison bratwurst sandwich. It closes early in shoulder season.

Bake Shop   FAST FOOD $
(Map p108; snacks $6; ⊘6:30am-10pm mid-May–Oct) For quick eats and simple breakfasts visit the Bake Shop in the lobby of the Old Faithful Lodge. It offers bison chili, pretzels, muffins and cinnamon rolls, and there's an ice-cream stand.

Bear Paw Deli   DELI $
(Map p108; snacks $7; ⊘10:30am-7:30pm) Just off the lobby of the Old Faithful Inn, the Bear Paw sells unappetizing prewrapped sandwiches, continental breakfasts and ice cream. Look for the original etched cartoon murals on the wall, which date from 1936, when this room housed the hotel bar.

Old Faithful Lodge Cafeteria
CAFETERIA $$

(Map p108; mains $9-15; ⊗11am-9pm mid-May–early Oct) It's factory-style functionality rather than fine cuisine, but this good-value place churns out solid standards like meatloaf and prime rib alongside lighter fare like the chicken wrap and a daily special. Get here early, before the buffet-style food gets too stewed. Most noteworthy are the views of Old Faithful from the side window and porch rockers. It doesn't serve breakfast.

Old Faithful Inn Dining Room
AMERICAN $$$

(Map p108; ☑307-545-4999; dinner mains $13-29, breakfast/lunch/dinner buffet $13/16/30; ⊗6:30-10:30am, 11:30am-2:30pm & 5-10pm early May–Oct; ✐) This buzzing dining room serves good-value steaks, salads and pasta, as well as breakfast, lunch and dinner buffets. The huge fireplace and wagon-wheel chandelier add to the rustic atmosphere and the classical music on the balcony is a classy touch. Without dinner reservations you'll end up eating dinner before 5pm or after 9pm; check the cancellations list around 3pm.

For post-geyser or après-ski cocktails, the attached **Bear Pit Lounge** (Map p108; ⊗from 11:30am) has microbrews and serves burgers.

Obsidian Dining Room
AMERICAN $$$

(Map p108; ☑307-344-7311; mains $15-33; ⊗6:30-10:30am and mid-Oct & mid-Dec–early Mar, lunch winter only) A quieter affair, the dining room at the Old Faithful Snow Lodge serves up a few unexpected dishes alongside bison ribs braised in Moose Drool Ale (the bison are farmed outside the Yellowstone-Ecosystem). The cozy fireside seats at the attached **Firehole Lounge** (Map p108; ⊗5-11pm winter) get snapped up quickly in winter.

✖ Lake Country

For the park's classiest corner, grab a predinner microbrew or glass of wine in the Lake Yellowstone Hotel lobby while listening to the string quartet.

Lake Yellowstone Hotel Deli
DELI $

(Map p100; sandwiches $7-11; ⊗6:30am-9pm mid-May–late Sep) The recently revamped deli offers superior breakfast bagels, bison brats, Starbucks coffee and carrot ginger soup, plus bottles of wine for a lakeshore picnic.

Fishing Bridge Yellowstone General Store
FAST FOOD $

(Map p100; mains $9-11; ⊗7:30am-8:30pm; ✈) This branch of the parkwide general stores has espresso coffee, Belgian waffles and root-beer floats served up at a fun retro soda-fountain counter that dates from 1931.

Lake Yellowstone General Store
FAST FOOD $

(Map p100; mains $9-11; ⊗7:30am-8:30pm) This branch of the general stores, behind the Yellowstone Lake Hotel, dates back 90 years and has a corner soda-fountain feel, down to the period 1938 counter stools. The simple food includes chili and nachos, with the same menu as the Fishing Bridge store.

Lake Lodge Cafeteria
CAFETERIA $$

(Map p100; dinner mains $12-16; ⊗6:30am-2:30pm & 4:30-10pm early Jun-early Oct) The affordable, rustic cafeteria at Lake Lodge offers hearty breakfasts and a limited range of precooked family fare such as prime rib, stuffed turkey and trout, plus lighter wraps and salads. Sipping something from the rustic lobby bar while watching the lake from the porch rockers is a pre-dinner highlight.

Grant Village Dining Room
AMERICAN $$

(Map p100; ☑307-344-7311; Grant Village; breakfast buffet $13.25, dinner $17-30; ⊗6:30-10am, 11:30am-2:30pm & 5-10pm late May-late Sep) The aroma emanating from this high-beamed lodge could draw a band of grizzlies, who would doubtless enjoy the elk sliders. Lunch offers deli fare, including a bison meatloaf sandwich. Dinner includes prime rib and a huckleberry crème brûlée. Dinner reservations are advised; grab a stool at the tiny Seven Stool Saloon for a cold brew while you wait.

Lake House
CAFETERIA $$

(Map p100; Grant Village; mains $8-15; ⊗6:30-10:30am & 5-10:30pm mid-Jun–late Sep) This quiet lakeshore spot offers build-your-own Italian or Asian noodles, dinner salads and the best lake views in the park in a casual pub-style environment. Try spicy peanut udon noodles with a seaweed salad. Walk down from the main parking area or marina to the lakeshore. It's closed for lunch.

★ Lake Yellowstone Hotel Dining Room
AMERICAN $$$

(Map p100; ☑307-344-7311; mains $14-40; ⊗6:30-10am, 11:30am-2:30pm & 5-10pm mid-May–Oct; ✐) Save your one unwrinkled outfit to dine in style at the dining room of the Lake Yellowstone Hotel. Lunch options include trout, a poached pear, cambozola and walnut salad and sandwiches. Dinner ups the ante with starters of lobster ravioli and mains of bison tenderloin, quail and rack of Montana lamb. Dinner reservations recommended. Breakfast is à la carte, or opt for the blow-out buffet ($15), including smoked salmon and blintzes.

YELLOWSTONE PARK: OPENING & CLOSING DATES

Yellowstone's opening schedule is complicated. Pin down specific opening and closing dates from www.nps/gov/yell and www.yellowstonenationalparklodges.com.

Year-round The North Entrance at Gardiner and the north road from Gardiner to Cooke City via Mammoth and Tower-Roosevelt Junction. Mammoth Campground is also open year-round.

Mid- to late April The first of the other roads to open are the West Entrance Rd and the western side of the Grand Loop Rd: Mammoth to Norris, Norris to Madison and Madison to Old Faithful. Norris to Canyon opens a week later. Old Faithful Snow Lodge opens.

Early May The South and East Entrances open, followed by the road between West Thumb and Old Faithful over Craig Pass (8262ft). Old Faithful Inn opens.

Mid-May Fishing Bridge RV Park, Mammoth Hotel, Old Faithful Lodge and Lake Yellowstone Hotel open.

End May The road between Tower and Canyon Junctions over Dunraven Pass (8859ft) is the last park road to open, usually by Memorial Day. The Beartooth Hwy between Red Lodge and Cooke City normally opens by Memorial Day, but can be delayed a week or more by heavy snowfall.

Early June Canyon Village, Lake Lodge and Roosevelt Lodge open. Lewis Lake and Grant Village campgrounds are the last to open.

September Park accommodations start to close, with Canyon Village and Roosevelt Lodge first to go.

Mid-October The Beartooth Hwy closes for the year, as do accommodations at Old Faithful. Slough Creek and Lewis Lake Campgrounds are the last to close at the end of the month.

November All park roads close on the first Monday in November, except for the Gardiner–Cooke City road.

Mid-December Entrances open to snowmobiles and snowcoaches from the third Wednesday in December through to the second Monday in March, when spring plowing starts. Roads are then closed to vehicles but are open to cyclists in April. Old Faithful Snow Lodge and Mammoth Hot Springs Hotel and Dining Room open for the winter until early March.

🛍 SHOPPING

The nonprofit **Yellowstone Association** (www.yellowstoneassociation.org) operates bookstores at the park's visitor centers and information stations, and at Norris Geyser Basin. Hiking maps and guidebooks are usually available. Members get a 15% discount.

❶ Park Policies & Regulations

➡ It is illegal to collect plants, flowers, rocks, petrified wood or antlers in Yellowstone.

➡ Firearms are now allowed in the park under valid state or federal laws, but are prohibited in park or concessionaire buildings.

➡ Swimming in water of entirely thermal origin is prohibited.

➡ Permits are required for all backcountry trips and activities such as boating and fishing.

➡ Drones are not allowed in the park.

❶ Dangers & Annoyances

Yellowstone is grizzly country. Bears that associate humans with food quickly become a problem, a danger and then a target, so keep all your food packed away in campgrounds, or strung up on a bear pole in the backcountry. We suggest carrying bear spray on all backcountry hikes. Two male hikers were killed in separate incidents in summer 2011 – one in the Canyon region, the other on the Geyser Country side of the Mary Mountain hiking trail. In 2015 a local employee was killed hiking off-trail near Elephant Back Mountain. The 2011 incidents were the first bear-related fatalities in the park for 25 years.

For all the focus on grizzlies, more people are injured by park bison (and even moose) each year than by bears. The golden rule is to keep your distance – 100yd from bears and 25yd from anything taller than a chipmunk.

The other main wildlife-related danger comes from slamming into the car in front of you while staring at a photogenic herd of roadside elk. Exercise caution whenever the desire to rubber-neck becomes irresistible and, if you must stop, make sure you pull completely off the road.

Theft from trailhead parking lots is not common, but it's not unheard of. Always lock your car and keep valuables out of sight.

For a catalogue of the least likely ways you can find trouble in the park, check out *Death in Yellowstone* by park historian Lee Whittlesey. The morbidly humorous book chronicles more than 300 deaths in the park over the last century, ranging from the horrifying (boiled alive in a hot spring; disemboweled by a grizzly) to the ridiculous (accidentally backing a car over the edge of the Grand Canyon of the Yellowstone; death from wild parsnips).

ⓘ Information

MEDICAL SERVICES

There are clinics at Mammoth, Old Faithful and Lake Village.

MONEY

There are 24-hour ATMs at Canyon Lodge, Canyon General Store, Fishing Bridge General Store, Grant Village General Store, Lake Yellowstone Hotel, Old Faithful Inn, Old Faithful General Store, Old Faithful Snow Lodge, Mammoth General Store and Mammoth Hot Springs Hotel.

POST OFFICES

The only year-round post office is at Mammoth. Seasonal post offices operate at Canyon, Lake Village, Grant Village and Old Faithful. All are open 8:30am to 5pm Monday to Friday.

SHOWERS & LAUNDRY

Canyon Village, Fishing Bridge RV Park and Grant Village provide laundry (7am to 10pm, last load 9pm; $2.75 per load) and showers (7am to 1:30pm and 3pm to 9:30pm; $3.90, plus $1.30 for a towel). Old Faithful Inn, Mammoth Hot Springs Hotel and Roosevelt Lodge offer showers only, and Lake Lodge and Old Faithful Snow Lodge have laundry only. Showers are included in campground fees at Canyon and Grant Village. All facilities close in winter.

TOURIST INFORMATION

Yellowstone's visitor centers and information stations are usually open 9am to 6pm, with extended hours from 8am to 7pm in summer. Most are closed or open reduced hours Labor Day to Memorial Day. The Albright Visitor Center (p89) in Mammoth is open year-round, and the Old Faithful Visitor Center (p107) is open in winter. Check the park newspaper for current hours of operation.

The park produces a series of informative pamphlets ($1) on Yellowstone's main attractions. These are available at visitor centers and in weatherproof boxes at the sites.

Ranger stations, open 8am to 4:30pm, are located at Grant Village, Lake Village, Lewis Lake, Bechler, Canyon, Mammoth, Bridge Bay, Tower Junction, Old Faithful, Madison, Lamar Valley and the West and South Entrances.

Yellowstone National Park Headquarters
(Map p88; ☑ 307-344-7381; www.nps.gov/yell) At Fort Yellowstone in Mammoth Hot Springs. Most of the park's brochures are downloadable from its website.

ⓘ Getting Around

Unless you're part of a guided bus tour, the only way to get around is to drive. There is no public transportation within the park, except for a few ski-drop services during winter.

DRIVING

The speed limit in most of the park is 45mph, dropping to 25mph at busy turnouts or junctions. In the words of writer Tim Cahill, anything faster than this is 'both illegal and silly.'

Gas and diesel are available at most junctions. Stations at Old Faithful and Canyon are open whenever the park is open to vehicles. The Roosevelt station closes at the beginning of September, Fishing Bridge in mid-September, Grant Village in late September and Mammoth in early October. Stations are manned from around 8am to 7pm and offer 24-hour credit-card service at the pump.

Towing, repair services and basic car parts are available at Sinclair gas stations at the following locations:

Old Faithful (☉ mid-Apr–early Nov)
Fishing Bridge (☉ late May-early Sep)
Grant Village (☉ late May–mid-Sep)
Canyon (☑ breakdown service 307-242-7644; ☉ May-early Oct)

Dial ☑ 307-344-2114 to check road and weather conditions prior to your visit, as road construction, rock or mudslides and snow can close park entrances and roads at any time.

ORGANIZED TOURS

Xanterra (p82) runs a slew of daily tours, all of which offer discounts for children aged 12 to 16 and are free for kids under 12. There are full-day tours of the upper and lower loops, as well as half-day afternoon wildlife trips and dawn photo safaris, as well as trips to the Tetons.

Most of these tours are on the wonderful Old Yellow Buses, a refurbished fleet of classic convertible 19-seater touring cars that plied the park's roads between 1936 and 1956, only to return to the park in 2007. They are guaranteed to add a touch of class to your sightseeing. See the 'Things to Do' section of Xanterra's website for details on all tours.

Around Yellowstone

Why Go?

The 43,750-sq-mile Greater Yellowstone Ecosystem doesn't suddenly end at the park fence. Enveloping the park kernel is a protective cushion of national forests and wilderness areas that offer almost as much scenic splendor as the park itself, but without the crowds and the pesky permits. Try to allocate at least a few days to explore this exceptional area.

Latched onto Yellowstone Park's northern boundaries, the three gateway towns of Gardiner, West Yellowstone and Cooke City serve as functional visitor hubs, good for a bed and a bite to eat, but it's the four corridors that radiate out from the park that offer the real scenic draws. Plan your itinerary to combine the stunning Beartooth and Gallatin routes, or the Beartooth, Wapiti and Chief Joseph Scenic Hwy via the Wild West town of Cody, and you'll have the ultimate add-on to a classic Yellowstone trip.

Best Places to Eat

➡ Yellowstone Valley Grill (p148)

➡ 2nd St Bistro (p145)

➡ Serenity Bistro (p165)

➡ Log Cabin Café (p138)

Best Places to Stay

➡ Murray Hotel (p145)

➡ Chamberlin Inn (p141)

➡ Rainbow Ranch Lodge (p158)

➡ Chico Hot Springs (p146)

➡ 320 Ranch (p158)

Road Distances (miles)

	Billings	Bozeman	West Yellowstone	Cody	Gardiner
Bozeman	145				
West Yellowstone	230	90			
Cody	110	210	135		
Gardiner	170	80	55	130	
Cooke City	130	140	100	75	55

Note: Distances are approximate

BEARTOOTH ROUTE

Billings

✍ 406 / POP 105,000 / ELEV 3300FT

Montana's largest city has more in common with the dusty plains of eastern Montana than the more-celebrated Rocky Mountain scenery out to the west of the state. It shouldn't be a priority on your Yellowstone itinerary, but it's not a bad place to overnight before heading to the park or catching your flight home.

Ernest Hemingway brought some excitement to Billings in November 1930 when he crashed his car on the way home from Yellowstone National Park. He broke his right arm and had to spend seven weeks in the town's St Vincent's Hospital.

◉ Sights

Western Heritage Center　　　　MUSEUM
(✍ 406-256-6809; www.ywhc.org; 2822 Montana Ave; adult/senior & child $5/3; ⊙ 10am-5pm Tue-Sat) If you have time in Billings, explore the changing exhibits and excellent artifact collection here, representing the various cultural traditions of Yellowstone Valley.

Yellowstone Art Museum　　　　GALLERY
(✍ 406-256-6804; www.artmuseum.org; 401 N 27th St; adult/child $6/3; ⊙ 10am-5pm Tue, Wed & Sat, to 8pm Thu & Fri, 11am-4pm Sun) Combining a collection of Western art with visiting exhibitions, the YAM is on the site of the 1916 Yellowstone County Jail. Admission is $1 on the first Saturday of the month.

Moss Mansion　　　　HISTORIC BUILDING
(✍ 406-256-5100; www.mossmansion.com; 914 Division St; adult/senior $10/7; ⊙ 10am-4pm Tue-Sat, 1-4pm Sun) Billings' most interesting historic home, the Moss was built in 1903 by local captain of industry PB Moss. The Moorish-style entryway and atmospheric staff kitchens are particularly interesting. Fans should attend the special behind-the-scenes tour ($25) every second Saturday.

The Rims　　　　AREA
Cycle or hike Chief Black Otter Trail from near the airport for the best overview of the city (great at dusk) as far as the distant Beartooth Mountains, and to visit the grave of Yellowstone Kelly, an early scout and guide.

🛏 Sleeping

Billings KOA　　　　CAMPGROUND $
(✍ 406-252-3104; www.billingskoa.com; 547 Garden Ave; tent/RV sites from $36/45, cabins from $85; ⊙ Apr-Oct; 🕸🏊) America's first KOA

campground is in a scenic spot by the Yellowstone River, 0.5 miles south of I-90, not far from downtown.

Dude Rancher Lodge　　　　MOTEL $
(✍ 800-221-3302; www.duderancherlodge.com; 415 N 29th St; d from $89; 🕸@🕸) Road-weary travelers will appreciate this downtown motor lodge, a fine and friendly motel with groovy oak furniture dating back to the 1940s, Western touches like split-log paneling and cattle-brand carpet, plus flat-screen TVs and in-room coffee. The attached diner is a local breakfast favorite.

Riversage Billings Inn　　　　MOTEL $
(✍ 800-231-7782; www.billingsinn.com; 880 N 29th St; r $72-96; 🕸) Most rooms here are updated to include a microwave, refrigerator and breakfast.

Cherry Tree Inn　　　　MOTEL $
(✍ 800-237-5882; www.billingscherrytreeinn.com; 823 N Broadway; r $65; 🕸🏊) Good-value, if somewhat dated; central location.

Northern Hotel　　　　HOTEL $$
(✍ 406-867-6767; www.northernhotel.com; 19 N Broadway; r $209; 🕸) The historic Northern was recently renovated, combing its previous elegance with fresh and modern facilities. Breakfast or lunch is in the attached 1950s diner, and the Ten restaurant offers one of best dinners in town.

Josephine's Bed & Breakfast　　　　B&B $$
(✍ 406-248-5898; www.thejosephine.com; 514 N 29th St; r $95-115, ste $135-170, all incl breakfast; @🕸) For those who prefer a more convivial experience, this B&B is down-home and attentive. All five rooms come with private bathroom.

🍴 Eating & Drinking

Some locals claim the Rex (www.therexbillings.com; 2401 Montana Ave; mains $17-37) serves the best steak in town, while others only eat beef at Jake's (www.jakesbillings.com; 2701 1st Ave N; mains $14-36).

McCormick Cafe　　　　BREAKFAST $
(www.mccormickcafe.com; 2419 Montana Ave; meals $7-10; ⊙ 7am-3pm Mon-Fri, 8am-3pm Sat, 8am-2pm Sun; @🕸🏠) For espresso, granola breakfasts, French-style crepes, good sandwiches and a lively atmosphere, stop by this downtown favorite.

Caramel Cookie Waffles　　　　EUROPEAN $
(www.caramelcookiewaffles.com; 1707 17th St W; mains $5-8; ⊙ 7am-5pm Tue-Sat; 🕸) Better known as the Dutch Brothers, this place

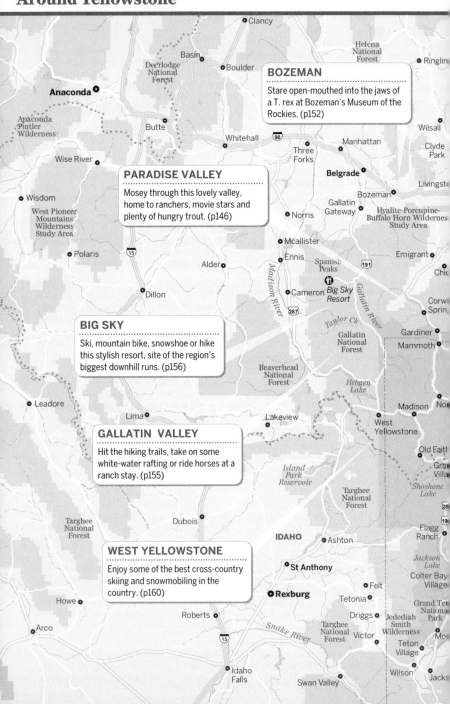

BOZEMAN

Stare open-mouthed into the jaws of a T. rex at Bozeman's Museum of the Rockies. (p152)

PARADISE VALLEY

Mosey through this lovely valley, home to ranchers, movie stars and plenty of hungry trout. (p146)

BIG SKY

Ski, mountain bike, snowshoe or hike this stylish resort, site of the region's biggest downhill runs. (p156)

GALLATIN VALLEY

Hit the hiking trails, take on some white-water rafting or ride horses at a ranch stay. (p155)

WEST YELLOWSTONE

Enjoy some of the best cross-country skiing and snowmobiling in the country. (p160)

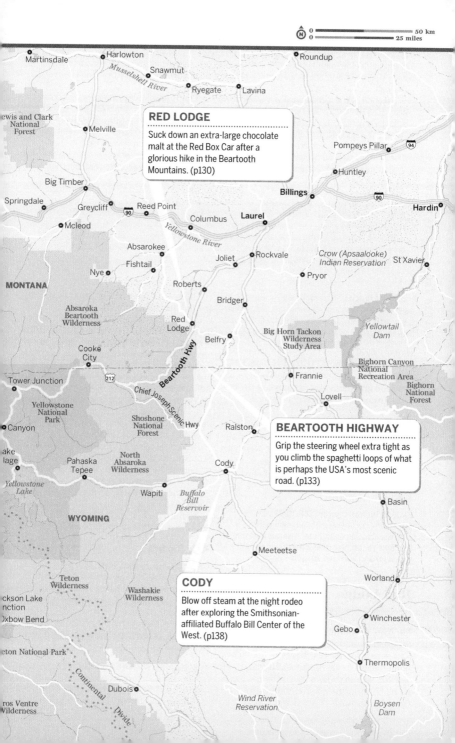

RED LODGE

Suck down an extra-large chocolate malt at the Red Box Car after a glorious hike in the Beartooth Mountains. (p130)

BEARTOOTH HIGHWAY

Grip the steering wheel extra tight as you climb the spaghetti loops of what is perhaps the USA's most scenic road. (p133)

CODY

Blow off steam at the night rodeo after exploring the Smithsonian-affiliated Buffalo Bill Center of the West. (p138)

BILLINGS BREWERY CRAWL

Billings has an impressive collection of craft breweries, all within a few downtown blocks. If you do decide to tackle the following walking tour in one gulp, arrange a taxi and start early – state law means that Montana taprooms can only serve until 8pm. Get a map of the walk at www.visitbillings.com.

Start off at the **Yellowstone Valley Brewing Company** (www.yellowstonevalleybrew. com; 2123 1st Ave N), referred to locally as the Garage, to sample its range of beers named after fishing flies. You'll often find good live music here. One block southwest is **Über- brew** (www.uberbrewmt.com; 2305 Montana Ave), the most polished (and our personal favourite) of the brewpubs and the best place to line your stomach with some pub food. The White Noise Hefeweizen here outsells the other brews three to one.

Continue down Montana Ave to grittier **Carter's Brewing** (www.cartersbrewing.com; 2526 Montana Ave), next to the railway tracks, for a De-Railed IPA or a four-taster flight decorated with a rail spike. From here continue down Montana Ave for four more blocks and swing north to **Angry Hanks** (20 N 30th St), where for $3 a pint you can enjoy an Anger Management Belgian Wheat, Street Fight Imperial Red or Head Trauma IPA on the patio. It's worth trying the brown ale just to order a pint of 'Dog Slobber.'

Finally, head up to the restaurant-style **Montana Brewing Company** (www.montana brewingcompany.com; 113 N Broadway; ⊙11am-2am) and toast your visit to the Little Big- horn Battlefield with a pint of Custer's Last Stout.

bustles at lunch with superb soups, European pastries and the eponymous *stroopwafels*. It's worth arranging your entire Yellowstone itinerary around the weekly seafood bisque.

Walkers Grill MODERN AMERICAN $$
(www.walkersgrill.com; 2700 1st Ave N; tapas $5-12, mains $15-36; ⊙5-10pm) Upscale Walkers of- fers good grill items and fine tapas at the bar (open from 4pm), in an elegant space.

🛍 Shopping

Base Camp OUTDOOR EQUIPMENT
(www.thebasecamp.com; 1730 Grand Ave) The place for last-minute outdoor gear, topo maps and that lost widget for your stove.

ℹ Information

Billings Visitor Center (☑800-735-2635, 406-245-4111; www.visitbillings.com; 815 S 27th St) Can help with hotel reservations and free bike rental. See also www.downtownbill- ings.com and www.billingsguide.com.

Red Lodge

☑406 / POP 2280 / ELEV 5555FT
A charming historic mining town lined with fun bars, restaurants, interesting shops and art galleries, and with great hiking, camping and skiing nearby, Red Lodge is the kickoff point for the scenic Beartooth Hwy and well worth a stop in its own right. The town gets its name from the painted red tipis of local Crow (Absaalooke or Absaroka) tribe.

The early town grew up so quickly around the coal mines that by 1910 its large- ly immigrant population was twice the size it is today. The hard-drinking, fist-fighting, bootlegging town must have been pretty rough-edged to have required one Jeremiah 'Liver-Eating' Johnson as its first constable, but this was perhaps spurred more by the 1897 attempted robbery of the central bank by Butch Cassidy's partner, the Sundance Kid. Most of the mines were closed by 1932, but the Beartooth Hwy opened four years later, just in time for the town.

Red Lodge celebrates its cosmopolitan early Scottish, Scandinavian and Slavic mining pop- ulation in the annual **Festival of Nationals** (www.festivalofnations.us) in August.

On the west bank of Rock Creek, Red Lodge is 60 miles south of Billings and 65 miles northeast of Cooke City and the north entrance to Yellowstone National Park.

◉ Sights

Carbon County Museum MUSEUM
(☑406-446-3667; www.carboncountyhistory.com; 224 N Broadway; adult/student $5/3; ⊙10am-5pm Mon-Sat, 11am-3pm Sun, closed Sun-Thu winter) Antique guns and mining disasters domi- nate the exhibits here, but it's the 1912 Mod- el T Ford, Yellowstone stagecoach and early electroshock machine that grab the attention.

Yellowstone Wildlife Sanctuary ZOO
(☑406-446-1133; www.yellowstonewildlifesanctuary .org; 615 2nd St E; adult/child under 12yr $7/3; ⊙10am-4pm Tue-Sun; ⊞) Families will love this

nonprofit refuge for 71 animals that can't be returned to the wild, including bears, wolves, a cougar and a sandhill crane called Niles. Check the website to time your visit with animal feeding. It's just northeast of town.

Carbon County Arts Guild Gallery GALLERY (☑406-446-1370; www.carboncountydepotgallery. org; 11 W 8th St; ⊙10am-5pm Mon-Sat, noon-5pm Sun) FREE The old railroad depot on 8th St, one block west of Broadway Ave, is where local artists exhibit paintings, sculptures and mixed media.

🏃 Activities

Hiking

A mile south of Red Lodge, just north of the Beartooth Ranger District Office, West Fork Rd turns southwest off US 212 and continues for a bumpy 12 miles up West Fork Creek. Trailheads along the road offer good hikes, including the **Timberline Lake Trail** (4½ miles, elevation gain 2000ft) and **Basin Lakes National Recreation Trail** (trail 61, 7.4 miles return, elevation gain 2000ft). Bear in mind that much of the upper valley was scarred by wildfires in 2008. Nearby **Wild Bill Lake** is a wheelchair-accessible trail to a lake with accessible fishing. The valley has two USFS campgrounds: Basin ($16) and Cascade ($12).

A rugged option further south is the short but strenuous 3.2-mile return trail to **Glacier Lake**, hidden high up in a glacial valley. Hikers have the option of continuing another mile to Little Glacier and Emerald Lakes. The trailhead is 8 miles southwest of Limber Pine Campground on rough, gravel Rock Creek Rd (Forestry Rd No 421). You need fairly high clearance to attempt this road.

The **Lake Fork Trail**, accessed from the end of Lake Fork Rd (turn off right about 2 miles before Parkside Campground), offers

excellent longer day hikes to Lost Lake (5 miles one way) and 1.5 miles further to Keyser Brown Lake.

For a rugged overnighter or three-day trek, continue over the 11,037ft **Sundance Pass** into the upper West Fork Valley (21 miles). The pass is only open from mid-July and you'll need to arrange a car shuttle between the two valleys.

Winter Sports

Red Lodge Mountain SKIING (☑800-444-8977, ski reports 406-446-2610; www. redlodgemountain.com; lifts adult $51, child $18-35; ⊙end Nov-early Apr) Six miles southwest of downtown, Red Lodge Mountain has a 2400ft vertical drop, serviced by eight lifts. A higher base elevation (7400ft) than any other Montana ski hill, it has some of the state's best spring skiing, particularly during February and March. Full rentals and excellent-value instruction packages are available.

Red Lodge Nordic Center SNOW SPORTS (☑406-425-1070; www.beartoothtrails.org; trail fee adult/child $5/free) Two miles northwest of Red Lodge on Hwy 78, this is Red Lodge's top cross-country resource and a good place for beginners. See the website for other local trails.

🛏 Sleeping

South of Red Lodge on US 212 are 10 USFS **campgrounds** (tent sites $15-16, $8 for second vehicle; ⊙May-late Sep). The nearest are small Sheridan and Rattin, 6 and 8 miles from Red Lodge, on the east side of the road. A little further, with shady creekside locations, are the nicer Parkside, Limber Pine and Greenough Lake campgrounds. All are reservable through www.recreation.gov. There's also lots of primitive camping nearby.

AROUND YELLOWSTONE RED LODGE

WORTH A TRIP

CUSTER'S LAST STAND

The best Billings day trip is to **Little Bighorn Battlefield** (☑406-638-3224; www.nps. gov/libi; US 212; per car $10; ⊙8am-9pm), the site of Custer's last stand, just an hour's drive (65 miles) east of town. You can drive around the battle sites or, better, take an hour-long bus tour in the company of a Crow guide with **Absalooke Tours** (☑406-638-3114).

If you're here for the last weekend of June, visit for the **Custer's Last Stand Reenactment** (www.littlebighornreenactment.com; adult/child $20/10), 6 miles west of Hardin. Pack your handlebar mustache and you can even attend the weekend ball; only those dressed in 1876 attire are allowed in!

On the way back, history buffs can pop into **Pompey's Pillar National Monument** (www.pompeyspillar.org; per vehicle $7; ⊙8am-8pm), home to the engraved 1806 signature of William Clark and the only physical evidence remaining of Lewis and Clark's famed transcontinental journey.

WACKY RACES

Southeast Montana is a proud home to some of the state's more surreal sports. In March Red Lodge hosts the national **ski-joring finals**, a not-quite-yet-Olympic sport that involves a horse towing a skier around an oval speed track. It's like water skiing. On snow. Except with a horse.

Equally silly is the annual **Running of the Sheep** at nearby Reed Point. Inspired by Pamplona's much more impressive Running of the Bulls, the significantly less dangerous herd of sheep thunders down six blocks of Main St every year during Labor Day weekend.

Finally, summer weekend evenings (Thursday to Sunday) see high-octane **pig racing** at the **Bear Creek Saloon** (☑406-446-3481; ⊙May-Sep & Dec-Mar), 7 miles east of Red Lodge on Hwy 308. Make a $2 bet, urge your porker over the finish line and round off the evening with a bacon sandwich (only kidding). Proceeds go to charity.

Yodeler Motel MOTEL $

(☑406-446-1435; www.yodelermotel.com; 601 S Broadway Ave; basement r from $60, upper level from $90; ⃰) A retro Bavarian theme livens up this friendly '60s-era hotel, down to the in-room wet steam showers and ski-waxing room. The spacious upper-level rooms with porches are roomier and brighter than the cheaper basement options. The hosts are enthusiastic hikers who gladly offer advice on local trails.

Pollard HISTORIC HOTEL $$

(☑406-446-0001; www.thepollard.net; 2 N Broadway Ave; r $150-195, ste $185-265; ⃰) Red Lodge's first brick building, dating from 1893, makes for a fun and elegant place to stay, even if you're paying more for the history than the quality of the room. The cozy lobby and restaurant are hubs of local activity.

Rock Creek Resort RESORT $$

(☑406-446-1111; www.rockcreekresort.com; d $130-190, ste $220-355; @⃰⃰) Red Lodge's most upscale accommodations has rooms, condos, suites and a decent restaurant at a quiet creekside location, 4.5 miles south of town, off US 212. The Beartooth Lodge rooms are the freshest and come with balconies.

✕ Eating

★**Red Box Car** BURGERS $

(1300 S Broadway; burgers $4; ⊙11am-9pm May-Sep; ⃰) Without doubt the Yellowstone region's best fast food is served out of a century-old railroad car at the south end of town. The malts and homemade onion rings are unbeatable.

Café Regis BREAKFAST $

(www.caferegis.com; cnr 16th St & Word Ave; mains $7; ⊙6am-2pm Wed-Sun) Locals know this as the best breakfast in town, with good-value blue-plate lunch specials and very pleasant garden seating.

Más Taco MEXICAN $

(306 Broadway Ave; mains $6-8; ⊙11am-7pm Tue-Sat) Authentic taqueria that serves fresh shrimp, carne asada or recommended *al pastor* (cooked on a gyros-style spit) chicken tacos, quesadillas or burritos, as well as homemade chips and salsa. It's quick, fresh and tasty. Outdoor seating is pleasant, or sit at the counter if the weather is chilly.

🍷 Drinking

Natali's Front Bar BAR

(www.thepizzaco.com; 115 S Broadway; ⊙4-11pm) Grab a pail of peanuts and choose from the many local microbrews on tap at this cool wooden bar. You can order in pizza from Red Lodge Pizza next door.

Red Lodge Ales BREWERY

(☑406-446-4607; www.redlodgeales.net; 1445 N Broadway; ⊙11am-9pm; ⃰) Sam's Tap Room lost some of its funkiness when it relocated to roomier, more family-friendly digs north of town, but at least there's outdoor seating now. Order the beer sampler ($6) to taste the six most popular brews, including our favorite, the grapefruit-infused Bent Nail IPA. Call in advance for a free brewery tour.

🛍 Shopping

It's worth setting aside an hour or two for browsing the shops and galleries along Broadway Ave.

Montana Candy Emporium FOOD

(7 S Broadway; ⃰) If you are old enough to remember cowtails and bubblegum cigarettes, or simply have a sweet tooth for taffy and chocolate truffles, you'll love this old-style candy store.

Sylvan Peak OUTDOOR EQUIPMENT

(☑406-446-1770; 9 S Broadway) Topo maps, outdoor gear and winter equipment rentals.

❶ Information

Red Lodge Visitor Center (☎888-281-0625; www.redlodge.com; 601 N Broadway; ◷10am-4pm Mon-Fri) On the north edge of town, with an RV dump station and road-condition information for the Beartooth Hwy. Check out 'Liver-Eating' Johnston's former cabin just outside.

Beartooth Highway

The breathtaking Beartooth Hwy connects Red Lodge to Cooke City and Yellowstone's Northeast Entrance along a soaring 68-mile road built in 1932. An engineering feat and the 'most beautiful drive in America,' according to the late journalist Charles Kuralt, this 'all-American' road is a destination in its own right and easily the most dramatic route into Yellowstone National Park. Motorcyclists in particular love the road, arriving en masse for the Sturgis-like Beartooth Rally in mid-July.

Covering 1474 sq miles, the Absaroka-Beartooth Wilderness stretches along the road, bordering Montana and Wyoming and crossing through Custer Gallatin and Shoshone National Forests, taking in two distinct mountain ranges: the Absarokas and the Beartooth Plateau (the Beartooths). Steep, forested valleys and craggy peaks characterize the Absarokas, while the Beartooths are essentially a high plateau of uplifted three-billion-year-old granite (some of the oldest rock in North America) dotted with more than 1000 lakes and tarns. Together they constitute the most visited wilderness area in the nation.

Most of the wilderness consists of high plateau above 10,000ft. Alpine tundra vegetation is the only thing that grows up here (where snow can last from October to mid-July), lending the landscape a desolate, otherworldly look. In fact, unless you are an outdoorsy type who makes frequent forays above 10,000ft, it probably is another world – you can't usually reach this kind of terrain by car. To really experience the surroundings, you must get out of the car, even if it's just for a few minutes, to suck in the thin, cold air.

The highway has a short driving season and is usually closed between mid-October and late May. For information on weather conditions, hikes and bear sightings, pull into the helpful Beartooth Ranger District Office (☎406-446-2103; ◷8am-4:30pm), just south of Red Lodge on Hwy 212.

There's gas at Red Lodge, Cooke City and, less reliably, along the highway at the Top of the World store. For more details see www.beartoothhighway.com and www.beartoothhighway.net.

The political landscape of the highway is as convoluted as the natural landscape. The highway starts and ends in Montana but dips into Wyoming en route. If you are fishing, you'll need to know exactly where you are so that you have the correct state fishing license.

Beartooth Highway Drive

Route Red Lodge to Cooke City

Distance 68 miles (3 hours)

Speed Limit Officially 70 mph, but more like 35mph

Summary From its starting point at Red Lodge, the highway climbs Rock Creek Canyon's glaciated valley before ascending the valley wall through a series of spaghetti-loop switchbacks, gaining an amazing 5000ft in elevation in just a few miles.

A parking area at Rock Creek Vista Point Overlook (9160ft), 20 miles from Red Lodge, has toilets and a short walk (wheelchair accessible) to superb views. The road continues up onto the high plateau, past 'Mae West Curve' and into Wyoming.

In another 7 miles the road passes Twin Lakes, where a parking area offers good views of the cirque and the ski lift that comprises the Beartooth Basin (www.beartoothbasin.com), an extreme early-summer ski run established by Austrians in the 1960s. Another 1.3 miles further, below the road, is Gardner Lake. After 0.7 miles, at the start of a series of switchbacks, look northwest across Rock Creek for views of the Hellroaring Plateau and the jagged Bear's Tooth (11,612ft; 'Na Piet Say' in the local Crow language), which lends the range its name. A mile later you'll crest the Beartooth Pass West Summit, the highest point along the highway at 10,947ft. You'll likely pass deep snowbanks here as late as June.

From this halfway point the road descends past Frozen Lake, Long Lake, Little Bear Lake (the last two with excellent fishing) and then the Chain Lakes (on the left) to the Island Lake and Beartooth Lake Campgrounds. Both offer excellent opportunities for a picnic, day hike or a canoe paddle. Between the campgrounds is the Top of the World Store (www.topoftheworldresort.com), which offers a reviving coffee (and a fishing license if you need one).

As the road descends, you'll see Beartooth Butte, a huge lump of the sedimentary rock that once covered the Beartooths. Two miles beyond Beartooth Lake Campground, 42 miles from Red Lodge, turn right up a 2.5-mile dirt road to the former fire watchtower at **Clay Butte Overlook** (no RVs or trailers). The views from here are fantastic: look for the 'Reef,' a snaking line of sedimentary rock that follows the entire valley, proving that this lofty region was once underwater.

Back on the main road, a mile further on, is an **overlook** offering views of Index Peak (11,313ft) and jagged Pilot Peak (11,708ft). At the height of glaciation, ice sheets would have covered the entire horizon except the very tip of these peaks. Index was originally given the somewhat unromantic name of Dog Turd Peak. Next up is the **Clarks Fork Overlook** (with toilets) and then a small turnout by Lake Creek Falls.

The turnoff left is for Chief Joseph Scenic Hwy, which leads 62 miles to Cody and accesses Yellowstone's East Entrance via the Wapiti Valley. The Beartooth Hwy descends to several excellent fishing areas on the Clarks Fork and re-enters Montana. Opposite Chief Joseph Campground is **Clarks Fork Trailhead**, a fine place for a picnic, a day hike and a look at the flume of the former mining power station. From here it's 4 miles to Cooke City, via the modest Colter Pass (8066ft).

🏃 Activities

Hiking & Backpacking
You can gain about 4000ft of elevation by car and begin your hike right from the Beartooth Hwy, but it's important to allow some time to acclimatize. Also be aware that the barren terrain offers little shade, shelter or wood. In order to protect the fragile alpine vegetation, hikers should not light campfires above the tree line. Grizzly and black bears are not that common in the higher elevations; hikers have a better chance of seeing bighorn sheep, mountain goats or elk.

August is the best month to hike the Beartooths. Snow remains in many places above the tree line at least until the end of July and starts to accumulate again after mid-September. Localized afternoon thunderstorms, with hail, are common in the Beartooths during June (the wettest month) and July. During early summer, you'll also need lots of bug repellent and waterproof shoes to cope with swampy trails. Don't be put off; just be forewarned. With proper preparation, the plateau offers some of Greater Yellowstone's very best hiking.

From Island Lake Campground you can take a wonderful and easy hour-long stroll along the **Beartooth High Lakes Trail** (trail 620) to Island Lake and beyond to Night Lake and Flake Lake. All lakes are popular fishing areas. If you can arrange a shuttle, continue downhill to Beauty Lake and then left (south) to Beartooth Lake for a fine half-day hike.

From Beartooth Lake Campground you can make a wonderful half-day 8-mile loop via **Beauty Lake**. Head up Beartooth Creek (trail 619) and then bear right, passing five lakes, including Claw Lake (trail 620), to the junction with the Beartooth High Lakes Trail. From here descend right past Beauty Lake (trail 621) back to Beartooth Lake. Parking is limited at the trailhead.

A longer, possibly overnight, option is the 11-mile **Beartooth National Recreation Trail** (trail 613) loop hike, accessed from the highway at Gardner Lake. The trail drops from the lake and loops around Tibbs Butte, initially along Little Rock Creek, past turnoffs to Deep Lake, Camp Sawtooth and Dollar Lake to arrive at Stockade Lake, a fine campsite. From here, continue around the loop past Losecamp Lake back to Gardner Lake, or cut east from Losecamp Lake for 3 miles past Hauser Lake to the Beartooth Hwy by a pullout overlooking Long Lake (this requires a shuttle).

Another easy day hike is the 6-mile return ramble to **Rock Island Lake**, which begins from the Clarks Fork Trailhead. After about 15 minutes, be careful to continue along Russell Creek Trail (trail 567) and *not* turn left along Broadwater Trail. The trail brushes Kersey Lake and branches right up to Rock Island Lake. An alternative hike branches right 1.3 miles from the trailhead up to Vernon Lake (trail 565).

The Clarks Fork Trailhead is also the start of the exciting multiday **Beartooth Traverse** (aka 'The Beaten Path') that runs along Russell Creek Trail to Fossil Lake and then across plateau trail 15 to Rosebud Lake (shuttle required). You need to be fairly experienced for this remote 26-mile wilderness trek.

The contoured 1:100,000 *Absaroka Beartooth Wilderness* map by Beartooth Publishing and the USFS 1:63,360 *Absaroka Beartooth Wilderness* map are both excellent. *Hiking the Absaroka-Beartooth Wilderness* and *Easy Day Hikes in the Beartooths,* both published by Falcon Press and written by Bill Schneider, are also useful.

🛌 Sleeping

There are 13 basic USFS campgrounds along the Beartooth Hwy between Red Lodge and Cooke City. **Island Lake** (tent sites $15) and

Beartooth Hwy

Red Lodge Nordic Center
Red Lodge
START
Yellowstone Wildlife Sanctuary
Beartooth Ranger District Office
Rock Creek Resort
Grizzly Peak (9416ft)
West Fork Rd
Sheridan Campground
Rattin Campground
Rock Creek Vista Point Overlook
Wyoming Creek
Lake Creek
Shoshone National Forest
Beartooth National Recreation Trail
MONTANA
WYOMING
Beartooth Hwy
Silver Run Plateau
Quinnebaugh Meadows
West Fork Rock Creek
Timberline Lake
Parkside Campground
M-K Campground
Twin Lakes
Gardner Lake
Frozen Lake
Stockade Lake
Limber Pine Campground
Greenough Lake Campground
Mt Rearguard (12,204ft)
Beartooth Pass West Summit
Little Bear Lake
Long Lake
Island Lake Campground
Sundance Pass
Bear's Tooth (11,612ft)
Silver Run Peak (12,500ft)
Glacier Lake
Night Lake
Island Lake
Top of the World Store
Sundance Lake
Beauty Lake
Beartooth High Lakes Trail
Beartooth Lake
Sylvan Peak (11,943ft)
Alpine
Sundance Glacier
Lake Creek
Beartooth Butte (10,482ft)
Beartooth Lake Campground
East Rosebud Lake
Rainbow Lake
Clay Butte Overlook
Beartooth Traverse Trail
Beartooth Plateau
Absaroka-Beartooth Wilderness
Lily Lake
296
Clarks Fork Overlook
Lake Creek Campground
Granite Peak (12,799ft)
Custer National Forest
Arch Creek
Fossil Lake
Crazy Lakes
Crazy Creek Campground
Upper Aero Lake
Lower Aero Lake
Lady of the Lake
Vernon Lake
Fox Creek Campground
Pilot Peak (11,708ft)
ROOSEVELT COUNTRY
West Rosebud Creek
Grasshopper Glacier
Goose Lake
Long Lake
Round Lake
Skyline Guest Ranch
Clarks Fork Trailhead
Colter Campground
Index Peak (11,313ft)
Gallatin National Forest
Stillwater River
Soda Butte Campground
212
Cooke City
END
Silver Gate
Chief Joseph Campground
North Absaroka Wilderness
Northeast Entrance Station
Tower Junction (29mi)
Yellowstone National Park

10 km
5 miles
N

Beartooth Lake (tent sites $15) – both open July to mid-September – are up on the high plateau; the latter has a boat launch. Further west are Crazy Creek (tent sites $10; ☉ late May-early Sep) and Fox Creek (tent sites with/ without electricity $20/15; ☉ mid-Jun–mid-Sep), the former with a small cascade nearby. These sites come under the Clarks Fork Ranger District of the Shoshone National Forest.

Closer to Cooke City, Colter and Soda Butte campgrounds are 2 miles and 1.5 miles east of town respectively. Only hard-sided vehicles are accepted following a fatal grizzly attack at Soda Butte in July 2010. Chief Joseph Campground, 4 miles from Cooke City, is currently closed due to budget issues. Contact the Custer Gallatin National Forest Gardiner District Office (p152) in Gardiner for details.

Skyline Guest Ranch   LODGE $$
(☎406-838-2380; www.flyfishyellowstone.com; 31 Kersey Lake Rd; d incl breakfast $120-164; @ ☎) The remote Skyline is perfect if you want to get away from it all, experience some Western hospitality and saddle up for some family horse riding ($30 per hour). Rooms in a three-story lodge are spacious and modern, with nice outside balconies, and the location – 3 miles outside of Cooke City – is officially the middle of nowhere.

Chief Joseph Scenic Highway

The wild and scenic Clarks Fork of the Yellowstone River runs along much of the Chief Joseph Scenic Hwy (Hwy 296), linking Cody (via Hwy 120 north) with the Beartooth Hwy and Yellowstone National Park's Northeast Entrance, 62 miles away. It's an astoundingly scenic and largely undiscovered corner of the Yellowstone region that links with the Beartooth Hwy to offer several potential loop itineraries. The highway is named for Chief Joseph of the Nez Percé tribe, who eluded the US Army and escaped through Clarks Fork here in 1877.

The paved highway is open year-round from Cody to just before the Beartooth Hwy, though not as far as Cooke City. The Beartooth Hwy itself is closed mid-October to late May. Fall colors are particularly lovely here.

The 47-mile Chief Joseph Scenic Hwy starts 16 miles north of Cody, enters the Shoshone National Forest after 8 miles and climbs to a spectacular viewpoint at Dead Indian Pass (8048ft). Native Americans used to ambush game that migrated through the pass between summer mountain pastures and winter ranges down in the plains. The pass is named for a Bannock brave killed here in skirmishes with the army in 1878.

As you descend from the pass, just 0.3 miles before Dead Indian Campground, an unsigned dirt road leads a couple of hundred yards to an unmarked trailhead that offers an excellent short hike to view the 1200ft-deep Clarks Fork Canyon. The trail leads north for 2 miles to a scenic overlook – watch for cairns marking the spot shortly after you first see the gorge. The views of the granite gorge and Dead Indian Creek waterfall are breathtaking. The canyon effectively separates the 50-million-year-old volcanic rock of the Absaroka Range from the two-billion-year-old granite of the Beartooth Plateau.

Back on the road, USFS Rd 101 branches southwest into the beautiful Sunlight Basin. Its upper branches end at a wall of peaks forming the remote eastern boundary of Yellowstone National Park. Writer Ernest Hemingway spent time grizzly hunting here in the 1930s and wrote an article on the subject for *Vogue* magazine.

Where Hwy 296 crosses Sunlight Creek is the terrific Sunlight Bridge, the highest in Wyoming. You can park and walk across the bridge for hair-raising views into the gorge (acrophobes beware!).

Just north of Crandall Creek (named after a pioneer miner who was beheaded by Native Americans), around Swamp Lake and below the Cathedral Cliffs, are six scenic ponds where you might spot sandhill cranes and trumpeter swans.

Hwy 296 continues northwest to the crossbar junction of US 212, where the Beartooth Hwy leads northwest to Cooke City and Yellowstone National Park or northeast to Red Lodge and Billings.

🛏 Sleeping

Shoshone National Forest has three simple campgrounds near the Beartooth Hwy. Contact the Clarks Fork Ranger District (☎307-527-6921; www.fs.fed.us/r2/shoshone) in Cody for details.

Lake Creek   CAMPGROUND $
(sites $10; ☉ late Jun-early Sep) Forested but lots of mosquitoes in July; 1 mile from the Beartooth Hwy. Six sites.

Hunter Peak   CAMPGROUND $
(☎877-444-6777; www.recreation.gov; sites $15; ☉ late May-Oct) Five miles from the Beartooth Hwy, with nine reservable sites.

Dead Indian Campground CAMPGROUND **$**
(sites $10) South from Hunter Peak, with one
loop and 10 sites open year-round. No water.

K Bar Z Guest Ranch RANCH **$**
(☑ 307-587-4410; www.kbarzguestranch.com; d
cabin $100) Family-run and 28 miles from
Yellowstone, this ranch offers horseback
rides from $35/175 per hour/day.

Hunter Peak Ranch RANCH **$$**
(☑ 307-587-3711; www.hunterpeakranch.com; cabin/
ste from $145/190) Just off Hwy 296, 24 miles
from Yellowstone, with plenty of summer-
time horseback riding and winter skiing.

7D Ranch RANCH **$$$**
(☑ 888-587-9885; www.7dranch.com; weekly per
person $1900; ⊘ Jun–mid-Sep) This guest ranch
has a fabulous location 8 miles up Sunlight
Valley, with 10 cabins and excellent horseback
riding and fishing opportunities. Early September is kid free and has discounted rates.

Cooke City

☑ 406 / POP 85 / ELEV 7800FT
Sandwiched spectacularly between two
forested ridges of the Beartooth Mountains, just 4 miles from Yellowstone's
Northeast Entrance, this one-street Montana town (population 85 in winter, 350
in summer) gets a steady flow of summer
visitors en route between the scenic splen-
dors of the Beartooth Hwy and the national park. There's not much here in the way
of shops, sights or even trailheads, but the
isolated town has a backwoods feel that's
more laid-back and less commercialized
than the park's other gateway towns.

Cooke City's isolation is due to geogra-
phy and the lack of a railroad link. Citizens
lobbied to bring the railroad to the original
mining town of Shoo-Fly, even going so far
as to rename the town in 1880 after the
Northern Pacific Railroad's Jay Cooke, but
even this blatant flattery failed to overcome
hard economics. Oddly, this enclave of Montana can only be reached from Wyoming.

In winter the road from Yellowstone is
only plowed as far as Cooke City, so visitors –
mostly experienced backcountry skiers and
snowmobilers – tend to check in and stay
awhile. Gas prices are the highest in the Yellowstone region. No cell coverage in town.

◉ Sights & Activities

In winter the network of mining roads
northeast of town are favorites of snowmobilers. Near Colter Campground, the un-

paved Lulu Pass–Goose Lake Rd, the Goose
Lake Track (trail 3230) and trails to Aero
Lakes are all popular, as is snowmobiling
the Beartooth Hwy. Several outfits in town
rent snowmobiles ($195 to $250 per day).

Cooke City General Store HISTORIC BUILDING
(www.cookecitystore.com; ⊘ 8am-7pm May-Sep)
This historic 1886 store dates from the
town's mining heyday and is a fun browse. It
sells fishing permits, topo maps and almost
anything else you can think of.

Yellowstone Trading Post MUSEUM
(⊘ 9am-9pm Mon-Sat; ⬛) Kids will like the
stuffed animal exhibits in this souvenir store
next to the Beartooth Café. It's normally
free; if not, the small admission fee can be
spent in the store.

Hemingway's Yellowstone CULTURAL TOUR
(www.hemingwaysyellowstone.com; tour with meal
per person $60-200) Literary travelers will
love this day tour focused on locations related to Ernest Hemingway's five summers in
the region, offering a unique insight into the
great man's work. Locations include Sunlight
Creek and the Range Rider in Silver Gate,
frequented by Hemingway and his wife in
1938 and 1939. An evening tour and a three-
day horse-packing trip are also offered.

Beartooth Powder Guides SKIING
(☑ 406-838-2097; www.beartoothpowder.com)
Come winter these are the people for guided
backcountry ski trips, based out of their wilderness yurt or backcountry cabin (accommodations $250 to $260 for six people).

🛏 Sleeping

Soda Butte (tent sites $9; ⊘ Jul-early Sep)
and **Colter** (tent sites $8; ⊘ Jul-Sep) camp-
grounds are just 1.5 miles and 2 miles from
town respectively.

Expect hefty discounts from mid-October
to mid-December and in April and May.

Alpine Motel MOTEL **$**
(☑ 406-838-2262; www.cookecityalpine.com; d $87-
106, ste $126-148; ⬛) Well-maintained and
spacious rooms are the hallmark of this good-
value motel, with laundry facilities, family
suites and discounted spring and fall rates.

Elkhorn Lodge HOTEL **$$**
(☑ 406-838-2332; www.elkhornlodgemt.com; s/d/
cabin $110/120/140; ⊘ May–mid-Oct & mid-Dec–
Mar; ⬛) Choose between six rooms in the
main building – with sitting area, coffeemak-
er and fridge – or the two pricier log cabins
with kitchenette. All are fresh and spacious.

High Country Motel
MOTEL **$$**

(🎯406-838-2272; www.cookecityhighcountry.com; d $110-120; 🕿) A good mix of cabins and motel-style rooms, some with kitchenettes and open year-round.

Antlers Lodge
CABIN **$$**

(🎯406-838-2432; www.cookecityantlerslodge.com; cabins $125-185; 🕿) This ramshackle collection of 17 old-style pine cabins has quarters in all shapes and sizes (most family-sized and with kitchenettes) and also offers several fresh and spacious motel rooms. The antler-horn chandeliers in the historic main lodge are a bit creepy.

Pine Edge Cabins
CABIN **$$**

(🎯406-838-2371; www.pineedgecabins.com; Silver Gate; cabins $100-165, apt $265; 🕿) If sleepy Cooke City is too urban for you, try this collection of cozy cabins at the nearly comatose community of Silver Gate (year-round population of 10), 2 miles west of Cooke City and just 2 miles from the park. Enquire at the general store.

✕ Eating

Cafe Cooke
AMERICAN **$**

(102 Main St; mains $6-10; ⊙noon-8pm Wed-Sun Jun-Sep; 🕿) The menu changes weekly here, with lots of great specials, but the common theme is simple: fresh, high-quality food made from scratch, even down to the house-made ice cream and fruit popsicles. Eat on the simple park tables, or take it to go for a park picnic. Cash only.

Bearclaw Bakery
BREAKFAST **$**

(mains $5-9; ⊙5-11:30am) If you plan to make an early start into the park, this down-home bakery offers pastries and coffee from 5am and fine scrambles, eggs Benedict and French toast from 6am.

★ Log Cabin Café
WESTERN **$$**

(🎯406-838-2367; www.thelogcabincafe.com; Silver Gate; lunch $10-14, dinner $15-30; ⊙6am-10pm mid-May–late Sep) In sleepy Silver Gate, this unexpectedly cool place serves excellent grilled trout, house-smoked salmon and homemade breakfast pumpkin bread. The cozy cabin dates back to 1937 and there are more cabins ($99 with breakfast) for rent out back.

★ Beartooth Café
AMERICAN **$$**

(www.beartoothcafe.com; lunch $9-13, dinner $16-25; ⊙11am-10pm late May-late Sep) A bright place for lunch sandwiches (such as a buffalo burger, a 'funk burger', or lighter portobello sandwich) served on the pleasant front

deck, washed down by a fine selection of 130 bottled microbrews. Dinner mains such as ribs, smoked trout and hand-cut steaks are double the lunchtime prices.

Bistro
EUROPEAN **$$**

(breakfast & lunch $10, dinner mains $20-25; ⊙7am-10pm) A popular place for breakfast, come nightfall the homey Bistro transforms into a demi-French restaurant with dishes such as escargot in garlic butter and seafood cassoulet. There's a nice terrace.

🛍 Shopping

Silver Gate General Store
OUTDOOR EQUIPMENT

(⊙8am-10:30pm) In Silver Gate, this store sells topo maps and rents spotting scopes ($35 per day).

ℹ Information

Bearclaw Mountain Recovery (🎯406-838-2040) Endorsed by the AAA, and the people to call if you have a breakdown. Montana fishing licenses are available.

Chamber of Commerce Visitor Center (🎯406-838-2495; www.cookecitychamber.org; 206 W Main; ⊙9am-5:30pm Mon-Sat, 10am-4pm Sun; 🕿) A helpful new visitor center with public restroom, free wi-fi and an interesting local museum featuring a replica miner's cabin out back. Historical talks take place around the back campfire most Saturdays.

WAPITI ROUTE

Cody

🎯307 / POP 9000 / ELEV 5095FT

Arrive in Cody at sundown and you'll find costumed gunslingers midbrawl, flanked by jezebels toiling under a career in false eyelashes. It's not a town to take too seriously. The spirit of showman Buffalo Bill still thrives in the town that he promoted with real-estate speculator George Beck in 1901. Beck and his backers milked Cody's fame to promote settlement, attract the railroad and lobby for a massive dam on the Shoshone River. But it's more than farce. Despite the corny cowboy themes, Cody feels like the real West, where graduation photos adorn shop counters, and stores stock more cowboy boots than Keens.

Cody is second only to Jackson as Wyoming's premier summer tourist town. Access to the great outdoors is excellent, and the mountain biking, rafting and boating are all good. But the town's ultimate blessing is its proximity to Yellowstone National Park, 51 miles to the west and connected by the scenic Wapiti Valley.

◉ Sights

★ **Buffalo Bill Center of the West** MUSEUM
(www.centerofthewest.org; 720 Sheridan Ave; adult/child $19/11; ☺8am-6pm May–mid-Sep, 8am-5pm mid-Sep–Oct, 10am-5pm Nov, Mar & Apr, 10am-5pm Thu-Sun Dec-Feb) Cody's major tourist attraction is the superb Buffalo Bill Historical Center. A sprawling complex of five museums, it showcases everything Western: from posters, grainy films and artifacts pertaining to Buffalo Bill's world-famous Wild West shows, to galleries showcasing frontier-oriented artwork, to museums dedicated to Native Americans. Its **Draper Museum of Natural History** explores the Yellowstone region's ecosystem with excellent results. The galleries are given regular overhauls to keep presentations fresh. There's also a daily (1pm) **raptor presentation**.

Entry is valid for two consecutive days. Save a couple of bucks by booking online.

Old Trail Town MUSEUM
(☑307-587-5302; www.museumoftheoldwest.org; 1831 DeMaris Dr; adult/child 6-12yr $9/5; ☺8am-7pm mid-May–Sep) The hideouts of Butch Cassidy, Kid Curry and the Sundance Kid comprise this unique museum, a collection of late-19th-century wooden buildings relocated here from all over Wyoming. Look for the bullet holes in the door of the Rivers Saloon and the grave of mountain man Jeremiah 'Liver-Eating' Johnson, reburied here in 1974 with Robert Redford as one of the pallbearers.

Buffalo Bill State Park PARK
(☑307-527-6076; www.bbdvc.org; day use $6; ☺8am-7pm Mon-Fri, 9am-5pm Sat & Sun May-Sep) This scenic state park, 6 miles west of Cody, centers on the Buffalo Bill Reservoir and Dam, unveiled in 1910 as the world's highest dam to provide the irrigation for expanding Cody. The reservoir is a hot spot for fishing, windsurfing and boating, and boat launches dot the north and southeast shores. The dam **visitor center** (no fee), just west of the dramatic Shoshone Canyon, offers interpretive exhibits on the dam, Bill and local wildlife.

🏃 Activities

No longer just for cowboys, Cody is an excellent base for outdoor pursuits. Apart from the activities mentioned here, Cody also offers some of the best winter **ice climbing** in the United States. See www.coldfear.com and www.codyiceclimbingfestival.com, or Inquire at Sunlight Sports.

Gradient Mountain Sports KAYAKING
(☑307-587-4659; www.gradientmountainsports.net; 1390 Sheridan Ave) If kayaking is your thing, head here for rentals, shuttles and information, plus instruction and guided trips. Kayaks, stand-up paddleboards (SUPs) and canoes cost $40 to $50 per day.

North Fork Anglers FISHING
(☑307-527-7274; www.northforkanglers.com; 1107 Sheridan Ave) Anglers should visit Tim Wade's place for local info, flies and guided trips. The website lists current fishing conditions.

Absaroka Bicycles MOUNTAIN BIKING
(☑307-527-5566; 2201 17th St, Kmart Plaza; ☺10am-6pm Mon-Thu, to 4pm Fri, to 2pm Sat) Ground central for mountain-bike rentals ($40 per day), repairs, tours (both cycling and hiking) and info on local fat-tire trails, including to the nearby Outlaw and Oregon Basin trail systems.

AROUND YELLOWSTONE CODY

WORTH A TRIP

HEARTLAND SECURITY

Following the Japanese bombing of Pearl Harbor, more than 110,000 Japanese Americans were interned in 10 camps across the US. Taking only what they could carry, around 11,000 Japanese Americans relocated from West Coast homes to the flimsy tar-paper rooms of **Heart Mountain Relocation Center** (☑307-754-8000; www.heartmountain.org; 1539 Rd 19, off Hwy 14A; adult/student $7/5; ☺10am-5pm mid-May–Sep, closed Sun-Tue Oct–mid-May) and made the best of three years of confinement here, setting up a newspaper, two theaters and a high school in what quickly became Wyoming's third-largest town.

Only the former hospital and chimney remain from the original buildings, but a memorial and barracks-style interpretive center tells the powerful story of how – temporarily seized by xenophobia – the US failed its own citizens 60 years ago. The center is 14 miles northeast of Cody.

Red Canyon

Wild Mustang Trips
WILDLIFE-WATCHING

(☑800-293-0148; www.codywyomingadventures.com; 1119 12th St; tour adult/child $33/31; ⊗May–mid-Oct) For something different take a morning or afternoon van tour out to the desert badlands of the McCullough Peaks Wild Horse Range, a refuge designated for 142 wild mustangs. Photo safaris are also possible. For more information on the horses, visit **FOAL** (www.friendsofalegacy.org).

Rafting

Just outside of town, the North Fork of the Shoshone River has scenic float trips and excellent class-II to class-IV white water. Bighorn sheep hang out on the cliffs, and eagles and moose are sometimes spotted. Prices range from $33 for family-oriented lower canyon trips to $75 for a half-day on the North Fork or Clark's Fork. The rafting season is mid-May to mid-September in the Red Rock and Lower Canyons, and late May to late June for the North Fork.

Red Canyon River Trips
RAFTING

(☑800-293-0148; www.codywyomingadventures.com; 1119 12th St) Also rents SUPs, kayaks and canoes.

River Runners
RAFTING

(☑307-527-7238; www.riverrunnersofwyoming.com; 1491 Sheridan Ave) Rafting company founded by Bill Cody's great-grandson.

Wyoming River Trips
RAFTING

(☑800-586-6661; www.wyomingrivertrips.com; 233 Yellowstone Ave) Rafting and inflatable-kayak trips.

☆ Festivals & Events

The **Cowboy Poetry & Range Ballads Festival** takes place the second week of April.

Spring into Yellowstone
OUTDOORS

(www.springintoyellowstone.net; ⊗mid-May) Four days of tours, talks, hikes and films, with an emphasis on wildlife-viewing, photography and even archaeology.

Cody

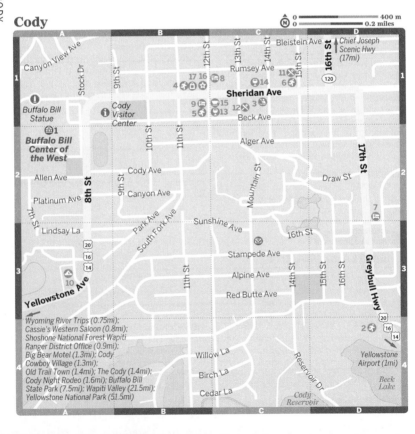

Plains Indians Powwow   CULTURAL
(Buffalo Bill Center of the West; adult/child 7-17yr $10/5; ⊗ mid-Jun) Drumming, dancing and ornate costumes mark this colorful gathering of Shoshone and other Northern Plains tribes.

Cody Stampede Rodeo   SPORTS
(www.codystampederodeo.com; admission $20-25; ⊗ Jul 1-4) Cody hosts the region's biggest rodeo on July 4 weekend.

🛏 Sleeping

Cody's accommodations are poor value in July and August. You'll get much better deals in spring and fall (summer rates are listed here).

Buffalo Bill State Park Campgrounds   CAMPGROUND $
(☑ 307-587-9227; http://wyoparks.state.wy.us; sites with/without electricity $16/11; ⊗ May-Sep) For the nicest camping, skip town for more scenic options along the banks of the Buffalo Bill Reservoir. The roadside **North Shore Bay** and **North Fork** Campgrounds, 6 miles west of Cody, are exposed and shadeless, but the former in particular offers lovely sunsets over the lake. Sites can be reserved online. Nonresidents will have to add on the $6 state-park entry fee.

Ponderosa Campground   CAMPGROUND $
(☑ 307-587-9203; www.codyponderosa.com; 1815 Yellowstone Ave; tent sites from $30, RV sites $35-49, cabins $60; ⊗ mid-Apr–mid-Oct; 🐾) Ponderosa edges out the competition with immaculate showers, laundry, cable TV and friendly service. Families can overnight in fun tipis ($31).

★ **Chamberlin Inn**   INN $$
(☑ 307-587-0202; chamberlininn.com; 1032 12th St; d/ste from $175/255) An elegant downtown retreat, this boutique hotel (built in 1903) has a library and a pretty inner courtyard. The old registry claims Hemingway crashed in room 18 ($275) on a 1932 fishing trip.

Irma Hotel   HISTORIC HOTEL $$
(☑ 800-745-4762; www.irmahotel.com; 1192 Sheridan Ave; r $132-152, ste $162-197) Built in 1902 by Buffalo Bill himself, and named for his daughter, this old-fashioned saloon has charming original historical suites named after past guests (Annie Oakley, Calamity Jane), plus less-inspiring modern rooms in an annex. The creaky hallways, dining room and lobby drip with atmosphere – the ornate cherrywood bar was a gift from Queen Victoria.

Cody Cowboy Village   CABIN $$
(☑ 307-587-7555; www.thecodycowboyvillage.com; 203 W Yellowstone Ave; cabins $155-165; ⊗ May–mid-Oct; 🐾🏊) Popular and well-run, the modern and stylish duplex cabins or standalone suites here come with small porch, plus there's a large outdoor plunge pool.

Carter Mountain Motel   MOTEL $$
(☑ 307-587-4295; www.cartermountainmotel.com; 1701 Central Ave; d $125-145; 🐾) An unpretentious mom-and-pop-style place, but well looked after and decent value, with cheery flowerpots, an upper-floor terrace and kitchenette suites.

Big Bear Motel   MOTEL $$
(☑ 307-587-3117; www.bigbearmotel.com; 139 W Yellowstone Ave; r $169; 🐾🏊🛏🏊) Despite the desolate parking lot, this is a friendly place,

AROUND YELLOWSTONE CODY

Cody

DON'T MISS

THE GHOSTS OF BUFFALO BILL

For a thick slice of classic Cody shtick join the crowds at 6pm on the porch of the Irma Hotel for the gunslingers' mock **shoot-out**. The shoot-out itself manages to be both hammy and cheesy (sounds delicious), but kids will enjoy watching costumed characters that include Wild Bill Hickok, Buffalo Bill and Wyatt Earp. It runs daily, except Sunday, June to mid-September.

After the shoot-out join the faux-cowboys in their 10-gallon hats for happy hour in the Irma Hotel's **Silver Saddle Saloon** or, better still, head next door to the atmospheric **Irma dining room** and grab a stool and a bottle of Bill Cody Beer at the 50ft-long imported French cherrywood bar. Presented to Bill by Queen Victoria, it was transported by stagecoach from Red Lodge and, at $100,000, cost more than the hotel itself.

It's well worth poking around the hallways of the atmospheric Irma Hotel (p141). Buffalo Bill built and named the hotel for his youngest daughter, Irma, calling it 'just the swellest hotel that ever was.' He kept two suites and an office for his personal use, and his ghost is said to frequent the creaking corridors.

though it's overpriced in high season (50% discounts in September). Ask for one of the newer east-block upper-story rooms. Kids will enjoy the pool and miniature pony rides.

The Cody HOTEL **$$$**
(☏ 307-587-5915; www.thecody.com; 232 W Yellowstone Ave; d incl breakfast $219-259;) Cody's most luxurious hotel combines New Western chic with green credentials, incorporating paneling made with recycled wood from park facilities and offering free bicycles to guests. Pay $10 extra for a balcony room away from the road, or $20 more for a king Jacuzzi suite.

✖ Eating

Slow-roasted prime rib and meatloaf are the signature dishes in the atmospheric dining room of the Irma Hotel (p141).

The Local MODERN AMERICAN **$$**
(☏ 307-586-4262; www.thelocalcody.com; 1134 13th St; lunch $10-13, dinner $30; ⊘ 8:30am-2pm & 5-9pm Tue-Sat) If you tire of Cody's cowboy cuisine, find the antidote in the stylish Local's fresh, organic and locally sourced dishes. Think gourmet sandwiches or a goat cheese and arugula salad for lunch, and mussels and pricier fish specials for dinner. Espresso is served throughout the day.

Pat O'Hara Brewing Company PUB FOOD **$$**
(1019 15th St; mains $10-13; ⊘ from 11am Wed-Mon; 🛜) The brew tanks sit proudly front and center at this friendly brewery, churning out two rotating home brews at a time. There's a full menu, including mussels, fish and chips and Irish bangers and mash, plus a wide range of local beers on draft, including from

Wyoming's Ten Sleep Brewery. Order a flight of six 5oz beer samples for $8.

Cassie's Western Saloon STEAK **$$**
(☏ 307-527-5500; www.cassies.com; 214 Yellowstone Ave; steaks $19-31) This classic roadhouse and former house of ill repute hosts heavy swilling, swingin' country-and-western tunes and the occasional bar fight. The attached supper club is one of the best places for a steak or walleye dinner, while out-of-towners can try the Rocky Mountain oysters.

Drinking & Nightlife

The Beta COFFEE
(1132 12th St; ⊘ 6:30am-6pm Mon-Sat, 9am-2pm Sun; 🛜) Join the locals on their daily espresso hit or breakfast wrap at this hip coffee shop opposite the Irma.

Silver Dollar Bar BAR
(1313 Sheridan Ave; mains $9-11; ⊘ 11am-late) The Silver Dollar Bar is a historic watering hole with lots of TV screens and live music or DJs nightly. The tap list is strong, with lots of great regional craft beers, and the burgers are tasty (the signature half-pounder goes for $15). In nice weather, an outdoor bar offers excellent views of street life.

Juniper WINE BAR
(www.junipershop.com; 1128 12th St; ⊘ 4-10pm Mon-Sat) This little oasis is part market and part stylish bar, serving up a sophisticated range of cocktails, wines and whiskeys, alongside house infusions and small plates of tasty charcuterie and cheeses. The delightful back garden terrace has live music Friday and Saturday evenings.

Entertainment

Cody Nite Rodeo SPECTATOR SPORT
(www.codystampederodeo.com; 519 W Yellowstone Ave; adult/child $20/10; ⏲8pm Jun-Aug) If you're wondering why Cody is known as the 'rodeo capital of the world,' check out this nightly event, where you'll see future (and some current) pro-rodeo superstars putting in the hours all summer. It's rain or shine, with fireworks at dusk.

Dan Miller's Cowboy Music Revue LIVE MUSIC
(☎307-272-7855; www.cowboymusicrevue.com; 1171 Sheridan Ave; admission $16; ⏲Mon-Sat May-Sep) The historic Cody Theater hosts this Branson-style family show, serving up folk music and cowboy poetry alongside thick slices of Old West nostalgia. Imagine Hannah Montana in cowboy boots, with a fiddle. A combo ticket, including a dinner buffet at the Irma, will save you a couple of bucks.

Shopping

Sunlight Sports OUTDOOR EQUIPMENT
(☎307-587-9517; www.sunlightsports.com; 1131 Sheridan Ave) Cody's best gear shop offers backpacking equipment rentals, bear spray, topo maps and local trail information. Its self-published hiking guide details 21 local walks, including the hike up Cedar Mountain, where many locals believe Buffalo Bill is buried.

Information

Cody Visitor Center (☎307-587-2777; www.codychamber.org; 836 Sheridan Ave; ⏲8am-7pm Jun-Aug, to 5pm Mon-Fri Sep-May) Information on Cody and the surrounding areas.

Shoshone National Forest Wapiti Ranger District Office (☎307-527-6921; www.fs.fed.us/r2/shoshone; 203a Yellowstone Ave; ⏲8am-4:30pm Mon-Fri) Ask for the useful recreation guide.

Wapiti Valley

Deemed the 'most scenic 52 miles in the United States' by Teddy Roosevelt, **Buffalo Bill Scenic Byway** (US 14/16/20) traces the North Fork of the Shoshone River through the Wapiti Valley from Cody to the East Entrance of Yellowstone National Park. You will find yourself twisting to gape at the volcanic Absaroka Range, a rugged canyon of eroded badlands that gradually gives way to alpine splendor.

The name Wapiti Valley translates as 'pale white rump' from the Algonquin language. Rather than being a jab at homesteaders' backsides, the term distinguishes the lighter-colored elk, or wapiti, from darker-colored moose.

The North Absaroka Wilderness Area sits to the north and the Washakie Wilderness Area (named after a revered Shoshone warrior and peacemaker) to the south. This vast wilderness is home to grizzlies, black bears, deer, elk, moose, bighorn sheep and a few bison. The extensive network of backcountry trails, easy access to Yellowstone National Park's Lake Country and a selection of the region's best dude ranches make the valley an excellent wild route into or out of the park.

Six miles west of Cody, US 14/16/20 emerges from the dramatic **Shoshone Canyon** and tunnel to views of the **Buffalo Bill Reservoir**. Past the tiny settlement of Wapiti, Wyoming's high-desert landscape and open ranchland closes in as the road enters Shoshone National Forest and becomes the Buffalo Bill Cody Scenic Hwy. The roadside information station at the **Wapiti Ranger Station** (☎307-587-3925) has a 3D map of the region, as well as information on grizzly sightings. The national forest here was the USA's first and the nearby 1903 ranger station is its oldest.

From here on, the Wapiti Valley is lined with eerie buttes and dark brown hoodoos. National forest campgrounds, trailheads and guest ranches crop up every few miles as the scenery becomes increasingly rugged.

Two miles before the East Entrance to Yellowstone is the gas station, store, restaurant, bar and corrals of Pahaska Tepee (p144) resort, a good place to refuel. Staff lead free tours of the original lodge, built by Buffalo Bill in 1904 as a hunting lodge, and there are local trail rides. Pahaska was Bill's Native American name and means 'Longhair' in the Sioux language, a reference to Cody's long white hair and extravagant goatee.

Activities

Most of the valley's guest ranches offer **horseback riding** (per hour/half-day from $40/100), horse-packing trips and cookouts to nonguests in addition to guests. Outstanding **fly-fishing** is easily accessed from the national forest and wilderness areas and campgrounds.

North Fork Nordic Trails (☎307-527-7701; www.nordicskiclub.com) offers 12 miles of groomed cross-country trails behind the Pahaska Tepee resort.

🛌 Sleeping

Camping

Nine USFS campgrounds line the Wapiti Valley, starting from 29 miles west of Cody. Overflow from Yellowstone fills up the campgrounds on July and August weekends, so try to arrive before late afternoon. All campgrounds border the river, offering easy access to trout fishing. Most are open June to early September but can close any time due to grizzly activity. Call the Shoshone National Forest Wapiti Ranger District Office (p143) for details. Four of the campgrounds are reservable at www.recreation.gov.

Most campgrounds have bear-resistant food storage.

Big Game Campground CAMPGROUND $
(sites $10; ☺ Jun–early Sep) Small but spacious and private, with no water. It's reservable.

Wapiti Campground CAMPGROUND $
(sites with/without electricity $20/15; ☺ mid-May–mid-Sep) More sites than the neighboring campgrounds but less space. It's the first in the valley to open (in May) and is reservable.

Elk Fork Campground CAMPGROUND $
(sites $10) Cramped and without potable water, but popular for hiking and horse-packing trips and open year-round.

Clearwater Campground CAMPGROUND $
(sites $10; ☺ late May–early Sep) Unreliable water supply but walk-in riverside sites make it good for those with tents.

Rex Hale Campground CAMPGROUND $
(sites with/without electricity $20/15; ☺ late May–early Sep) Exposed, but has six sites with electrical hookups. Reservable.

Newton Creek Campground CAMPGROUND $
(sites $15; ☺ mid-May–late Sep) Woodsy and pleasant. Hard-sided campers only, due to grizzly activity.

Eagle Creek Campground CAMPGROUND $
(sites $15; ☺ late May–late Sep) Hard-sided campers only.

Threemile Campground CAMPGROUND $
(sites $15; ☺ Jul–early Sep) Hard-sided campers only; the closest campground to the park and the last to open.

Lodging

Wapiti Valley's lodges and guest ranches make a great base for exploring Yellowstone or Cody. Most offer fishing, hiking and guided horseback rides. Luxury in proximity to the park doesn't come cheap, but discounted rates are the norm before May and after September.

Lodges East of
Yellowstone Valley ACCOMMODATION SERVICES
(☎ 307-587-9595; www.yellowstone-lodging.com) Provides information on the Wapiti Valley's numerous family-owned member dude ranches and lodges.

Pahaska Tepee CABIN $$
(☎ 307-527-7701; www.pahaska.com; 183 Yellowstone Hwy; cabins $160-180, ste $220; ☺ May–mid-Oct) The historic lodge is close to Yellowstone National Park and a popular place for lunch before entering the park. Despite a great location, the cabins themselves are generally old-fashioned and musty. The cheapest A-frame cabins wouldn't fit a grizzly, but considering the location, that might just be a good thing.

PARADISE VALLEY ROUTE

Livingston

🚗 406 / POP 6800 / ELEV 4503FT

In the late 1880s the Northern Pacific Railroad laid tracks across the Yellowstone River and began building Livingston as the main jumping-off point for Yellowstone National Park. Visited by Clark (of Lewis and Clark fame) and at one point a temporary home to one whip-crackin' Martha Canary (otherwise known as Calamity Jane), Livingston is an excellent departure point for rafting and fly-fishing trips on the Yellowstone River.

Bozeman's overflow has brought upscale restaurants, antique shops and art galleries to Livingston's picturesque old buildings, as well as a growing community of writers and artists (think Russell Chatham, Jim Harrison, Thomas McGuane and Tim Cahill), but generally it retains its no-fuss, small-town feel.

Livingston is at the north end of Paradise Valley, where I-90 meets US 89. The latter heads south to Gardiner and Yellowstone National Park, 53 miles away.

⊙ Sights & Activities

Livingston is home to over a dozen galleries ('13 galleries; 3 stop lights'). View them on the afternoon art walk on the fourth Friday of the month in summer. You can get details and a map at any of the art galleries in town.

Depot Center
MUSEUM

(☑406-222-2300; www.livingstondepot.org; 200 W Park St; adult $5; ⊙10am-5pm Mon-Sat, 1-5pm Sun late May-early Sep) The original Northern Pacific Railroad depot, built in 1902 by the architects who designed New York's Grand Central Station, is now home to a railroad history and arts museum. Don't miss the collection of Montana movie trivia upstairs.

Yellowstone Gateway Museum
MUSEUM

(☑406-222-4184; www.yellowstonegatewaymu seum.org; 118 W Chinook St; adult/child $5/free; ⊙10am-5pm Jun-Sep, Thu-Sat only Oct-May) Livingston's collection of historical and archaeological treasures is housed in a century-old schoolhouse. Exhibits include a pioneer kitchen and an early Yellowstone stagecoach.

Yellowstone Fly Fishing School
FISHING

(☑406-223-0918; www.yellowstoneflyfishingschool. com; 416 N 8th St) Offers a half-day fly-fishing class for $275/325 for one/two people, as well as land-based casting lessons by the hour and a women's one-day fly-fishing school ($250 per person). There are also youth classes and Yellowstone National Park fishing clinics.

Dan Bailey's Fly Shop
FISHING

(☑800-356-4052; www.dan-bailey.com; 209 W Park St) Built on a legacy of Goofus Bugs, Humpy Flies, Green Drakes and Hair Wing Rubber Legs (to name but a few), Dan Bailey's is one of the world's best fly-fishing shops. It offers rentals, guided trips and on-line fishing reports. It's opposite the Depot Center.

George Anderson's Yellowstone Angler
FISHING

(☑406-222-7130; www.yellowstoneangler.com; Hwy 89) Good fly-fishing store, with equipment rental and guide service, located 1 mile south of town.

Rubber Ducky River Rentals
BOATING

(☑406-222-3746; www.riverservices.com; 15 Mt Baldy Dr) For canoe and kayak rentals and info on local rivers, head to Rubber Ducky, just north of I-90.

Timber Trails
BICYCLE RENTAL

(☑406-222-9550; www.timbertrailsmontana.com; 309 W Park St; ⊙noon-6pm) For maps and outdoor gear, including mountain bike ($30), ski and snowshoe rentals.

🛏 Sleeping

The nearest Forestry Service campground is Pine Creek (p148), 15 miles south in the Paradise Valley. Consider also the other excellent options in the Paradise Valley (p147).

★ Murray Hotel
HISTORIC HOTEL $

(☑406-222-1350; www.murrayhotel.com; 201 W Park St; r $89-98, ste $149-179; ☎) Central to Livingston's history since 1904, the Murray is the place to bed down with the ghosts of gunslinger Calamity Jane and director Sam Peckinpah (who lived in a suite for over a year, occasionally shooting holes in the ceiling). The hand-crank lift, original sinks and creaky wood floors set the tone, but the 25 rooms are fresh and modern.

Osen's RV Park & Campground
RV PARK $

(☑406-222-0591; www.montanarvpark.com; 20 Merrill Lane; tent/RV sites from $30/34, cabins $55; ☎) Just south of I-90, this place has laundry and showers and is open year-round.

🍴 Eating & Drinking

Mark's In and Out
FAST FOOD $

(cnr Park & 8th Sts; burgers $4; ⊙11am-10pm Mar-Nov) If your tastes are less merlot and more chocolate milk, Mark's has been churning out quality never-frozen burgers, foot-long chilli dogs and malts since 1954, the latter made with Livingston's very own Wilcoxson's ice cream. Roller-skating carhops lay on an extra scoop of nostalgia most summer Friday and Saturday evenings.

Mustang Catering
DELI $

(www.mustangcatering.com; 112 N Main St; mains $8; ⊙10am-6pm Mon-Fri, 11am-3pm Sat; 🖊) For a top-shelf picnic en route to Yellowstone, combine a fabulous ciabatta sandwich, gourmet salad or hot daily special from this top-notch cafe with a wine-and-cheese grab from the Gourmet Cellar (next to Depot Center) and make a beeline for the Paradise Valley.

★ 2nd St Bistro
BISTRO $$

(☑406-222-9463; www.secondstreetbistro.com; 123 N 2nd St; mains $18-29; ⊙from 5pm Wed-Sat) Our personal favorite, located in the historic Murray Hotel, with a superb range of appetizers, cocktails and draft beers, this is a classy but relaxed bistro with an emphasis on quality locally sourced and housemade food. From the pear-and-pumpkin-seed salad to the European-style mussels and fries, you can't go wrong, and there's more vegetarian fare than the average Montanan restaurant.

Chadz
COFFEE

(www.chadzmt.com; 104 N Main St; ⊙6am-2:30pm, to 9pm Fri; ☎) Lose yourself in the comfy sofas for a light lunchtime panini and reviving espresso at this funky coffeehouse.

Katabatic Brewing MICROBREWERY
(www.katabaticbrewing.com; 117 W Park St; ⊗ noon-8pm) Suitably named in incessantly windy Livingston, this dog- and family-friendly brewpub has stylishly exposed brick walls and live music on Saturday and Wednesday. There are normally eight brews on tap, including a crisp pale ale.

ℹ Information

Chamber of Commerce (⊅ 406-222-0850; www.livingston-chamber.com; 303 E Park St) Has a very useful website. Try also www.livingstonmontana.com.

Custer Gallatin National Forest Livingston Ranger District (⊅ 406-222-1892; 5242 Hwy 89 S; ⊗ 8am-4:30pm Mon-Fri) One mile south of town on I-90, next to Yellowstone Angler.

Paradise Valley

With Livingston as a railroad stop, Paradise Valley became the first travel corridor to Yellowstone National Park. Gardiner, 50 miles south of Livingston and just north of Yellowstone's North Entrance, is still one of the park's most popular entry points. The valley is mostly ranchland, but has also included at various times such famous residents as Peter Fonda, Jeff Bridges, Dennis Quaid, Tom Brokaw and John Mayer. And yes, a river, the Yellowstone, does run through it.

US 89 follows the Yellowstone River through this broad valley, flanked by the Gallatin Range to the west and the jagged Absaroka Range to the east. If you have time, the scenic East River Rd offers a recommended parallel and quieter alternative to busy US 89. Amazingly in retrospect, plans were afoot in the 1960s to dam the Yellowstone River and flood much of the lovely valley.

Chico Hot Springs

Thirty miles from Yellowstone National Park, just south of Pray at the mouth of Emigrant Canyon, **Chico Hot Springs** (⊅ 406-333-4933; www.chicohotsprings.com; 1 Old Chico Rd, Pray; 2-person cabins $237, main lodge r $61-98; ⊗ 7am-11pm; 🛜 🐾) was established in 1900 as a luxurious getaway for local cattle barons. The Victorian elegance has been restored, with great attention to rustic detail. It's worth a visit just to poke around and take a plunge in the large outdoor **pool** (adult/child 3-6yr $7.50/3.50; ⊗ 8am to 11pm), fed from hot springs and a toasty 103°F (39°C).

Smallish, creaking rooms in the main lodge, with shared bath, are the cheapest

options ($61 to $77), with motel-style fisher's cabins and modern high-ceiling rooms with a porch around double those rates. Chalets up the hill have mountain views and mostly sleep four to six. Suites with private Jacuzzi are a great luxury.

Chico's activity center offers **horseback riding** (half-day rides $90) and **raft trips** ($41) down the Yellowstone. It also offers cross-country ski trips and there's a full spa attached to help you recover. Dogsled tours are operated from Thanksgiving to March through **Absaroka Dogsled Treks** (⊅ 406-333-4933; www.extrememontana.com; per person $125-450).

🍴 Eating

Chico Inn Restaurant AMERICAN $$$
(dinner mains $25-32, Sun brunch $16) The restaurant at Chico is renowned throughout the region, though there's slim pickings for vegetarians. The beef Wellington ($60 for two) gets rave reviews, as does the Sunday brunch, between 8:30am and 11:30am.

The Poolside Grill is cheaper and more casual, with sandwiches, pizzas and ribs. The rollicking saloon has microbrews on tap and live music on Friday and Saturday night.

Southern Paradise Valley

South of the Tom Miner turnoff, US 89 winds through Yankee Jim Canyon, a narrow gorge cut through folded bands of extremely old rock (mostly gneiss) that look a bit like marble cake. Yankee Jim George hacked out a toll road through the canyon in the 19th century and made a living from Yellowstone-bound stagecoaches until the railroad put him out of business. This stretch of the Yellowstone River is the valley's hottest white-water spot.

A couple of miles further toward Yellowstone look for the roadside hot springs, which were once channeled into an elegant, turn-of-the-century resort at nearby Corwin Springs. Across the river is the headquarters of the Church Universal and Triumphant (CUT), which built a huge underground nuclear shelter here in the 1980s after its leader, Elizabeth Prophet, predicted the end of the world.

Further south, a pullout offers fine views of the **Devil's Slide**, a superbly named, salmon-pink landslide area consisting of 200-million-year-old rock. Keep an eye out for bighorn sheep here.

Activities

Hiking & Backpacking

Paradise Valley's most popular trail is the 10-mile round-trip hike to **Pine Creek Lake**. The trail starts from the Pine Creek Campground parking area and leads 1.2 miles to Pine Creek Falls, where the crowds thin out for the next 3.8 miles to the lake, gaining around 3000ft en route. Budget at least four hours for the return hike, which is also a good overnighter.

Further south, down Mill Creek Rd, is the trailhead for **Elbow Lake**, 3500ft above the trailhead at the base of 11,206ft Mt Cowen, the highest peak in the Absaroka Range. The strenuous 18-mile round-trip hike (along trails 51 and 48) is best done as an overnighter. From the lake you can continue northeast to a second lake and ascend the ridge on the left for views of Mt Cowen.

Further south, there are more hiking opportunities on the east side of the Gallatin Range. A popular day hike from Tom Miner Campground takes you 3 miles uphill (gaining 1400ft) to meadows at **Buffalo Horn Pass** (clear of snow from July). A viewpoint five minutes' walk south offers excellent views of the Gallatin Valley; Ramshorn Peak (10,289ft) beckons to the north.

Other Activities

The Yellowstone River winds past 19 **fishing** access sites along Paradise Valley, most of which have boat ramps. Experienced anglers can pit themselves against challenging private spring creeks such as Nelson's, Armstrong's and Depuy's. For bookings, fees and conditions contact Livingston's fishing shops.

The Montana Department of Fishing, Wildlife & Parks runs basic **campgrounds** (www.fwp.mt.gov; sites with/without a Montana

fishing license $7/12) at the Mallard's Rest, Loch Leven and Dailey Lake fishing access sites. Primitive overnight camping is permitted free of charge at the Bureau of Land Management Carbella and Paradise fishing access areas, by the Tom Miner and Miller Creek turnoffs respectively, but the limited and primitive sites get snapped up quickly. All other access areas are day-use only.

Paradise Valley has some of the best **cycling** in the Yellowstone region. The paved East River Rd from the junction with Hwy 89 to Chico Rd and Chico Hot Springs is a scenic and smooth ride of 24 miles. For something more suited to fat tires, try the 17-mile gravel Gardiner Back Rd between Gardiner and Tom Miner Rd. This route starts from just behind the Yellowstone Heritage and Research Center as a dedicated bike path and follows the old railroad bed and stagecoach road past the Devil's Slide, the narrows of Yankee Jim Canyon and several primitive camping spots. To shorten the ride, turn off at Corwin Springs after 8 miles. Combine these routes, and you'll get a complete traverse of the valley.

Bearpaw Outfitters　　HORSEBACK RIDING
(☑ 406-222-6642; www.bearpawoutfittersmt.com; 136 Deep Creek Rd) This operation, 8 miles south of Livingston, organizes horse-pack trips in the Absaroka-Beartooth Wilderness (half-day $95) and day rides in Yellowstone Park (from $225), plus fly-fishing in Yellowstone's Slough Creek.

🛏 Sleeping

There are several useful campgrounds in the Paradise Valley. Pine Creek and Snowbank Campgrounds serve as springboards to local hikes. Snowbank closes first, early in September.

WORTH A TRIP

TOM MINER BASIN

To get off the beaten track, head west of US 89 on Tom Miner Rd, 17 miles north of Gardiner and 35 miles south of Livingston, into one of the prettiest pockets of land in the area. The washboard road ends 12 miles west of the highway at secluded 16-site **Tom Miner Campground** (sites $7; ⊘ Jun-Oct), which has potable water and toilets.

Trails from the campground lead up through the **Gallatin Petrified Forest**, where remnants of 35- to 55-million-year-old petrified redwood and oak trees lie scattered among the Absaroka's volcanic rocks. A 0.5-mile interpretive trail near the campground winds around volcanic bluffs of fused ash (bear right where a sign says 'Hiker Trail Only') and peters out by a remarkable piece of petrified wood that is lodged in the roof of a small cave. Visitors are allowed to keep one small piece of petrified wood (maximum 20 cubic inches), with a free permit available at the Gardiner, Bozeman or Livingston ranger offices (and maybe the Tom Miner Campground hosts).

AROUND YELLOWSTONE PARADISE VALLEY

The USFS also operates two simple year-round cabins. **Big Creek Cabin** (cabins $50) sleeps 10 and is set a half-mile from Mountain Sky Guest Ranch, up FS Rd 132, on the west side of the valley. **Mill Creek Cabin** (cabins $45) which sleeps four, is on the east side of the valley, 12 miles up E Mill Creek Rd, near Snowbank Campground. It has an electric stove and lights, but no mattresses. Call the Livingston Ranger District (p146) for information. Reserve these from six months to three days in advance at www.recreation.gov.

Pine Creek Campground　　CAMPGROUND $
(sites $14; ⊘ mid-May–Sep) This reservable Forestry Service campground has pit toilets, water and 24 sites. Head 4 miles south of Livingston on East River Rd, then climb up Luccock Park Rd, 3 miles east.

Snowbank Campground　　CAMPGROUND $
(sites $14; ⊘ mid-May–Sep) Quiet 10-site campground, somewhat inconveniently located 12 miles up unpaved Mill Creek Rd.

Canyon Campground　　CAMPGROUND $
(sites $7; ⊘ year-round) This roadside, 15-site campground is waterless, but does have picnic tables, fire rings and an accessible toilet. It's in Yankee Jim Canyon, 15 miles from Yellowstone, and isn't reservable.

KOA　　CAMPGROUND $
(☑ 406-222-0992; www.livingstonkoa.com; 163 Pine Creek Rd; tent/RV sites from $29/47, cabins $70-163; ⊘ May–mid-Oct; 🛜 ▣) Nicely situated by Pine Creek between US 89 and the East River Rd, 10 miles south of Livingston, this peaceful spot offers an indoor heated pool, cabins and laundry room. Some spots offer prime river access.

Mountain Sky Guest Ranch　　RANCH $$$
(☑ 800-548-3392, 406-333-4911; www.mtnsky.com; daily/weekly rates per person from $370/3890; 🛜 ▣) The western flanks of the valley hide this professionally run dude ranch, 4.5 miles up Big Creek Rd and 30 miles from Yellowstone. Rates include food and everything from fly-fishing to fun kids' programs. The dawn horseback rides to catch sunrise over Emigrant Peak are a highlight. There's a one-week minimum stay June to August. Shoulder-season months are adults only.

Yellowstone Valley Lodge　　LODGE $$$
(www.yellowstonevalleylodge.com; 3840 Hwy 89 S; d $229-289, ste $399; 🛜) Anglers love this row of modern duplex cabins right on the banks

of the Yellowstone River. You can almost cast your line from your private balcony.

Eating

⭐ **Yellowstone**
Valley Grill　　MODERN AMERICAN $$$
(☑ 406-222-4815; www.yellowstonevalleylodge.com; 3840 Hwy 89 S; mains $25-34; ⊘ 5:30-9pm Tue-Sun) Sustainable local ingredients, fresh Napa Valley cuisine and fine views of Emigrant Peak and the Yellowstone River combine to make this the valley's top restaurant. Reservations are recommended, and try a table outside on summer evenings. The restaurant is 14 miles south of Livingston, just below the Yellowstone Valley Lodge.

Gardiner

📍 406 / POP 800 / ELEV 5134FT

A quintessential gateway town founded and fed on tourism, Gardiner, Montana, is the only entrance to Yellowstone National Park open to automobile traffic year-round. The park starts just where the souvenir stores peter out at the south end of town. Mammoth Hot Springs is only 5 miles away.

The town is named after Johnson Gardner, an 'illiterate and brutal trapper' who worked the area in the 1830s. Gardiner only made it onto the map, misspelled, in the 1880s when the Northern Pacific Railroad unveiled its Park Branch Line from Livingston to nearby Cinnabar. Stagecoaches ferried passengers on the last leg of the journey to the park, and Gardiner grew as a transit stop. By 1883 the town's 200 thirsty residents could stagger between 21 saloons.

These days the friendly and unpretentious town sticks to its ranching, mining and outfitting roots. The rodeo still pulls into town five times during the summer and the plaid shirts and pickups haven't yet given way to microbrews and art galleries.

⊙ Sights

Roosevelt Arch　　LANDMARK
Gardiner's most photographed sight is the park's northwestern entry gate, dedicated by Teddy Roosevelt himself on April 25, 1903, and inscribed with Congress' words: 'For the benefit and enjoyment of the people.'

Yellowstone Heritage
& Research Center　　MUSEUM
(☑ 307-344-2664; www.nps.gov/yell/historyculture/collections.htm; ⊘ library 9am-4pm Tue-Fri) FREE

The park's abundant archives (over five million items and growing) moved from Mammoth to this research facility in 2004. Drop-in visitors can peruse the lobby displays on painter Thomas Moran and the ground-breaking Hayden Expedition of 1871. Alternatively, reserve one of the hour-long tours that run at 8am on Tuesday and Thursday (Memorial Day to Labor Day) and take you into the museum and rare-book archives.

🏃 Activities

Several outfitters run fishing trips, horseback rides and pack trips into Yellowstone and other nearby mountain areas, though all are primarily hunting operations. Rides start at around $105/170 per half-/full day. Outfitters include Yellowstone Rough Riders (406-223-3924; www.yellowstoneroughriders.com) and Hell's A-Roarin' Outfitters (406-848-7578; www.hellsaroarinoutfitters.com; Jardine), which also does cabin rentals, luxury tent accommodations and steak cookouts, courtesy of the Johnson family.

Parks' Fly Shop   FISHING
(406-848-7314; www.parksflyshop.com; 202 S 2nd St) Old-school owner Richard Parks sells flies (specifically designed for park waters), rents gear and offers float trips, and is the author of the much-respected *Fly Fishing Yellowstone National Park* (Falcon Press). In winter the action switches to cross-country ski and snowshoe rental.

Rafting

Half-a-dozen companies operate family-friendly rafting trips on the Yellowstone River through the class II to III rapids of Yankee Jim Canyon, one of Montana's more famous white-water spots. Half-day rafting trips operate from mid-May to mid-September and start from $40/30 for adults/children aged five to 12, or $80/60 for a full day. Most companies also offer half-day 'paddle and saddle' combos for around $100/90.

Yellowstone Raft Company   RAFTING
(800-858-7781; www.yellowstoneraft.com; half-day adult/child $42/32) With over 30 years of local experience, this company also has half-day kayaking lessons on the river and offers helmet video cams.

Wild West Whitewater Rafting   RAFTING
(406-848-2252; www.wildwestrafting.com; Scott St W) Rafting and gentler scenic floats in the upper Paradise Valley and inflatable kayak trips, with a climbing wall.

Montana Whitewater   ADVENTURE TOUR
(406-848-7398; www.montanawhitewater.com; 603 Scott St W; ⊗ May-Sep) In addition to rafting and sit-on kayaks, it offers horseback riding and zip-lining ($59 to $79), with various combo options. There's a branch (p157) in the Gallatin Valley.

Flying Pig Adventures   ADVENTURE TOUR
(406-848-7510; www.flyingpigrafting.com; 511 Scott St W) Rafting shop that also offers horseback rides, cowboy cookouts, Yellowstone nature safaris and an outdoor-gear shop that stocks bear spray.

River Source   RAFTING
(888-406-2214; www.paddleyellowstone.com; Hwy 89) Located nine miles north of Gardiner, with rafting, kayaking and stand-up paddleboards.

🛏 Sleeping

Camping

Custer Gallatin National Forest offers three first-come, first-served primitive campgrounds just northeast of Gardiner. Timber Camp and Bear Creek Campgrounds are free but somewhat inconvenient, being 10 and 12 miles respectively from Gardiner and without water.

Eagle Creek Campground   CAMPGROUND $
(Map p88; sites $7; ⊗ year-round) Has 16 woodsy sites and pit toilets but no water. It's located 2 miles northeast of Gardiner on unpaved Jardine Rd.

Rocky Mountain RV Park   RV PARK $
(877-534-6931; www.rockymountaincampground. com; 14 Jardine Rd; RV sites from $51.50, cabins $50-125; ⊗ mid-Apr–mid-Oct; 🐾) This friendly place overlooking the river offers showers, laundry, full hookups and fine panoramas of Yellowstone, but little shade. Ask about the simple one- or two-room cabins that can sleep up to six.

Yellowstone RV Park   RV PARK $
(406-848-7496; www.ventureswestinc.com; 117 Hwy 89; tent/RV sites $31/54; 🐾) At the northwest end of town, this RV park has 46 fairly cramped riverside sites with full hookups, plus showers and a laundry.

Lodging

About half of Gardiner's accommodations close between October and May and those that remain cut their rates by around 50%. Chain places (all with free breakfast) include

Gardiner

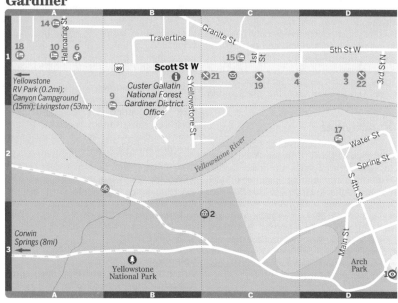

Gardiner

Comfort Inn (☑406-848-7536; www.choice hotels.com; d $195; 🕾), **Super 8 Motel** (☑406-848-7401; www.yellowstonesuper8.com; d $160; 🕾🖳🐾) and the **Rodeway Inn & Suites** (☑406-848-7520; www.yellowstonerooms.com; 1102 Scott St; d $180-260; 🕾).

Hillcrest Cottages   MOTEL $
(☑800-970-7353;   www.hillcrestcottages.com; 200 Scott St W; d $85-110, 2-room cottages $150;

⊙May-Sep; 🕾) This slightly cramped mini-village features a variety of pleasant if old-fashioned 1950s-era cottages. Most come with kitchenettes and sleep two to seven.

Yellowstone River Motel   MOTEL $
(☑406-848-7303; www.yellowstonerivermotel.com; 14 E Park St; d $86-110, ste $155; ⊙May-Oct; 🕾) This is one of the better-run motels, clean and friendly with picnic tables and a BBQ area

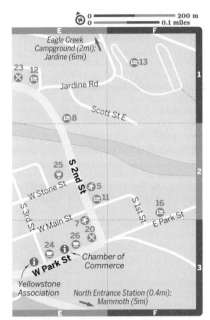

ard Parks at the next-door fly-fishing shop. Breakfast is a serious family-style affair.

Yellowstone Village Inn   MOTEL $$

(☑ 800-228-8158; www.yellowstonevinn.com; 1102 Scott St W; d/ste incl breakfast from $159/209; 🛜 ▣) Standing alone at the entrance to Gardiner, this locally owned motel is pretty good value, with spacious rooms and a few family suites featuring a private porch.

Best Western by Mammoth Hot Springs   HOTEL $$

(☑ 406-848-7311; www.bestwestern.com/mammoth hotsprings; 905 Scott St W; d $205; 🛜 ▣) It's not 'by Mammoth Hot Springs' (they're 5 miles away), but once you get past that tiny fib this is a solid choice, with spacious modern rooms and an in-house tour company. Pay $15 more for a mountain-view room, or $35 for a river-side view or hot tub in your room.

🍴 Eating

Fill up on park supplies at the **Gardiner Market** (701 Scott St W; ⊙ 7am-10pm) across from the Super 8 Motel.

Tumbleweed Bookstore & Cafe   CAFE $

(501 Scott St W; wraps $8.50; ⊙ 6am-9pm; 🛜) Browse the selection of Yellowstone books over a fresh wrap, salad or espresso at this bookstore with a fine terrace. Gluten-free and vegan options are available.

Yellowstone Grill   SANDWICHES $

(404 Scott St W; mains $8-10; ⊙ 7am-2pm Tue-Sun, to 9pm Thu) This reliable place serves up fine burritos, salads and wraps in a coffeehouse-style industrial brick interior, or on the outdoor terrace. It's also good for coffee and morning cinnamon rolls, or as a grab-and-go option for a park picnic. Opening hours change frequently, so check its Facebook page in advance.

The Corral   BURGERS $$

(711 Scott St W; burgers $11-15; ⊙ 11am-10pm Apr-Oct) This old-style malt-and-greasy-burger stand has been proudly clogging arteries since 1960. It's neither gourmet nor all that cheap, but really, where else are you going to dive into a half-pound elk burger followed by a huckleberry shake? New ownership has revitalized the place in recent years.

Rosie's Grill   AMERICAN $$

(206 Park St; mains $12-17; ⊙ 7-11:30am & 5-9:30pm) Dining out in Gardiner is generally a disappointment. That said, Rosie's is

overlooking the river. The renovated new-block rooms are bigger, with a fridge and microwave, but all are fresh and good value.

Absaroka Lodge   HOTEL $$

(☑ 800-755-7414; www.yellowstonemotel.com; S 2nd St; r $150-175; 🛜) Modern, but surprisingly unobtrusive hotel. The best thing about the rooms are the fine balconies overlooking the rushing Yellowstone River.

Yellowstone Suites   B&B $$

(☑ 406-848-7937; www.yellowstonesuites.com; 506 S 4th St; d with/without bath $150/120; @ 🛜) There's plenty of privacy in this well-appointed, four-room, 100-year-old B&B, which makes a nice antidote to motel over-load. There are cozy sitting spaces and views of Electric Peak, but only two rooms have attached bathrooms. Get a deal by renting an entire floor (two rooms).

Gardiner Guesthouse   B&B $$

(☑ 406-848-9414; www.gardinerguesthouse.com; 112 E Main St; d incl breakfast $95-135; 🛜 🐾 ▣) Kid-friendly, pet-friendly and pretty much everyone-friendly, this homey century-old B&B offers two rooms with shared bath and one suite available in the main house, as well as a rustic cabin ($165) in the back – perfect for anglers hooking up with owner Rich-

probably the best dinner option in town, with good pastas, salmon and trout dinners and fine pancake breakfasts, in a surfeit of pine furniture.

Drinking

Grab your morning espresso at either **Hi Country Trading** (W Park St; ⏱7:30am-9pm), which has some outdoor seating, or **Yellowstone Perk** (208 W Park St; ⏱from 7am), which also offers ice cream and a pharmacy.

Iron Horse Bar & Grill
BAR
(20 Spring St; ⏱11am-midnight) The interior here isn't much to look at (is that a cougar skin on the wall?!), but the real draw is the great sundeck overlooking the Yellowstone River. There are lots of local drafts to sample and the bar food is a notch above average, featuring elk nachos or tacos for lunch, and elk bolognaise and bison meatloaf for dinner.

Information

Chamber of Commerce (☑406-848-7971; www.gardinerchamber.com; 220 W Park St; ⏱9am-4pm Mon-Fri, to 1pm Sat & Sun; 🛜) Tourist information, free wi-fi and a public bathroom.

Custer Gallatin National Forest Gardiner District Office (☑406-848-7375; 805 Scott St; ⏱8am-noon & 1-4:30pm Mon-Fri) Campground and hiking information.

Sinclair Gas Station (Scott St W) Sells Montana state fishing licenses.

Yellowstone Association (www.yellowstone association.org; W Park St; ⏱8am-8pm) Former general store that houses a bookstore and information desk with a map of recent wildlife sightings in the park. Rent binoculars/spotting scopes here for $15/25 per day. Some Yellowstone Institute (p261) courses are held here.

GALLATIN ROUTE

Bozeman

☑406 / POP 37,000 / ELEV 4700FT

The hip college town of Bozeman, only an hour's drive north of Yellowstone, is regularly voted one of America's best outdoor towns, and with good reason. With excellent restaurants and shops, one of the region's best museums and outdoor opportunities that beckon from every corner, the town is well worth a stop en route to the more rustic delights of the parks. The town is named af-

ter John Bozeman, who guided settlers here along his namesake Bozeman Trail, a spur of the Oregon, from 1864.

Highlights of the cultural year include the independent film and arts festival **Hatchfest** (www.hatchfest.org) in October and the artsy **Sweetpea Festival** (www.sweetpeafesti val.org), with lots of food, art and live music, in August.

Sights

★ Museum of the Rockies
MUSEUM
(☑406-994-2251; www.museumoftherockies.org; 600 W Kagy Blvd; adult/child $14.50/9.50; ⏱8am-8pm Jun-Aug, 9am-5pm Mon-Sat, noon-5pm Sun Sep-May; P♿) Montana State University's museum is the most entertaining in Montana and shouldn't be missed, with stellar dinosaur exhibits, early Native American art and laser planetarium shows, as well as a living-history outdoors section (closed in winter) and various temporary exhibits. Guided tours happen more or less constantly and are recommended for families with young children, as they let kids get more interactive with some of the displays.

Emerson Cultural Center
ARTS CENTER
(☑406-587-9797; www.theemerson.org; 111 S Grand Ave; ⏱most galleries closed Mon) **FREE** Known around town as 'the Emerson,' this nonprofit center is the place to plug into Bozeman's art scene, with retail galleries, exhibits, studios and a fine cafe/restaurant.

Pioneer Museum
MUSEUM
(☑406-522-8122; www.pioneermuseum.org; 317 W Main St; adult/under 12yr $5/free; ⏱10am-5pm Mon-Sat Memorial Day-Labor Day, 11am-4pm Tue-Sat rest of year) The former town jail does a good job presenting local history and famous residents (including one Gary Cooper).

Activities

Spire Climbing Center
ROCK CLIMBING
(☑406-586-0706; www.spireclimbingcenter.com; 13 Enterprise Blvd; day pass $15; ⏱noon-10pm Mon-Thu, to 9pm Fri, 10am-6pm Sat & Sun) Hone your climbing skills on the indoor wall here before heading off to tackle Grand Teton. Good-value private lessons and weekly classes are offered.

Bozeman Angler
FISHING
(☑406-587-9111; www.bozemanangler.com; 23 E Main St; 1-day class adult/child $125/75; ⏱9am-5:30pm Mon-Sat, to 4pm Sun) If you are new to fly-fishing, this downtown shop offers a

MONTANASAURUS REX

It's amazing how much drama you can find in a single 50-million-year-old slab of rock at Bozeman's Museum of the Rockies (MOR). From the group of teenage diplodocus who suffocated when their legs became stuck in river mud, to the dinosaur skeleton surrounded by the teeth of the pack of predators that devoured it, these are fossils that come alive before your eyes. We challenge you to stare at the terrifying claws of a deinonychus without feeling a slight shiver run down your spine.

Like all good museums, MOR also shatters preconceptions, reminding you that many dinosaurs were in fact clad in feathers and that sharks once swam the tropical seas covering current-day Montana. Then there's the scale of the beasts – 9ft-long rib bones stand in the corner near huge 20ft-tall reconstructions of horned torosaurus and Montanoceratops (we kid you not). On display here is the world's largest collection of T. rex skeletons.

Even the curator is larger than life. Paleontologist Jack Horner is widely believed to have been the model for the character Dr Alan Grant in the book *Jurassic Park* and served as technical adviser to all the films. And yes, they *are* extracting soft tissue from tyrannosaur thigh bones, right here in Bozeman.

one-day fly-fishing class on the second Saturday of the month (May to September). Kids eight and up have their own day camp every Tuesday (July to mid-August), learning basic fly-tying and casting techniques. Nonbeginners can polish their skills in a private casting or fly-tying lesson ($40 per hour).

Bangtail Bikes BICYCLE RENTAL
(406-587-4905; www.bangtailbikes; 137 E Main St) Bozeman's best for buying and renting bikes and cross-country skis.

🛏 Sleeping

Camping
There are three USFS campsites (all sites $14) 25 minute's drive southeast of town near the Hyalite Reservoir: Langhor (10 sites), Hood Creek (18 sites) and Chisholm (10 sites). Take Forestry Rd No 62 from south Bozeman. Reserve sites at www.recreation.gov.

Bozeman KOA CAMPGROUND $
(406-587-3030; tent/RV sites from $31/39, cabins $63-73; 🔄🏊) Off I-90, 8 miles west of Bozeman in the Gallatin Valley and next to Bozeman Hot Springs, this is the only campground in the area open year-round.

Bear Canyon Campground CAMPGROUND $
(800-438-1575; www.bearcanyoncampground.com; I-90 exit 313; tent sites $20, RV sites $30-40; ☺May–mid-Oct; 🔄🏊) Bear Canyon Campground is on top of a hill 3 miles east of Bozeman, with great views of the surrounding valley. There's even a pool.

Lodging

Lewis & Clark Motel MOTEL $
(800-332-7666; www.lewisandclarkmotelbozeman.com; 824 W Main St; r $94-179; ✳@🔄) For a drop of Vegas in your Montana, stay at this flashy, locally owned motel. The large rooms have floor-to-ceiling front windows and the piped 1950s music adds to the retro Rat Pack vibe. With hot tub and steam room. Prices go up on weekends in summer.

Royal 7 Motel MOTEL $
(800-587-3103; www.royal7inn.com; 310 N 7th Ave; d $70-100; @🔄) This little inn really tries. It's dated (squint and it's almost retro cool) but spacious rooms offer large TV, microwave, fridge, continental breakfast, laundry service and a handful of DVDs for rent. Add $20 in July and August. Swings are set up in a grassy space for the kiddies.

The Lark MOTEL $$
(866-464-1000; www.larkbozeman.com; 122 W Main St; r $169-209; 🔄) With its fresh yellow palette and modern graphic design, this hip new designer place is a big step up from your average grungy motel. Rooms are fresh and the fine location puts it in walking distance of downtown's bars and restaurants.

Other positives include the two family rooms with kid-friendly bunk beds and the public patio set around a fireplace. Room rates are $20 higher on weekends.

Lehrkind Mansion Bed & Breakfast B&B $$
(406-585-6932; www.bozemanbedandbreakfast.com; 719 N Wallace Ave; d incl breakfast $159-229; 🔄) This sophisticated nine-room Victorian B&B was built by a Swiss-German master

brewer and is steeped in period furniture and history (the bricks were actually soaked in beer before construction). The 7ft Regina music box (one of only 25) is a highlight, as are the organic breakfasts and claw-foot bathtubs. If they are around, the owners can fill you in on all the park's hidden spots; they are former Yellowstone Park rangers.

Howlers Inn B&B $$

(406-587-5229; www.howlersinn.com; 3185 Jackson Creek Rd; r $145-160, 2-person cabins $205;) Wolf-watchers will love this beautiful sanctuary 15 minutes outside of Bozeman. Rescued captive-born wolves live in enclosed natural areas on 4 acres, supported by the profits of the B&B. There are three spacious Western-style rooms in the main lodge and a two-bedroom carriage house. With luck, you will drift off to sleep serenaded by howls. Take exit 319 off I-90.

Eating

Only Jackson can compete with Bozeman's range of excellent restaurants. The Ale Works also offers good food.

★**Community Co-Op** SUPERMARKET $

(www.bozo.coop; 908 W Main St; mains $7-12; 7am-10pm Mon-Sat, 8am-10pm Sun;) This beloved local market and deli is the best place to stock up on organic and bulk foods, as well as hot meals, salads and soups to eat in or take away. There's another branch at 44 E Main St.

Granny's Gourmet Donuts BAKERY $

(3 Tai Lane; donuts 75¢; 7am-2pm) The donuts here are utterly addictive, so come in the morning before they sell out and don't be stupid like us and buy only one; you'll only have to return later for more. Look for local Flathead cherry or huckleberry toppings in late summer.

La Parrilla SANDWICHES $

(1624 W Babcock St; wraps $7-9; 11am-9pm) Join the local MSU students for a top lunch of gourmet California-style fish tacos, burritos and exotic wraps, strong on the cilantro and wasabi.

Cateye Café BREAKFAST $

(www.cateyecafe.com; 23 N Tracy Ave; mains $8-10; 7am-2pm) The banana-bread French toast and daily specials make the hip and quirky Cateye our favorite Bozeman breakfast. Expect to queue on weekends, but at least you can sip on a coffee while you wait.

★**John Bozeman's Bistro** AMERICAN $$

(406-587-4100; www.johnbozemansbistro.com; 125 W Main St; mains $12-28; 11:30am-2:30pm & 5-9:30pm Tue-Sat) Bozeman's best restaurant, this pretty blonde-and-gold space offers Thai, Creole and pan-Asian slants on the cowboy dinner steak, plus globally influenced soups and starters and a weekly 'superfood' special ($14.95). Service is classy, friendly and unpretentious. Lunchtime offers an $8 menu of healthy salads and sandwiches. The beer taps are all local; sample five for $8.75.

Dave's Sushi SUSHI $$

(www.davessushi.com; 115 N Bozeman Ave; rolls $6-15; 11am-9:30pm Sun-Thu, to 10pm Fri & Sat) Recently expanded wooden house, one-and-a-half blocks north of Main St, with a cool counter and patio, offering the best rolls and freshest line-caught fish for miles around. Try a Widespread Panic roll, with spicy crab, mango, avocado, cucumber and chili sauce.

Starky's DELI $$

(www.starkysonline.com; 24 N Tracy Ave; mains $10-20; 8am-9pm) Offering great New York–style deli lunches, including chicken matzoh-ball soup and a mean Reuben pastrami on rye, served on a sunny patio. It's perfect for a late lunch that slowly slips into happy hour (4pm to 6pm).

Drinking & Nightlife

For a rundown of what's playing where, pick up a copy of free local papers *Lively Times* (www.livelytimes.com) or the *Bozone* (www.bozone.com), or visit www.bozemanevents.net. **Cactus Records** (29 W Main St), the region's best music store, has the lowdown on musical happenings.

College dive hangouts include the pumping **Haufbrau** (22 S 8th Ave), with frequent live music, and the smaller next-door **Molly Brown** (www.mollybrownbozeman.com; 703 W Babcock).

★**Montana Ale Works** PUB

(www.montanaaleworks.com; 611 E Main St; 4-11pm Sun-Thu, to midnight Fri & Sat) Bozeman's former Northern Pacific freight warehouse brings industrial chic to this ever-reliable bar-restaurant, with excellent food (mains $11 to $24), pool tables and people-watching. Staff are happy to let you taste any of the 30 microbrews on tap, including the local Bozones.

ROCKY MOUNTAIN BREWS

The Yellowstone states of Wyoming and Montana are fast developing a reputation among beer hounds for hosting some of the country's best microbreweries.

Snake River Brewing Co (p217) in Jackson is perhaps the region's most popular brew-pub. Flagship beers include the crisp Snake River Pale Ale, the dark and creamy Snake River Zonker Stout and the Austrian-style Jenny Lake Lager, part of the proceeds of which go to park improvements at Jenny Lake.

Also popular are brews from Teton Valley's **Grand Teton Brewing Company** (www.grandtetonbrewing.com), which uses local spring water to produce its smooth Old Faithful and Amber ales.

Missoula's **Bayern Brewing** (www.bayernbrewery.com) is the only German microbrewery in the Rockies, serving up amber, pilsner, Killarney and Hefeweizen beers. **Big Sky Brewing** (www.bigskybrew.com), also of Missoula, produces Montana's best-selling microbrew, Moose Drool, a creamy brown ale with hints of coffee.

There are dozens of other microbreweries in the Greater Yellowstone Region and many are listed in this guide. Bozeman alone has seven microbreweries, three of which opened in 2015. Fans of walking and drinking will want to take the Billings Brewery Crawl (p130), a walking tour of six breweries in an eight-block radius. If you are keen on tracking down more Montana craft breweries, try the following:

Lone Peak Brewery (www.lonepeakbrewery.com; Meadow Village, Big Sky; ⊙11am-10pm) A kid-friendly brewpub equipped with a fine shuffleboard and light food menu. The Lone Peak IPA and Nordic Blond are the most popular, or try the Brewski Rack of 4oz samples.

Bozeman Brewing Company (www.bozemanbrewing.com; 504 N Broadway, Bozeman; ⊙4-8pm Mon-Thu, Sat & Sun, 12:30-8pm Fri) Drink Bozone brews at the source at this bustling taproom. The four-glass sampler is served on a downhill ski.

406 Brewing (www.406brewing.com; 101 E Oak St, Suite D, Bozeman; ⊙noon-8pm) A relaxed place with cool wooden bar benches, a hoppy Hop Punch IPA and darker English-style EKG bitter, plus house-distilled spirits.

Bridger Brewing   MICROBREWERY
(www.bridgerbrewing.com; 1609 11th Ave; ⊙11:30am-9pm, last beer order 8pm) This well-run and friendly brewpub draws a loyal combination of beer hounds and local MSU students. The Lee Metcalfe Pale Ale is a firm favorite and there are lots of food specials, including great pizza and Wednesday-night mussels. Don't miss the hidden upstairs deck. Happy hour is 2pm to 4pm.

Wild Joe's   CAFE
(www.wildjoescoffee.com; 18 W Main St; ⊙6.45am-7pm Mon-Thu, to 9pm Fri & Sat, 7.30am-6pm Sun) Everything a coffeehouse should be: pressed-tin ceilings and comfy sofas in a century-old building, live music on the weekends, pizza by the slice and a fine community spirit. Oh, and great coffee and chai.

🔒 Shopping

Northern Lights   OUTDOOR EQUIPMENT
(☎866-586-2225; www.northernlightstrading.com; 1716 W Babcock) Good but pricey gear store, offering demos and rentals.

REI   OUTDOOR EQUIPMENT
(☎406-587-1938; www.rei.com/bozeman; 2220 Tschache St) Yellowstone topo maps, backpacking rentals and popular weekly workshops.

ℹ Information

Custer Gallatin National Forest Bozeman Ranger District (☎406-522-2520; www.fs.usda.gov/gallatin; 3710 Fallon, Suite C; ⊙8:30am-4:30pm Mon-Fri) Tricky to find in the west of town, with info on campsites and cabins, plus it sells USGS topo maps.

Gallatin Valley

A broad ribbon snaking through big valleys, the Gallatin River leaves its headwaters in the northwest corner of Yellowstone National Park to cascade through the narrow, craggy Gallatin Valley. US 191 traces its path, eventually meeting the Madison, Jefferson and Missouri Rivers at Three Forks. Sandwiched between the scenic Madison and Gallatin Ranges, the route – first forged by Lewis and

Clark – is peppered with enough trailheads to make return hikers and skiers arthritic. The commercial heart of the valley is the broad opening connecting Big Sky Resort.

On a clear day, look for a distinct cluster of summits exceeding 10,000ft rising sharply out of the silhouette of the Gallatin Range, west of US 191. These are the Spanish Peaks, the valley's premier hiking and backcountry-ski destination and part of the Lee Metcalf Wilderness.

Big Sky

Commercial development hits hyperdrive near the turnoff to Big Sky, the Gallatin Valley's main attraction, 18 miles north of Yellowstone National Park and 36 miles south of Bozeman. This world-class winter and summer resort attracts a cosmopolitan crowd more partial to an organic pinot noir than a can of Bud Lite, and multi-million-dollar homes continue to sprout like milkweed.

Big Sky spreads from US 191 to the base of Lone Mountain in four areas: Gallatin Canyon, Town Center/West Fork Meadows, Meadow Village and Mountain Village. Meadow Village and West Fork Meadows offer the bulk of the services, including a dozen restaurants. All are connected by a bike trail and a free shuttle service.

Activities

Big Sky Resort (406-995-4486; www.bigskyresort.com; Big Sky; lift tickets adult $103, child over/under 10yr $83/53) is comprised of Andesite Mountain (8800ft), Lone Peak (11,166ft) and Moonlight Basin (www.moonlightbasin.com), offering an awesome 5500 acres of terrain, with a 4350ft vertical drop, a 15-passenger tram, a gondola and multiple high-speed lifts.

From June to September the Swift Current lift (10:30am to 3:30pm) shuttles people and bikes to 10,000ft for $19 ($35 for a day pass), from where mountain bikers can choose from a dozen advanced downhill rides. Thrill seekers will love the giant swing ($13), high ropes course ($65) and zip lines ($65 to $85).

For the region's biggest hike, take the Swift Current lift and then walk to the top of Lone Peak. Figure on a couple of hours to the top, which is generally clear from snow by the middle or end of July. Nonhikers can cheat by taking the tram to the summit ($85). Big Sky's other prime hike is the 6.5-mile return to Beehive Basin at the base of the Spanish Peaks range.

Lone Mountain Ranch SNOW SPORTS
(406-995-4644; www.lonemountainranch.com; day trail passes adult/teen/child 12yr & under $20/10/free) Tucked into sagebrush meadows, this is one of the country's top Nordic resorts, with 47 miles of groomed cross-country trails, 20 miles of dedicated snowshoe trails and a full-service, high-end lodge. The 'first-timer' package ($60) is a bargain, including group lesson, trail fee and gear rental. Other standouts include prime-rib-dinner sleigh rides and ski and snowshoe tours of Yellowstone's northwest.

East Slope Outdoors SKIING
(406-995-4369; www.eastslopeoutdoors.com; town center) Among the many rental shops around Big Sky, this place tends to have the best prices, with downhill/cross-country ski rentals from $22/12 per day. The attached Orvis store is full of fly-fishing equipment for rent or sale and there are guided fishing trips in summer.

Sleeping & Eating

Inquire about condo, cabin or house rentals in Big Sky through **East West Resorts** (877-527-1817; www.eastwestresorts.com) or **Big Sky Central Reservations** (800-548-4486; www.bigskyresort.com); ski packages are available throughout the winter season.

Hungry Moose Market MARKET $
(www.hungrymoose.com; town center, West Fork Meadows; sandwiches $9; 6:30am-10pm) If a good cabernet and hot, made-to-order panini would spice up the picnic, check out Big Sky's favorite post-ride or pre-ski stop. There are also hot breakfasts, espresso, smoothies, bulk food and groceries leaning toward the organic and natural. Take your order to go or use the wi-fi on the patio.

Information

Big Sky Chamber of Commerce (800-943-4111; www.bigskychamber.com) Visitor center by the turnoff to Big Sky on Hwy 191.

Big Sky to West Yellowstone

After passing the Gallatin Canyon, Hwy 191 briefly enters the far northwestern corner of Yellowstone National Park (there is no entry booth here). Several remote park trails offer quiet day hikes and ambitious multiday backpacking trips across the Gallatin Range to the Mammoth region. **Specimen Creek Trailhead** leads to Gallatin's petrified forest, created 50 million years ago when lava, ash and mudflows swallowed trees and other vegetation. The Bighorn Pass and Fawn Pass Trails beckon with more good hiking and hot-springs soaks.

The road leaves the headwaters of the Gallatin River at Divide Lake. The Madison Range and Taylor Peaks of the Lee Metcalf Wilderness lie to the west.

About 12 miles before reaching West Yellowstone you'll see the turnoff to Hebgen Lake (Hwy 287).

🏃 Activities

Hiking & Backpacking

Hiking trails – all open to mountain biking – head into the mountains along numerous creek drainages from both sides of US 191. Trails are marked on Beartooth Publishing's *Bozeman & Big Sky's Essential Dayhikes* map, available at local sports stores. It also produces a mountain-bike version.

A favorite dining-and-hiking combo is to hike up to the fire lookout at the top of the Cinnamon Creek Trail (6.6 miles return, gaining 2675ft), then have a post-hike beer or dinner at the Cinnamon Lodge, opposite the trailhead across US 191.

The most well-trodden hikes are in the northern half of the valley. The popular 6-mile round-trip hike to Lava Lake offers decent trout fishing. The trailhead is at a tight turnoff on a dangerous curve in Hwy 191. The trail climbs about 1600ft, crossing Cascade Creek several times to meadows and then continues up more switchbacks. Good campsites flank Lava Lake's northeast shore, but fires are banned within 0.5 miles of the lake.

A trailhead on Squaw Creek Rd accesses several trails. The 2.5-mile climb to the top of the Storm Castle Trail (trail 92) offers great views, but the 1900ft climb is unrelenting, with the last quarter-mile, across loose scree, especially strenuous and tricky.

The equally demanding 8-mile round-trip Garnet Lookout Trail (trail 85) leads off in the opposite direction, gaining 2850ft to the top of Garnet Peak, where there is a USFS lookout tower that can be rented as a cabin (bring your own water).

One of the best backpacking destinations is the Spanish Peaks area, accessed at the end of USFS Rd 982, about 22 miles south of Bozeman. Camping is allowed at the trailhead and there's a USFS cabin nearby. Most routes are overnighters or multiday loops. A popular loop leads up Falls Creek to the Jerome Rock Lakes (8 miles) and then back down the South Fork. Longer loops take in the Spanish

Lakes (8.5 miles from the trailhead) or Mirror Lake (7.5 miles) and return via Indian Ridge and Little Hellroaring Creek.

Other Activities

Scenes from the film *A River Runs Through It* were filmed on the beautiful Gallatin River, where local anglers swear that the sweet spot is anywhere you cast a line. You will also find fishing access sites at Greek Creek, Moose Creek Flat and Red Cliff Campgrounds.

The Gallatin Valley also offers the best white-water rafting around Yellowstone – most exciting during June's high water. For inspiration, check out the 'mad envie' of white water visible from the main road after the Cascade Creek bridge.

Geyser Whitewater Expeditions   RAFTING
(☑ 406-995-4989; www.raftmontana.com; US 191)
This well-run operation, 1 mile south of the Big Sky turnoff, offers white-water rafting (half/full day $60/96) and kayaking (half-day $75). Its excellent-value Epic Pass (adult/child $144/134) includes a half-day raft trip, a day-long ropes course and a week of cruiser-bike rentals, paddle boarding and indoor climbing.

Montana Whitewater   RAFTING
(☑ 406-763-4465; www.montanawhitewater.com; Hwy 191 Mile 64, Gallatin Valley; half-/full day $56/92)
Runs white-water trips and scenic floats, as well as a half-day introduction to fly-fishing ($60 per person), zip-lining ($59 to $88) and activity combos. See also www.yellowstone zip.com. It has an office in Gardiner (p149).

Jake's Horses   HORSEBACK RIDING
(☑ 406-995-4630; www.jakeshorses.com; 200 Beaver Creek Rd) Horseback trips, costing about $37 for an hour or $83/140 per half-/full day, plus a steak-dinner ride and horseback trips in Yellowstone National Park. It's 2.5 miles south of Big Sky.

Gallatin Riverguides   FISHING
(☑ 406-995-2290; www.montanaflyfishing.com; Hwy 191) Fly-fishing shop, just south of the Big Sky turnoff, that offers guided fly-fishing trips, equipment rentals and some women-only trips and tuition.

🛏 Sleeping

Camping

Numerous USFS campgrounds (open mid-May to mid-September) snuggle up to the base of the Gallatin Range along US 191. All have potable water and vault toilets.

The USFS operates four sweet but simple little cabins in the valley: Little Bear, Spanish Creek, mountaintop Garnet Mountain and Windy Pass. The last three are accessible by hiking, skiing or snowmobile only. Great value for self-sufficient groups, most cabins are available year-round for $30 per night, sleep four and are equipped with stoves, firewood, cooking supplies and blankets. Contact the **Bozeman District Office** (☑406-522-2520) for information. Cabins and campgrounds can be reserved at www. recreation.gov.

Spire Rock Campground CAMPGROUND $
(sites $11) Secluded and away from the road, 26 miles south of Bozeman, then 2 miles east on Squaw Creek Rd No 1321. Has 17 sites, but no water.

Greek Creek Campground CAMPGROUND $
(sites $14) Doubles as a fishing access site, 31 miles south of Bozeman, with a total of 15 sites on both sides of the highway. Western riverside sites fill early.

Swan Creek Campground CAMPGROUND $
(sites $14) Secluded and popular, with 13 sites backing onto Swan Creek. It's 32 miles south of Bozeman and 1 mile east on paved Rd No 481.

Moose Creek Flat Campground CAMPGROUND $
(sites $14) Riverside with good fishing and 14 sites, but very close to the road. It's 9 miles north of Big Sky.

Red Cliff Campground CAMPGROUND $
(sites with/without electricity $16/14) Ample availability with 63 sites, some with electrical hookups, 48 miles south of Bozeman.

Lodging

Cinnamon Lodge CABIN $
(☑406-995-4253; www.cinnamonlodgeandadventures.com; dm $15, cabins $50-150, cottages $250) This budget roadside establishment attracts a hodgepodge of RVers, families and fly-fishers. The modest but tidy cabins are perhaps the best value in the valley. It's on the Gallatin River 11 miles south of the Big Sky turnoff.

320 Ranch RANCH $$
(☑406-995-4283; www.320ranch.com; Hwy 191 Mile 36; cabins incl breakfast from $180) This historic 19th-century ranch occupies a beautiful swath of the Gallatin, 12 miles south of Big Sky by the Buffalo Horn Creek trailhead. Guests stay in spacious duplex log cabins with access to a fishing pond (casting les-

sons $35), outdoor hot tub and trail rides (activities are open to nonguests). Couples should splash out on the historic McGill cabin ($260).

★**Rainbow Ranch Lodge** RESORT $$$
(☑800-937-4132; www.rainbowranchbigsky.com; r $295-400) Rustic but ultra-chic, Rainbow Ranch offers a select group of pondside or riverside rooms, most with roaring stone fireplaces, balconies and access to the romantic outdoor hot tub. The Pondside Luxury rooms are easily the most stylish. The lodge is 5 miles south of the Big Sky turnoff and 12 miles north of Yellowstone National Park.

Covered Wagon Ranch RANCH $$$
(☑406-995-4237; www.coveredwagonranch.com; 34035 Gallatin Rd; r & board per night per person with/without horseback riding $360/240) Three miles from Yellowstone National Park, near Taylors Fork, this 1925 ranch feels more rugged than some of the rhinestone-cowboy ranches around. With a strong emphasis on riding, a top offer is the small pack trips into Yellowstone.

✖ Eating

★**320 Ranch** AMERICAN $$
(www.320ranch.com; Hwy 191 Mile 36; saloon mains $10-16, mains $24-42; ⊙5:30-9:30pm May-Sep; 🖶) This rustic ranch-house restaurant and saloon is heavy on game, but the real draws are the fun weekly specials. Mondays bring a good-value pig roast ($15), while the popular Wednesday steak chuckwagon dinners start off with a two-hour horseback ride (adult/child $85/75) or 20-minute hay-wagon ride ($55/35). Book the latter in advance.

Cinnamon Lodge MEXICAN $$
(www.cinnamonlodgeandadventures.com; mains $15-28; ⊙dinner) The Western bar and Mexican steakhouse at the Cinnamon Lodge serves excellent food, including good chile rellenos and bacon-wrapped cream-cheese jalapeños, plus there's a nice sun deck to sample Lone Peak brews from Big Sky. Taco Tuesdays also bring $4 margaritas.

Rainbow Ranch Lodge MODERN AMERICAN $$$
(www.rainbowranchbigsky.com; mains $32-60; ⊙dinner Tue-Sun) The gourmet restaurant attached to its upscale lodge is the best in the valley and the place for a blowout. You won't find Montana morels, fiddlehead ferns or responsibly sourced New Zealand alpine tahr anywhere else.

Hebgen & Quake Lakes

If the Yellowstone park boundary had been drawn differently, this broad lake valley surrounded by snowcapped peaks would be mobbed with tourists. As it is, visitors with a mind to meander will find wild and beautiful backcountry and a slew of recreational opportunities with a fraction of Yellowstone's crowds.

Connected to Quake Lake by a scenic stretch of the Madison River, Hebgen Lake easily merits a few lazy days of hiking, angling and boating. Motorboats are permitted, and are available for rent at the **Madison Arm Resort & Marina** (www.madisonarmresort.com) on the south shore and the **Yellowstone Holiday** (www.yellowstoneholiday.com) and **Kirkwood Resort** (www.kirkwoodresort.com) marinas on the north shore.

🏃 Activities

Between the Earthquake Lake Visitor Center and the dam, Beaver Creek Rd turns north off the highway through an area notorious for grizzly sightings, and heads 3 miles to the **Avalanche Lake/Blue Danube Lake trailhead** (trail 222/152). Both Avalanche (11-mile round trip) and Blue Danube (12.5-mile round trip) Lakes make excellent dayhike destinations from July onward; the trail splits 4.5 miles from the trailhead.

Further along Beaver Creek the road finishes at Potamogeton Park, the trailhead for an excellent midsummer overnight trip up Sentinel Creek to the dozen-or-so alpine lakes of the **Hilgard Basin** (trail 202/201, 7 miles, 2700ft elevation gain) in the Lee Metcalf Wilderness.

Along the western shore of Hebgen Lake, a couple of miles past Spring Creek Campground, is the trailhead for Watkins Creek and the 10-mile round-trip day or overnight hike (gaining 1700ft) to **Coffin Lakes** (trail 215/209).

The useful 1:63,360 USFS *Lee Metcalf Wilderness & West Yellowstone Vicinity* map marks these and many other trails, as does Beartooth Publishing's *Bozeman & Big Sky's Essential Dayhikes* map.

🛏 Sleeping & Eating

On the southwest side of Hebgen Lake, three remote USFS campgrounds serve boaters and anglers. Four miles down a tarmac road, **Lonesomehurst** (sites with/without electricity $24/16; ☉ mid-May–end Sep) is the most accessible, with lovely lake views, potable water and a boat ramp. Another 2 and 6 miles, respectively, down a dirt road that turns to rough washboard, are lakeshore Cherry Creek and Spring Creek (no fee), both primitive sites with pit toilets but no drinking water and reputations as places for teenagers to party. Reach them by turning north off Hwy 20 about halfway between Targhee Pass and West Yellowstone on Denny Creek Rd (USFS Rd 176).

On the southeast shore of the lake is **Rainbow Point Campground** (sites with/without electricity $22/16; ☉ mid-May–end Sep), 10 miles from West Yellowstone. Rainbow Point and Lonesomehurst are reservable at www.recreation.gov.

Closer to Quake Lake are two scenic concession-run USFS campgrounds: **Cabin Creek** (sites $14; ☉ mid-May–mid-Sep), 23 miles from West Yellowstone, and the larger, nicer and nearby **Beaver Creek** (sites $14; ☉ late May–late Sep), near some scenic beaver ponds. Both are reservable at www.recreation.gov. See also www.hebgenbasincampgrounds.com.

Call the **Hebgen Lake Ranger District** (☏ 406-823-6961) in West Yellowstone for information on all of these.

Beaver Creek Cabin   CABIN $
(www.recreation.gov; cabins $30; ☉ year-round) A superb base for hiking north of Hebgen Lake, accessible by car in summer, this simple forestry cabin offers bunk beds sleeping four, a stove, utensils, firewood and an ax.

Campfire Lodge Resort   CABIN $
(☏ 406-646-7258; www.campfirelodgwestyellowstone.com; tent sites $23, RV sites $30-40, cabins $85-220; ☉ Jun-Sep) Just across from Cabin Creek Campground, near Quake Lake, the riverside cabins here sleep up to seven, and there are RV and tent sites, a fly shop and showers. The popular riverside cafe (7am to 2pm) is worth a visit for breakfast or lunch.

Parade Rest Ranch   CABIN $$$
(☏ 800-753-5934; www.paraderestranch.com; 7979 Grayling Creek Rd; per adult/child $273/217; ☉ mid-May–Sep) Ten miles from West Yellowstone, northeast of Hebgen Lake, this historic 1935 ranch offers 15 cabins and plenty of activities. Daily rates include lodging, meals, horseback riding and fly-fishing on Graying Creek. There's a three-night minimum, but discounts of 40% in spring and fall.

WORTH A TRIP

QUAKE LAKE: THE NIGHT THE MOUNTAINS MOVED

Just before midnight on August 17, 1959, an earthquake measuring 7.5 on the Richter scale ripped the landscape of the Upper Madison Valley. As two huge fault blocks tilted and dropped, a massive 80-million-ton landslide pulverized two campgrounds, before rising halfway up the opposite valley wall.

The slip caused Hebgen Lake's north shore to drop 18ft, flooding lakeshore houses and lodges. Gaps opened up in highways, and cars crashed into the gaping holes in classic disaster-movie style.

Hurricane-force winds caused by the slide then rushed down the valley, tearing off campers' clothes from their bodies and creating a huge wave on the lake. Mini-tsunamis called seiches sloshed up and down the lake for the next 12 hours, pouring over the Hebgen Lake Dam, which, amazingly, held firm.

The slide blocked the Madison River, and the waters of newborn Quake Lake soon started to fill, as engineers worked around the clock to cut a spillway and avoid a second catastrophic flood. In a final fanfare, several hundred of Yellowstone's thermal features simultaneously erupted.

After the dust settled, it was discovered that 28 people had been killed, mostly in the Rock Creek campsite. Nineteen bodies were never found, presumably entombed under the slide. The quake had been felt in California, and water tables were affected as far away as Hawaii.

Viewing the Site

The best way these days to get to grips with the enormity of the quake, the largest ever to hit the Rockies, is to visit the **Earthquake Lake Visitor Center** (Quake Lake visitor center; ☑ 406-682-7620; ⊗ 10am-6pm Memorial Day-Labor Day) **FREE**, atop the landslide area at the end of Quake Lake. Drive or hike up the interpretive trails for a vista of the dramatic slide area and a memorial boulder inscribed with the names of the 28 campers killed in the slide. A dock at the eastern end of Quake Lake allows boaters to glide past the surreal submerged treetops. The following sites, listed west–east, can be seen on the drive back to West Yellowstone:

Refuge Point This is where many of the quake survivors were rescued. In summer rangers often lead a 1.5-mile guided walk from here for an overview of Ghost Village; call the visitor center to check. The ski loop here makes for a great 2.3-mile hike in summer, but the trail is faint so you need to keep a close eye on the blue diamond tree markers.

Ghost Village A half-dozen cabins of the former Halford's Camp lie stranded in the plain here, deposited by the rising waters of the new lake. To get here turn off the highway toward Campfire Lodge and then branch right down a dirt road. The cabins are on the other side of the river.

Cabin Creek Scarp Area Highlights a 21ft-tall scarp that opened up along the Hebgen Lake fault line. One campsite actually straddled the fault, with the picnic table left above the scarp and the fire ring 21ft below.

The Lake that Tilted Ten miles further east along Hwy 287, a road leads off to a parking area and a short trail to Hebgen Lake, where you can see three partly submerged cabins destroyed by the slide.

Happy Hour Bar & Restaurant AMERICAN **$$** (www.happyhourbar.com; Mile 4, Hwy 287; meals $8-18; ⊗ noon-midnight Wed-Sat, from 4pm Mon & Tue, from 9:30am Sun) It's hard to think of a better end to the day than grabbing a basket of shrimp and watching the sun sink over Hebgen Lake from the boat-shaped deck. Drawing locals, fly-fishers, cyclists and campers, it's a colorful slice of rural Montana, down to the collection of eyebrow-raising boob shots on the walls. Wednesday is crab night.

West Yellowstone

☑ 406 / POP 1500 / ELEV 6600FT

Seated a scant quarter-mile from Yellowstone National Park, the old rail terminus of West Yellowstone is the most popular gateway to Yellowstone. It's tiny as towns go, but offers its own brand of diversity, from endless variations on the burger joint and souvenir shop to live wolves and grizzlies, RV villages, taxidermy clinics and snowmobile shops. Stop for a quality bison burger, double licks of tart huckleberry ice cream and enough diversions to fill a day's sightseeing.

West Yellowstone is the regional hub for snowmobiling, as well as a launch pad for snowcoach tours into the park. Most locals battled the National Park Service's proposed ban on snowmobiling in Yellowstone National Park, and some are still not happy with the limits imposed. Outside the park, unrestricted snowmobiling continues and is an important winter business.

'West' bustles with park traffic from June to September, but even then the surrounding wilderness remains lightly used. Ride a bike, paddle a canoe, fly-fish or click on skis – even at the height of tourist season, you can have the waterways, lakes and trails mostly to yourself.

History

In the early 1900s the Union Pacific Railroad built a rail line to the western edge of the park, then a fledgling community called Riverside. In 1908 Eagle's General Store (still on Yellowstone Ave today) was established, joined by the Madison Hotel in 1912. The frontier-style town, soon rechristened Yellowstone, became a hub of activity fueled by the railroad, until the rise of automobile travel put the line out of business in 1960. The entrepreneurial spirit ruled even during prohibition, when the town exported potent 'Yellowstone Spring Water.'

In 1920 the community changed its name to West Yellowstone after pressure from Yellowstone's other gateway towns.

◉ Sights

Ranger talks are given daily at 2pm at either the Yellowstone Historic Center or the Grizzly & Wolf Discovery Center. There are also two weekly ranger-led slide shows at 7pm, and a daily 9am wildlife talk at the Chamber of Commerce Visitor Center.

Grizzly & Wolf Discovery Center ZOO
(406-646-7001; www.grizzlydiscoveryctr.org; 201 S Canyon; adult/child 5-12yr $11.50/6.50; 8:30am-8:30pm, closes earlier in winter;) Offering an afterlife to 'pest' grizzlies facing ex-

termination, this nonprofit center grants a chance to see captive wolves and bears if you failed to see any in the park. The indoor bear exhibit is good, and there is an information wall with clippings of recent bear encounters, as well as the latest wolf-pack locations. The daily programs on hiking safely in bear country and using bear spray are excellent primers for the park.

Yellowstone Historic Center MUSEUM
(406-646-1100; www.yellowstonehistoriccenter. org; 104 Yellowstone Ave; adult/child $6/3; 9am-9pm mid-May–early Oct) Housed in the 1909 Union Pacific depot, this small museum explores early stagecoach and rail travel. Look for the highly unstable-looking early snowmobile with a propeller and three skis parked outside. It closes earlier in May and September.

Oregon Short Line Railway Car HISTORIC SITE
FREE This wonderfully preserved 1903 Pullman car, once used by railroad executives, perfectly sums up the golden age of Western travel. Decked out in velvet, gas lamps and even stained glass, it sits beside the Branch restaurant at the Holiday Inn.

Eagle's Store HISTORIC BUILDING
(406-646-9300; www.eagles-store.com; 3 Canyon St) Grab an old-fashioned soda at the antique 1910 fountain while stocking up on a motley collection of fishing supplies and cowboy hats at this century-old stalwart.

🏃 Activities

West Yellowstone hosts a range of cultural and sporting events, from evening rodeo (www.yellowstonerodeo.com; adult/child from $12/6; mid-Jun–Aug) and August's mountain-man rendezvous to the Spam Cup, a series of ski races in which the lucky winner receives a free can of preserved-pork products.

Summer

Both the Rendezvous and Riverside trail systems offer great mountain biking and trail running from mid-June to mid-October.

West Yellowstone has some of the best fishing shops in the Rockies for information, equipment, rentals and guides.

Arrick's Fly Shop FISHING
(406-646-7290; www.arricks.com; 37 Canyon St) Gear, reports and trips.

Bud Lilly's Trout Shop FISHING

(☎ 406-646-7801; www.budlillys.com; 39 Madison Ave) Rents fishing equipment and offers one-day float and walk trips (from $245 per person in a group of two).

Jacklins Fly Shop FISHING

(☎ 406-646-7336; www.jacklinsflyshop.com; 105 Yellowstone Ave) Offers good fishing reports and a free weekly casting clinic on Sundays at 7:30pm.

Free Heel & Wheel ADVENTURE SPORTS

(☎ 406-646-7744; www.freeheelandwheel.com; 33 Yellowstone Ave; ☺9am-6pm Mon-Sat, to 5pm Sun) The place for maps, gear and advice on cycling and skiing conditions. In addition to renting mountain bikes ($35 per day), skis and snowshoes ($20), it offers touring and skate-ski lessons and organizes free women's rides.

Parade Rest Ranch HORSEBACK RIDING

(☎ 406-646-7217; www.paraderestranch.com; 1279 Grayling Rd) Nine miles from West Yellowstone, who this dude ranch offers horseback rides from one to four hours ($55 to $125 per person, Monday to Saturday), including sunset rides and corral rides for kids under seven. There are also fun Western cookouts on a section of the old Bannock Trail overlooking Hebgen Lake on Monday and Friday evenings (adult/child $59/25).

Old Faithful Cycle Tour CYCLING

(www.cycleyellowstone.com; entry $65) The chamber of commerce sponsors this fall cycle tour to Old Faithful, with part of the proceeds going to charity. The fully supported trips (with a van and repair assistance) are a lot of fun and are geared toward a range of abilities.

Yellowstone Aerial
Adventures ADVENTURE SPORTS

(☎ 406-646-5171; www.yellowstoneparkzipline.com; 105 S Faithful St; adult/child under 12yr $49/45, full day $79; ☺9am-8pm Jun-Sep) This high ropes course is a hit with adventurous kids, who

West Yellowstone

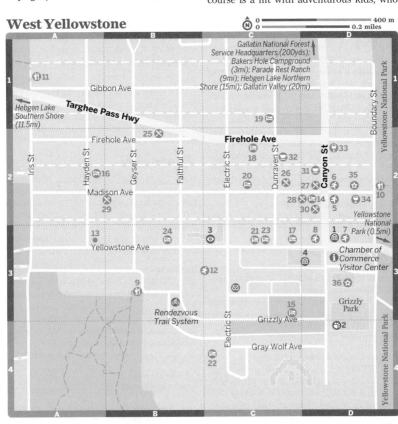

inch across rope bridges and throw themselves down zip lines, while their parents look on nervously. Kids under 12 can do some of the elements, while even adults will struggle with the upper level.

Winter

Many of the hotels rent snowmobiles and offer good-value winter lodging and rental packages. Guided snowmobile day tours to the park cost around $200 per person. Several agencies rent snowmobiles for outside the park for $120 to $160 per day, excluding clothing, including **Rendezvous Snowmobile Rentals** (☑406-646-9564; www.yellowstone vacations.com; 415 Yellowstone Ave) and **Two Top Snowmobile Rentals** (☑800-522-7802; www.twotopsnowmobile.com; 645 Gibbon Ave).

Rangers lead free snowshoe walks along Riverside Trails from West Yellowstone's Chamber of Commerce Visitor Center (2pm weekends).

Rendezvous Ski Trails　　　　　SKIING
(www.rendezvousskitrails.com; day/season pass $8/40; ⊙Dec-Mar) In November this world-class network of trails becomes the training ground for US Olympic cross-country ski teams, with 30 miles of groomed Nordic skiing and skating trails. Grooming goes through March, when the Rendezvous Marathon Ski Race draws hundreds of skiers.

There are also special kids' loops. For more information, visit Free Heel & Wheel.

Riverside Trails　　　　　SKIING
This small network of trails follows an old stagecoach road for 1.5 miles to emerge on Yellowstone National Park service roads and trails alongside the Madison River. It's also a good short summer mountain-bike ride.

Hellroaring Ski Adventures　　　SKIING
(☑406-570-4025; www.skihellroaring.com) Powder hounds keen to get off the grid should try the Centennial Mountains, 25 miles from West Yellowstone. From $200 per person (in a group of up to four), you get a shuttle, guide, meals, avalanche-rescue equipment, climbing skins, hut accommodations and excellent backcountry terrain. Hut rental, for a maximum of six experienced skiers, costs $250 per night.

☞ Tours

Buffalo Bus Touring Company　BUS TOUR
(☑800-426-7669; www.yellowstonevacations.com; 415 Yellowstone Ave; tour adult/child $75/65) Summertime tours pick up from local campgrounds and motels for a full day of the park's upper or lower loops. In winter it also runs full-day guided snowcoach tours to Old Faithful (adult/child $114/94) or Canyon

West Yellowstone

($124/104) in the park, which you can use as ski drops.

Yellowstone Alpen Guides TOUR
(☎800-858-3502; www.yellowstoneguides.com; 555 Yellowstone Ave; adult/child $125/115) Runs 10-person snowcoach tours to Old Faithful, departing daily from mid-December through mid-March. Guided or independent skiing, snowshoeing and kayaking options on Hebgen Lake are also available, as are summer van tours of the park and multiday tours.

🛏 Sleeping

Considering the number of motel signs, there is precious little variety in accommodations. Book well in advance and expect hefty discounts October to May.

Camping

Tent camping in town means cramming between rows of powered-up RVs. For more breathing space, don't forget the national forest campsites on Hebgen Lake (p159).

Bakers Hole Campground CAMPGROUND $
(sites with/without electricity $22/16; ⊙mid-May–end Sep) The nearest forestry service campground has 73 pleasant sites on the banks of the meandering Madison River, just 3 miles north of West Yellowstone. There are no reservations and it fills up most summer afternoons.

Yellowstone Grizzly RV Park RV PARK $
(☎406-646-4466; www.grizzlyrv.com; 210 S Electric St; RV sites $58-68, cabins $99-145; ⊙end May–mid-Oct; 🛜) This RV metropolis is pricey but professional and the friendly service includes help with tours and rentals. Facilities include showers, laundry, cable TV and a recreation room.

Lodging

Lazy G Motel MOTEL $
(☎406-646-7586; www.lazygmotel.com; 123 Hayden St; r $92-109, ste $131; 🛜) Nothing flash here, but good-value motel rooms with fridges, some with kitchenettes, in a quiet part of town. No pets.

Madison Hotel HOSTEL $
(☎406-646-7745; www.madisonhotelmotel.com; 139 Yellowstone Ave; dm $42, r $99-129, without bathroom $69-79; ⊙late May–mid-Oct; @🛜) It's hard to picture President Hardy or Clark Gable snuggled in one of the basic timber rooms here, but it's this sense of history that might just draw you to this creaky 1912

hostel. Rooms are simple and clean but with thin walls and most share a bathroom. Nonguests are free to poke around unoccupied rooms before 6pm.

Alpine Motel HOTEL $$
(☎406-646-7544; www.alpinemotelwestyellowstone.com; 120 Madison Ave; r $90-115, ste $140-175; ⊙mid-May–Oct; 🛜) The friendly and well-tended Alpine has a rather cramped courtyard, but remains one of the best-value places in town. The suites come with a kitchen and can sleep up to six.

One Horse Motel MOTEL $$
(☎406-646-7677; www.onehorsemotel.com; 216 Dunraven St; s $79, d $119-129; ⊙May-Sep; 🛜) Friendly, fresh and family-run. The singles are small.

Moose Creek Cabins CABIN $$
(☎406-646-9646; www.moosecreekinn.com; 220 Firehole Ave; r $140-210; ⊙Apr-Oct; 🛜) This friendly mix of 1950s-era wooden cabins and modern rooms is a good choice. Reception is in the nearby motel with the same name.

Explorer Cabins CABIN $$$
(☎406-646-7075; www.visityellowstonepark.com; 201 Grizzly Ave; r $285-399; 🛜🏊🛏🐾) If you fancy a Yellowstone cabin vibe, but can't imagine life without a dishwasher, this group of 50 luxury suburban suites comes with a fireplace, porch and even a DIY s'more kit, as well as a kitchen (and, yes, a dishwasher).

Three Bear Lodge LODGE $$$
(☎800-646-7353; www.threebearlodge.com; 217 Yellowstone Ave; main lodge d $239-299, motel d $179-209; 🛜🏊🐾) Rebuilt with reclaimed original wood after a 2008 fire, this friendly lodge once again offers spacious, stylish hotel rooms, as well as a cheaper motel option. Kids will go nuts over the themed 'Goldilocks and the Three Bears' suite ($309).

Stage Coach Inn HOTEL $$$
(☎800-842-2882; www.yellowstoneinn.com; 209 Madison Ave; r $189-289; 🛜🏊) A longtime hub, the Stage Coach has eye-catching stuffed wildlife in the lobby, a sauna and an indoor pool. Deluxe rooms are bigger and fresher than the historic rooms. Winter rates drop as low as $60.

🍴 Eating

Pick up groceries at the **Food Roundup** (cnr Madison Ave & Dunraven St; ⊙7am-9pm) supermarket.

Running Bear Pancake House BREAKFAST $
(cnr Madison Ave & Hayden St; mains $8-11; ⊙6am-
1:30pm; 🍴) Serves up small and large stacks,
eggs and sausage links – a family favorite.

Ernie's SANDWICHES $
(www.erniesbakery.com; 406 Hwy 20; sandwiches
$10-12; ⊙7am-2pm; 🐾) An unpretentious
sandwich maker on the highway between
Geyser and Hayden Sts, Ernie's is a popular local stalwart and does good breakfasts,
though things get busy at rush hour.

★Serenity Bistro MODERN AMERICAN $$
(☑406-646-7660; www.serenitybistro.com; 38
N Canyon St; mains $17-26; ⊙5-10pm mid-Apr–Nov)
An island of modern upscale cuisine in a sea
of chicken-fried steak and gravy, sophisticat-
ed Serenity is the place to turn to for a pear-
and-walnut salad or orange Thai curry. The
dining area is small and intimate so reserve a
table, either inside or on the back patio.

**Madison
Crossing Lounge** MODERN AMERICAN $$
(☑406-646-7621; www.madisoncrossinglounge.
com; 121 Madison Ave; mains $14-24; ⊙5-10pm)
West Yellowstone's 1918 school building
houses this classy restaurant and bar. Stand-
out dishes include the mussels and chorizo,
bison steak salad and blueberry white chocolate pudding, alongside the standard trout
and burgers.

Old Town Café AMERICAN $$
(128 Madison Ave; dinner mains $14-20; ⊙7am-
10pm) Grab a counter stool or a booth at this
laid-back local diner-bar and feast on au-
thentic down-home beef and trout dinners,
or a breakfast of hotcakes, bacon and syrup.

Drinking

For a strong shot of espresso, hit **Morning
Glory** (129 Dunraven St; ⊙7am-3pm Fri-Wed) cof-
fee roasters, or settle into the sofa of Mocha
Mamas at Free Heel & Wheel (p162) and get
the lowdown on local ski or bike trails.

Slippery Otter Pub PUB
(139 N Canyon St; ⊙11:30am-11pm) Beer snobs
will want to head here for the region's wid-
est selection of craft beers on tap (over 20).
Settle in with a selection of five 6oz tasters
for $12.50.

Wild West Saloon BAR
(www.wildwestpizza.com; 14 Madison Ave; ⊙10am-
2am) Live honky-tonk rock packs this divey

but fun place on summer weekends, plus
you can order in the best pies in town from
the attached pizzeria (pizzas $12).

Book Peddler CAFE
(106 Canyon St; ⊙8am-10pm summer) A good
selection of books and fine espresso, with
some outdoor seats.

☆ Entertainment

Playmill Theater THEATER
(☑406-646-7757; www.playmill.com; 29 Madi-
son Ave; tickets $19.50-24; ⊙Mon-Sat Memorial
Day-Labor Day; 🍴) Churning out light musi-
cals, melodramas and comedies for 40 years,
the Playmill is a local institution. Reserve
your tickets in advance.

Yellowstone Giant Screen Theater CINEMA
(☑406-646-4100; www.yellowstonegiantscreen.
com; 101 S Canyon St; adult/child $9/6.50; ⊙hour-
ly showings 9am-9pm May-Sep, 1-9pm Oct-Apr; 🍴)
If it's raining head indoors for *Yellowstone,
Lewis & Clark* and other films on a screen
six stories high.

ℹ Information

There are slightly rundown public showers at
Canyon Street Laundry (312 Canyon St, 7am to
9pm). Six-minute showers cost $4.50.
Chamber of Commerce Visitor Center
(☑406-646-7701; www.westyellowstonecham-
ber.com; Canyon St; ⊙8am-8pm; 🐾) Friendly
traveler assistance, convenient parking and
free wi-fi. There's also a ranger-staffed park
desk and backcountry office. See also www.
destinationyellowstone.com.
**Gallatin National Forest Service Headquar-
ters** (☑406-823-6961; www.fs.fed.us/r1/
gallatin; Canyon St; ⊙8:30am-noon & 1-4:30pm
Mon-Fri) Two blocks north of Firehole Ave, for
information on Hebgen Lake campgrounds and
trails.

ℹ Getting There & Away

Budget (☑406-646-7882; www.budget-yellow
stone.com; 131 Dunraven St) and **Big Sky Car
Rentals** (☑800-426-7669; www.westyellow
stonecarrental.com; 415 Yellowstone Ave) offer
car rentals from $50 a day.
Karst Stage (☑406-556-3540; www.karst
stage.com) runs buses daily, December to
April, from Bozeman airport to Big Sky ($51,
one hour) and West Yellowstone (around
$63.50, two hours). Summer service is by
charter only.

Grand Teton National Park

Why Go?

Rough-cut summits rising sharply from a lush valley floor, the Tetons are a sight to behold. Simply put, this is sublime and crazy terrain, crowned by the dagger-edged Grand (13,770ft), a giant in the history of American mountaineering. And there's much more to explore here, from sagebrush flats and wildflower meadows to the hundreds of alpine lakes and fragrant forests trodden by bear, moose, grouse and marmot.

While the park is dwarfed by neighboring Yellowstone, it can offer visitors a more immediate intimacy with the landscape and more varied and scenic hiking. Climbers, boaters, anglers and other outdoor enthusiasts find plenty to do, and lovers of alpine scenery find that the Tetons' visual impact far exceeds that of Yellowstone's. Whichever way you wander, these rock spires exercise a magnetic attraction on your gaze.

Best Hikes

➡ Leigh & Bearpaw
Lakes (p173)

➡ Phelps Lake (p180)

➡ Taggart & Bradley Lakes
(p175)

➡ Teton Crest Trail (p183)

➡ Table Mountain (p176)

Best Places to Stay

➡ Jenny Lake Lodge (p204)

➡ Triangle X Ranch (p203)

➡ Climbers' Ranch (p204)

➡ Jackson Lake Lodge (p203)

➡ Gros Ventre Campground
(p204)

Road Distances (miles)

	Jackson	Moose	Colter Bay (GTNP)	Grand Targhee Resort (ID)
Moose	15			
Colter Bay (GTNP)	40	30		
Grand Targhee Resort (ID)	45	55	85	
Old Faithful (Yellowstone)	100	85	60	130

Note: Distances are approximate

Entrances

The park begins 4.5 miles north of Jackson. There are three entrance stations. The closest to Jackson is the South Entrance at Moose on Teton Park Rd, west of Moose Junction. From Teton Village, the Southwest Entrance is a mile or so north via the Moose–Wilson Rd. If driving south from Yellowstone, take the North Entrance, 3 miles inside the park on US 89/191/287 north of Moran Junction.

In winter the 15-mile section between Taggart Lake Trailhead and Signal Mountain Lodge is closed to vehicles. For seasonal road closures, consult with the park.

DON'T MISS

Don't miss sunrise from the deck of a canoe. Leigh Lake, our favorite, requires some effort but it's well worth a short haul in first light to see Mt Moran hulking in these still, clear waters. More visitors arrive with each hour of the day but this one is yours.

First, paddle String Lake, entering just off the trailhead. After a short canoe portage you're on Leigh. Either come early with headlamps or reserve a paddle-in backcountry campsite to make a night of it – though it's only a short trip, the off-trail setting feels marvelously rugged and wild. Bring binoculars to spot wildlife.

Canoes can be rented from Adventure Sports (p191) in Moose, along with life jackets and accessories. Acquire canoe and backcountry permits (both are required) at Craig Thomas Discovery & Visitor Center (p207).

When You Arrive

➡ To drive on Teton Park Rd, park entrance permits are required. They are valid for seven days for entry into both Grand Teton and Yellowstone National Parks; the fee is $30 per vehicle, $25 per motorcyclist and $15 for cyclists or hikers on foot. Winter day use has a lower fee, currently under review. An annual pass costs $60.

➡ Keep your receipt to be able to reenter the park if you leave.

➡ There is no charge to transit the park on Hwy 26/89/191 from Jackson to Moran and out the East Entrance to the Togwotee Pass. This area encompasses the access road to Jackson Hole Airport.

➡ Visitors receive a free orientation map and copy of the park newspaper, *Grand Teton Guide,* which details ranger-led activities, road closures and park news.

➡ Bring bear spray and know how to use it. It's sold at park gift shops and outdoor stores.

PARK POLICIES & REGULATIONS

Backcountry permits are required for all overnight backcountry trips in Grand Teton.

Permits are required for boating and fishing.

Fast Facts

➡ Area: 484 sq miles

➡ Highest elevation: 13,770ft

➡ Lowest elevation: 6109ft

Reservations

Lodging should be reserved as far in advance as possible, especially for peak-season dates. Grand Teton Lodge Company accepts reservations for the following season starting November 1. Most campgrounds are first-come, first-served but some allow a limited number of reservations. See websites for details.

➡ Grand Teton Lodge Company (www.gltc.com)

➡ Spur Ranch Log Cabins (www.dornans.com)

➡ Signal Mountain Lodge (www.signalmountainlodge.com)

➡ Flagg Ranch Company (www.gtlc.com/headwaters-lodge.aspx)

Resources

➡ **National Park Service** (www.nps/grte) Official park website.

➡ **Official park blog** (www.gtnpnews.blogspot.com) With current updates.

➡ **Official online ranger station** (www.tetonclimbing.blogspot.com)

GRAND TETON NATIONAL PARK

Grand Teton National Park

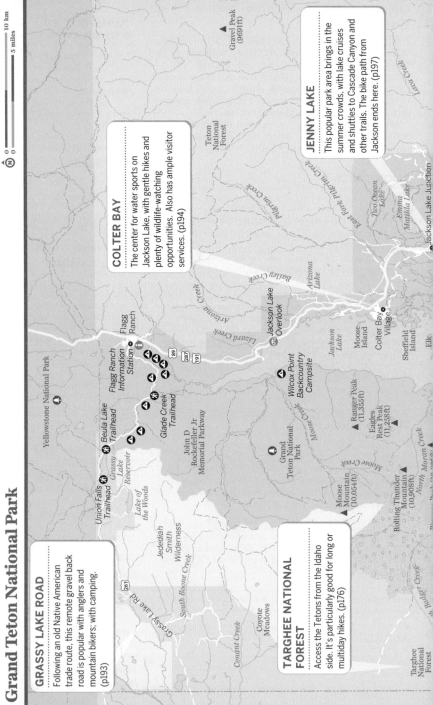

GRASSY LAKE ROAD

Following an old Native American trade route, this remote gravel back road is popular with anglers and mountain bikers; with camping. (p193)

COLTER BAY

The center for water sports on Jackson Lake, with gentle hikes and plenty of wildlife-watching opportunities. Also has ample visitor services. (p194)

JENNY LAKE

This popular park area brings in the summer crowds, with lake cruises and shuttles to Cascade Canyon and other trails. The bike path from Jackson ends here. (p197)

TARGHEE NATIONAL FOREST

Access the Tetons from the Idaho side. It's particularly good for long or multiday hikes. (p176)

Yellowstone National Park

Union Falls Trailhead

Grassy Lake Reservoir

Beula Lake Trailhead

Flagg Ranch

Flagg Ranch Information Station

Glade Creek Trailhead

Lake of the Woods

Jedediah Smith Wilderness

South Boone Creek

Comant Creek

Coyote Meadows

Grassy Lake Rd

John D Rockefeller Jr Memorial Parkway

Lizard Creek

Arizona Creek

Bailey Creek

Arizona Lake

Jackson Lake Overlook

Wilcox Point Backcountry Campsite

Grand Teton National Park

Moose Creek

Ranger Peak (11,355ft)

Eagles Rest Peak (11,258ft)

Jackson Lake

Moose Island

Colter Bay Village

Sheffield Island

Elk I

Moose Creek

Moose Mountain (10,054ft)

Rolling Thunder Mountain (10,908ft)

North Moran Creek

Teton National Forest

Pilgrim Creek

East Fork Pilgrim Creek

Two Ocean Lake

Emma Matilda Lake

Jackson Lake Junction

Lava Creek

Gravel Peak (9691ft)

Targhee National Forest

Badger Creek

10 km
5 miles

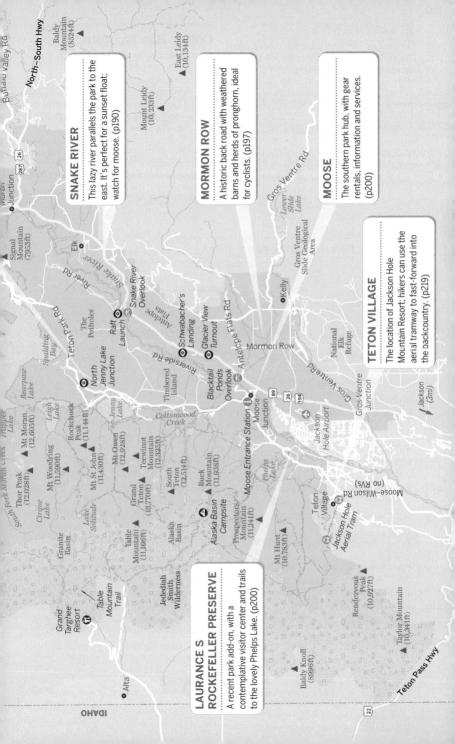

SNAKE RIVER

This lazy river parallels the park to the east. It's perfect for a sunset float; watch for moose. (p190)

MORMON ROW

A historic back road with weathered barns and herds of pronghorn, ideal for cyclists. (p197)

MOOSE

The southern park hub, with gear rentals, information and services. (p200)

TETON VILLAGE

The location of Jackson Hole Mountain Resort; hikers can use the aerial tramway to fast-forward into the backcountry. (p219)

LAURANCE S ROCKEFELLER PRESERVE

A recent park add-on, with a contemplative visitor center and trails to the lovely Phelps Lake. (p200)

Buffalo Valley Rd

North–South Hwy

Baldy Mountain (8524ft) ▲

East Leidy (10,134ft) ▲

Mount Leidy (10,233ft) ▲

Moran Junction

287 26

Signal Mountain (7953ft)

Elk

River Rd

Snake River

The Potholes

Spalding Bay

Teton Park Rd

Snake River Overlook

Antelope Flats

Raft Launch

Schwabacher's Landing

Glacier View Turnout

Mormon Row

Gros Ventre Rd

Lower Slide Lake

Gros Ventre Slide Geological Area

Kelly

National Elk Refuge

Bearpaw Lake

Leigh Lake

Trapper Lake

South Fork Moran Creek

Thor Peak (12,028ft) ▲

Mt Moran (12,605ft) ▲

Mt Woodring (11,590ft) ▲

Rockchuck Peak (11,144ft) ▲

North Jenny Lake Junction

Jenny Lake

Riverside Rd

Timbered Island

Blacktail Ponds Overlook

Cottonwood Creek

Antelope Flats Rd

Moose Junction

89 26 191

Jackson Hole Airport

Gros Ventre Rd

Gros Ventre Junction

Jackson (3mi)

Cirque Lake

Lake Solitude

Mt St John (11,430ft) ▲

Mt Owen (12,928ft) ▲

Teewinot Mountain (12,325ft) ▲

South Teton (12,514ft) ▲

Buck Mountain (11,938ft) ▲

Moose Entrance Station

Moose

Phelps Lake

Moose-Wilson Rd (no RVs)

Granite Basin

Table Mountain (11,106ft) ▲

Grand Teton (13,770ft) ▲

Alaska Basin

Alaska Basin Campsite

Prospectors Mountain (11,241ft) ▲

Jedediah Smith Wilderness

Teton Village

Jackson Hole Aerial Tram

Mt Hunt (10,783ft) ▲

Table Mountain Trail

Grand Targhee Resort

Rendezvous Peak (10,927ft) ▲

Baldy Knoll (8906ft) ▲

Taylor Mountain (10,341ft) ▲

Teton Pass Hwy

Alta

IDAHO

22

🏃 DAY HIKES

The Tetons' extreme verticality means that flat and easy rambles are few. The rating standard of the hikes reflects the difficulty. Most easy-to-moderate day hikes are suitable for families and most walkers. Hikers should adjust the distance they walk to their satisfaction.

Paved **wheelchair-accessible trails** include the Jenny Lake shoreline, String Lake shoreline, Colter Bay Lakeshore Trail and the southern edge of Jackson Lake Dam.

Colter Bay Region

Birds, animals and wildflowers all feature in this popular section of the park.

A nice evening or early-morning stroll is the 45-minute Colter Bay Lakeshore Trail, which traces a figure eight across a causeway onto a small island. Take the forest trail that dips onto the beach or just walk along the shore. The trail starts on a paved road beside Colter Bay Marina, or you can access it from the amphitheater next to the visitor center. Finish the hike at the amphitheater by 7pm or 9pm to catch the evening ranger talk.

GRAND TETON NATIONAL PARK HIKES

NAME	REGION	DESCRIPTION
Taggart & Bradley Lakes (p175)	Central Tetons	Glacial lakes set in wildflower meadows and pine forest
Leigh & Bearpaw Lakes (p173)	Central Tetons	A fun, flat, family outing to crystal-clear swimming holes
Paintbrush Divide (p182)	Central Tetons	This pretty grind lifts you into the alpine scenery
Lake Solitude (p173)	Central Tetons	This ultra-popular grind scales to a mountain lake via a gradual climb
Table Mountain (p176)	Central Tetons	Wildflowers and high-alpine scenery without the crowds
Devil's Staircase to Alaska Basin (p177)	Central Tetons	Long day loop with stunning views
Surprise & Amphitheater Lakes (p174)	Central Tetons	A classic leg-burner with valley views
Avalanche Canyon & Lake Taminah (p176)	Central Tetons	This challenging hike rewards with lake swims and killer views
Garnet Canyon (p175)	Central Tetons	The climbers' route to the Grand
Teton Crest (p183)	Central Tetons	The epic hike of Grand Teton National Park
Two Ocean Lake & Grand View Point (p172)	Colter Bay Region	Lush forest, wildflowers and good bird-watching
Hermitage Point (p171)	Colter Bay Region	A wild and windswept point facing the multifanged Mt Moran
Phelps Lake (p180)	Moose-Wilson Rd	A lovely and flat forested amble around a beautiful lake
Death Canyon (p180)	Moose-Wilson Rd	An ethereal river valley flanked by granite climbing walls

 Wildlife-Watching   View   Great for Families Waterfalls   Restrooms

🚶 Hermitage Point

Duration 4 hours (shorter loop 1¾ hours)

Distance 9.2 miles (shorter loop 3 miles)

Difficulty Easy–moderate

Elevation Change Negligible

Start/Finish Hermitage Point Trailhead

Nearest Town/Junction Colter Bay Village

Summary A wild and windswept point with outstanding views of the multifanged Mt Moran.

From the Colter Bay Visitor Center follow the parking lot to the southern end. At first the trail's signage may seem a little unclear, but throughout the hike the junctions are well marked. The trail itself starts by a sign that reads 'Foot Trail Only, No Road.' It follows a former road for less than 10 minutes, turns right, and then turns right again to climb up to the Jackson Lake Overlook.

The trail descends and passes along the left (eastern) side of lily-filled Heron Pond, where you can look for moose, trumpeter swans and cranes. It branches right then right again for 2.2 miles to the cairn marking Hermitage Point (4.4 miles, 1¾ hours).

This lesser-hiked leg is densely forested and without views. Be sure to announce

GRAND TETON NATIONAL PARK DAY HIKES

DIFFICULTY	DURATION	ROUND-TRIP DISTANCE	ELEVATION CHANGE	FEATURES	FACILITIES
easy-moderate	3hr	5.9 miles	560ft		
easy-moderate	3½hr	7.4 miles	negligible		
moderate	2-3 days	17.8 miles	3775ft		
moderate-difficult	6-7hr	14.4 miles	2240ft		
moderate-difficult	6hr	12 miles	3906ft		
moderate-difficult	1-2 days	15.7 miles	2200ft		
difficult	5-6hr	9.6 miles	3000ft		
difficult	6-7hr	11 miles	2300ft		
difficult	9hr	12 miles	4800ft		
moderate-difficult	4-5 days	31-40 miles	6000ft		
easy-moderate	4hr	6.4 miles	400ft		
easy-moderate	4hr	9.2 miles	negligible		
easy-moderate	3½hr	7 miles	negligible		
moderate	5hr	8-10 miles	1360ft		

 Ranger Station
 Backcountry Campsite
 Boat Shuttle
 Picnic Sites
 Drinking Water

your presence when approaching blind corners in case of bears. The return leg (4.8 miles, two hours) loops back, taking a right to **Third Creek** and then a left past **Swan Lake**. Keep a watchful eye out for beavers munching on lily pads.

If you don't have the time to tackle the entire Hermitage Point loop, then turn left at the southeast end of Heron Pond to Swan Lake and back for a 3-mile, 1¾-hour loop, which is commonly used by horseback riders and ideal for families with small children.

This is also an easy and enjoyable destination for overnight backpacking. Reserve ahead for backcountry campsite No 9 at Hermitage Point.

🚶 Two Ocean Lake & Grand View Point

Duration 4 hours

Distance 6.4 miles

Difficulty Easy–moderate

Elevation Change 400ft

Start/Finish Two Ocean Lake Trailhead

Nearest Town/Junction Jackson Lake Junction

Summary On this unique hike views take a backseat to the beauty of Two Ocean Lake and the lush surrounding forest.

The park's wildflowers peak in July, when abundant huckleberries and chokeberries make the area prime black-bear territory. The tall grass means long trousers are a good idea. Set out by 8am to take advantage of a calm lake and great bird-watching opportunities. Grizzlies frequent this area, so be bear aware.

To reach the trailhead turn north onto the smooth, gravel Pacific Creek Rd around 1 mile west of Moran Junction. After 2 miles turn left onto the rougher Two Ocean Lake Rd and follow it for 2.5 miles to the parking area.

Follow a clear trail counterclockwise around **Two Ocean Lake** through lovely wildflower meadows with aspens and Teton views. At the west end of the lake (1¼ hours from the trailhead) the trail branches to the right; at the next junction, turn left to continue around the lake. Another option is to take the right branch and then a left branch for 1.3 miles uphill to **Grand View Point** (7586ft).

The second hill boasts the best views of Mt Moran, as well as Two Ocean and Emma Matilda Lakes. Return to the main lake trail via the same route.

From the lake junction take a right turn and continue around Two Ocean Lake. Sometimes the trail follows the lakeshore and sometimes it's through conifer forest and open meadow. It's about an hour to the trailhead.

Colter Bay Region – Day Hikes

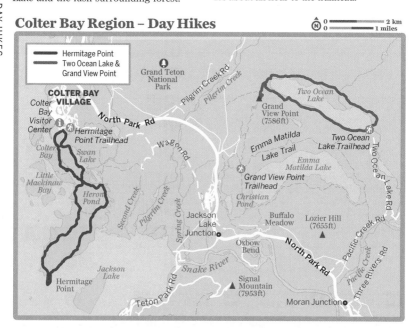

Central Tetons

There's something for everyone here: lakes, waterfalls, glaciers, canyons and viewpoints.

🚶 Leigh & Bearpaw Lakes

Duration 3½ hours

Distance 7.4 miles

Difficulty Easy–moderate

Elevation Change Negligible

Start/Finish Leigh Lake Trailhead

Nearest Junction North Jenny Lake Junction

Summary A fun, flat family outing skirting forest-clad, crystal-clear swimming holes.

The Leigh Lake Trailhead is at the end of the side road off Jenny Lake Dr; don't confuse it with the String Lake Trailhead. Try to get an early start on this trail, as it's very popular, particularly with young families. Canoeing these lakes (with short portages) is an excellent option on a hot summer's day. Always keep track of your picnic food, since bears are frequently spotted here.

The trail quickly joins String Lake. After around 20 minutes a trail branches left across the outlet to Paintbrush Canyon (and a possible loop of String Lake). Instead, take the right branch and then turn right again to Leigh Lake. You may see people carrying their canoes over this portage area.

As you continue north along Leigh Lake, your surroundings open up to fine views of Mt Moran and its Falling Ice and Skillet Glaciers. The dark central stripes in both Mt Moran and Middle Teton consist of 1.5-billion-year-old lava-injected rock called diabase, which extends 7 miles west into Idaho.

Continue past the lovely lakeside campsites 12A (group site), 12B and 12C, which make easy camping destinations for families with small children. Ten minutes further along the trail you'll pass a picturesque beach, with views of Mystic Island and, from left to right, Rockchuck Peak, Mt Woodring, Mt Moran and Bivouac Peak.

After an hour (about 2 miles) of Leigh Lake views, the trail heads into forest to a meadow junction; take the central path to the west side of Bearpaw Lake and campsites 17A and 17C. The trail then veers away from the lake for 0.5 miles to Trapper Lake. Before you descend too far on the trail back to Bearpaw Lake, watch for a faint path that veers to the left. This drops through forest

and over a log bridge to campsite 17B, looping back to join the earlier junction. Return to String Lake the way you came.

Several backcountry campsites are outstanding. On Leigh Lake the most popular sites are 12B and 12C – you'll need to reserve these well in advance. Remoter sites 13 and 15 are accessible by foot on an unmaintained trail that leads north from the bridge over Leigh Lake outlet. The nicest site at Bearpaw Lake is 17B, which has fine views of Rockchuck Peak. Site 17A is on the lakeshore below the path; 17C is more private but a bit uphill. Trapper Lake offers the quietest site (18A). These sites are among the few in Teton where campfires are allowed (in fire grates only).

🚶 Lake Solitude

Duration 6–7 hours

Distance 14.4 miles with boat shuttle, 18.4 miles without

Difficulty Moderate–difficult

Elevation Change 2240ft

Start/Finish Jenny Lake Boat Shuttle

Nearest Junction South Jenny Lake Junction

Summary This ultra-popular hike scales to a mountain lake via a gradual climb.

Thanks to wide patronage, this rewarding trail (particularly its beginning) lacks its namesake solitude, but still provides a rewarding challenge. Though a long hike with a large elevation gain, it is not especially tough since the grade is quite gradual. Gear up for steep sections at the beginning near Inspiration Point and just before Solitude Lake. Moose and bear frequent the area.

The Cascade Canyon (west) dock on Jenny Lake meets a network of trails. Head left to pass Hidden Falls after 0.2 miles and ascend to Inspiration Point in another 0.5 miles. Climbers complete the scenery – Exum Guides uses this area for training. Soon afterward, the horse trail from String Lake joins from the right.

The Cascade Canyon Trail continues straight, past a lovely beach and a high cascade, with fine views. About two hours (4.5 miles) from the dock the valley splits. The left branch leads to South Fork and Hurricane Pass. Turn right and climb gently for 30 minutes to enter the Cascade Camping Zone (12 sites), which stretches for the next 30 minutes. From the zone's end it's 10 minutes up to the lake, past a small cascade

Central Tetons – Day Hikes

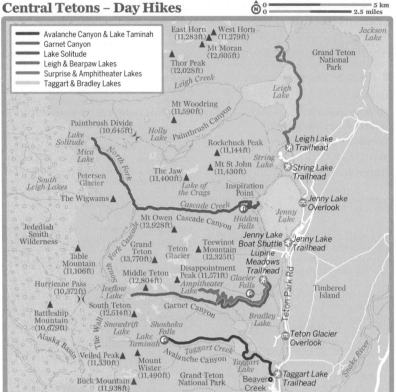

Avalanche Canyon & Lake Taminah
Garnet Canyon
Lake Solitude
Leigh & Bearpaw Lakes
Surprise & Amphitheater Lakes
Taggart & Bradley Lakes

N   0   5 km
     0   2.5 miles

East Horn (11,283ft)
West Horn (11,279ft)
Mt Moran (12,605ft)
Thor Peak (12,028ft)
Leigh Creek
Grand Teton National Park
Jackson Lake
Leigh Lake
Mt Woodring (11,590ft)
Paintbrush Divide (10,645ft)
Holly Lake
Paintbrush Canyon
Lake Solitude
Mica Lake
North Fork
Rockchuck Peak (11,144ft)
Leigh Lake Trailhead
String Lake
Mt St John (11,430ft)
String Lake Trailhead
South Leigh Lakes
Petersen Glacier
The Jaw (11,400ft)
Lake of the Crags
Inspiration Point
The Wigwams
Jenny Lake Overlook
Jedediah Smith Wilderness
Cascade Creek
Cascade Canyon
Hidden Falls
Jenny Lake
Mt Owen (12,928ft)
South Fork Cascade
Table Mountain (11,106ft)
Grand Teton (13,770ft)
Teton Glacier
Teewinot Mountain (12,325ft)
Jenny Lake Boat Shuttle
Jenny Lake Trailhead
Hurricane Pass (10,372ft)
Iceflow Lake
Middle Teton (12,804ft)
Disappointment Peak (11,571ft)
Lupine Meadows Trailhead
Glacier Falls
Timbered Island
Battleship Mountain (10,679ft)
South Teton (12,514ft)
Amphitheater Lake
Garnet Canyon
Bradley Lake
Teton Park Rd
Alaska Basin
Snowdrift Lake
Shoshoko Falls
Teton Glacier Overlook
The Wall
Lake Taminah
Avalanche Canyon
Taggart Creek
Veiled Peak (11,330ft)
Mount Wister (11,490ft)
Taggart Lake
Taggart Lake Trailhead
Buck Mountain (11,938ft)
Grand Teton National Park
Beaver Creek
Snake River

and a hitch rail marking the end of the line for horses. It's about three hours (7.2 miles) from here back to the dock.

Rimmed by fir and pines and sporting ice until midsummer, Lake Solitude (9035ft) is a great spot to loll around (but probably not to swim). To the northeast, the diagonal slash leading up the hillside leads to Paintbrush Divide (p182). Camping is prohibited at the lake.

Return to the boat dock the way you came. The terrain, shaded most of the afternoon, is all downhill, affording full views of Mt Owen and Grand Teton.

🚶 Surprise & Amphitheater Lakes

Duration 5–6 hours

Distance 9.6 miles (10.2 miles with Glacier Overlook extension) round-trip

Difficulty Difficult

Elevation Change 3000ft

Start/Finish Lupine Meadows Trailhead

Nearest Junction South Jenny Lake Junction

Summary One of the park's oldest, this trail is a classic leg-burner. Expect company: great views make it very popular.

Even before cubicle fever existed, two 1920s businessmen built this trail. The route should be free of snow by late June. Bring plenty of water since none is available between the trailhead and the two lakes near the top of the climb. There are three designated campsites at Surprise Lake for those who want to stay overnight; however, due to heavy use, some areas are off limits for regeneration.

The well-worn trail gently winds through pine forest until it mounts a shoulder and the ascent begins in earnest. A junction with the Taggart and Bradley Lakes Trail lies atop the shoulder, 1.7 miles (40 minutes) from the start. Keep right and tackle the series of switchbacks up the flank of **Disappointment Peak**. The route offers views over Taggart Lake and Jackson Hole. About 1½ hours (3 miles) from the trailhead there is a signed junction with the Garnet Canyon trail.

The switchbacks ease shortly before the lakes, and after 2¼ hours of solid climbing, you'll finally reach the inviting, gemstone waters of **Surprise Lake**. Set in a hollow beneath jagged white rocks and cliffs, it is a resplendent payoff for your efforts. The slightly bigger and starker **Amphitheater Lake** lies just 0.2 miles further along the trail. Return the way you came.

SIDE TRIP: TETON GLACIER OVERLOOK

To reach the **Teton Glacier Overlook**, follow the trail around the northeast shore of Amphitheater Lake, staying right at several indistinct forks. Climb between the rocks to the top of a shoulder for breathtaking views into the valley, sweeping down from the Grand Teton. A shattered ridgeline between the razor-sharp spires of Teewinot and Mt Owen to the north contrasts with the flatlands visible between sheer valley walls south. Vertigo sufferers beware!

Retrace your steps to the trailhead.

🚶 Garnet Canyon

Duration 9 hours

Distance 12 miles

Difficulty Difficult

Elevation Change 4800ft

Start/Finish Lupine Meadows Trailhead

Nearest Junction South Jenny Lake Junction

Summary This climbers' route hauls hikers into the world of rock and ice. You must be fit and well acclimatized.

It's possible to hike this trail in a day, but it's best done as an overnighter, camping at either the Meadows or South Fork sites. Set off at first light since afternoon weather is notoriously fickle up here.

For the first 3 miles follow the Surprise & Amphitheater Lakes hike description. At the signed trail junction branch left instead of right. From this junction the trail curves around the hillside to dramatic views of Garnet Canyon and Middle Teton (12,804ft). Just over a mile from the junction the maintained trail stops and the sometimes indistinct **climbers' path** continues over boulder fields for 20 minutes to the Meadows campsite. If you aren't confident with bouldering

and trail finding, this spot makes a good terminus (8.4 miles round-trip, five hours).

The path splits right to Spalding Falls and the base camp for **Grand Teton** and left through indistinct boulder fields to switchback up to a small saddle, where you'll find a couple of campsites. From here the trail traverses a small snowfield (present until August) and heads up the valley over a series of false saddles. With several indistinct trails at your disposal, finding the right one involves some guesswork and bouldering. About 2 miles from the meadows you'll finally reach the **saddle** between Middle and South Teton, with fabulous views down to Iceflow Lake and across to the Wall and Hurricane Pass. You will likely meet groups of climbers heading to Middle Teton.

From the saddle it's a 3½- to four-hour return the way you came. Take great care on the rocks and snowfields as you return, as you'll be tired; this is no place to sprain an ankle or worse.

🚶 Taggart & Bradley Lakes

Duration 3 hours

Distance 5.9 miles

Difficulty Easy–moderate

Elevation Change 560ft

Start/Finish Taggart Lake Trailhead

Nearest Town/Junction Moose Junction

Summary An easy amble. This pair of glacial lakes sits at the base of the Tetons, surrounded by grassy areas thick with summer wildflowers and fragrant pine forest.

These lakes were named after surveyors of the 1872 Hayden Expedition. The terrain is open from earlier fires, so it's a bit easier to spot wildlife, particularly moose. The trails here offer several easy loop options ranging from 3 to 5 miles total. Plan an early start in summer since much of the trail lacks shade. Don't forget your bathing suit.

The **Taggart Lake Trailhead** is just off Teton Park Rd, 5 miles north of Moose. Follow the trail northwest, past horse corrals, and take the first left at a marked signpost after 0.2 miles. Although this trail is only slightly longer, it receives far less traffic than the other option. After another 1.4 miles, turn right and climb open slopes to a point on the moraine wall overlooking the beautiful rusty-green **Taggart Lake**. Descend the short distance to the lakeshore and use a wooden footbridge to cross the outlet creek. A small, rocky outcropping makes a fine point to swim from. The views of the Tetons are fantastic.

The trail winds around the east shore of Taggart Lake, passing a signposted trail junction for the parking area (a shortcut back if you're tired) to your right. Climb steadily away from Taggart Lake and crest the moraine wall separating Taggart and Bradley Lakes. Descend through the trees to reach the thickly forested shores of Bradley Lake. You'll reach a junction just before the trail reaches the shores. Turn right to begin the trip back to the parking area or forge ahead to explore the perimeter of the lake before returning to this junction. The campsite at Bradley Lake is reserved for hikers on multiday loops of the Valley Trail.

If it's still early and you're brimming with energy, consider forging on to Avalanche Canyon and Lake Taminah. You might want to combine your hike with the ranger-led wildflower and naturalist walks that depart every morning from the Taggart Lake Trailhead.

🏃 Avalanche Canyon & Lake Taminah

Duration 6–7 hours

Distance 11 miles

Difficulty Difficult

Elevation Change 2300ft

Start/Finish Taggart Lake Trailhead

Nearest Junction Moose Junction

Summary This challenging hike runs the gamut of good stuff: lake swims, waterfalls and killer views.

Park at the Taggart Lake Trailhead, where there's a convenient toilet. Take the shortest route to Taggart Lake, branching right initially then left after 1.1 miles. At Taggart Lake branch right toward Bradley Lake.

Curving around the north side of Taggart Lake, you'll lose sight of the lake shortly before the faint left-hand turnoff to Avalanche Canyon – if you start to climb the moraine hill to Bradley Lake, you've gone too far.

The trail heads up Avalanche Canyon, past steep fern-thick inclines, with views ahead to 11,490ft Mt Wister. As the trail becomes increasingly wet, you'll first hear and then see Taggart Creek. There's a good chance of spotting moose here. At the head of the valley, about 2½ hours from the trailhead, look for the waterfalls up both branches of the valley – you are headed right for Shoshoko Falls.

The trail winds up a steep talus slope to the right of the falls and, once you have gained most of the elevation, swings left up a small gully to meet remote Lake Taminah. Approach the falls to get great views down the valley. The ascent takes about 3½ hours.

Return the way you came. At the junction with the main Taggart-Bradley Lake Trail, you can head back to the trailhead, though it's worth detouring to Bradley Lake on the Bradley Lake Trail – this only adds an extra 0.7 miles (30 minutes) and it provides more secluded swim spots. From Bradley Lake it's 2 miles back to the trailhead.

The Tetons via Idaho

🏃 Table Mountain

Duration 6 hours

Distance 12 miles

Difficulty Moderate–difficult

Elevation Change 3906ft

Start/Finish Teton Canyon Campground

Nearest Junction Driggs

Summary This outstanding hike, starting in the Targhee National Forest, offers solitude, wildflowers galore and stunning high-alpine scenery without the crowds on the eastern side. It is a long haul and its stream crossings and steep sections make it advisable for experienced hikers. The trail is optimal after snowpack has melted (early July through September). The final scramble onto Table Mountain can be slippery – tread carefully.

Heading north through Driggs, take a right at the traffic light (toward Targhee Ski Resort). Take a right onto a gravel road (6.5 miles) toward Teton Campground; just past here are two parking lots. Park in the first and follow the trail for Table Mountain. Teton Campground (7200ft) provides a good base.

The first section is a thigh-burner. Ascend a steep forested trail to a lovely wildflower meadow dotted with aspens and frequented by moose. The next segment is mellower, with a slow ascent that requires crossing the north fork of Teton Creek. Hiking poles and sandals are a great help here.

After the stream crossing, the trail winds through a tall pine forest giving way to the open cirque below Table Mountain. Here you ascend steeply – the trail zigzags with breathtaking views of the valley below and the Jedediah Smith Wilderness. Step carefully over patches of snow.

Once you achieve the ridge, the rounded knob of **Table Mountain** (11,106ft) appears so close! But it is still about 1½ hours to its summit. Sighting marmots along the way, follow the trail as it bends left toward Table Mountain. Once there, ascend the steep, crumbly rock with care, using the least steep path.

The flat-top summit of Table Mountain affords great gawping views of the Grand Teton, Alaska Basin and the western slope of the peaks. Spend some time drinking it all in. Photographer William H Jackson took the first photos of the Grand Teton here, during the 1872 Hayden Survey. Head back at a reasonable hour since snowmelt will increase the runoff in the streams and make the crossing more challenging as the day goes on.

🏃 Devil's Staircase to Alaska Basin

Duration 1 or 2 days

Distance 15.7 miles

Difficulty Moderate–difficult

Elevation Change 2200ft

Start/Finish Teton Canyon Campground

Nearest Junction Driggs

Summary This long day loop can be done

in either direction, but by hitting it counter-clockwise you'll encounter fewer people in the early leg of the hike and quickly achieve stunning views after ascending the Devil's Staircase. Beware of snowpack in early summer; consult first with Targhee National Forest rangers. You can savor this epic trek by overnighting in Alaska Basin.

This sensitive alpine terrain receives heavy use. Practice leave-no-trace principles, stay on trails and observe fire restrictions. Permits are not required to camp, but campers must be at least 200ft from lakes and 150ft from streams. To get here from Driggs, head toward Targhee Ski Resort. Take a right onto a gravel road (6.5 miles) when the road forks toward Teton Campground. Just past the campground there are two parking lots. Park in the second parking lot with pit toilets. Bring water tablets or a purifier, sandals for river crossings and ample sunscreen.

Set aside at least nine hours. The first 2.7 miles follow an old jeep track at a mellow grade through fir and lodgepole pine. The south fork of Teton Creek parallels the trail. When the trail forks for Alaska Basin and Devil's Staircase, take the right hand fork, which quickly gets steep. After a few switchbacks, you end up on a gently up-sloping high meadow with views. Heading toward **Mt Meek Pass**, look for Dall sheep on the

Tetons via Idaho – Day Hikes

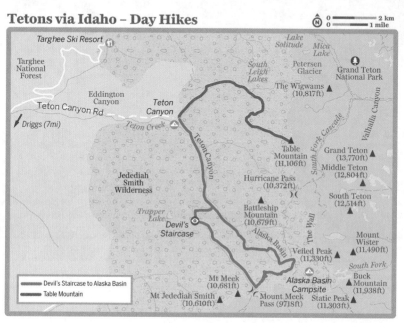

1. Wildflowers (p249)
June and July are the best times to view the park's vivid blooms.

2. Elk (p244)
Keep an eye out for this graceful species of large mammal, one of the most abundant in the region.

3. Jackson Lake (p190)
Take in the stunning alpine scenery from canoe on Grand Teton's largest lake.

cliffs that tower to the right. A gurgling brook parallels most of this section, steeped in wildflowers.

The trail splits, with the right fork heading toward Mt Meek Pass and the left dropping down the Sheep Steps into Alaska Basin. Savor the views of Mt Meek, Buck Mountain (11,938ft) and South Teton (12,514ft). Take the fork to Alaska Basin (9200ft). This high-alpine area resembles Alaska's open tundra. There are many good campsites and over-nighters have extra time to explore the Basin Lakes. The rest of the hike follows the valley downhill through switchbacks and stream crossings (either shallow or with stepping stones or a bridge). Polished rock outcrops show evidence of glacial movement. This rocky and sometimes steep forested section can be somewhat tough on the knees.

From Alaska Basin to the signed junction with Devil's Staircase it is 5 miles. Continue toward the parking lot via the entrance trail. If you're hot and sweaty, take advantage of the great swimming holes off short paths to the creek.

Moose–Wilson Road

At the southern extreme of the park, these hikes are more likely to offer solitude.

In addition to the two hikes below, another day-hike loop starts from the top of the tram down the South Fork into Granite Canyon and back to Teton Village (15 miles).

🦶 Death Canyon

Duration 5 hours

Distance 8–10 miles

Difficulty Moderate

Elevation Change 1360ft

Start/Finish Death Canyon Trailhead

Nearest Junction Moose Junction

Summary Lesser-known Death Canyon offers moderate hiking up an ethereal river valley flanked by granite climbing walls.

To reach the Death Canyon Trailhead, take the turnoff 3 miles south of Moose on Moose–Wilson Rd. Go right 1.6 miles down a narrow dirt track, which is in poor condition. The small parking area is often crowded with climbers' and backpackers' vehicles. Nearby, the White Grass Ranger Station was once an outfitters' cabin.

The trail climbs 0.9 miles to Phelps Lake Overlook (7200ft) and then descends 0.7 miles through lovely aspen forest to a junction; go right here. As you enter the towering gorge, the ascent kicks in – a relentless uphill climb over rocky switchbacks that quickly joins the river, which cascades over large boulders. After a hard slog of about 1.5 miles the path flattens out. Devoid of the river's roar, the valley seems impressively serene.

The trail hits a junction by an old patrol cabin, 3.7 miles from the trailhead. The right branch climbs steeply to Static Divide; if you have the energy, switchback up the trail to the treeline for great views of the peaks and plains (a two-hour detour). Or continue straight on the main trail up Death Canyon, through riverside willows in prime moose habitat. The trail crosses a log bridge and enters a lush forest filled with berries, which indicate bear territory. The campsites of the Death Canyon Camping Area pop up occasionally, as do views of the Death Canyon Shelf, an impressive layer of sedimentary rock atop harder granites and gneiss. You can continue along this trail as long as you wish, perhaps using one of the campsites as a picnic spot, though a good turnaround point comes where the trail crosses the stream.

To exit, retrace your steps. Consider descending to the pine-rimmed Phelps Lake for a dip before the final grind, a 1.6-mile hike back up the moraine hill, which somehow seems a lot longer at the day's end.

🦶 Phelps Lake Trail

Duration 3½ hours

Distance 7-mile loop

Difficulty Easy–moderate

Elevation Change negligible

Start/Finish Phelps Lake Trailhead

Nearest Town/Junction Moose

Summary A lovely and flat forested amble around a beautiful lake.

The trail leaves the Laurance S Rockefeller Preserve Center and splits. If you go left over the bridge, you will be on the Lake Creek Trail. Go right for the Woodland Trail. Before long it crosses the main road and continues in a gentle, winding ascent through pine forest and aspens, hitting the junction of the Boulder Ridge Trail at 0.7 miles. Continue straight; soon after, views open up and you get a glimpse of Static Peak and Buck Mountain on its right. It should take 30 or 45 minutes total to reach Phelps Lake. Go the extra 20yd to the lake viewpoint for gorgeous views of the headwall across the lake; there are benches here for resting.

Start the Phelps Lake Trail loop counter-clockwise. The trail intersects again with the longer Boulder Ridge Trail; continue on the lake loop, going through forested and sometimes bouldery terrain with lake views on the left. About one hour in you'll reach Jump Rock, an immense boulder used for launching swimmers into the lake. It's a fine spot to rest or picnic. The rock itself has a 23ft drop and the water is about 30ft deep here, so it's perfect for jumping in.

Ten minutes on, there are campsites 2 and 1 (respectively) to the right side of the trail. If you want to stay here, obtain a backcountry permit ahead of time. Shortly you will reach the opposite side of the lake. Hikers can get easily turned around here, since a nearby avalanche created some trail detours. If you pay close attention, the route is clear. Briefly turn onto Valley Trail, which ascends a humid aspen grove with a waterfall within earshot.

Two short paths veer toward the lake; keep right and continue rounding the lake, looking up to your right to see the waterfall. This area is popular with moose, so keep an eye out for them. A muddy section has round log stepping stones. Ascend away from the lake to a trail sign that marks the halfway point. Go left here and cross a bridge over the stream. The trail ascends, surrounded by ferns, and on the left you will have a view of the creek feeding the lake. Keep ascending and reach the trail's highest point, the intersection of Valley Trail with Phelps Lake Trail. Veer left here, and it's 3 miles to the Laurance S Rockefeller Preserve Center.

The trail has views across the lake to Jackson Peak. A mile on, consider taking the short left-hand trail to lakeside Huckleberry Point if it's berry season – they flourish here. Rejoin the trail, which passes over marshlands on a steel boardwalk. Continue straight at another intersection with the Boulder Ridge Trail. Soon after, you will

Moose–Wilson Road – Day Hikes

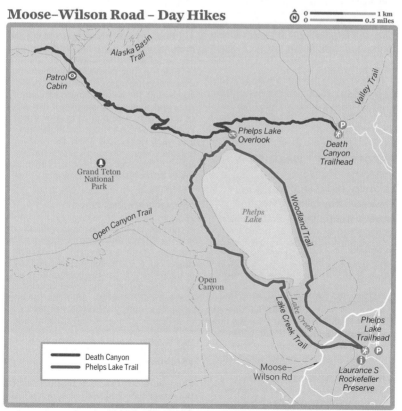

GRAND TETON NATIONAL PARK DAY HIKES

reach the road: cross carefully as it's a blind curve. The trail crosses the river before ending at the Visitor Center.

John D Rockefeller Jr Memorial Parkway

From Flagg Ranch, Polecat Creek offers a pleasant stroll. The trail leads across Grassy Lake Rd from the main parking lot, passing two turnoffs to the right and an employee-housing loop before branching right to peaceful Oxbow Meadows. From here you can take a left at the next junction over a small creek to Huckleberry Hot Springs. The NPS advises against bathing here due to high radiation levels in the water (caused by naturally occurring radon), but this hardly deters locals taking post-work alfresco soaks. You can also get to the springs from a parking lot 1 mile west of Flagg Ranch, though you need to ford Polecat Creek on this route, so bring water shoes. This former road used to lead to a hot-springs resort that was torn down in 1983.

A fairly interesting hiking trail also runs beside the volcanic walls of Flagg Canyon, northeast of Flagg Ranch. Get the brochure *Flagg Ranch Area Trails* from the Flagg Ranch information station.

Along Grassy Lane Rd, 2.2 miles west of Flagg Ranch, is the Glade Creek Trailhead, which accesses the rarely visited northwest corner of the park and its Berry Creek and Moose Creek Trails.

SPOTS TO SPY WILDLIFE

Hunker down at dusk or dawn with a spotting scope or binoculars to feast your eyes at the following sites.

Oxbow Bend (p196) A scenic river bend populated with moose, elk, sandhill cranes, ospreys, bald eagles, trumpeter swans, Canada geese, blue herons, white pelicans and...oh, yeah, abundant mosquitoes.

Willow Flats Turnout (p194) Views of a freshwater marsh that's home to birds, moose, elk and beavers.

Blacktail Ponds (p187) Features ospreys, eagles and moose.

Antelope Flats (p188) Bison and pronghorns at home on the range.

Swan Lake (p172) The spot to see beavers, trumpeter swans and geese.

OVERNIGHT HIKES

Paintbrush Divide

Duration 2–3 days
Distance 17.8-mile loop
Difficulty Moderate
Elevation Change 3775ft
Start/Finish String Lake Trailhead
Nearest Town/Junction North Jenny Lake Junction
Summary This pretty grind lifts you into the alpine scenery above tree level.

This is the Teton's most popular backpacking trip. If you like some social atmosphere with your backcountry, make sure you reserve a campsite in advance or keep an open itinerary. Uber-athletes could zip through it on an epic day hike.

DAY 1: STRING LAKE TRAILHEAD TO HOLLY LAKE
4 HOURS / 6.2 MILES / 2540FT ASCENT
From the String Lake parking lot take the trail that curves south around String Lake. It climbs gently until the left-hand junction with Paintbrush Canyon, 1.6 miles in. This steeper but moderate trail borders a stream flowing over granite boulders, passing through the Lower Paintbrush Camping Zone and some stock campsites. It reaches an upper basin surrounded by snowy peaks. The first lake isn't Holly; continue right of it to reach Holly Lake. There are two shady designated campsites at the lake's southeast corner. If these sites are booked, camp in the Upper Paintbrush Canyon Camping Zone.

DAY 2: HOLLY LAKE TO NORTH FORK CASCADE CAMPING ZONE
3 HOURS / 3.2 MILES / 1235FT ASCENT
Ascend steeply to join the main trail; it's one hour to Paintbrush Divide (10,645ft). The pass may be snowy into early July – consult a ranger before going. An ice tool could come in handy here. Enjoy the outstanding views before descending along broad switchbacks to reach Lake Solitude after another hour or so. Camp in the nearby North Fork Cascade Camping Zone or head straight back.

DAY 3: NORTH FORK CASCADE CAMPING ZONE TO STRING LAKE TRAILHEAD
4–5 HOURS / 8.4 MILES / 2000FT DESCENT
Continue down Cascade Canyon to either the String Lake Trailhead or to Jenny Lake via the shuttle boat.

Paintbrush Divide Loop

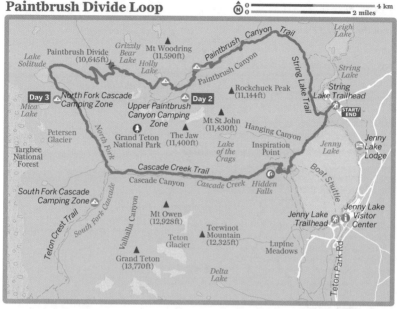

🥾 Teton Crest Trail

Duration 4 or 5 days

Distance 31.4 or 39.9 miles

Difficulty Moderate-difficult

Elevation Change 6000ft

Start String Lake

Finish Granite Creek Trailhead or Teton Village

Nearest Junction North Jenny Lake Junction

Summary This epic trail takes hikers rambling over the lofty spine of the Tetons for jaw-dropping views and a fair share of high exposure.

This classic route is one to remember. Dipping in and out of the neighboring Jedediah Smith Wilderness, the route has numerous outs – the canyons and passes that access the trail on either side. Hikers must arrange for a shuttle or have two cars to leave at the start and end points. Bring plenty of sunscreen – there is almost no shade.

DAYS 1 & 2

Day one is the same as the Paintbrush Divide loop. Day two continues to follow this route until the junction between the North and South Forks of Cascade Canyon, where the trail branches up the South Fork to the **South Fork Cascade Camping Zone** (19 campsites). You can start the hike from Jenny Lake and spend night one at the South Fork Camping Zone after hiking up Cascade Creek Trail; this shaves off a day.

DAY 3: SOUTH FORK CASCADE CAMPING ZONE TO ALASKA BASIN
3–3½ HOURS / 6.1 MILES / 1992FT ASCENT

The trail climbs up to **Avalanche Divide** junction: head right (southwest) to **Hurricane Pass** (10,372ft), which has unsurpassed views of the Grand, South and Middle Tetons. (An excursion from the Avalanche Divide junction leads 1.6 miles to the divide, a scenic overlook above Snowdrift Lake.) From the pass the trail descends into the Jedediah Smith Wilderness, past Sunset Lake, into the **Basin Lakes** of the Alaska Basin, where you'll find several popular campsites. No permits are needed here since you're outside the park, but you must camp at least 300ft from lakes and 50ft from streams.

DAY 4: ALASKA BASIN TO MARION LAKE
4½ HOURS / 8.2 MILES

The trail crosses South Fork Teton Creek on stepping stones and switchbacks up the Sheep Steps to the wide saddle of **Mt Meek**

Teton Crest Trail

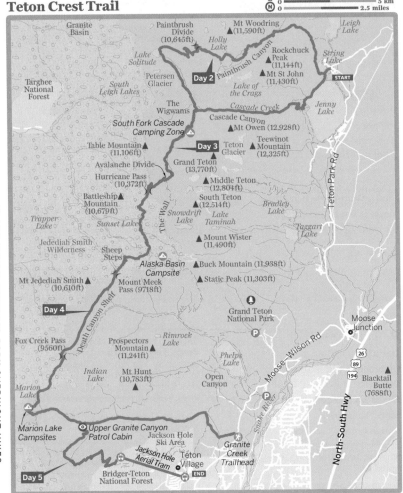

Pass (9718ft) to reenter the park. The trail dips for the next 3 miles into the stunning plateau of **Death Canyon Shelf** and camping zone. Past the turnoff to Death Canyon, it climbs to **Fox Creek Pass** (9560ft) and continues southwest over a vague saddle to **Marion Lake** and its designated campsites.

DAY 5: MARION LAKE TO TETON VILLAGE
5 HOURS / 9.7 MILES

The trail descends into the Upper Granite Canyon Camping Zone and continues past the Upper Granite Canyon patrol cabin to the junction with the Valley Trail. From here

continue south to the Granite Canyon Trailhead or straight on to Teton Village.

OTHER COMBINATIONS

The Teton Crest Trail can be accessed from the east by several steep canyons. Trailheads (south to north) are: Granite Canyon, Death Canyon, Taggart Lake, Lupine Meadows, Jenny Lake and String Lake/Leigh Lake. Hike canyon-to-canyon to make a combination hike of any length. Options include the following:

Open Canyon to Granite Canyon One-night 19.3-mile loop from the Granite Creek Trailhead.

Granite Canyon to Death Canyon A two- to three-night 25.7-mile loop via the Teton Crest Trail.

Death Canyon to Open Canyon A 24.7-mile loop from the Death Canyon Trailhead.

🚶 Marion Lake & Death Canyon

Duration 2 days

Distance 18 miles (or 23.5-mile loop)

Difficulty Moderate

Elevation Change 3850ft descent (from top of tram to Death Canyon Trailhead)

Start Teton Village

Finish Death Canyon Trailhead

Nearest Town Teton Village

Summary Downhill but not a downer, this hike's tram shortcut gets you quickly steeped in the backcountry.

DAY 1: JACKSON HOLE AERIAL TRAM TO MARION LAKE

4 HOURS / 6.6 MILES / 1400FT DESCENT

This hike starts with a considerable boost: after reopening in 2008, the Jackson Hole Aerial Tram (p219) to the top of Rendezvous Mountain gains 0.8 miles of elevation. From the tram, descend to a junction at the park boundary and turn right to descend into the South Fork of Granite Canyon. Take a left at the next junction and then a right at the next two junctions to descend into the North Fork of Granite Canyon. From here it's a short climb to lovely Marion Lake, 6.6 miles from the trailhead, where you'll find three designated campsites.

DAY 2: MARION LAKE TO DEATH CANYON TRAILHEAD

6 HOURS / 11.3 MILES / 2450FT DESCENT

Today it's 2.3 miles up to Fox Creek Pass, then it's all downhill for 9 miles through the forests of Death Canyon to Phelps Lake Overlook and the Death Canyon Trailhead. To avoid a car shuttle, hike south at the junction before Phelps Lake along the Valley Trail to Teton Village (5.5 miles).

By choosing to hike in the opposite direction you can save a few bucks (the downhill tram ride is free of charge), but you'll gain a lot more elevation.

🚶 Other Central Tetons Hikes

Other good options for overnighting include camping at Marion Lake (13-mile round-trip) from the Jackson Hole Aerial Tram. For an easy overnighter, check out the Hermitage Point hike (p171) or the Leigh & Bearpaw Lakes hike (p173). Also check out Alaska Basin from the Idaho side.

Marion Lake & Death Canyon

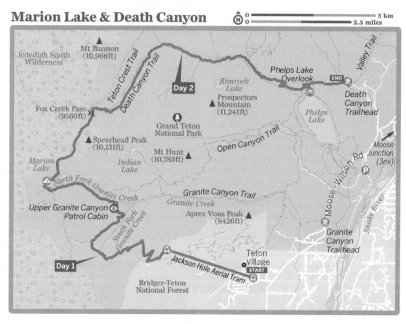

BACKCOUNTRY PERMITS

Backcountry permits are required for all overnight backcountry trips in Grand Teton. Permits for walk-ins are $25, given on a first-come, first-served basis, 24 hours in advance, from the backcountry offices at Craig Thomas and Colter Bay Visitor Centers (p207) or Jenny Lake Ranger Station (p207). For best results, apply early in the morning the day before your intended departure. A notice board at Craig Thomas Discovery & Visitor Center indicates which backcountry sites are full each day.

About a third of the backcountry sites can be reserved from the first Wednesday in January to May 15 via www.recreation.gov, for a nonrefundable $35 fee.

Park-approved bear-resistant food-storage canisters are required. Backpackers can check one out for free when securing their permit.

Backcountry camping is restricted to camping zones. Hikers (with backcountry permits) can choose their own sites inside many of these areas, but in the most heavily used zones all sites are designated (indicated by marker posts). Fires are prohibited, except at some lakeshore sites, so bring a camp stove. Campsites must be at least 200ft from waterways.

No permits are required for backcountry camping in the John D Rockefeller Jr Memorial Pkwy, though campers must stay a minimum of 1 mile from roads and 100ft from water sources. Fires are generally allowed, but check current regulations at the information station. No bikes or pets are permitted on trails.

CYCLING

Cyclists are in less danger from motorists in the Tetons than in Yellowstone because the roads are wider and more open, but it is still best to venture out early to avoid traffic. Grand Teton National Park gets little traffic from September to early October, and the cool temperatures make for pleasant pedaling. In April, Teton Park Rd is open only to cyclists and pedestrian traffic. This is a great time to bike if the snow has cleared.

The best spot for cycling in the park is the multiuse pathway, bordering the Teton Park Rd between Jackson and Jenny Lake (a 20-mile stretch). Riders can also park at the lot just after the Moose Entrance Station. Construction is underway to extend the path north to Antelope Flats.

For a mellow, scenic ride, try Mormon Row, a 16-mile loop including terrain beyond Mormon Row, which starts and finishes in Gros Ventre Junction. While part of this ride is paved, the 3-mile Mormon Row section, bumpy and unpaved, is not great for road bikes. This trail follows an abbreviated version of the Hole in One driving loop (p188). Start at Gros River Junction. Go right at the turnoff, heading northeast with Blacktail Butte to your north. Take a left at Mormon Row, and another left at Antelope Flats Rd. It ends at Hwy 191; take the highway south to return to the start.

If you are on a road bike, check out the various driving-route options. Biking tours require mountain-bike treads, but only Shadow Mountain is steep and may require suspension.

Snake River Road

Duration 2–3 hours

Distance 15 miles one way

Difficulty Easy–moderate

Elevation Change Negligible

Start Riverside Rd at Cottonwood Creek

Finish Signal Mountain Summit Rd

Nearest Junction Moose Junction

Summary Explore the incredible riparian landscape on a short mountain-bike ride.

The gravel River (RKO) Rd parallels the west side of the Snake River between Signal Mountain and Cottonwood Creek. Those doing the ride one way can park at the turn-out near Cottonwood Creek. There is no shade here and it gets quite hot in summer, so bring plenty of water or come early. Wildlife is prolific, especially bison. Maintain a safe distance of 300ft and never pass through a herd. Wait until they move away or bike around.

Be prepared for a bumpy, uneven ride. The road parallels braided channels of the scenic Snake River, one of the most heavily used rivers in the west. Binoculars would be useful: the river is critical habitat for beaver and river otter. Osprey and eagle are here too, fishing for cutthroat trout, and moose and deer frequent the willows. The track rejoins Teton Park Road just south of the Signal Mountain Rd turnoff. Arrange a vehicle shuttle or be prepared to cycle the 12 miles south on the paved Teton Park Rd back to Cottonwood Creek.

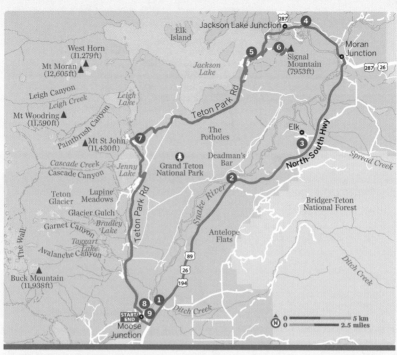

Driving Tour
Plains & Panoramas

DURATION 1.5 HOURS
DISTANCE 45-MILE LOOP
START/FINISH MOOSE JUNCTION
NEAREST TOWN MOOSE
SPEED LIMIT 30–45MPH

This scenic loop offers fantastic views of the Teton Range from the flats of Jackson Hole Valley. With some luck, you will spot pronghorn, deer or moose. Each year animals are killed on this road, so drive cautiously and watch for animals bounding across the road.

Begin the tour 8 miles north of Jackson at Moose Junction. Follow Hwy 191 north past ❶ **Blacktail Ponds Overlook** and Glacier View Turnout. Seven miles after Moose Junction, ❷ **Snake River Overlook** has views of the braided channels of the Snake. Dense cottonwoods, willows and Engelmann spruce provide an excellent habitat for moose and deer. Spotted sandpipers should be easy to pick out. Make a stop at ❸ **Cunningham Cabin**, the site of an 1892 shootout when a band of self-deputized locals sought to root out rumored horse thieves.

At Moran Junction bear left (continuing on 191). The hulking peak of Mt Moran looms to the west, bearing five glaciers. Stop about 3.5 miles later at ❹ **Oxbow Bend** to look for fishing eagles and ospreys, and trumpeter swans. Long-legged great blue herons stalk the shallows. Head south along Teton Park Rd at Jackson Lake Junction. The ❺ **Log Chapel of the Sacred Heart** follows. On your left you will see a sign for ❻ **Signal Mountain Road**, a 5-mile climb. You can detour here or continue straight ahead.

Turn on the one-way ❼ **Jenny Lake Scenic Drive**, twisting through a forested area with the spires of the Tetons just above you. It will deposit you back on Teton Park Rd where, on the left, you will see ❽ **Menor's Ferry** historic area. The brainchild of Bill Menor, the ferry provided the only transportation across the river. In late summer, when tourists crossed the river to pick berries, Menor charged them 'Huckleberry Rates.' The log ❾ **Chapel of the Transfiguration**, built in 1914, still holds church services (detour slightly). Return to the main road and follow it until it exits the park at Moose Junction.

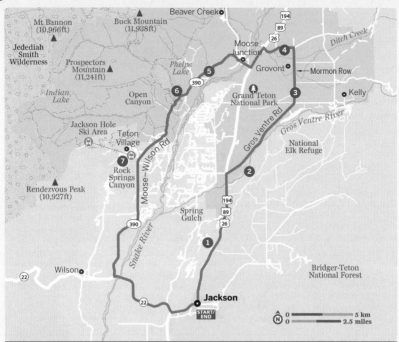

Driving Tour
Hole in One

DURATION ONE HOUR PLUS STOPS
DISTANCE 40-MILE LOOP
START/FINISH JACKSON
NEAREST TOWN JACKSON
SPEED LIMIT 15–45MPH

A scenic drive through sagebrush flats and forest with picturesque barns and Teton panoramas. You could say Gros Ventre Butte ruined it for Jackson – there are no Teton views from the park's main hub due to the blockage created by this hump. But this driving tour, not suitable for RVs or other oversize vehicles, is just the remedy.

Head out of Jackson on Hwy 191. First stop: the ❶ **National Museum of Wildlife Art**. You may ask, why do this when you have the real thing? Just look. The way these masters envisioned this landscape will change the way you see it yourself.

Continue north on Hwy 191. At the Gros Ventre Junction, take a right and drive along Gros Ventre Rd, skirting the ❷ **Gros Ventre River**, lined with cottonwoods, juniper, spruce and willows. The river ecology contrasts

sharply with the dry sagebrush flats north of it, where pronghorn can often be seen, bounding at speeds up to 60mph. At the next junction, take a left to drive north on ❸ **Mormon Row**, a picturesque strip that includes a much-photographed rambling barn. At the end of the row loop left on ❹ **Antelope Flats Road**, from which you may be able to see bison and more pronghorn. It soon meets Hwy 191: go left, then right at Moose Junction.

Before the park entrance gate, take a left on the small ❺ **Moose–Wilson Road**. Squeeze to the side when you face oncoming traffic: this is why oversize vehicles are banned. Mind the blind curves, twisting through dense foliage. You will pass a dirt road to Death Canyon Trailhead and later the Granite Canyon Trailhead, both on your right. If you're keen on a swim, detour to the latter, which will take you to ❻ **Phelps Lake** (in a few hours). This short section of the road is unpaved but even.

The road spills out near ❼ **Teton Village**, where you can take a gondola to the top for views or grab lunch at Mangy Moose Saloon. Follow the Moose–Wilson Rd south to Hwy 22. Go left to return to Jackson.

🚲 Shadow Mountain

Duration 2½–3 hours

Distance 6-mile loop

Difficulty Difficult

Elevation Change 1300ft

Start/Finish Antelope Flats Rd

Nearest Junction Moose Junction

Summary Challenge yourself with this strenuous but quick ascent and descent.

Just east of the park in Bridger-Teton National Forest, the forested Shadow Mountain offers a strenuous 6-mile round-trip loop. Set off along a gravel road from the parking lot at the end of paved Antelope Flats Rd. A steady climb, the road is rutted and rocky at points. Open sections offer excellent Teton views. Just over half a mile past the summit there's a single-track path to the left. It splits, and your best option is to stay left, although all trails do lead to the bottom. Be alert for fallen logs, which cross the path in places. After this exciting downhill run, join the fire road. Watch for muddy conditions, which make this section a lot trickier. A webbed network of trails here means it is easy to get turned around. For topographical maps, visit Hoback Sports (p211) in Jackson.

🚲 Hole in One

Duration 5 hours

Distance 33-mile loop

Difficulty Moderate

Elevation Change 340ft

Start/Finish Jackson, Wyoming

Nearest Town Jackson

Summary Scoot past Jackson Hole highlights on this loop with long, flat stretches.

This trail follows an abbreviated version of the Hole in One driving loop. Start in Jackson and head north on Hwy 191 to Moose Junction. Go left here and left again to the narrow and winding Moose–Wilson Rd. While it is paved, there are some deep potholes, so stay alert. Horned owls nest along this section. Approaching Teton Village, the road becomes smooth and stays that way. Continue on the flats of Moose–Wilson Rd until you hit a juncture with Hwy 22; turn left here. There will be a lot of car traffic on Hwy 22. An early start will help you avoid traffic on the narrows of Moose–Wilson Rd.

SUMMER ACTIVITIES

Rock Climbing & Mountaineering

Jenny Lake Ranger Station (p207) is ground zero for climbing information. It sells climbing guidebooks, provides information and has a board showing campsite availability in Garnet Canyon. An excellent resource and the spot to meet outdoor partners in crime, the American Alpine Club's Climbers' Ranch (p204) has been a climbing institution since opening. It also offers lodging. The ranch is just south of the Teton Glacier turnout.

Garnet Canyon ROCK CLIMBING

Garnet Canyon is the gateway to the most popular scrambles to Middle and South Tetons, and the technical ascent of Grand Teton. These nontechnical climbs can be handled as day hikes from bases at the Meadows, South Fork, Caves or Moraine campsites, but you need to know what you're doing and be with someone familiar with the routes.

Grand Teton ROCK CLIMBING

The Grand Teton is cherished by climbers as a classic climb. It starts with a strenuous hike up Garnet Canyon (4000ft-plus) and making camp. Day two requires an alpine start. The Owen-Spaulding route is the most popular, but there are many others. There's 2700ft of elevation gain, fun scrambling, three easy 5th-class pitches and an exciting rappel. Very fit nonclimbers can complete the climb with an outfitter and some training beforehand.

Those staying overnight need a backcountry use permit. Call ☎307-739-3604 for recorded climbing information.

Horseback Riding

Horseback riding is possible at Jackson Lake, Colter Bay and the Flagg Ranch area. Children are charged the same as adults and must be at least eight years old.

Boating

Colter Bay Lake Cruises CRUISE

Daily scheduled cruises (1½ hours adult/child $30/13.50) as well as breakfast or lunch cruises (three hours adult/child $45/23) and dinner cruises (adult/child $54/37).

String & Leigh Lakes CANOEING

Perfect for a family canoe trip or even just splashing about. Start on String Lake and make a 120ft portage before Leigh Lake. Leigh Lake offers the most scenic day and overnight paddles. Six beautiful backcountry campsites flank the lakeshore, three of which (16, 14A and 14B) are only accessible by boat. It is 3 miles one way from the portage point at the outlet of Leigh Lake to the furthest campsite (16). Leigh Lake also offers quality fishing. String Lake's canoe-only put-in is just before the Leigh Lake Trailhead parking lot.

Jackson Lake   BOATING
A fun, mellow activity for families or groups is to rent a motorboat for a day and explore Jackson Lake, stopping to picnic and swim at uncrowded inlets and islands. Though they cover less terrain, canoes and kayaks are also wonderful, but those rented at the marinas may not be paddled beyond Colter Bay or Half Moon Bay (from Colter Bay) or Dornan's Island (from Signal Mountain).

Fishing

Anglers must carry a valid Wyoming fishing license. Fishing licenses are issued at Moose Village store, Signal Mountain Lodge (p202) and Colter Bay Marina. The Snake, Buffalo Fork and Gros Ventre Rivers are closed November 1 to March 31. In general, anglers are limited to six trout per day, with varying size limitations. Get a copy of the park's fishing brochure for details.

Jackson Lake   FISHING
Cutthroat, brown and lake trout cruise the waters of Jackson Lake. On fishing excursions, your catch can be cleaned and most fine-dining restaurants within the park will cook it up for you too. Jackson Lake is closed to fishing in October.

Tour Operators & Equipment Rental

Exum Mountain Guides   ROCK CLIMBING
(Map p198; ☑307-733-2297; www.exumguides. com) The region's oldest climbing school, the excellent Exum Mountain Guides runs climbing schools at Hidden Falls on Jenny Lake's west shore and has a base camp at Grand Teton's Lower Saddle (11,600ft).

Jackson Lake
Lodge Activities Desk   ADVENTURE TOUR
(☑307-543-2811; Jackson Lake) Offers guided horseback rides (two hours $75) that loop around the local trails, as well as breakfast and dinner rides by horseback or wagon. Also organizes Colter Bay lake cruises.

Colter Bay Corral   HORSEBACK RIDING
(☑307-543-2811; 1½-/2½-hour trail rides $42/65; ☺7am-8pm) Offers short rides around Swan Lake. Children are charged the same rates. Families with small children can check out the breakfast wagon rides (adult/child $40/29). Make reservations at the activities booth next to the Colter Bay grocery store a few days in advance.

Flagg Ranch Company   ADVENTURE SPORTS
(☑1-800-443-2311; www.gtlc.com/headwaters -lodge.aspx; Flagg Ranch) Runs pony rides and hour-long horseback riding trips ($40) hourly from June to September. Eight-hour fly-fishing trips ($549 for two) go to different locations, depending on conditions.

WORTH A TRIP

THE SNAKE RIVER

Ansel Adams immortalized the Snake as a luminous ribbon retreating from sharp snow-bound peaks. With outstanding wildlife-watching, this iconic river is a prime spot for boating. Float trips (averaging adult/child $70/40) start after Jackson Lake Dam and meander through park wilderness; the wildest white water flows south of the town of Jackson. Usually kids must be six years or older to participate.

Barker-Ewing Float Trips (☑307-733-1000; www.barker-ewing.com; meeting area, 945 West Broadway, Jackson) Offers float trips from Deadman's Bar to Moose, free for four- and five-year-olds.

Solitude Float Trips (☑307-733-2871, 888-704-2800; www.solitudefloattrips.com; Moose) Recommended; runs Deadman's Bar-to-Moose trips and sunrise trips, plus shorter 5-mile floats.

Triangle X Float Trips (☑307-733-2183; http://trianglex.com/river-trips) Offers dawn, daytime and sunset floats, plus a four-hour early-evening float and cookout.

BOATING REGULATIONS

All private craft must obtain a one-year nonmotorized/motorized craft permit $10/40. Nonmotorized craft are rafts, canoes and kayaks. The Craig Thomas and Colter Bay Visitor Centers and Buffalo Fork Ranger Station at Moran Junction issue permits. Display yours on the port side of the vessel at the rear. Permits for Yellowstone are valid for Grand Teton (and vice versa) but must be registered at either Moose or Colter Bay Visitor Centers.

The state of Wyoming also requires boaters to purchase an aquatic invasive species decal for watercraft over 10ft long to help fund prevention efforts against invasive quagga and zebra mussels. The cost is $10/5 for motorized/nonmotorized watercraft registered in Wyoming, and $30/15 for motorized/nonmotorized watercraft owned by nonresidents. Decals are sold by the Wyoming Fish and Game Department (www.gf.state.wy.us) online and at automated license agents.

Motorized craft (maximum 7.5HP) are allowed only on Jackson, Phelps and Jenny Lakes. On Jenny Lake, crafts with over 10HP are prohibited. Hand-propelled nonmotorized craft are permitted on Jackson, Two Ocean, Emma Matilda, Bearpaw, Leigh, String, Jenny, Bradley, Taggart and Phelps Lakes, as well as the Snake River 1000ft below Jackson Dam. Sailboats, water skis and sailboards are permitted only on Jackson Lake. Jet skis are not allowed in the park.

Floating is prohibited within 1000ft of Jackson Lake Dam. Only hand-powered rafts, canoes and kayaks are allowed on the Snake River. Watercraft are forbidden on other rivers.

On Jackson Lake, fires are forbidden along the east shore from Spalding Bay to Lizard Creek and otherwise permitted only below the high-water mark.

See the park's *Boating* and *Floating the Snake River* brochures.

OARS
WATER SPORTS
(Outdoor Adventure River Specialists; ☎800-346-6277, 209-736-4677; www.oars.com; 2-day kayaking trip from $389) Guides trips kayaking around Jackson Lake with instruction for beginners, as well as multiday rafting trips on the Snake River.

Signal Mountain Marina
BOAT RENTAL
(Map p195; ☎307-543-2831; ⊙7am-7:30pm mid-May–early Sep) Rents canoes ($17/85 per hour/day), kayaks ($15/79), motorboats ($36/175) and pontoon cruisers ($80/480). Also guides fly-fishing on the lake (two people $94/290 per hour/half-day).

Colter Bay Marina
BOAT RENTAL
(Map p195; ☎307-543-2811; ⊙8am-5pm) Provides fishing gear and licenses, as well as boat rentals. Offers motorboats ($35/175 per hour/day), rowboats and canoe rentals ($15 to $17 per hour). Also offers guided lake fishing ($92 per hour, two-hour minimum) plus fly-fishing half-day trips ($450 for two).

Leek's Marina
WATER SPORTS
(☎307-543-2494) A simple affair, north of Colter Bay Junction, with a gas dock, three-day parking for boat trailers and vehicles and overnight buoys.

Adventure Sports
OUTDOORS
(Dornan's; ☎307-733-3307; www.dornans.com/adventures; Moose Village, WY; ⊙9am-7pm) Rents kayaks, canoes and paddleboards ($50 per day), mountain and road bikes ($40–$65 per day), as well as kids' bikes and racks, with discounted weekly rates. Winter rentals include Nordic skis, snowshoes and sleds.

WINTER ACTIVITIES

With the crowds gone, bears tucked away in their dens and powdery snow blanketing the pines, the Tetons make a lovely winter destination. Moose is the focus of winter activities and the Craig Thomas Discovery & Visitor Center has information on ski-trail, weather, road and avalanche conditions. Teton Park Rd is plowed from Jackson Lake Junction to Signal Mountain Lodge and from Moose to the Taggart Lake Trailhead.

Grand Teton National Park brochures for Nordic skiing (appropriate for snowshoeing) and snowmobiling can be downloaded from www.nps.gov/grte/planyourvisit/brochures.htm.

Nordic Skiing

The park grooms 15 miles of track right under the Tetons' highest peaks, between Taggart-Bradley Lakes parking area and Signal Mountain. Lanes are available for ski touring, skate skiing and snowshoeing. The NPS does not always mark every trail: consult at

TETON WINTER FACILITIES

In Grand Teton National Park much is closed for winter. Get information on weather, road, ski and avalanche conditions from the Jackson Visitor Center (p218). Spur Ranch Log Cabins (p204) sits close to the center. There is limited tent and RV camping near the Colter Bay Visitor Center (p207). On the eastern edge of the national park, Triangle X Ranch (p203) has wood cabins at discount winter rates.

the ranger station to make sure that the trail you plan to use is well tracked and easy to follow. Remember to yield to passing skiers and those skiing downhill. You can find rentals in Jackson.

Taggart Lake to Beaver Creek   SKIING
A moderate to difficult trail with some climbing. It's 3 miles round-trip to Taggart Lake or 4 miles round-trip to do the Beaver Creek Loop, climbing through a glacial moraine. Use care on the return descent, the trail may be icy. Park at the Taggart Lake parking area.

Jenny Lake   SKIING
An easy 8-mile round-trip. Park at the Taggart Lake parking area. Follow the Jenny Lake trail parallel to Cottonwood Creek and return via Teton Park Rd. There are great views of the Tetons throughout.

Moose–Wilson Road   SKIING
Park at the entrance to Death Canyon Rd. To ski Moose–Wilson Rd, it's an easy 5.8 miles round-trip, with some climbing. A 2-mile loop detours to the edge of Phelps Lake. You can also approach via Teton Village, parking at Granite Canyon trailhead. Pets are allowed on Moose–Wilson Rd but not on the trails into the park.

Snowshoeing

Snowshoers may use the Nordic skiing trails described previously. For an easy outing, try Teton Park Rd (closed to traffic in winter). Remember to use the hardpack trail and never walk on ski trails – skiers will thank you for preserving the track!

From late December through to mid-March rangers lead free two-hour 1.5-mile snowshoe hikes from the Craig Thomas Discovery & Visitor Center. Snowshoes are provided, it's open to eight-year-olds and up.

Polecat Creek   SNOW SPORTS
Park at the Flagg Ranch Lodge. Traveling clockwise, this easy 2.5-mile loop soon arrives at Polecat Creek and Huckleberry Hot Springs. After crossing power lines, in 0.4 miles another trail intersects. Stay right on the loop, continuing south to the lodge.

Snowmobiling

In the park, snowmobiling is only allowed on the frozen surface of Jackson Lake. Snowmobilers will have more options in Yellowstone and West Yellowstone. Snowmobilers must have a valid driver's license and vehicles must have Best Available Technology (BAT) and meet requirements listed on the NPS snowmobiling brochure. On the John D Rockefeller Jr Memorial Pkwy, Grassy Lake Rd is open to snowmobiles without BAT requirements.

Flagg Ranch Company   SNOW SPORTS
(☑ 307-543-2861; www.gtlc.com/headwaters-lodge .aspx; ⊙ Dec-Mar) Offers guided snowmobile tours to Old Faithful and the Grand Canyon of the Yellowstone, departing at 6:30am. Since the resort is closed to guests, Flagg Ranch offers hotel pickups in Jackson for its snowmobilers. Flagg Ranch information station does stay open in winter for those using the trails.

Backcountry Skiing

There is excellent backcountry skiing here, but skiers should have adequate knowledge of avalanche safety and use a transceiver, or book a guided tour.

Teton Backcountry Guides   SNOW SPORTS
(☑ 307-353-2900; http://tetonbackcountryguides. com; 2-person downhill/XC tour $420/300) Guides small groups of one to four on backcountry ski and snowboarding tours for all abilities. Day trips and multiday tours available. It also operates the only hut system in the Tetons and runs safety clinics.

◉ SIGHTS

◉ John D Rockefeller Jr Memorial Parkway

This NPS-managed parkway is a 7.5-mile corridor linking Yellowstone and Grand Teton National Parks. Congress recognized Rockefeller's contribution to the creation of Grand

Teton National Park by designating this 24,000-acre parkway in his honor in 1972. Here, the Tetons taper to a gentle slope, and rocks from volcanic flows in Yellowstone line the Snake River. A transitional zone between the two national parks, the area combines characteristics of both, though it's less spectacular than either. Activities focus around historic Flagg Ranch, which was established as a US Cavalry post in 1872.

North–south US 89/191/287 is the main road through the parkway. The turnoff to Flagg Ranch Rd is 2 miles south of Yellowstone's South Entrance Station and 15 miles north of Colter Bay Village. The turnoff to Grassy Lake Rd, which leads west to Ashton, Idaho, is just north of Flagg Ranch.

The **Flagg Ranch Information Station** (☏307-543-2401; ☺9am-6pm Jun-Sep) is near the Grassy Lake Rd turnoff. Flagg Ranch Resort offers parkway accommodations, dining, gas and activities. Once a popular winter launch pad into Yellowstone National Park, the resort now closes in winter since stricter snowmobiling regulations have been put in place. Winter trails can still be accessed here.

Grassy Lake Road

The 52-mile, east–west Grassy Lake Rd links US 89/191/287 to US 20 at Ashton, Idaho, offering a remote back way into the national parks. This bumpy gravel road, also a good mountain-biking route, follows an old Native American trade and hunting route. In late fall it closes and snowmobiles take over.

Heading west from US 89, Flagg Ranch is the first landmark on the road. Shortly after crossing the Polecat Creek Bridge, the pavement ends. The graded gravel road parallels the north bank of the Snake River. Camping is restricted to designated sites, and is popular with anglers, hunters and those headed west along the rough Reclamation Rd (USFS Rd 261) to the Cascade Corner in Yellowstone's lush Bechler region.

Sandwiched between the Winegar Hole and Jedediah Smith Wildernesses, this region is peppered with lakes with great fishing options. The most accessible are the roadside **Indian Lake** and **Loon Lake**, 1 mile down a bumpy track off Reclamation Rd. Further east there's a turnoff for the rough road to stunning **Lake of the Woods**, site of the Boy Scouts' Loll Camp. A mile further east is the 0.5-mile detour south to Tilley Lake. Beyond, the expansive and popular **Grassy Reservoir** has boating, fishing and dispersed campsites. Just after the reservoir the road enters the Rockefeller Pkwy. There are eight free campsites further along Grassy Lake Rd (USFS Rd 261).

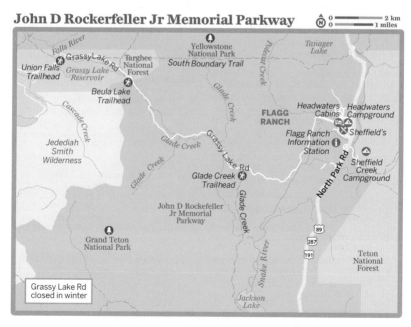

John D Rockerfeller Jr Memorial Parkway

Grassy Lake Rd closed in winter

◎ Colter Bay Region

The road south from Yellowstone drops off the Yellowstone plateau at the end of the Rockefeller Pkwy, where a startling view of the Tetons soaring above Jackson Lake comes into play. Past Lizard Creek Campground several beaches tucked into nooks offer some of the park's best picnic areas.

Jackson Lake is a natural glacial lake that has been dammed, so water levels fluctuate, dropping considerably toward the end of the summer. Mt Moran (12,605ft), named after landscape painter Thomas Moran, dominates the north end of the park. After Moran first traveled this way with Hayden's geological survey in 1871, his grand depictions forever became synonymous with the area.

Two Ocean and Emma Matilda Lakes sit east of Jackson Lake, tucked into the hills. Visitor services are concentrated at Colter Bay Village.

Colter Bay

Ask at the visitor center about early-morning bird-watching walks. Rangers also lead a daily 8am morning walk from Colter Bay Visitor Center to Swan Lake (3 miles, three hours) and campfire programs in the evening. South of the visitor center is the marina and trailhead for hikes to Swan Lake and Hermitage Point. A popular picnic and swimming area sits just north of the visitor center, though there are countless other secluded swimming and sunbathing spots dotted around Jackson Lake.

Indian Arts Museum MUSEUM
(Map p195; ☑1-800-299-0396; ⊙8am-5pm)
FREE Displays 80 pieces from the vast collection of David T Vernon (other pieces are under restoration). Artifacts include beautiful beadwork, bags and photographs. The visitor center offers books on Native American history and lore. There's also a visiting guest artist each summer showing modern Native American works and Shoshone elder talks.

Around Jackson Lake Lodge

The elegant Jackson Lake Lodge is worth a stop, if only to gape at the stupendous views through its 60ft-tall windows. In cold weather the cozy fireplaces in the upper lobby are blazing. In summer you can drink in fine Teton views and a cold Snake River Lager while sitting outdoors.

Rangers answer questions on the back deck of Jackson Lake Lodge daily from 6:30pm to 8pm, and there is a free talk on the history of the lodge every Sunday at 8pm.

The willow flats below the hotel balcony are a top spot to catch a glimpse of moose, which flock to willow as a critical food source, particularly in winter. Since the area has become popular with calving elk and bears, it now has a seasonal closure between mid-May and mid-July. During that time you can still enjoy the nearby Willow Flats turnout (Map p195), with views of Mt Moran, Bivouac Peak, Rolling Thunder Mountain, Eagles Rest Peak and Ranger Peak.

A short walk from the lodge, Christian Pond is a good place to spot riparian birdlife. The trail to the pond crosses the main road by a bridge just south of the lodge.

About a mile north of Jackson Lake Lodge a rough dirt road branches east off the main road to a trailhead, from which it's a 1-mile walk one way (with a steep climb at the end) to 7586ft Grand View Point (Map p195), which offers fine views of both the Tetons and Two Ocean Lake. You can also visit the viewpoint as part of the Two Ocean Lake hike.

Colter Bay Region

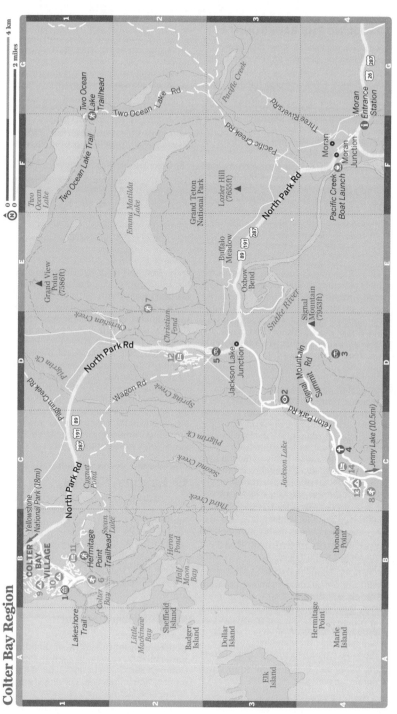

Colter Bay Region

PADDLING THE BACKCOUNTRY

Overnight boaters can use backcountry campsites around **Jackson Lake** at Deadman Point, Bearpaw Bay, Grassy Island, Little Mackinaw Bay, South Landing, Elk Island and Warm Springs. Book these sites in advance, especially on summer weekends when the lake is chockablock with powerboats, sailboards, sailboats and canoes. There is a maximum three-night stay.

With dramatic close-ups of the toothy Mt Moran, **Moran Bay** is the most popular destination from Colter and Spalding Bays. While boating you can stop at Grassy Island en route. The following sample distances start from Signal Mountain: Hermitage Point (2 miles), Elk Island (3 miles) and Grassy Island (6 miles); from Colter Bay to Little Mackinaw Bay it's 1.5 miles.

Alternatively, you can paddle from Lizard Creek Campground to remote backcountry trails on the northwest shore. Wilcox Point backcountry campsite (1.25 miles from Lizard Creek) provides backcountry access to Webb Canyon along the Moose Basin Divide Trail (20 miles). For a longer intermediate-level trip, paddle the twists and turns of the **Snake River** from Flagg Ranch to Wilcox Point or Lizard Creek.

Predominant winds from the southwest can be strong, especially in the afternoon, when waves can swamp canoes. Morning is usually the best time to paddle.

One of the most famous scenic spots for wildlife-watching is **Oxbow Bend**, 2 miles east of Jackson Lake Junction, with the reflection of Mt Moran as a stunning backdrop. Early morning and dusk are the best times to spot moose, elk, sandhill cranes, ospreys, bald eagles, trumpeter swans, Canada geese, blue herons and white pelicans. The oxbow was created when the river's faster water eroded the outer bank while the slower inner flow deposited sediment.

Heading south on Teton Park Rd, you'll find interpretive displays along the west shoulder near **Jackson Lake Dam** (Map p195). Built in 1916, the dam raises the lake level by 39ft and was paid for by Idaho farmers who still own the irrigation rights to the top 39ft of water. The dam was reinforced between 1986 and 1989 to withstand earthquakes.

South of here is the **Log Chapel of the Sacred Heart** (Map p195). Open to visitors, it's also a pleasant picnic area.

Signal Mountain Summit Road

This 5-mile paved road (no RVs) east of Teton Park Rd winds up to the top of **Signal Mountain** for dramatic panoramas from 800ft above Jackson Hole's valley floor. Below, the Snake River, the valley's only drainage, runs a twisted course through cottonwood and spruce. Abandoned dry channels demonstrate the changing landscape.

Views are superb at sunrise, but the best vistas are actually from three-quarters of the way up at **Jackson Point Overlook** (Map p195), a short walk south from a parking area. William Jackson took a famous photo-

graph from this point in 1878, when preparing a single image could take a full hour, using heavy glass plates and a portable studio.

The mountain's name dates from 1891, when Robert Ray Hamilton was reported lost on a hunting trip. Search parties lit a fire atop Signal Mountain after he was found a week later, floating in Jackson Lake. A 6-mile round-trip hiking trail leads to the summit from Signal Mountain Campground, through groves of scrumptious huckleberries.

In winter Signal Mountain Rd offers Nordic skiing with stunning views and a fun 5-mile downhill return run. To reach the turnoff, ski 1 mile south from Signal Mountain along a snowmobiling trail.

⊙ Eastern Slopes

Hwy 26/89/191 traverses the park's eastern flank for about 25 miles from the Moran Junction to the park's southern gate past sagebrush flats and the occasional ranch – always with the Tetons' sharp spires diverting your gaze westward. The hardscrabble lives of Jackson Hole's early homesteaders are reflected in the valley's characteristic lodgepole buck and pole fences.

Moran to Blacktail Butte

Ranchers Pierce and Margaret Cunningham, early major supporters of Grand Teton National Park, cultivated a cattle ranch at **Cunningham Cabin** in 1890, located 6 miles south of Moran Junction. The property is one of the best surviving examples of a homestead cabin; a short trail casts light on local homesteading.

Four miles south, the Snake River Overlook offers good panoramas of the Tetons and opportunities for wildlife-watching, though forest growth means the photo ops aren't quite as good as when Ansel Adams immortalized the shot.

A better place for photos is Schwabacher's Landing, a popular rafting put-in 4 miles further south. The jagged Tetons reflected in the meandering river ranks as some of the park's most sublime scenery. Access the landing via a short dirt road.

East of Blacktail Butte, an unpaved road great for cycling connects Antelope Flats Rd to the north with Gros Ventre Rd to the south (when not washed out). Its scenic collection of ranches with pioneer barns and cabins is known as Mormon Row, where 10 settlers took up residence in the 1890s. A resident bison herd, gorgeous post-dawn light and superb Teton views make this area exceptionally popular with photographers. Two barns sit north of the junction and two south, currently under restoration.

Gros Ventre Rd leads east to the Gros Ventre Slide.

◉ Central Tetons

South of Signal Mountain, Teton Park Rd passes the Potholes, sagebrush flats pockmarked with craterlike depressions called kettles. The kettles were formed slowly by blocks of orphaned glacial ice that were stranded under the soil, left by receding glaciers. Just south is the Mt Moran turnout.

Jenny Lake Scenic Drive

Seven miles south of Signal Mountain, the Jenny Lake Scenic Dr branches west to begin the park's most picturesque drive.

The Cathedral Group turnout boasts views of the central Teton spires, known as the Cathedral Group. Interpretive boards illustrate the tectonic slippage visible at the foot of Rockchuck Peak, named for its resident yellow-bellied marmots. String Lake is the most popular picnic spot, with dramatic views of the north face of Teewinot Mountain and Grand Teton from sandy beaches along its east side. The road becomes one way beyond String Lake, just before exclusive Jenny Lake Lodge.

Perched on the lake's glacial moraine, Jenny Lake Overlook (Map p198) offers good views of the Tetons and tall Ribbon Cascade

to the right of Cascade Canyon, and shuttle boats headed for Inspiration Point. Be careful not to miss the turnout, as you can't back up on this one-way road.

Jenny Lake

The scenic heart of the Grand Tetons and the epicenter of Teton's crowds, Jenny Lake was named for the Shoshone wife of early guide and mountain man Beaver Dick Leigh. Jenny died of smallpox in 1876 along with her children.

The Jenny Lake Visitor Center (p207) is worth a visit for its geological displays and 3D map of Jackson Hole. The cabin was once in a different location, as the Crandall photo studio. The Jenny Lake area is undergoing a massive $17 million restoration to trails and infrastructure, planned to be ready for 2017. In the meantime, watch for temporary trail closures and the relocation of services.

From the visitor center a network of trails leads clockwise around the lake for 2.5 miles to Hidden Falls and then continues for a short uphill run to fine views at Inspiration Point. Once you're here, it's worth continuing up Cascade Canyon for as long as you can, since you've already finished most of the hard climb. From here you can return via the way you came or continue clockwise to the String Lake Trailhead to make a 6-mile circle around the lake. If you're on the Jenny Lake Trail in the early morning or late afternoon, detour approximately 15 minutes (about 0.5 miles) from the visitor center to Moose Ponds for a good chance of spotting moose.

TETON NAMES

Impressions are everything... French Canadian fur trappers named the three Tetons – South, Middle and Grand – 'les Trois Tetons' (the Three Breasts), most likely in a lonely moment of Western wandering and reflection.

Trapper Osborne Russell claimed their Shoshone moniker was 'Hoary Headed Fathers.' Teewinot means 'Many Pinnacles' in Shoshone – it now describes the range as well as Teewinot Mountain.

The Snake River gets its name from the local Shoshone people, though the name Snake was mistakenly given to the Shoshone when the weaving sign for the Shoshone (who called themselves the people of the woven grass huts) was confused with the sign for a snake.

Central Tetons

GRAND TETON NATIONAL PARK

N

0   2 miles
0   4 km

Cathedral Group Turnout

Jenny Lake Scenic Drive

Leigh Lake

Leigh Lake Trailhead

String Lake Trailhead

String Lake

String Lake Trail

Teton Park Rd

Jenny Lake

Lupine Meadows

Jenny Lake Trailhead

Glacier Gulch

Glacier Falls

Lupine Meadows Trailhead

Timbered Island

Teton Park Rd

Climber's Ranch Rd

Taggart Lake

Taggart Creek

Hanging Canyon

Inspiration Point

Hidden Falls

Rockchuck Peak (11,144ft)

Mt St John (11,430ft)

Lake of the Crags

Paintbrush Canyon Trail

Paintbrush Canyon

Mt Woodring (11,590ft)

Holly Lake

The Jaw (11,400ft)

Cascade Creek

Cascade Creek Trail

Cascade Canyon

Teewinot Mountain (12,325ft)

Mt Owen (12,928ft)

Teton Glacier

Disappointment Peak (11,571ft)

Delta Lake

Amphitheater Lake

Surprise Lake

Garnet Canyon Trail

Garnet Canyon

Bradley Lake

Avalanche Canyon Trail

Paintbrush Divide (10,645ft)

North Fork Cascade Canyon

North Fork

Petersen Glacier

The Wigwams

Grand Teton (13,770ft)

Middle Teton (12,804ft)

South Fork Cascade

Iceflow Lake

South Teton (12,514ft)

Lake Taminah

Shoshoko Falls

Mount Wister (11,490ft)

Lake Solitude

Mica Lake

Table Mountain (11,106ft)

Hurricane Pass (10,372ft)

Snowdrift Lake

The Wall

Granite Basin

South Leigh Lakes

Jedediah Smith Wilderness

Battleship Mountain (10,679ft)

Teton Canyon

Table Mountain Trail

Targhee National Forest

Trapper Lake

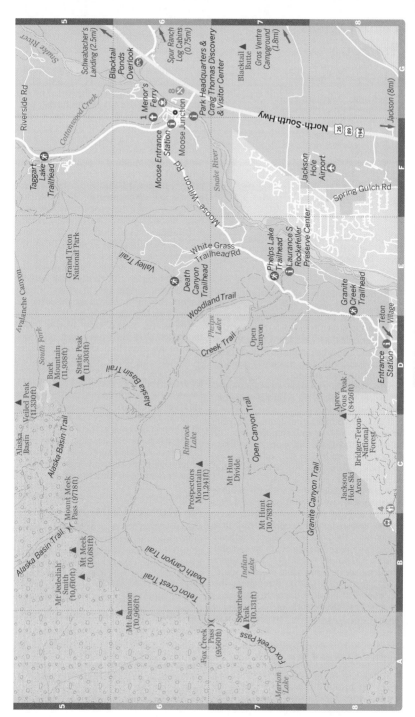

GRAND TETON NATIONAL PARK

Central Tetons

⦿ Sights

1 Chapel of the Transfiguration	F6
2 Jenny Lake Overlook	G2

⦿ Activities, Courses & Tours

3 Exum Mountain Guides	F3
4 Jackson Hole Mountain Resort	C8

⦿ Sleeping

5 Climbers' Ranch	F4
6 Jenny Lake Campground	F3
7 Jenny Lake Lodge	F1

⦿ Eating

8 Dornan's Chuckwagon	G6
Dornan's Grocery Store	(see 8)
Jenny Lake Lodge Dining Room	(see 7)
Pizza Pasta Company	(see 8)

Alternatively, **Jenny Lake Boating** (☑307-734-9227; www.jennylakeboating.com; 1-way shuttle adult/child 8-12yr $9/6; ⊙7am-7pm Jun-late Sep) runs shuttles across Jenny Lake between the east-shore boat dock near Jenny Lake Visitor Center and the west shore boat dock near Hidden Falls, offering quick (12-minute) access to Inspiration Point and the Cascade Canyon Trail. Shuttles run every 15 minutes, but expect long waits for return shuttles between 4pm and 6pm.

Rangers lead hikes from Jenny Lake Visitor Center at 8:30am to Inspiration Point (2 miles, 2½ hours) via the Jenny Lake ferry. Numbers are limited to 25, and places are first-come, first-served; arrive at the visitor center by 8am to secure a spot.

Canoes, kayaks and boats with motors less than 8HP are allowed on Jenny Lake. The put-in is by the east-shore boat dock and is accessed by a separate road that branches off the Lupine Meadows Trailhead road. Jenny Lake Boating rents kayaks and canoes ($20/75 per hour/day). It also offers hour-long scenic Jenny Lake cruises (adult/child 7 to 11 years $19/11) throughout the day. Inquire at the dock or call to reserve.

Jenny Lake also offers good fishing and is stocked with lake, brown, brook and Snake River cutthroat trout.

South of Jenny Lake

Just south of Jenny Lake, Teton Park Rd passes the turnoff to the Lupine Meadows Trailhead, for hikes to Surprise Lake and Garnet Canyon. On the east side of the road watch for **Timbered Island**, an enclave of forested glacial soils stacked atop poorly drained sedimentary soils.

Two miles south of here, Teton Glacier turnout offers some of the best views of **Teton Glacier**, the largest in the park. The Taggart Lake Trailhead is 1.5 miles further on.

A short trail and the homestead cabin of William Menor sit half a mile north of Moose Village, off a paved road. Menor was alone on the west bank of the Snake River for 10 years, building a pontoon raft that provided a vital crossing for mule teams and riders who hunted, picked mushrooms and berries, and cut lumber on the Teton side. In 1910 he sold the property to entrepreneur Maude Noble, who started charging a then-brazen $1 to locals and $2 for those with out-of-state plates to cross. Today you can cross in a replica of **Menor's Ferry** (Map p198; ⊙early Jul-Aug). Old photographs, restored buggies and the original settlers' wagon offer insight into the lives of early settlers. Stop by the obligatory old-fashioned period store (9am to 4:30pm).

The nearby 1924 **Chapel of the Transfiguration** (Map p198) has aspen pews and views of the Tetons through the altar window. In summer Episcopal services are held on Sundays. Just beyond is **Moose Entrance Station** (Map p198) and the Craig Thomas Discovery & Visitor Center (p207), offering interpretive displays, an auditorium hosting excellent speakers and events, and the largest selection of books in the park. The park's southern hub, **Moose** also offers accommodations, restaurants and shops, and serves as the jumping-off point for many park activities. It is also the center for wintertime park activity.

⦿ Moose–Wilson Road

Moose–Wilson Rd is a partially paved 15-mile route (its southernmost 3 miles are gravel) that connects Teton Village to Moose. RVs and trailers are not allowed on this road inside the park, which is quite narrow in sections.

Laurance S Rockefeller Preserve

For solitude coupled with the most stunning views that don't include the Grand, visitors should definitely check out this newer section of Grand Teton National Park. Once the JY Ranch, an exclusive Rockefeller family retreat, these 3100 acres around Phelps Lake were donated in full in 2001 by Laurance S

Rockefeller. His grandfather John D Rockefeller had been an early park advocate, purchasing the first tracts of land to donate in 1927. Despite strong local opposition, by 1949 he had donated some 33,000 acres of former ranchland to Grand Teton National Park.

With this sector, Laurance Rockefeller's vision was to create a space of refuge and renewal. In contrast to other visitor centers, the beautiful **Laurance S Rockefeller Preserve Center** (Map p198; ☑307-739-3654; Moose-Wilson Rd; ⊙8am-6pm Jun-Aug, 9am-5pm Sep-May) is a meditative experience. Sparely furnished and LEED-certified, it features quotes from naturalists and writers etched into walls, giant picture windows to admire the views and a library with leather armchairs and books on conservation and nature to browse. The center also hosts a full board of ranger programs.

Little trace is left of the ranch. Homes and cabins have been torn down, roads left to revegetate and an 8-mile network of nature trails has been created. By design, the preserve promotes an intimate experience. To prevent overcrowding, there is no parking allowed nearby on the shoulder of the Moose–Wilson Rd and the parking lot only accommodates 40 vehicles – come before 10am or after 3pm in summer to ensure a spot. It's 4 miles south of Moose Junction.

🛏 SLEEPING

Most campgrounds and accommodations are open from early May to early October, depending on the weather conditions. Camping inside the park is permitted in designated campgrounds only and is limited to 14 days (seven days at popular Jenny Lake). The NPS operates the park's six **campgrounds** (National Park Service Campgrounds; ☑800-628-9988; www.nps.gov/grte/planyourvisit/camping.htm) on a first-come, first-served basis.

Demand for campsites is high from early July to Labor Day, and most campgrounds fill by 11am (checkout time). Jenny Lake fills by about 8am, followed by Signal Mountain. Colter Bay is a large site and fills later; Gros Ventre fills last, if at all.

Signal Mountain is a popular base because of its central location. Colter Bay and Jenny Lake have tent-only sites reserved for backpackers and cyclists.

Group sites (for up to 75 people) available at Gros Ventre and Colter Bay Campgrounds can be reserved only by calling park concessionaire Grand Teton Lodge Company (p207). Reservations are only taken for groups, up to one year in advance.

🛏 John D Rockefeller Jr Memorial Parkway

The parkway is a handy place to stay en route between Yellowstone and Grand Teton National Parks.

Headwaters Campground   CAMPGROUND $
(Flagg Ranch Campground; tent/RV sites $35/69, 4-person cabins $73; ⊙May-early Oct) Among the most expensive campgrounds around. It features pull-through sites, propane for sale, 24-hour showers, laundry and a nightly campfire program. Sites are generally available the same day, but RV campers should reserve a week or more in advance (reserve through Flagg Ranch Company; p190).

Headwaters Cabins   CABIN $$
(Flagg Ranch Resort; ☑800-443-2311, 307-543-2861; www.gtlc.com/headwaters; r $195-295; ⊙mid-May–mid-Sep; ⛺🐾) Since its occupation by the US Cavalry, this 1910 resort has seen improvements: walkways lead to prim log duplexes featuring rooms with phones, coffeemakers and patio rockers. Pet-friendly ($17 extra), it's popular with families and couples stopping between parks. The lodge offers upscale dining, a minimarket and an activities desk. Shuttles go to Jackson and the Jackson Hole Airport.

DITCH THE CROWDS

Parking lots at popular trailheads and areas such as Jenny Lake, String Lake, Lupine Meadows and Granite Canyon are often packed before 11am. The Death Canyon Trailhead parking stays full since overnight backpackers leave cars for multiple days. Cascade Canyon hums with day-trippers to Solitude Lake in August.

Get an alpine start on your hike (leave before most of your neighbors think of breakfast) to beat the crowds. It's a good way to see more wildlife too.

Jenny Lake Campground is perennially full, and Signal Mountain Campground fills up early in the day. You can avoid the campground crowds by choosing less-popular campgrounds such as Lizard Creek or Gros Ventre.

Two Ocean and Emma Matilda Lakes, in the northeast section of the park, offer excellent hiking without the crowds.

🛏 Colter Bay Region

Camping

At campgrounds run by the Grand Teton Lodge Company (GTLC), walk-in hikers and bicyclists pay only $10 per person, with specific sites reserved for them.

Lizard Creek Campground   CAMPGROUND $
(☑800-672-6012; www.nps.gov/grte; sites $22; ⊙Jun–early Sep) Snug in a forested peninsula along Jackson Lake's north shore, about 8 miles north of Colter Bay Junction, these secluded woodsy sites (60 total) are a great option. Register early since it's popular with boaters. Vehicle length limited to 30ft.

Signal Mountain
Campground   CAMPGROUND $
(Map p195; ☑800-672-6012; www.signalmtn lodge.com; Teton Park Rd; sites $22; ⊙early May–mid-Oct) This popular campground with 86 sites looks out on lovely sunsets on Jackson Lake from 5 miles south of Jackson Lake Junction. Sites can be cramped but are convenient: a restaurant, bar, grocery store and marina are nearby. Vehicle size is limited to 30ft. There's a dump station for RVs.

Colter Bay Campground   CAMPGROUND $
(Map p195; www.gtlc.com; US 89/191/287; sites $22; ⊙mid-May–mid-Sep) The pros and cons of this large, noisy campground (350 sites) on the east shore of Jackson Lake relate to its size. It should always have available spots and there's a separate RV park, grocery store, laundromat and hot showers available at nearby Colter Village. Propane is available, and there's a dumping station. It's 3 miles north of Jackson Lake Junction.

Colter Bay RV Park   CAMPGROUND $
(Map p195; ☑800-628-9988, reservations 307-543-2811; www.gtlc.com; sites $65; ⊙mid-May–mid Sep) Sewer, electrical and water connections are perks at these long pull-through sites (112 total). There's a surcharge for vehicles that are over 38ft.

Lodging

Signal Mountain Lodge   LODGE $$
(Map p195; ☑307-543-2831; www.signalmtnlodge. com; r $221-326, cabins $173-233, ste $350, tent/ RV sites $22/45; ⊙May–mid-Oct) 🍴 This spectacularly located place at the edge of Jackson Lake offers cozy, well-appointed cabins and rather posh rooms with stunning lake and mountain views.

GRAND TETON NATIONAL PARK CAMPGROUNDS

CAMPGROUND	LOCATION	DESCRIPTION	NO OF SITES	ELEVATION (FT)
Gros Ventre (p204)	Central Tetons	Spacious and shady, with plenty of ample spaces; tent sites are on separate loops	372	6783
Jenny Lake (p203)	Central Tetons	The most coveted camp spot amid boulders and trails; tents only	51	6803
Colter Bay (p202)	Colter Bay	Enormous but wooded, with ready conveniences; buzzing with activity	350	6820
Colter Bay RV Park (p202)	Colter Bay	RV zones are separate with electrical connections	112	6820
Lizard Creek (p202)	Colter Bay	A secluded spot with shade and lake access	60	6768
Signal Mountain (p202)	Colter Bay	Close to shops and restaurants, with lake access and forest shade	86	7593
Headwaters (at Flagg Ranch; p201)	Rockefeller Pkwy	Features dining and conveniences nearby but not a haven for tenters	175	6300

 Drinking Water   *Restrooms*   *Ranger Station*   *Wheelchair Accessible*   *Grocery Store Nearby*

Colter Bay Village
CABIN **$$**

(Map p195; ☑ 307-543-2811; www.gtlc.com; tent cabins $66, cabins with bath $155-290, without bath $85; ☺ Jun-Sep) Tent cabins (June to early September) are very basic log-and-canvas structures sporting Siberian gulag charm. Expect bare bunks, a wood-burning stove, picnic table and outdoor grill. Bathrooms are separate and sleeping bags can be rented. The log cabins, some original, are much more comfortable and a better deal, available late May through September.

★ Jackson Lake Lodge
LODGE **$$$**

(Map p195; ☑ 307-543-2811; www.gtlc.com; r & cottages $289-385; ☺ mid-May–Sep; 🛜🦽🐕) With soft sheets, meandering trails for long walks and enormous picture windows framing the luminous peaks, this lodge is the perfect place to woo. Yet, you may find the 348 cinder-block cottages overpriced. Has a heated pool and pets are OK.

🛏 Eastern Slopes

★ Triangle X Ranch
RANCH **$$$**

(☑ 307-733-2183; www.trianglex.com; 2 Triangle X Rd, Moose; weekly all-inclusive per person double occupancy $1820, winter cabins per person $140) With a stunning Teton backdrop, this 1926 ranch on the eastern flanks of the park is still run by its founders, the Turner family. There are immaculate wood cabins and activities – from square dancing and trout fishing to Dutch-oven cookouts – to keep you out in the fresh air. Cabins have one to three bedrooms.

Moose Head Ranch
RANCH **$$$**

(☑ 307-733-3141; www.mooseheadranch.com; all-inclusive per person double occupancy $410; ☺ Jun-Aug) Families rave about this ranch, which has modern log cabins, friendly young staff, a varied and tasty menu and a slew of activities for adults and kids alike. Rides are for all abilities. Visits require a five-night minimum and children get discounted rates. It's located between the Tetons and Yellowstone, 18 miles north of Jackson, at 6800ft.

🛏 Central Tetons

Camping

At Jenny Lake Campground and Gros Ventre Campground, walk-in hikers and bicyclists pay $8 per person, with specific sites reserved for them.

Jenny Lake Campground
CAMPGROUND **$**

(Map p198; Teton Park Rd; tent sites $22; ☺ mid-May–late Sep) This congenial and popular tent-only campground (51 sites) sits among the evergreens and glacial boulders 8 miles

GRAND TETON NATIONAL PARK SLEEPING

OPEN	RESERVATION REQUIRED?	DAILY FEE	FEATURES & FACILITIES
late April– mid-Oct	no	$24	
mid-May– late Sep	no	$22	
mid-May–mid-Sep	no	$22	
mid-May–mid-Sep	no	$65	
early Jun-early Sep	no	$22	
early May–mid-Oct	no	$22	
late May-late Sep	yes	tent/RV $35/64	

   Dogs Allowed (on Leash)   *Payphone*   *Summertime Campfire Program*   *RV Dump Station*

❶ CAMPING ON THE CHEAP

Some lesser-known, first-come, first-served sites near the park may have fewer amenities, but they also have openings when NPS campgrounds are bursting, and charge a third to half of the price.

Hidden **Sheffield Creek Campground** (sites $5; ⊘ late Jun-Nov) is a five-site USFS campground 2.5 miles south of Yellowstone's South Entrance and just south of Flagg Ranch, across the Snake River Bridge, then a half-mile east on a rough dirt road from a subtly signed turnoff.

Located 7 miles north of Kelly on the shores of Slide Lake, **Atherton Creek Campground** (Gros Ventre Rd, Slide Lake; sites $12) has 20 sites, drinking water and pit toilets.

Eight free, minimally developed, first-come, first-served campgrounds are strung out along the bumpy unpaved **Grassy Lake Road**, which begins just west of the parking lot at Flagg Ranch. The first (and most popular) campground is 1.6 miles along the road and has four riverside campsites. Each of the next three riverside campgrounds, in the 1.5-mile stretch past Soldiers' Meadow, has two sites. The last four campgrounds, spaced out along the next 3.5 miles, are useful for hikes into Yellowstone's southern reaches. All sites have toilets and trash service but no potable water. Camping is only allowed in designated sites.

The hidden eight-site **Pacific Creek Campground** (sites $10; ⊘ mid-Jun–Dec) is 12 miles up the graveled Pacific Creek Rd (USFS Rd 30090) from Grand Teton's Moran Ranger/Entrance Station. It's generally used as a base for backpacking trips into the Teton Wilderness.

Several free dispersed campsites sit on **Shadow Mountain**, on the east edge of the valley. This spot has a dedicated following, so show up early. Don't expect water or toilets, and there's a two-day maximum stay. It's a rough drive anywhere, but you'll be rewarded with stunning dawn views of the Tetons.

north of Moose Junction. Convenient to many trailheads, it is almost always full. Only vehicles less than 14ft long are allowed, and trailers are prohibited.

⭐**Gros Ventre Campground** CAMPGROUND $
(Gros Ventre Rd; sites $24; ⊘ late Apr–mid-Oct) Sprawling but secluded, this 372-site campground sits near the Gros Ventre River, 11.5 miles from Moose. With the tall cottonwoods for shade and a nearby river, it's very attractive. It tends to fill up later in the day, with the more private sites west of the loops going first. There's an RV dump but no hookups.

Lodging

⭐**Climbers' Ranch** CABIN $
(Map p198; ☑ 307-733-7271; www.americanalpine-club.org; Teton Park Rd; dm $25; ⊘ Jun-Sep; 🐾) Started as a refuge for serious climbers, these rustic log cabins run by the American Alpine Club are now available to hikers who can take advantage of the spectacular in-park location. There is a bathhouse with showers and sheltered cook station with locking bins for coolers. Bring your own sleeping bag and pad (bunks are bare, but still a steal).

⭐**Jenny Lake Lodge** LODGE $$$
(Map p198; ☑ 307-733-4647; www.gtlc.com; Jenny Lake; cabins from $699; ⊘ Jun-Sep) Worn timbers, down comforters and colorful quilts

imbue this elegant lodging off Teton Park Rd with a cozy atmosphere. It doesn't come cheap, but includes breakfast, a five-course dinner, bicycle use and guided horseback riding. Rainy days are for hunkering down at the fireplace in the main lodge with a game or book from the stacks.

🛏 Moose

Spur Ranch Log Cabins CABIN $$
(☑ 307-733-2522; www.dornans.com; cabins $195-285; ⊘ year-round) Gravel paths running through a broad wildflower meadow link these tranquil duplex cabins on the Snake River in Moose. Lodgepole-pine furniture, Western styling and down bedding create a homey feel, but the views are what make it.

✕ EATING & DRINKING

Visitors dine in the park for the convenience or the stunning views, but generally not for the food. The better restaurants face the challenge of getting chefs on a seasonal basis – the quality of your meal will depend largely on their success. For foodies, it's worth a trip to nearby Jackson. Other options include taking a Jackson Lake dinner and breakfast cruise or packing a picnic basket with five-star goodies. Dornan's (p206) in Moose offers an impressive selection of wines.

✕ John D Rockefeller Jr Memorial Parkway

Sheffield's   AMERICAN $$
(☎800-443-2311; mains $10-27; ☺6:30am-9:30pm, bar until 11pm) Hungry travelers flock to this eatery at Flagg Ranch, the area's sole dining option. Breakfast and lunches are casual at this handsome lodge while dinner goes Western with grilled steaks, meatloaf and chicken pot pie. Whiskey and local brews are served at the Burnt Bear Saloon. The adjoining minimart has a deli (open 1:30pm to 5:30pm).

✕ Colter Bay Region

Colter Bay

For the cheapest nearby picnic fixings, hit the deli counter at the Colter Bay grocery store.

Leek's Pizzeria   PIZZA $
(Map p195; ☎307-733-5470; mains $4-12; ☺11am-10pm) Pizza and draft beer on the patio is a fine way to end an active day. North of Colter Bay Village, this casual but cozy eatery also serves soup, salad and sandwiches, and has a basic kids' menu. Open-mic nights are on Monday, and live bands play every two weeks.

**John Colter Café
Court Pizza & Deli**   CAFETERIA $
(Map p195; mains $7-12; ☺11am-10pm) An airy, plain cafeteria offering salads, burritos, picnic takeout and grill staples. Kids will like this place. The service is friendly and the grilled free-range chicken tacos are tasty.

Ranch House   AMERICAN $$
(breakfast $9-15, lunch $11-15, dinner $9-30; ☺6:30am-9pm May-Sep; ☝) Serving wild game, salmon and flank steak, this Western dining room with a branded bar offers a more formal setting, serving wine and beer. Vegetarians are appeased (but barely) with veggie burgers or tofu lo mein. The all-you-can-eat breakfast buffet is a pre-hike institution.

Jackson Lake Lodge

Blue Heron   BARBECUE $
(Map p195; ☎307-543-2811; mains $10-12; ☺6-8pm Sun-Fri Jul-Aug) An outdoor casual grill attached to an attractive cocktail lounge, with a caffeination station that serves lattes and espressos from 6am and alcohol and appetizers from 11am to midnight. Occasionally you'll hit on live music. To fully appreciate the patio, sip a huckleberry margarita while watching the alpenglow on Mt Moran.

Pioneer Grill   DINER $$
(Map p195; ☎307-543-1911; mains $9-25; ☺6am-10:30pm; ☝) A casual classic diner with a row of leatherette stools, the Pioneer serves up wraps, burgers and salads. A Mt Owen – an oversized profiterole topped with ice cream, hot fudge and whipped cream – takes the burn off hiking Cascade Canyon. There's takeout, boxed lunches (order a day ahead) and room-service pizza for pooped hikers (5pm to 9pm).

Mural Room   MODERN AMERICAN $$$
(Map p195; ☎307-543-1911; mains $22-44, lunch mains $12-20; ☺7am-9pm) The ambience could hardly be heightened: in addition to stirring views of the Tetons and moose ambling in the willow flats, the walls are adorned with the romantic Rendezvous Murals, depictions of 19th-century life by Carl Roters. Gourmet selections include game dishes and juicy vegetable Wellington. Breakfasts are very good; dinner reservations are recommended.

Signal Mountain

Trapper Grill   CAFE $$
(Map p195; ☎307-543-2831; Signal Mountain Lodge; mains $10-19; ☺7am-10pm) With an encyclopedic menu, the Trapper Grill should please each picky member of the family, offering choices from grass-fed burgers and tacos to gourmet sandwiches and ribs. Breakfast, with sides of ham, bacon or buffalo sausage, are gut busters. You could also grab a Philly steak and a pint of Snake River Lager at Deadman's Bar, named after the site of an unsolved murder in 1886.

Peaks   AMERICAN $$$
(Map p195; ☎307-543-2831; Signal Mountain Lodge; mains $18-38; ☺5:30-10pm) Dine on selections of cheese and fruit, local free-range beef and organic polenta cakes. Small plates, like wild-game sliders, are also available. While the indoor ambience is rather drab, the patio seating, starring sunsets over Jackson Lake and top-notch huckleberry margaritas, gets snapped up early.

✗ Central Tetons

Jenny Lake Lodge
Dining Room MODERN AMERICAN $$$
(Map p198; ☑307-543-3352; Jenny Lake Lodge; breakfast $26, lunch mains $11-15, dinner prix-fixe $88; ⊙7am-9pm) A real splurge, this may be the only five-course wilderness meal of your life, but it's well worth it. For breakfast, crab cake eggs Benedict is prepared to perfection. Trout with polenta and crispy spinach satisfies hungry hikers, and you can't beat the warm atmosphere snuggled in the Tetons. Dress up in the evening, when reservations are a must. There's live classical guitar most evenings in the lobby.

✗ Moose

Dornan's Grocery Store MARKET, DELI $
(Map p198; ☑307-733-2415; Moose Village) The park's best-quality selection. Has an excellent deli with imported cheeses, sandwiches, espresso counter and wildly popular ice cream. The Wine Shoppe offers 1700 selections as well as monthly wine tasting.

Pizza Pasta Company PIZZA $
(Map p198; mains $9-18; ⊙11:30am-9:30pm) Packed with crowds nightly, this unpretentious pizza parlor is simple yet so satisfying. Crusty pizza, pastas and nachos are offered with beer, wine and snappy service. Guests line up and make their orders at a counter.

Dornan's Chuckwagon BARBECUE $$
(Map p198; ☑307-733-2415, ext 213; Moose Village; breakfast & lunch $7-12, dinner $17-32; ⊙7:30-11am, 11:30am-3pm & 5-9pm Jun–mid-Sep, closed Fri & Sat evening) At this family favorite, breakfast means sourdough pancakes and eggs off the griddle while lunchtime offers light fare and sandwiches. Come dinner, Dutch ovens are steaming. There's beef, ribs or trout, along with a bottomless salad bar. Picnic tables have unparalleled views of the Grand. Kids get special rates. The bar boasts zinging margaritas and Snake River Lager on tap. Locals and travelers flock to the Monday-night Hootenanny, an open-mic event, heavy on the folk tunes and Appalachian jams. Bring your own beer and blanket.

❶ Orientation

Just south of Yellowstone National Park, Grand Teton National Park stretches 40 miles along the compact, 15-mile-wide range. Its western boundary merges with the Jedediah Smith Wilderness within Targhee National Forest. The Bridger-Teton National Forest sits east. The steep eastern flank overlooks Jackson Hole valley, where Jackson Lake catches the Snake River flowing south from its source in Yellowstone National Park. On the western side of the range, Idaho's Teton Valley features more gradual slopes.

MAIN REGIONS

Jackson Lake dominates the northern half of the park with the Tetons to the west. The popular central Teton peaks, ringed by alpine lakes, are concentrated in the southwest. The most remote and least visited area of the park is the northwest region, accessible only by multiday backpacking. This is the Tetons' prime grizzly habitat, although sightings have extended south and east through other parts of the park.

Before crossing into Idaho, the Snake River winds through flat glacial deposits on the south side of the park. The quieter, less visited east side is bordered by the forested hills of the Bridger-Teton National Forest and the remote trails of the Teton Wilderness.

MAJOR ROADS

The main north–south route through the park is US 26/89/191, contiguous with the east bank of the Snake River between Jackson and Moran Junction. At Moran Junction US 89/191 joins US 287 heading north along Jackson Lake to the Rockefeller Memorial Pkwy; US 26 joins US 287 heading east to Dubois via Togwotee Pass.

Teton Park Rd links Moose Junction to Jackson Lake Junction and US 89/191/287 via Jenny and Jackson Lakes. The 5-mile Jenny Lake Scenic Dr connects North Jenny Lake and South Jenny Lake Junctions; the road is two way to Jenny Lake Lodge and one way south of it. Gros Ventre Rd heads east from US 26/89/191 at the south end of the park to Kelly and out of the park into the Gros Ventre Valley. Antelope Flats Rd is 1 mile north of Moose Junction, east of US 26/89/191. The narrow Moose–Wilson Rd connects Teton Village to Moose; no RVs or trailers are allowed.

FOLLOW THE PARK

➡ www.facebook.com/GrandTetonNPS

➡ twitter.com/GrandTetonNPS

➡ instagram.com/GrandTetonNPS

➡ www.youtube.com/user/GrandTetonNP1

➡ http://tetonapp.com

VISITOR SERVICE HUBS

The southern hub is Moose, with a new visitor center, a gas station, accommodations, restaurants, groceries and equipment rental. The nearby Laurance S Rockefeller Preserve Center is south on the Moose–Wilson Rd.

Further north on Teton Park Rd, Signal Mountain has accommodations, a grocery store, a gas station and a restaurant. Jackson Lake Lodge has shops and restaurants.

Colter Bay hosts the highest concentration of visitor services, with a visitor center, gas station, grocery store, restaurants, laundromat, showers, campground, RV park and marina.

Information

Three park concessionaires operate various accommodations, restaurants, marinas and activities: **Dornan's** (☑ 307-733-2522; www.dornans.com; Moose Village), **Grand Teton Lodge Company** (GTLC; ☑ 307-543-3100, 800-628-9988; www.gtlc.com) and Signal Mountain Lodge (p202).

MEDIA

Grand Teton Association (☑ 307-739-3606; www.grandtetonpark.org) This nonprofit organization sells books and maps at all park visitor centers. It funds educational materials, learning programs, research grants, and host art events and more.

POST

Post office (Moose Village)

RANGER STATIONS

Colter Bay Visitor Center (☑ 307-739-3594; ⊙ 8am-5pm early–mid-May & Sep-early Oct, 8am-7pm Jun-early Sep) On US 89/191/287, 6 miles north of Jackson Lake Lodge. Issues backcountry permits and offers crafts demonstrations and tours of its Indian Arts Museum. Newcomers can get their bearings at 'Teton Highlights,' a daily 30-minute ranger talk at 11am at the auditorium.

Craig Thomas Discovery & Visitor Center (Map p198; ☑ 307-739-3399, backcountry permits 307-739-3309; Teton Park Rd; ⊙ 8am-7pm Jun-Aug, to 5pm Sep-May; 🛜)

Jenny Lake Ranger Station (☑ 307-739-3343; ⊙ 8am-6pm Jun-Aug) Also offers backcountry permits and climbing information.

TOURIST INFORMATION

Flagg Ranch Information Station (☑ 307-543-2327; ⊙ 9am-4pm Jun-early Sep, closed for lunch) Provides park information, rest rooms and a small bookstore. Located 2.5 miles from Yellowstone's South Entrance.

Jenny Lake Visitor Center (☑ 307-739-3343; ⊙ 8am-7pm Jun-Aug, to 4:30pm Sep-May) On Teton Park Rd, 8 miles north of Moose

❶ DANGERS & ANNOYANCES

Though people are the greater nuisance, be aware that black bears and a growing population of grizzlies live in the park.

Mid-October to early December is elk-hunting season in areas east of US 26/89/191, west of US 26/89/191 along the Snake River between Moose and Moran Junctions, and the Rockefeller Memorial Pkwy. If you must venture into these areas during hunting season, exercise caution: don a bright-orange vest and avoid elk-like behavior. The National Park Service (NPS) *Elk Ecology & Management* pamphlet offers more details and a map.

Junction. Facilities include a store, lockers, geology exhibits, a relief model, restrooms and telephones. With in-depth information on backpacking and trails, it's also the meeting place for guided walks and talks.

❶ Getting Around

DRIVING

The speed limit on US 26/89/191 is 55mph; elsewhere it's generally 45mph. Watch for wildlife at dusk, as well as cyclists crossing sections of the multiuse pathway on Teton Park Rd. Gas stations are open year-round at Moose (24 hours, credit card only 8pm to 8am) and Flagg Ranch Resort, and summers only at Colter Bay, Signal Mountain and Jackson Lodge.

ORGANIZED TOURS

Grand Teton Lodge Company (☑ 800-628-9988; www.gtlc.com; adult/child 3-12yr Grand Teton $65/30; Yellowstone $106/63) Half-day Grand Teton tours, full-day tours of Yellowstone or a combination of both parks.

Gray Line National Park Tours (☑ 800-443-6133, 307-733-3135; www.graylinejh.com; adult/child $100/50) Full-day park tours from Jackson.

PUBLIC TRANSPORTATION

Alltrans Park Shuttle (☑ 800-443-6133, 307-733-3135; www.alltransparkshuttle.com; daily pass $15; ⊙ 7am-7pm Jun-Sep) Operates several buses a day in summer between Jackson, Moose, Jenny Lake Lodge, Signal Mountain Lodge, Jackson Lake Lodge and Colter Bay. Riders can pay with cash or credit cards. Rides are unlimited on the daily pass. The service is free for guests of GTLC properties.

Around Grand Teton

Best Places to Eat

➡ Persephone (p216)

➡ Snake River Grill (p217)

➡ Teton Thai (p220)

➡ Nora's Fish Creek Inn (p216)

Best Places to Stay

➡ Alpine House (p215)

➡ The Hostel (p220)

➡ Turpin Meadow Ranch (p222)

➡ Buckrail Lodge (p214)

➡ Rock Spring Yurt (p220)

Why Go?

Outside the park boundaries, the landscape doesn't suddenly turn dull. The rampage of beauty continues with cold clear rivers, winding singletracks and steep powder runs. Visit this region in winter and you will find Jackson Hole and Grand Targhee resorts serving up deep, pillowy snow. Lodges light roaring fires and the wilderness becomes a haven for dogsledding, snowshoeing, ski touring and frozen fun.

Posh and popular Jackson serves as the regional hub and base camp, where you can browse for Western baubles, down pints of fresh organic lager or wrap yourself in honey and rose petals. The foodie scene is among the best in the West, with an emphasis on local, farm-raised food. On the Idaho side, rural Teton Valley is another world. If you have come to embrace every scrap of solitude, a trip west across the divide might be in order.

Road Distances (miles)

	Jackson	Teton Village	Moose	Victor, ID
Teton Village	15			
Moose	15	10		
Victor, ID	25	25	35	
Grant Village (Yellowstone)	80	75	65	100

Note: Distances are approximate

Jackson

📞 307 / POP 10,135 / ELEV 6234FT

Beautiful and studiedly rustic, this town, technically in Wyoming, has the highest per-capita income in the US: with no income tax, it's a haven for millionaires. Once a diamond in the rough, it nowadays has McMansions spreading like brucellosis. This is the new West, a human confluence that includes ranchers, rhinestone cowboys, mountain athletes and an army of service workers. As the community evolves, tensions sometimes flare over wilderness issues, since 97% of Teton County is, in fact, public land.

Yet Jackson is abuzz with life: trails and outdoor opportunities abound, fresh sushi is flown in daily and generous purse strings support a vigorous cultural life. When it becomes a little much, just skip the souvenir shops and dwell in the glorious backyard called Grand Teton National Park.

Jackson marks the intersection of Hwy 22 (heading west to Teton Pass) and US 26/89/191. The main drag follows East-West Broadway into the downtown area, where it turns north onto Cache Dr at the town square, the heart of the pedestrian-oriented commercial district. Hwy 390 (Moose–Wilson Rd) leads north 7 miles to Teton Village.

◎ Sights

★**National Museum of Wildlife Art** MUSEUM

(📞307-733-5771; www.wildlifeart.org; 2820 Rungius Rd; adult/child $14/6; ⊙9am-5pm, from 11am Sun spring & fall) If you visit one area museum, make it this one, with major works by Bierstadt, Rungius, Remington and Russell. It's worth driving up just for the outdoor sculptures and the building itself (inspired by a ruined Scottish castle). The **discovery gallery** has a kids' studio for drawing and print rubbing that adults plainly envy. Check the website for summer film-series and art-class schedules.

National Elk Refuge WILDLIFE RESERVE

(📞307-733-9212; www.fws.gov/refuge/national_elk_refuge; Hwy 89; ⊙8am-5pm Sep-May, to 7pm Jun-Aug) FREE This refuge protects Jackson's herd of several thousand elk, offering them a winter habitat from November to March. During summer, ask at the Jackson visitor center for the best places to see elk. An hour-long horse-drawn sleigh ride is the highlight of a winter visit; buy tickets at the visitor center.

Center for the Arts ARTS CENTER

(📞307-733-4900; www.jhcenterforthearts.org; 240 S Glenwood S) One-stop shopping for culture, attracting big-name concert acts and featuring theater performances, classes, art exhibits and events. Check the calendar of events online. Students get discounts on performances.

Jackson National Fish Hatchery FISH HATCHERY

(📞307-733-2510; 1500 Fish Hatchery Rd; ⊙8am-4pm) FREE Just north of the elk refuge, with daily tours.

🏃 Activities

Goodwin Lake & Jackson Peak HIKING

This 9-mile round-trip is one of the closest summits to Jackson with cross-valley Teton views. The bare, pointed summit of Jackson Peak (10,741ft) sits above a lake. Its most secure approach winds left up a gradual saddle. Continue past Goodwin Lake heading southeast, crossing an open field. Take a right at a well-worn but narrow trail marked with cairns. Climb steeply to the ridge, crossing snow patches and rocky outcrops to the peak.

To get here, drive east on East Broadway until it ends, turning left into the National Elk Refuge. The road switchbacks. Bear right at Curtis Canyon for Goodwin Lake (after 9.2 miles) and drive 2.7 miles to the parking lot. The trail climbs steadily through a field of wildflowers, topping out on a level hilltop, and passing through fragrant forests of Douglas fir. Approach the forested shores of Goodwin Lake (880ft), a nice spot for a swim or trout fishing.

Return via the same route. Dogs allowed.

Mill Iron Ranch HORSEBACK RIDING

(📞888-808-6390, 307-733-6390; www.millironranch.net; 5 US Hwy 89; 2hr ride $60) This fourth-generation operation of a Wyoming ranch family is the real deal. Climbing 2000ft, its two-hour ride in the Bridger-Teton National Forest is rated the number-one trail ride in the US. It also offers dinner rides, sleigh rides and barn dances. To get there, drive south from Jackson on Hwy 89.

Jackson Hole Mountain Guides ROCK CLIMBING

(📞307-733-4979, 800-239-7642; www.jhmg.com; 1325 US 89, Suite 104) With world-class climbing at your fingertips, Jackson is an ideal center for instruction or guided climbs. This place offers guided Teton rock climbing and programs for kids.

Around Grand Teton

Yellowstone
Lake

Grant
Village

Flat
Mountain

Shoshone
Lake

Lewis
Lake

Yellowstone National Park

Channel
Mountain

Mount
Sheridan
(10,308ft)

Overlook
Mountain

Snow Creek
Butte

Bechler River

Targhee
National
Forest

Birch
Hills

Chipmunk Creek

Yellowstone

Teton Range

Winegar
Hole
Wilderness

Flagg Ranch

John D. Rockefeller Jr.
Memorial
Parkway

Huckleberry
Mountain
(9615ft)

Teton
Wilderness

Survey Peak
(9277ft)

Pacific Creek

TETON VALLEY

On the Idaho side of the Tetons, towns such as Victor and Driggs offer rural charm and outdoor activities galore. (p222)

Moose
Mountain
(10,054ft)

Ranger
Peak
(11,355ft)

Colter Bay
Village

WYOMING

Jackson Lake Junction

Oxbow Bend

Terrace
Mountain

Grand
Teton
National
Park

Jackson
Lake

Felt

Tetonia

Teton River

Driggs

IDAHO

Squirrel
Mountain
(7769ft)

Victor

Mt Moran
(12,605ft)

Signal
Mountain
(7953ft)

Baldy
Mountain
(8524ft)

Mt Woodring
(11,590ft)

Leigh
Lake

Teton
National
Forest

Grouse
Mountai

Mt St John
(11,430ft)

Jenny
Lake

Table
Mountain
(11,106ft)

Grand Teton
(13,770ft)

Shadow
Mountain
(8299ft)

East Leidy
(10,134ft)

Green
Mountain
(9695ft)

Jedediah
Smith
Wilderness

Moose

Blacktail
Butte

Lower
Slide Lake

Snake River

Mt Hunt
(10,783ft)

Phelps
Lake

Gros Ventre River

JACKSON

Not your typical old West town, with gourmet fare, luxuriant lodgings and a host of summer events. (p209)

Teton
Village

JACKSON HOLE
MOUNTAIN RESORT

This legendary ski area defined steep and deep, but it also offers festivals, mountain biking and hiking access via tram. (p219)

Wilson

Jackson

Crystal
Peak

Jackson
Peak
(10,741ft)

Wind River Range

Gros
Ventre
Wilderness

Snake River

Taylor
Mountain
(8022ft)

Munger
Mountain
(8294ft)

Needle Peak
(8438ft)

Caribou
National
Forest

Palisades
Reservoir

Targhee
National
Forest

Cream
Puff Peak
(9639ft)

WILSON

A last haven for red barns, cowboys and cowgirls, good for country breakfasts and live bands at the Stagecoach. (p216)

Beaver
Mountain
(9731ft)

Teton
National
Forest

GRANITE HOT SPRINGS

Soak away your muscle aches at this natural hot springs area south of Jackson. (p221)

Rendezvous Sports KAYAKING
(Jackson Hole Kayak School; ☑ 307-733-2471; www.
jacksonholekayak.com; 945 W Broadway) Offers
kayak and stand-up paddleboard (SUP)
rentals and instruction in addition to multiday paddling trips to Yellowstone Lake.

Wyoming Balloon Co BALLOONING
(☑ 307-739-0900; www.wyomingballoon.com; per
person $325; ☺ mid-Jun–mid-Sep) The ultimate
float trips are these hour-long flights over
the Tetons. Flights are weather-dependent.

Scenic Safaris WILDLIFE-WATCHING
(☑ 307-734-8898; www.scenic-safaris.com; 545 N
Cache St; half-day tour adult/child $125/95) Guid-
ed wildlife safaris in Grand Teton National
Park, with spotting scopes and binoculars
provided. Also has Yellowstone options.

Winter Activities

**Continental Divide
Dogsled Adventures** TOUR
(☑ 307-455-3052; www.dogsledadventures.com;
half-day $248) Iditarod veteran Billy Snod-
grass and his team of Alaskan racing dogs
sled through the beautiful winter backcountry. Half- and full-day trips are run near
Grand Teton National Park.

Snow King Resort SNOW SPORTS
(☑ 800-522-5464, 307-733-5200; www.snowking.
com; 400 E Snow King Ave; lift ticket adult/child
$47/30) Sling the skis over your shoulder and
walk to this tiny 400-acre resort from downtown. Three lifts serve ski and snowboard
runs with a vertical drop of 1571ft (15% beginner, 25% intermediate, 60% advanced).
This north-facing slope catches less snow
than other resorts but is convenient and well
suited to families. In summer it offers a host
of great activities.

Also popular in winter is night skiing
(adult/child $25/20; 4:30pm to 8:30pm
Monday to Saturday) and tubing (adult/
child per hour $20/15). The best value is
the 'Ski All Three' package, which includes
three nights' lodging with breakfast and two
full-day lift tickets for Snow King, Jackson
Hole Mountain Resort and Grand Targhee,
and transfers to and from the airport and
between the resorts.

In summer, the new Treetop Adventure
(adult/child aged 7 to 12 $69/39), an ad-
venture park designed by pro mountain
guides, opens all its attractions (mid-May
to early October, 10am to 4pm). It features
a fun series of tree-to-tree aerial challenges
including wobbly bridges, climbing walls,
zip lines, moving skateboards and Tarzan
swings that snake through the pine forest
with spectacular Teton views. The course
has variations for adults and children, and
should take between two and four hours.
Rates include use of a 2500ft alpine slide.
There is also a bungee trampoline and paragliding onsite.

New in 2015, the coaster carries riders
400 vertical feet up the mountain before
speeding downhill at up to 25 miles per
hour up to 23ft off the ground, over six
bridges and four loops. It runs in both summer and ski season, with options to drive
yourself or go along as a passenger (driver/
passenger $24/9).

The scenic 20-minute Snow King Chairlift
ride (adult/child $17/12) goes up to 7751ft.
Follow the nature trail at the top through
wildflower fields and aspen groves.

Cycling
There is excellent mountain biking here.
Popular rides in the area include Cache
Creek, southeast of Jackson into the Gros
Ventre; Game Creek, along USFS Rd 30455
east off US 26/89/191; and Spring Gulch
Rd, west of and parallel to US 26/89/191
between Hwy 22 and Gros Ventre Junction.
Hard-core riders can try Old Pass Rd, the old
route over Teton Pass, south of Hwy 22.

Hoback Sports BICYCLE RENTAL
(☑ 307-733-5335; 520 W Broadway Ave; per day
from $49; ☺ 9am-7pm) Offers regular and
performance road bike and mountain-bike
rentals, tours, repairs and maps of area biking trails.

White-Water Rafting & Floating

Snake River Canyon RAFTING
(half-day adult/child 6-12yr from $80/70;
☺ May-early Sep) A splashy paddle down
the class-III Snake River Canyon, south of
Jackson along US 89/26 between Hoback
Junction and Alpine, is a popular summer
pastime. Half-day trips put in at West Table
Creek and take out at Sheep Gulch (8 miles).
Full-day trips put in at Pritchard Creek, upstream from West Table Creek, and take out
at Sheep Gulch (16 miles). The best white
water is in June. Reserve ahead.

Snake River Float Trips RAFTING
(half-day adult/child 4-12yr from $75/65) Half-
day scenic float trips on a 13-mile section of
the swift-flowing Snake River put in south
of Grand Teton National Park and take out
north of Hoback Junction, passing through

Jackson

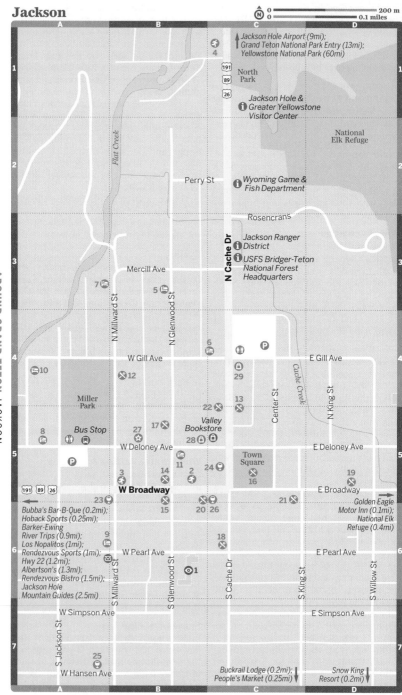

0 — 200 m
0 — 0.1 miles

Jackson Hole Airport (9mi);
Grand Teton National Park Entry (13mi);
Yellowstone National Park (60mi)

191
89
26

North Park

Jackson Hole &
Greater Yellowstone
Visitor Center

National
Elk Refuge

Flat Creek

Perry St

Wyoming Game &
Fish Department

Rosencrans

N Cache Dr

Jackson Ranger
District

USFS Bridger-Teton
National Forest
Headquarters

Mercill Ave

7

5

W Gill Ave

6

E Gill Ave

Cache Creek

N Millward St

N Glenwood St

12

29

13

E Gill Ave

Center St

N King St

Miller
Park

22

17

Valley
Bookstore

27

28

8

Bus Stop

W Deloney Ave

11

2

24

Town
Square

16

19

E Deloney Ave

3

14

W Broadway

E Broadway

191 89 26

23

15

20 26

21

Golden Eagle
Motor Inn (0.1mi);
National Elk
Refuge (0.4mi)

Bubba's Bar-B-Que (0.2mi);
Hoback Sports (0.25mi);
Barker-Ewing
River Trips (0.9mi);
Los Nopalitos (1mi);
Rendezvous Sports (1mi);
Hwy 22 (1.2mi);
Albertson's (1.3mi);
Rendezvous Bistro (1.5mi);
Jackson Hole
Mountain Guides (2.5mi)

9

18

S Millward St

W Pearl Ave

S Glenwood St

E Pearl Ave

1

S Cache Dr

King St S

S Willow St

W Simpson Ave

E Simpson Ave

S Jackson St

25

W Hansen Ave

Buckrail Lodge (0.2mi);
People's Market (0.25mi)

Snow King
Resort (0.2mi)

the Jackson Hole wetlands, which are rich with bird- and wildlife-viewing opportunities.

Barker-Ewing River Trips RAFTING
(☑307-733-1000; www.barker-ewing.com; 45 W Broadway) A reputable outfitter.

Dave Hansen Whitewater RAFTING
(☑307-733-6295; www.davehansenwhitewater.com; 225 W Broadway) Gets rave reviews from families.

★ Festivals & Events

Jackson Hole Rodeo RODEO
(☑307-733-2805; http://jhrodeo.com; 447 Snow King Ave; adult/child 3-15yr from $20/15; ☺summer) Held at Teton County Fairgrounds, this popular rodeo saddles up at 8pm Wednesdays and Saturdays June through August, with some Friday shows.

ElkFest FAIR
(Antler Auction; http://elkfest.org; ☺late May) If an ungulate rack would provide the finishing touch to your home decor, check out this unique Jackson event which takes place every May around the town square. Boy Scouts collect and sell the shed antlers during the festival to raise money to buy pellet winter feed for the elk – thus the elk financially support themselves during the winter.

Teton County Fair FAIR
(www.tetonwyo.org/fair; 447 Snow King Ave; ☺late Jul) From pig wrestling to live music and 4-H animal shows, it does not get more

Wyoming than this. The Teton County Fair takes over the Teton County Fairgrounds in late July.

Jackson Hole Fall Arts Festival ART
(www.jacksonholechamber.com/fall_arts_festival; ☺Sep) Features live auctions, artist talks and samples of local chefs' culinary wizardry.

Jackson Hole Shootout THEATER
(☺6:15pm Mon-Sun summer) Kids shouldn't dodge this street theater. The longest-running shootout in the country happens on Jackson Town Sq, where costumed good guys and bad guys face off from Memorial Day to Labor Day.

🛏 Sleeping

Unfortunately, budget lodgings in Jackson have gone the way of the stagecoach. The best deals come during the shoulder seasons (from October 1 until the opening of ski season in late November, and after spring snowmelt in early April until Memorial Day, when rooms are as much as 50% less than high-season prices quoted here. Those on a tight budget should plan to camp or stake out the bargain off-season ski lodgings over the pass in Idaho.

Advance reservations are essential during holiday periods. For more options, contact Jackson Hole Central Reservations (p221), which has listings for the town of Jackson as well as Teton Village.

AROUND GRAND TETON JACKSON

Jackson

Rates quoted here are for doubles with private bathroom, since single rates are often not available. Walk-in rates can be up to 20% lower than rack rates, especially during slow periods when it pays to shop around. Check online for special seasonal package deals.

Camping

For more information on campgrounds in the Jackson Ranger District call ✏ 1-800-342-CAMP.

Curtis Canyon Campground   CAMPGROUND $
(sites $12; ☺ late May-Sep) Conveniently located, this popular 12-site campground, on gravel USFS Rd 30440 (off Elk Refuge Rd), sits 7 miles northeast of Jackson at 6900ft, with splendid views of the Tetons.

East Table Campground   CAMPGROUND $
(sites $30; ☺ late May-early Sep) Toward Idaho on the southeast side of US 26/89 is this roadside, 18-site campground, 24 miles south of Jackson at 5900ft.

Hoback Campground   CAMPGROUND $
(sites $15; ☺ late May–mid-Sep) Along the Hoback River, 8 miles east of Hoback Junction and 22 miles southeast of Jackson (6600ft), is this shady, 13-site campground.

Kozy Campground   CAMPGROUND $
(sites $12; ☺ late May-Sep 10) On the east side of US 189/191 is this riverside, eight-site campground, 30 miles southeast of Jackson at 6500ft.

Granite Creek Campground   CAMPGROUND $
(sites $15; ☺ late May-Sep) The signed turnoff for this 52-site campground is 1 mile north of Kozy Campground. The campground itself is 35 miles from Jackson, 9 miles northwest of US 189/191 up (often washboard)

gravel USFS Rd 30500, nestled deep in the Gros Ventre Mountains at 6900ft. Has drinking water, flush toilets and shade.

Station Creek Campground   CAMPGROUND $
(sites $15; ☺ late May-Sep) One mile west along the Snake River from Granite Creek Campground is 16-site Station Creek, 25 miles south of Jackson at 5900ft.

Snake River KOA   CAMPGROUND $
(✏ 307-733-7078; www.srpkoa.com; tent sites $34-45, RV sites $44-95; ☺ late May-Sep) Grassy Snake River is 12 miles south of Jackson off US 26/89/191 near Hoback Junction. Cheaper, recommended public US Forest Service (USFS) campgrounds are outside town.

Lodging

Anvil Motel   MOTEL $
(✏ 307-733-3668; www.anvilmotel.com; 215 N Cache Dr; r $77-245) Friendly and well scrubbed, the barn-red Anvil offers good value, is centrally located and has one Jacuzzi suite. Passes are available to the local recreation center with pool, sauna and hot tub. Nonguests can shower here ($6).

Pony Express   MOTEL $
(✏ 307-733-3835; www.ponyexpresswest.com; 1075 W Broadway; r $79-129; ✳ 🛜 🏊) A proud little motel that's hidden behind the gas station. Fresh and spacious rooms have pine walls and tucked-away bunks. Outdoors there's a plush lawn with tables and a heated pool. Cyclists can make use of the cleaning buckets and rags.

★ **Buckrail Lodge**   MOTEL $$
(✏ 307-733-2079; www.buckraillodge.com; 110 E Karns Ave; r $93-162; ✳ 🛜) With spacious and charming log-cabin-style rooms, this steal is

---

SPLURGE: SPRING CREEK RANCH

Embodying every Western fantasy, this rustic resort (✏ 800-443-6139; www.spring-creekranch.com; Spring Creek Rd; resort fee $20, r/ste incl breakfast $380/445; @ 🛜 🏊) gazes smack at the Tetons from the top of a butte ringed in sagebrush. The views are unreal and the vibe is oh-so-relaxed. Guests can rent sprawling mountain villas or little studios with fireplaces. Trails crisscross the property, where you can also ride horses. Naturalist programs take visitors on dawn or dusk safaris to see bison, wolves and other wildlife. Then grab a juniper massage or mineral-rich seaweed wrap from the lauded Wilderness Adventure Spa.

If staying here is out of your price range, consider heading to the resort's gourmet restaurant Granary for happy hour (4pm to 7pm), live jazz on Fridays or piano bar on Saturdays. Staff also mix tasty house cocktails, talked up by *Wine Spectator* magazine, at the copper bar with wild mountain panoramas. To get there, take Hwy 22 from Jackson; the Spring Creek Rd is on your right.

centrally located, with hanging flower baskets and rockers outside each room and an outdoor Jacuzzi. Has a sprawling lawn and wooden swing and is a good bet for families.

Cowboy Village
CABIN **$$**

(☎800-962-4988, 307-733-3121; www.townsquare inns.com/cowboy-village; 120 S Flat Creek Dr; cabins $109-299; ❄🛜❄) Though they're in an urban lot, these cozy log cabins have a spark of yesteryear, snugly furnished with knotted pine, bark beds and animal carvings. It's family friendly, all rooms have kitchenettes and there's a fitness center, outdoor grills and an indoor pool. It's just off W Broadway.

Golden Eagle Motor Inn
MOTEL **$$**

(☎307-733-2042; www.goldeneagleinn.com; 325 E Broadway; d $130-160; ❄) Run by a friendly Jackson native and just far enough out of the fray, this refurbished motel is a reliable choice in the center.

Rawhide Motel
MOTEL **$$**

(☎800-835-2999, 307-733-1216; www.rawhide motel.com; 75 S Millward St; r $169; ❄🛜) New Berber carpets and pine furniture spruce up these typical motel rooms, which also have flat-screen TVs, hair dryers and coffeemakers. Staff are friendly and one basement room runs $30 cheaper.

★ Alpine House
B&B **$$$**

(☎307-739-1570; www.alpinehouse.com; 285 N Glenwood St; r $240-330, cottages $330-515; @) Two former Olympic skiers have infused this downtown home with sunny Scandinavian style and personal touches, like great service and a cozy mountaineering library. Amenities include plush robes, down comforters, a shared Finnish sauna and an outdoor Jacuzzi. Save your appetite for the creative breakfast options, like lemon-ricotta blueberry pancakes or eggs Benedict.

Rusty Parrot Lodge & Spa
LODGE **$$$**

(☎888-739-1749; www.rustyparrot.com; 175 N Jackson St; r incl breakfast from $470) With a collection of Remington sculptures and amazing Western art, this elegant lodge is excruciating in its luxury. Service is top-notch and rooms pamper with well-tended bedroom fireplaces and a plush teddy bear posed on the bed. Those who don't ski will get distracted at the spa, where the arnica sports massages and herbal lavender wraps are pure hedonism. The gourmet restaurant prepares innovative international cuisine.

Inn on the Creek
INN **$$$**

(☎800-669-9534, 307-739-1565; www.innonthe creek.com; 295 N Millward St; r incl breakfast $259-599; @) Elegant and intimate, this stone inn offers nine handsome rooms. Details include recessed fireplaces, top-quality linens on comfy beds and views of a gurgling creek out back. Some rooms have hot tubs. It's wedged into the edge of town, handy to restaurants and shopping.

Wort Hotel
HOTEL **$$$**

(☎800-322-2727, 307-733-2190; www.worthotel. com; 50 N Glenwood St; r $409-699; ❄@🛜) Western themes run amok, but in a good way, at this historic 1940s English Tudor. It's gussied up with lodgepole-pine beds and cowboy-motif sheets, with full-size baths and Jacuzzis. It has, hands down, the best concierge service in Jackson, with great outdoor tips. The attached bar and restaurant features an antique S bar encrusted with silver dollars and painted bordello scenes.

Snow King Resort
HOTEL, CONDO **$$$**

(☎800-522-5464, 307-733-5200; www.snowking. com; 400 E Snow King Ave; r from $309) This expanding resort offers a variety of options ranging from condominiums to luxury suites, with the advantage of being slopeside. Inquire about the attractive seasonal package deals.

Parkway Inn
INN **$$$**

(☎800-247-8390, 307-733-3143; www.parkwayinn. com; 125 N Jackson St; r $249-389; ❄) You may feel like you're spending the weekend at grandma's (except the wolf remains in Yellowstone). This Victorian-themed lodging – really a glorified motor inn – offers ample suites decked in chintz with quilted brass beds. Perks include a well-stocked continental breakfast, indoor lap pool, hot tub and fitness facility.

✖ Eating

Jackson's fare boasts sophistication – even if that means garnishing your burger with a basil leaf. Those hungry for exotic options won't come away disappointed: all manner of game and international cuisine are present, particularly if you're willing to pony up. Pick up a free *Jackson Hole Dining Guide*, found in shops and hotel lobbies, for menus.

Travelers who plan to pack a cooler can shop at grocery stores.

★ **Persephone** BAKERY $
(145 E Broadway; mains $5-15) With rustic breads, oversize pastries and excellent coffee drinks, this French bakery is an obvious pick for breakfast or lunch. The BKT (bacon, kale and tomato jam) sandwich comes on multigrain bread with a spread of ricotta. If you're truly feeling French, go for wine out on the ample deck seating.

Coco Love DESSERTS $
(☑ 307-733-3253; 55 N Glenwood St; desserts $5-10; ☺ 9am-8pm) Master dessert chef Oscar Ortega shows off his French training with a pastry case of exquisite objet d'art desserts and handmade chocolates. Do it.

Los Nopalitos MEXICAN $
(945 Alpine Ln; mains $7-15; ☺ 11am-9pm) For anything more authentic you would need a passport stamp. This informal, bare-bones eatery thrives with the local Latin population, especially at lunchtime before the daily specials have run out. The enormous red mole features tender beef, whole vegetables and corn cobs. There's also tacos you can dress up at the topping bar. Serves beer and cold watermelon juice.

Pica's Mexican Taqueria MEXICAN $
(1160 Alpine Ln; mains $8-15; ☺ 11am-10pm; 🐾) Cheap and supremely satisfying, with Baja tacos wrapped in homemade corn tortillas or *cochinita pibil* (chili-marinated pork), served with Mexican sodas. Locals love this place; it's the best value around. It's just around the corner from Albertson's.

Dog BREAKFAST $
(25 S Glenwood; burritos $6; ☺ 7am-2pm) For bomber breakfast burritos, you would be hard-pressed to beat this tiny shack whose expert eggman serves them fresh and wrapped in a grilled tortilla, surefire fuel for the slopes.

Pearl Street Meat Co DELI $
(260 W Pearl Ave; sandwiches $7-15; ☺ 7am-7pm Mon-Fri, 8am-7pm Sat, 11am-6pm Sun) Jackson's answer to Dean & Deluca is this busy deli stocked with artisan cheeses, gourmet products, natural local meats and takeout sandwiches.

Bunnery Bakery & Restaurant CAFE $
(☑ 307-733-5474; 130 N Cache St; mains $9-12; ☺ 7am-3pm & 5-9pm summer) A family favorite. Lunch and breakfast at this buzzing cafe offer an assortment of hearty fare, including all-day eggs and great vegetarian options. The dessert case tempts with mammoth slices of chocolate cake, pecan pie and caramel cheesecake.

Jackson Whole Grocer HEALTH FOOD $
(☑ 307-733-0450; www.jacksonwholegrocer.com; 1155 S Hwy 89; ☺ 7am-10pm; 🐾🚗) A health-food market and deli, this is a good place to load up for a day's hiking or skiing adventure. There's even wine and beer by the glass, so you can sip while you shop.

Albertson's SUPERMARKET $
(105 Buffalo Way; 🅿) Grocery store.

WORTH A TRIP

WILSON

Big barns and open range make this little outpost 13 miles from Jackson feel more like cowboy country, even though the median home price passes a cool million. It's a popular stop before that last push over the pass to Idaho, especially for cyclists and skiers going to Grand Targhee Ski Resort.

A popular mainstay of live music, mingling cowboys with rhinestone cowgirls, hippies and hikers, Wilson's **Stagecoach Bar** (☑ 307-733-4407; www.stagecoachbar.net; 5800 W Hwy 22; ☺ 11am-late) is worth the short drive. Daily happy hours start at 4:30pm, Thursday is disco night and every Sunday the house band croons country and western until 10pm.

Local institution **Nora's Fish Creek Inn** (☑ 307-733-8288; 5600 W Hwy 22; mains $7-35; ☺ 6am-2pm & 5-9:30pm) reels 'em in with heaping country breakfasts. You can skip the wait by taking a seat at the counter. Lunch and dinner feature prime rib, fresh trout prepared five ways and homemade cobbler.

Pizzeria Caldera
PIZZA $$

(☎307-201-1472; www.pizzeriacaldera.com; 20 W Broadway; slices $4-5, pizzas $13-17; ⊙11am-9:30pm; ⍾) ⌀ Fresh and unpretentious, this upstairs pizzeria serves its pies on the thinner side. Try topping yours with briny kalamata olives or fragrant bison sausage with sage, which begs to be eaten with one of the beers on tap. Salads use locally grown arugula and beets. Slices available until 6pm.

Bubba's Bar-B-Que
BARBECUE $$

(☎307-733-2288; 100 Flat Creek Dr; mains $7-23; ⊙7am-10pm; ⍾) Get the biggest, fluffiest breakfast biscuits for miles at this friendly and energetic diner. Later on, bring your own bottle (BYOB) and settle in for some BBQ ribs and racks.

Lotus Cafe
VEGETARIAN $$

(☎307-734-0882; www.tetonlotuscafe.com; 145 N Glenwood; mains $7-24; ⊙8am-10pm; ⍾) You can hardly swing a cat in this town without hitting a primo steak, but good veggie fare is harder to find. The Lotus solves that with things like kale-avocado salad, veggie lasagna and giant grain-and-veg bowls. (There is some meat on the menu too, all organic.)

★Snake River Grill
MODERN AMERICAN $$$

(☎307-733-0557; 84 E Broadway; mains $23-51; ⊙from 5:30pm) With a roaring stone fireplace, an extensive wine list and snappy white linens, this grill creates notable American haute cuisine. Try the wild game Korean hot bowl, with venison and spring veggies in spicy black-bean sauce. Or munch on a cast-iron bucket of truffle fries. Splurge-desserts like buttermilk *panna cotta* or homemade ice cream easily satisfy two.

Rendezvous Bistro
MODERN AMERICAN $$$

(☎307-739-1100; 380 S Broadway; mains $14-42; ⊙5:30-10pm Mon-Sat) A sure bet for sophisticated bistro food. The happy-hour menu hits the mark with well-priced sophisticated small plates, such as oyster shooters, foie gras with fig jam and a creamy chipotle corn dish that's out of this world. Mains also show good variety, from comfort foods like a local steak frites to fish with spicy roasted grits.

Blue Lion
FUSION $$$

(☎307-733-3912; 160 N Millward St; mains $19-43; ⊙from 6pm) In a precious cornflower-blue house, the Blue Lion offers outdoor dining under grand old trees on the deck. Its renowned rack of lamb, served in peppercorn rosemary cream sauce, may take a while but wins rave reviews. Or there's tenderloin with kimchi butter. Also has early bird specials.

🍸 Drinking & Nightlife

Jackson isn't exactly a wild-night-out kind of town; our guess is that most folks are tuckered from playing all day. But happy hours are exceptionally lively, and a good way to sample the finer restaurants with small plates at cheap prices.

★Bin 22
WINE BAR

(☎307-739-9463; www.bin22jacksonhole.com; 200 W Broadway; ⊙11:30am-10pm Mon-Sat, 3-10pm Sun) Tucked into a wine store stacked deep with wooden crates of the good stuff, this wine bar and tapas restaurant delivers with wonderful wines accompanied by earthy small plates of housemade sausage, organic salads and sumptuous cheeses. Grab a stool at the bar for better service; there's also a pleasant hidden patio.

Snake River Brewing Co
MICROBREWERY

(☎307-739-2337; www.snakeriverbrewing.com; 265 S Millward St; pints $4-5; ⊙11:30am-midnight) With an arsenal of more than 20 microbrews crafted on the spot, some award-winning, it's no wonder this is a local favorite. Food includes wood-fired pizzas, bison burgers and wild-game stew (mains $11 to $14).

Million Dollar Cowboy Bar
BAR

(☎307-733-4790; 25 N Cache Dr; ⊙from 11am) Touristy to the gills, but you kind of have to give it a whirl. Plunk your hindquarters on a saddle stool and order a shot of Wyoming whiskey or a pint of the bar's namesake beer. Most nights there's Western swing dancing, and there's an upscale steakhouse downstairs (reservations recommended).

The Rose
COCKTAIL BAR

(therosejh.com; 50 W Broadway; cocktails $9-14; ⊙5:30pm-2am) A swank little lounge upstairs inside the Pink Garter theater, with red-leather booths, low lighting and chandeliers, the Rose is the place for craft cocktails in Jackson.

Hayden's Post
LOUNGE

(☎307-733-5200; 400 E Snow King Ave) Popular nightspot at Snow King Resort that features live acid jazz on Saturday nights.

DON'T MISS

FARMERS MARKETS

Get a massage, watch a chef demo and sample some gourmet grub while you're at it. These bustling markets run from late June/early July to mid-September.

People's Market (http://jhpeoples market.org; base of Snow King Resort; ⊘4-7pm Wed) At the base of Snow King, this popular farmers market even sells local beer in reusable glasses. It doesn't get much more Jackson that that.

Farmer's Market (www.jacksonhole farmersmarket.com; Jackson Town Sq, Jackson; ⊘8am-noon Sat) Local vendors sell produce, cheeses and natural meats and there are live music performances.

Entertainment

The free weekly *Jackson Hole Weekend Guide* appears Friday and reviews local entertainment options, as does the *Stepping Out* insert.

Jackson Hole Playhouse   THEATER
(☑307-733-6994; www.jhplayhouse.com; 145 W Deloney Ave) Local theater troupes stage acclaimed Broadway-style musical comedies and provide dinner.

Shopping

Teton Mountaineering   OUTDOOR EQUIPMENT
(☑307-733-3595; 170 N Cache St) Stocks a good range of books and outdoor gear. Singles seeking climbing partners can check the bulletin board.

Skinny Skis   OUTDOOR EQUIPMENT
(☑307-733-6094; 65 W Deloney Ave) One of the best backcountry ski shops in the US, with Nordic ski rentals, quality hard goods and a huge selection of the best women's outdoor clothing. Also knowledgeable about trails.

ℹ Information

Tune to 90.3 FM (NPR), 93.3 (KJAX) or 96.9 (KMTN) for the local lowdown. Free newspapers include the *Jackson Hole Daily* (liberal) and the *Daily Guide* (conservative).

Bank of Jackson Hole ATM (990 W Broadway, cnr E Broadway & S Cache)

Jackson Hole & Greater Yellowstone Visitor Center (☑307-733-3316; www.jacksonhole chamber.com; 532 N Cache Dr; ⊘9am-5pm) Provides information, books, restrooms, an ATM and a courtesy phone for free local calls.

Jackson Ranger District (☑307-739-5450; www.fs.fed.us/btnf; 25 Rosencranz Ln; ⊘8am-4:30pm Mon-Fri) Side by side with the USFS Bridger-Teton National Forest Headquarters.

St John's Medical Center (☑307-733-3636; 625 E Broadway)

Teton County Library (☑307-733-2164; www. tclib.org; 125 Virginian Ln; ⊘10am-9pm Mon-Thu, 10am-5pm Fri & Sat, 1-5pm Sun) Great resource for topo maps and local information, with free internet and wi-fi.

USFS Bridger-Teton National Forest Headquarters (☑307-739-5500; www.fs.fed.us/ btnf; 25 Rosencranz Ln) Office in the Jackson Ranger District; information available at the visitor center.

Wyoming Game & Fish Department (☑307-733-2321; 25 Rosencranz Ln; ⊘8am-5pm Mon-Fri) For fishing licenses and required decals on motorcraft.

ℹ Getting There & Away

Jackson Hole Airport (JAC; Map p198; ☑307-733-7682; www.jacksonholeairport.com) is 7 miles north of Jackson off US 26/89/189/191 within Grand Teton National Park. Daily flights serve Denver, Salt Lake City, LA, San Francisco, Chicago, Dallas and Houston.

Alltrans' Jackson Hole Express (☑307-733-3135; www.jacksonholebus.com; ⊘park shuttle mid-May–Oct) buses provide a shuttle to Grand Teton National Park ($14 per day) and the airport ($16). Buses also depart at 6:30am daily from Maverik County Store (on the corner of Hwy 89 S and S Park Loop Rd) for Salt Lake City ($75, 5½ hours).

ℹ Getting Around

Southern Teton Area Rapid Transit (START; ☑307-733-4521; www.startbus.com) operates an around-town shuttle and two routes (Red Line and Workers' Special) between Jackson and Teton Village. One-way fares are free within town limits and $3 to Teton Village; exact change is required. Check maps and timetables posted at stops for current routes and schedules.

Major car-rental agencies have outlets at the airport.

Alltrans (☑800-443-6133, 307-733-3135) Taxi service.

Hertz (☑800-654-3131, 307-733-2272; www. hertz.com) Counter at Jackson airport.

Jackson Hole

Now that the valley is clad in faux fur, Stetsons and trophy homes, it's hard to remember that the first settlers of Jackson Hole wrangled with harsh winters and a short growing season, not to mention the horse thieves, poachers and elk tuskers that roamed the rural valley.

This is one of the most breathtaking destinations in the country. Moose, elk and bison roam the valley floor against the rugged backdrop of the Tetons. Eagles and osprey fish the cold, crystalline streams and lakes. Surrounding the valley, the mountainous 3.4-million-acre Bridger-Teton National Forest is the second-largest forest in the lower 48.

Dubbed 'hole' by early European visitors, the broad valley is bounded by the Gros Ventre (grow-vant: 'big belly' in French) and Teton Ranges to the east and west, respectively, and the Yellowstone lava flows and Hoback and Wyoming Ranges to the north and south. The communities of Jackson, Teton Village, Kelly, Moose and Wilson, as well as much of south Grand Teton National Park, lie within the Hole. (Some of these are inside the Grand Teton National Park.)

Downhill skiing rules winter, but summertime visitors find no shortage of things to do.

Teton Village & Jackson Hole Mountain Resort

Long runs, deep powder and a screeching 4139ft vertical drop may have earned it infamy, but Jackson Hole has quickly become the pet resort of a tony, jet-setting crowd. There are real athletes here too, though, and those with any interest in playing outdoors can revel in the fair-weather pursuits of hiking, cycling, white-water rafting, fly-fishing, mountain biking and faux cowboying. This modern year-round resort is at the foot of Rendezvous Mountain, 12 miles northwest of Jackson.

◉ Sights

Jackson Hole's lifts provide a high-altitude piggyback to the high-country trails in Grand Teton National Park. Tickets can be purchased from guest services (p221).

Aerial Tram   CABLE CAR
(☑ 307-729-2654; adult/child 6-17yr $32/17, mountain biking pass $37, free descent; ☺9am-5pm Jun-Sep) The 60-passenger tram travels 2.5 miles in 10 minutes to the top of Rendezvous Mountain (10,450ft), offering great views of Jackson Hole. Hikers should note that they can hike up (or in via Grand Teton National Park) and take the tram down for free. Paragliding is done from here too.

Bridger Gondola   CABLE CAR
(mountain biking pass $37; ☺ Sun-Fri mid-Jun–Sep)
FREE Offers rides to the headwall (which is 1355ft lower than Rendezvous Mountain) and hiking trails. It's open in the evening to bring diners up to Couloir. Mountain bikers pay for a pass for both lifts.

Teewinot Quad   CABLE CAR
(mountain biking pass $37; ☺9am-5pm daily mid-Jun–Aug, Sat & Sun Sep) This high-speed chairlift provides access to downhill mountain-bike trails. The resort distributes free bike trail guides. Passes are for all lifts.

🏃 Activities

Hiking and mountain biking are the big summer activities. Resort lifts give a head start into high country. From the Rendezvous summit, hikers can either descend Granite Canyon Trail or choose from a series of shorter trails: the 0.5-mile Summit Nature Loop, 3-mile Cody Bowl Trail or the 4.25-mile Rock Springs Bowl.

Pick up free bike trail guides at guest services and rental bikes at the ski shops. Downhill trails can be accessed via the Teewinot Quad. On Friday nights (5pm to 7pm) mountain bikers can get a lift pass for $10.

★**Jackson Hole**
Mountain Resort   SNOW SPORTS
(Map p198; ☑307-733-2292; www.jacksonhole. com; day pass adult/child $121/75; ☺late Nov-early Apr) 'The Hole' is all about vertical, boasting a continuous vertical rise of 4139ft – beaten only by Big Sky, by 41ft (we're sure that some front loader is poised to adjust this injustice). Among the world's top ski destinations, the resort has 2500 acres of ski terrain blessed by an average of 380in of snow annually.

Jackson Hole Mountain
Sports School   COURSE
(☑307-733-4505, 800-450-0447; www.jackson hole.com/mountain-sports-school) For downhill or snowboard lessons and clinics, check out this school; its top-dollar draw is skiing with Olympic gold medalist Tommy Moe.

Jackson Hole Paragliding   PARAGLIDING
(☑307-690-7560, 307-739-2626; www.jhparaglid ing.com; tandem flight from $245) Tandem rides take off from Jackson Hole Mountain Resort or Snow King. No experience is necessary.

Teton Village   AMUSEMENT PARK
(☑307-739-2654; www.jacksonhole.com; Grand Adventure pass $79; ☺10am-5pm late Jun-Labor Day) Kids can bounce on a bungee trampoline,

scramble up a climbing wall or fish for free at Crystal Springs Pond. Adults may want to join in for disc golf, free to all guests. To do it all, the Grand Adventure pass includes the bike park and aerial adventure course, with unlimited tram rides. Purchase tickets from guest services.

Jackson Hole Nordic Center SKIING
(☑307-739-2629; www.jacksonhole.com/nordic. html) Offers 20 miles of groomed track and wide skating lanes with rentals and instruction.

High Mountain Heli-Skiing SKIING
(☑307-733-3274; www.heliskijackson.com; per person $1200) Delivers advanced skiers and snowboarders to ungroomed backcountry powder. Rates are for one day and six heli-skiing runs – about 12,000 vertical feet.

Jackson Hole Sports OUTDOORS
(☑307-739-2687; Bridger Center; ⊙8:30am-6pm) Rents and sells downhill gear. In the summer it tunes and rents mountain bikes and can offer the lowdown on area rides.

✨ Festivals & Events

Grand Teton Music Festival MUSIC
(☑307-733-1128; www.gtmf.org; Walk Festival Hall, Teton Village; ⊙Jul-Aug) Considered one of the best venues for classical music in summer. While it can get expensive, there are free family concerts, student tickets without cost and rehearsal tickets for only $10.

🛏 Sleeping

Rates vary widely and seasonally; some hotels also levy a resort fee. Rates drop up to 50% in the shoulder seasons (when it is too warm to ski but too muddy to mountain bike). The village has extensive lodging options.

★Hostel HOSTEL $
(☑307-733-3415; www.thehostel.us; 3315 Village Dr, Teton Village; dm $34-40, r $79-119; @✋) The area's only budget option, this old ski lodge in Teton Village offers private doubles and bunk-bed rooms with renovated showers for up to four. The spacious lounge with fireplace is ideal for movies or Scrabble tournaments and there's a playroom for tots. There's a microwave and outdoor grill, coin laundry and ski-waxing area. Rates drop in fall and spring.

Fireside RV Resort & Cabins CAMPGROUND $
(☑307-732-2267; www.firesidejacksonhole.com; 2780 N Moose-Wilson Rd; RV sites $79-125, cabins $339-389; ⊙May-Oct; 🐾) Probably the highest-end RV sites you could find, 2 miles north of Hwy 22 on Hwy 390. Cabins are rustic chic, with luxury bedding, flat-screen TVs, fireplaces and private outdoor fire pits.

★Rock Spring Yurt YURT $$$
(☑307-739-2654; www.jacksonhole.com/yurt.html; up to 8 people half-board $500) If you're craving a wilderness experience without the hassle, trek to this modified Central Asian–style tent equipped with a wood-burning stove and gas lamps. An expert guide cooks your food and does the dishes (but you tell the bedtime stories). A porter ($100) is extra. The hut is reached via a 2.5-mile hike (or ski) from Teton Village.

Alpenhof Lodge HOTEL $$$
(☑307-733-3242; www.alpenhoflodge.com; r incl breakfast $199-319) The classic Tyrolean Alpenhof has snug gable rooms with thick duvets, hand-painted furniture and cozy wood paneling. The cozy bistro specializes in wild game and schnitzel. The après-ski scene is popular with the fortysomething crowd.

🍴 Eating & Drinking

★Teton Thai THAI $
(☑307-733-0022; http://tetonthaivillage.com; 7342 Granite Loop Rd; mains $8-18; ⊙noon-10pm) Maybe it's the long hike that kick-started your hunger, but it would be hard to find a more satisfying food stop with craft beer on tap. Chopped laab salad gives just the right bite and the velvet curries burst with flavor. Portions are generous. There's indoor/outdoor seating and takeout for those who wish to torture nearby campers. With vegan options.

Calico Italian Restaurant & Bar ITALIAN $$
(☑307-733-2460; Hwy 390; mains $14-29; ⊙from 5pm) 🌿 Serves original salads, earthy minimalist pizzas, roast chicken and hearty pastas in a renovated 1905 church. Greens come from the organic vegetable garden out back, and there's also lovely porch seating, a good wine list and $3 kids' meals.

Mangy Moose Saloon PUB FOOD $$
(☑307-733-4913, music hotline 307-733-9779; www.mangymoose.net; lunch mains $8, dinner mains $14-29; ⊙7am-9pm; 🐾) A cavernous pub serving baskets of nachos and buffalo burgers to hungry families. Après-ski gets busy and dinner features pizzas, steaks from local farms and a good salad bar. Check the website for big-name live music.

Bar J Chuckwagon   BARBECUE **$$**
(📞 307-733-3370; www.barjchuckwagon.com; Hwy 390; adult/child from $24/12; ⏰ 7pm Memorial Day weekend-Sep) We know it's corny, but all who visit rave about the sing-along chuck-wagon suppers, featuring BBQ beef, biscuits and beans. Pork ribs or steak cost a bit more. Dinner is followed by an hour of stories and songs from the wranglers. Lap-sized kids go free. Reservations are recommended.

★**Couloir**   MODERN AMERICAN **$$$**
(📞 307-739-2675; www.couloirrestaurant.com; 4-course meal $95, incl wine $155; ⏰ from 5pm) Dashed with exotic influences and located in the grandest of settings, Couloir does innovative American food well worth the trek (or ride). Greens with sage-roasted cashews and fresh manchego cheese, Wagyu beef with red onion marmalade and truffle crusted halibut are just some sublime options. In summer, local farms supply free-range meat and organic produce. It's at the summit of Bridger Gondola.

A lucky few can reserve to dine in-kitchen with Chef Hamilton, with a custom menu and wine pairings.

Cascade Grill House & Spirits   BAR
(📞 307-732-6932; ⏰ 7am-10pm) A popular stop for après-ski cocktails in the Teton Mountain Lodge. The menu is upscale Western.

ℹ Information

Jackson Hole Central Reservations (📞 888-838-6306; www.jacksonholewy.com) Lodging with off-season specials and package deals.
Jackson Hole Guest Services (📞 888-333-7766, 307-739-2753; Clock Tower Bldg) Information on activities and tours, located near the tram ticket office in Teton Village. Pick up a free *Jackson Hole Mountain Map & Guide* here.
Jackson Hole Resort Lodging (📞 800-443-8613, 307-733-3990; www.jhrl.com; 3200 W McCollister Dr) Property manager with listings ranging from studio condos to two-bedroom town homes as well as multiple-bedroom houses.

Gros Ventre Slide Area

On June 23, 1925, a vast slide of 50 million cubic yards of rock, one of the world's largest recent movements of earth, plummeted 2000ft down the side of the Gros Ventre Mountains to form a 225ft-high dam, creating a lake atop the Gros Ventre River. Two years later when the dam suddenly gave way, it created a monster wave that killed six and washed away the downstream town of Kelly.

Today the **Gros Ventre Slide Geological Area** offers a 0.5-mile interpretive trail with views over the slide. Amazingly, some trees survived the fall, 'surfing' the slide to reroot on the valley floor. The resulting Upper and Lower Slide Lakes attract anglers and boaters. The turnoff to the slide area is 1 mile north of Kelly. Not far from the junction is the **Kelly Warm Spring**, an undeveloped pool of warm (80°F) water.

The slide sits outside Grand Teton National Park, but is most easily accessed through it by taking Gros Ventre Rd east off Hwy 26/89/191.

Three very attractive and economical **USFS campgrounds** (📞 Jackson Ranger District 307-739-5400; sites $15; ⏰ early Jun-Sep) are spread out along Gros Ventre Rd beyond the Gros Ventre Slide Geological Area (18 to 23 miles northeast of Jackson). Sites have pit toilets and water but no RV hookups. Twenty-site Atherton Creek Campground, 5.5 miles along Gros Ventre Rd at Lower Slide Lake, at the end of the paved road, has a boat dock. If your car can take rough roads, check out the five-site Red Hills Campground, 4.5 miles further east, fronting the Gros Ventre River; the six-site Crystal Creek Campground is 0.5 miles further east.

A 7-mile round-trip day hike heads up to Grizzly Lake from near the Red Hills Campground.

Granite Hot Springs

The signed turnoff for the developed **Granite Hot Springs Swimming Pool** (📞 307-734-7400; www.granitehotsprings.mountainmancountry.com; Hwy 191, Pinedale; adult/child $6/4; ⏰ 10am-6pm summer, to 5pm winter) and Granite Creek Campground (p214) is 35 miles southeast of Jackson on Hwy 189/191. Free camping is allowed along the road to the hot springs, but not within 2 miles of the hot springs. In winter, the springs (a delicious 112°F) are accessible by snowmobile or skiing only. In summer the water temperature drops to 93°F. The route south through Hoback Canyon affords views of the stunning south face of the Gros Ventre Mountains.

The campground bumps up against the **Gros Ventre Wilderness** and offers good hiking up Granite Creek. Within walking distance of the campground is the undeveloped **Granite Falls Hot Springs**, accessed from the dirt parking area just below the falls. Reaching the hot springs (on the east bank of the creek) requires an often tricky and always chilly ford, and water levels only allow for soaking from around late May until spring snowmelt submerges the pool. Winter access is by snowmobile or cross-country skis. Please respect the place and enjoy one of Wyoming's best natural soaks.

Upper Wind River Valley

Part of the Wyoming Centennial Scenic Byway, US 26/287 climbs east from Grand Teton National Park's Moran Junction up the slopes of Bridger-Teton National Forest to Togwotee Pass (*Toe*-ga-tee; 9658ft), before dropping into the upper Wind River Valley. To the north is the 914-sq-mile Teton Wilderness; to the south is the more distant Gros Ventre Wilderness. Dubois is the only town in the upper valley, east of which the landscape yields to the semi-arid red sandstone Dubois badlands.

The Bridger-Teton National Forest **Buffalo Ranger District Blackrock Ranger Station** (☑307-739-5600, 307-543-2386), 8 miles east of Moran Junction, has general information and free maps of the region.

Moran Junction to Togwotee Pass

About 3 miles east of Moran Junction, the paved Buffalo Valley Rd forks off the main highway to offer a 4-mile detour northeast up the Buffalo Fork to the Turpin Meadow Recreation Area, a popular launching pad for local outfitters. There's a USFS campground here and lots of dispersed camping.

For a true wilderness getaway or some of the best Nordic terrain in the region, check out **Turpin Meadow Ranch** (☑855-231-0786; www.turpinmeadowranch.com; 24505 Buffalo Valley Rd, Moran; ste/cabins from $237/350; 🐾), a luxury dude ranch offering acres of cross-country skiing right outside the cabin door, in addition to fat-bike touring and snowmobiling. In summer there's mountain biking, horseback riding, pack trips and wildlife watching. Cabins feature smart retro decor and fireplaces. Pets may be welcome for a fee.

The road loops south as the unpaved USFS Rd 30050 to rejoin US 26/287. Three miles from this junction, just past Togwotee Cowboy Village, a short detour to the left leads to a **scenic overlook** with fine views back to the Tetons. A second viewpoint, the **Togwotee Pass Vista View**, is 5 miles further along; the actual pass is another 12 miles from here. The pass, named for a Shoshone medicine man who led the US Army Corps of Engineers here in 1873, marks the Continental Divide. Just by the pass, the lovely **Wind River Lake** makes a perfect picnic spot.

Six miles downhill, the turnoff to Falls Campground offers access to pretty **Brooks Lake Creek Falls**, with fine views up to the breccia (lava and ash) cliffs of the Pinnacle Buttes.

Across from Falls Campground, unpaved Brooks Lake Rd (USFS Rd 515) winds uphill for 5 miles to gorgeous **Brooks Lake**, a popular base for camping, canoeing, fishing and hiking set at the base of dramatic Pinnacle Buttes. The road passes Pinnacle Campground before it descends to **Brooks Lake Campground** (tent/RV sites $10/15), a boat ramp and a trailhead. From the Brooks Lake turnoff it's 23 miles to Dubois and 31 miles back to Grand Teton. For information about the campground call the **Wind River Ranger District** (☑307-455-2466).

Idaho's Teton Valley

The west face of the Teton Range soars above this broad valley, which is warmer, sunnier and more tranquil than its well-known Wyoming neighbor. Most of the valley lies in Teton County, Idaho, though a small portion (up to the Teton crest) is in Teton County, Wyoming. In Jackson it's dubbed the Tetons' backside, while in Idaho it's dubbed the 'sunny side.'

Teton Valley (6200ft) was first frequented by Blackfoot, Bannock, Shoshone, Nez Percé and Crow Indian tribes as a summer hunting ground. Lewis and Clark expedition member John Colter stumbled upon it in 1808 while hunting for beaver, finding them in abundance. The valley soon became known as Pierre's Hole, a favored mountain-man rendezvous, until a violent battle with a band of Blackfoot in 1832 caused the fur company's abandonment. Trade ended when beaver hats fell out of fashion (although some await their return with anticipation).

Mountains surround the valley: the Targhee National Forest and the Teton Range to the west, the Snake River Range to the south and the Big Hole Mountains to the southwest. Farming has been the valley's mainstay since Mormon families settled here in the late 19th century, but these once-sleepy ranching towns are now a year-round mecca for outdoor adventure and summer music festivals, with fabulous skiing, hiking, mountaineering and mountain-biking. North of Driggs, however, the classic Fords and antique grain silos hark back to days of yore.

Victor & Driggs

A friendly feel, the great outdoors and a growing number of good eats make Victor, Idaho a growing draw, especially for those who work in Jackson and can't afford to live there.

Rapidly growing Driggs (population 1439) is the valley's tourist nerve center and the access point for Grand Targhee Resort.

Activities

Habitat   BICYCLE RENTAL
(☑208-787-7669; www.ridethetetons.com; 18 N Main St; bike rental $45; ⊘9am-6pm) A hip full-service bike shop that also rents kid carts. Check out its group rides on Tuesday and Thursday, and Saturday chaperoned rides. Features ski and snowboard gear too.

Eating

Provisions Local Kitchen   CAFE $
(☑208-354-2333; http://provisionsdining.com; 95 S Main St; mains $7-12; ⊘7am-2pm) A busy mainstreet cafe with friendly service and heaping plates of steak and eggs, bison burgers and quinoa salads for the health-conscious. Supports local farms.

Forage Bistro   CAFE $$
(☑208-354-2858; www.forageandlounge.com; 285 E Little Ave, Suite A, Driggs; mains lunch $10-18, dinner $14-36; ⊘4pm-late Tue-Sun; ☑) ✦ A little cafe with a crisp and vibrant atmosphere serving small plates and locally farmed meat and vegetables. Dishes like dill trout or bacon and egg salad with fresh greens are simple but stand up. There are vegan options too; happy hour is 4pm to 7pm.

Scratch   MODERN AMERICAN $$
(☑208-787-5678; 185 W Center St, Victor; mains $8-22; ⊘8am-9pm Wed & Fri, to 11:30pm Thu, to 1pm Sat & Sun) ✦ In a rambling red house, this sustainable eatery serves up jalapeño cornbread, local elk burgers and sweet-potato fries with a touch of cinnamon and chipotle spice. It's wildly popular for breakfast.

Drinking & Entertainment

Knotty Pine   PUB
(☑208-787-2866; 58 S Main St, Victor) Cranks out an eclectic summer music lineup that yanks crowds on their feet for frantic fun. It is known for its burgers, microbrews and relaxed local vibe.

Spud Drive-In Theater   CINEMA
(☑208-354-2727; www.spuddrivein.com; 231 S Hwy 33, Victor; adult/child 6-12yr $7/4; ⊘Mon-Sat summer) A classic shot of Americana. Grab a malt and fries and get the kids in their jammies for the full experience. Look for the monstrous potato on the back of the vintage flatbed between Victor and Driggs.

Shopping

Victor Outdoors Seconds   OUTDOOR EQUIPMENT
(☑208-787-2887; ⊘10am-6pm Mon-Sat) Outdoor gear, quality used items and seconds.

Information

Driggs Geotourism Center (☑208-354-2607; www.tetongeotourism.us; 60 S Main St, Driggs; ⊘9am-5pm Mon, Tue, Thu & Fri, 10am-4pm Sat, noon-4pm Sun) A new information center focused on the culture, heritage, food, art, geology and music of the area. There are plentiful maps and brochures.

Targhee National Forest Teton Basin Ranger District (☑208-354-2312; www.fs.usda.gov/ctnf; 525 S Main St, Driggs; ⊘8am-4:30pm Mon-Fri) Information on trails and campgrounds, and offers free travel-planner maps.

Grand Targhee Ski & Summer Resort

On the west side of the Teton Range, Grand Targhee Resort (☑307-353-2300, 800-827-4433; www.grandtarghee.com; Alta; lift ticket adult/child 6-12yr $75/32) is revered for its incredible powder stashes (more than 500in of snow falls each winter) and its easygoing vibe. Base elevation is 8100ft, and four high-speed lifts to the top of Fred's Mountain (10,200ft) access 1500 acres of runs, with a total vertical drop of 2200ft in 3.2 miles. The runs are suited for families and intermediate-level skiers.

The ski season runs from mid-November to mid-April. Targhee lift tickets are a bargain compared with the competition. The ski and snowboard schools offer private and group instruction, as well as telemark and skate clinics. Performance demos and rentals are available. Amenities include a full spa, kids' programs and day care.

In summer it is most famous as a top-notch mountain-biking destination, with extensive trails, a bike park and big-name competitions. Don't be confused by the location: while it is accessed via Driggs, Idaho, it's actually over the Wyoming line.

🏃 Activities

Wilderness snowcat powder skiing leads intermediate and advanced skiers to Peaked Mountain (10,230ft) for breathless powder runs that average 2000 vertical feet. There are 10 miles of groomed Nordic trails (adult/child $10/6) and skating tracks. Other winter activities include snowshoeing, tubing, skating and dogsledding.

When the snow melts, and muddy trails then wildflower fields replace it, the valley becomes a haven for hiking, climbing and biking. The mountain offers scenic chairlift rides (adult/child $15/10; ☉ late Jun-early Sep) to the summit of Fred's Mountain, with higher rates for lift-served mountain biking (day pass $35); a downhill bike is a must.

The resort's horseback riding (1hr rides $40) takes advantage of the stunning scenery at Grand Targhee. Riders amble the dusty trails rimmed by wildflowers in the shadow of the Tetons. Pack trips and lessons on Western and English riding are also available. A one-hour hike affords a spectacular vista of Grand Teton itself; ride the lift down for free.

Frisbee fans take note: there's also free 18-hole disc golf. Kids will enjoy the climbing wall and Eurobungy (a hybrid trampoline-bungy). The activity pass ($25) includes a scenic chairlift ride. The staff naturalist provides excellent free naturalist outings (☉ 10:30am & 1:30pm Thu-Sun) on topics ranging from wolves to botany and geology. Register via the resort activity center.

Amenities include a full spa, kids' programs and day care.

🎊 Festivals & Events

Targhee Fest   MUSIC
(☉ mid-Jul) Part of a larger summer music festival, this annual event at Targhee Resort bursts with dancing and merrymaking to a range of music, from hip-hop and alt music to funk.

Grand Targhee
Bluegrass Music Festival   MUSIC
(☉ early Aug) A huge summer music festival with bluegrass, folk and alt rock.

🛏 Sleeping & Eating

Rates vary seasonally; contact Grand Targhee Resort (☏ 800-827-4433; www.grandtarghee.com) about off-season specials and package deals. Kids under 15 stay for free. All lodgings are ski-in, ski-out.

Teewinot Lodge   LODGE $$
(d $205; @ �widehat 💺) Snug and luxurious, with deluxe doubles, flat-screen TV, phone, huge indoor Jacuzzi, outdoor heated pool and ski-in location.

Targhee Lodge   HOTEL $$
(d $150; @ �widehat 💺) Standard rooms slopeside with two queen-size beds, full bath, TV and phone.

Tower   HOTEL $$$
(6-person apt $619; @ �widehat 💺) The newest lodgings at the resort, these spacious VIP residences are decked in hardwood, with leather armchairs, a fireplace and full kitchen.

Sioux Lodge   CONDO $$$
(studios $250; @ 💺) A steal in summer, these are recently remodeled, bright, four-person studios and eight-person two-bedroom units with flat-screen TV, microwave, mini-fridge and full bath. Ideal for families and groups.

ℹ Getting There & Away

From Driggs head 4 miles east on USFS Rd 025 (toward Alta) to the Idaho-Wyoming state line and continue east 8 miles to Targhee. From the second switchback en route to the resort you get the first glimpse of Grand Teton and an overlook of the Teton Basin. Sunset colors are wonderful from here.

Sno'Scape Ski Shuttle (☏ 208-529-6597; from Idaho Falls $20) Weekly shuttle from Idaho Falls to Grand Targhee Resort, run on Wednesdays in winter.

Targhee Express (☏ 800-443-6133; www.jacksonholealltrans.com; from Jackson $54, combo shuttle & lift ticket $99) Operates a daily winter bus service between Jackson, Teton Village and Targhee. Reservations are required.

Understand Yellowstone & Grand Teton

The Parks Today

Created by the *Yellowstone National Park Act* (1872) as a 'public park or pleasuring-ground for the benefit and enjoyment of the people,' this mother of all national parks straddles a tense line between preservation and recreation, access and excess, encapsulating along the way the very best and worst of the national parks system.

Best in Print

Lost in My Own Backyard (Tim Cahill) Engaging, funny and our personal favorite.

Travels in the Greater Yellowstone (Jack Turner) Gorgeous nature essays; also check out Turner's *Teewinot*.

Walking Down the Wild (Gary Ferguson) Account of a local writer's 500-mile walk through Greater Yellowstone.

Free Fire (CJ Fox) Yellowstone thriller featuring Mammoth, Bechler, Grand Prismatic Spring and Old Faithful Inn.

Best Documentaries

Silence and Solitude (2003) Follows photographer Tom Murphy's journey into the Yellowstone backcountry.

The National Parks: America's Best Idea (2009) Ken Burns' engaging visual history.

Yellowstone (1994) IMAX big-screen movie shown daily at West Yellowstone.

Best Maps

Beartooth Publishing (www.bear toothpublishing.com) 1:113,730 – *Yellowstone National Park.*

Trails Illustrated 1:63,360 – four hiking maps: *Mammoth Hot Springs, Tower/ Canyon, Old Faithful, Yellowstone Lake.*

Trail Illustrated 1:78,000 – *Grand Teton National Park*, with a 1:24,000 inset of the Grand Teton climbing area.

Too Close for Comfort?

In a rare, wild place like this it's hard not to feel that you have come face to face with the eternal. But the truth is that the Greater Yellowstone Ecosystem is a dynamic, changing environment. Climate change is already having visible consequences, which are more pronounced in the park than in other regions. Human impact is another force that is shaping not only the environment but our experience of it.

Yellowstone and Grand Teton now attract more than three million visitors annually – a volume that writer Edward Abbey termed 'industrial tourism.' On Grand Loop Rd, grazing bison or elk regularly create mob scenes. Unattended picnics habituate bears to dangerous behavior. Wildlife selfies have become extreme, with bison butting the bold posers who got too close. Debate rages over how best to manage this human influx. While the democratic approach to public access remains the parks' greatest strength, we may be destroying the very assets that draw us to these wild places.

Seeking Balance

If you want to spark an argument in Yellowstone country, simply start a conversation on any of the following: wolf reintroduction, the park's fire policy, bison hazing, grazing rights, oil drilling or the health advantages of tofu over Angus steak. Fractured regional politics means that a cloud of legal challenges descends over almost every major wildlife policy decision made in Yellowstone. It also makes it hard for Yellowstone to pursue coherent policies.

The 1996 reintroduction of wolves to Yellowstone has been considered a success story of restoring ecological balance and integrity to the park, and is wildly popular among park visitors. Yet recent debates among scientists question whether it has really righted the ecosystem, and opponents include many ranchers and elk hunters. In 2011 the wolf finally lost its federally protected status, to howls and cheers from the respective sides. There are now around 100 wolves in the park.

The policy of hazing wandering bison back into the park each winter (directing them with noises, helicopters etc) in an attempt to stop brucellosis entering the Montana cattle industry remains controversial. In the name of disease risk management, more than 3200 bison have been slaughtered this decade just outside the park. Yet the claim that bison spread brucellosis remains undocumented. Yellowstone bison research is now thriving, with some scientists suggesting a focal shift to managing contact between livestock and contaminated elk.

In 2013, the snowmobiling debate was finally put to bed, with new regulations that restrict snowmobile access to 51 groups per day, of no more than 10 participants each. The snowmobiles must meet much more stringent pollution standards than before to reduce noise and air pollution.

Preserving an American Icon

In 2016 the National Park Service will celebrate 100 years in service. Individual parks are gearing up for this milestone with renovations, reflection and renewed energy for their mission. Arriving at a time when visitation is hitting record numbers, the centennial is a chance to lace up our boots, leave the cars and RVs behind and enjoy this unparalleled public resource.

Over the coming decades, the park planners' understanding of Yellowstone's complex ecological web will be tested like never before, as climate change affects everything from grizzlies dependent on thinning white-bark pines to bison grazing drying meadows. Already, the park is gearing up to face these changes, despite a budget shortfall of $23 million. Our response to these challenges will define the parks' second century.

Yet Yellowstone and Grand Teton still deliver in big ways. Exciting technological leaps and scientific investigation have brought more understanding to the intricate inner workings of this supervolcano. From spurting geysers to the jagged Tetons, the parks have become an essential part of the US national consciousness, loved and treasured by millions. Long may they prosper.

AREA: **34,375 SQUARE MILES (GREATER YELLOWSTONE)**

ELEVATION: **AVERAGE ABOVE 7500FT**

STATES: **WY, MT, ID**

WILD BISON: **4900**

THERMAL FEATURES: **APPROX 10,000**

if 100 people come to Yellowstone

69 visit in Summer
9 visit in Spring
19 visit in Fall
3 visit in Winter

Yellowstone
(% of landscape)

80 Forest

5 Water

15 Grassland

population per sq mile

MONTANA   WYOMING   USA

≈ 1 person

History

As the world's oldest national park, Yellowstone holds a key place in both the historical development of the US National Park Service and the spread of protected wilderness areas across the globe. This is hallowed ground to both environmentalists and tourists, and the tensions between the two form the major theme of the past, present and, doubtless, the future of Yellowstone and Grand Teton.

First Peoples

To experience Native American culture locally, attend the Crow Fair or the Plains Indians Powwow in Cody; visit Cody's Plains Indian Museum or Colter Bay Indian Arts Museum; or join a Crow interpreter tour of the Battle of Little Bighorn outside Billings.

Recent archaeological evidence unearthed near Pinedale, Wyoming, and excavations from Osprey Beach on Yellowstone Lake suggest that human inhabitation of the Greater Yellowstone region began soon after the Pinedale Glaciation period ended, between 12,000 and 14,000 years ago. Only a few thousand years before that, the Yellowstone region was almost completely covered in glaciers.

Archaeologists divide Greater Yellowstone's first inhabitants – ice-age hunter-gatherers who chased spectacular megafauna such as bear-size beavers, enormous camels, gigantic moose, massive mastodons and 20ft-tall bison – into two distinct cultures, Clovis and Folsom, based on the uniquely shaped stone spearheads they fashioned.

The human presence in Greater Yellowstone increased dramatically 1500 to 2000 years ago, coinciding with a more favorable climate, resurgent large mammal populations and development of the bow and arrow, which replaced the *atlatl* (spear-thrower). Sheep traps and *pishkun* (buffalo jumps) were the weapons of choice in the Rockies and Great Plains, respectively. Obsidian from Yellowstone (still visible at Obsidian Mountain on the Mammoth–Norris road) made such durable spear and arrow tips that they were traded for hundreds of miles.

The Tukudika (or Sheepeaters) – a Shoshone-Bannock people who hunted bighorn sheep in the mountains of Yellowstone – were the region's only permanent inhabitants before white settlement, though surrounding tribes such as the Crow/Absaroka (to the northeast), Shoshone (east), Bannock (south and west), Blackfeet/Siksikau (north) and Gros Ventre (south) hunted, traded and traveled seasonally through the region.

TIMELINE	9000 BC–AD 1870	1797	1805–06
	Native American inhabitation of area now known as Greater Yellowstone. Most only enter the high mountains on summer hunting trips to collect food and medicinal plants.	French map makes first reference to the 'R des Roches Jaunes,' or Yellow Stone River, itself a translation of the Minnetaree word *Mi tsi a-da-zi* that described the yellow bluffs around Billings, Montana.	Lewis and Clark expedition passes north of Yellowstone; Clark carves his name on Pompey's Pillar near Billings – today it is the only surviving physical evidence of the expedition.

The Tukudika never acquired horses or iron tools and are often portrayed as a simple and undeveloped people, but they were proficient tanners whose composite sheep-horn bows were powerful enough to send an arrow straight through a bison (it's thought the Tukudika made the horns more pliable by soaking them in Yellowstone's boiling hot springs). The Tukudika, who never numbered more than about 400, spent the summers in camps of *wikiups* (tepee-like frames of leaning lodgepole branches), using dogs to transport their gear. The last of the Tukudika were hustled off the new park territory into the Wind River Reservation in the early 1870s to come under the control of the Shoshone chief Washakie.

One of the region's most extraordinary modern episodes involving Native Americans was the 1877 flight of the Nez Percé, led by Chief Joseph. The Nez Percé fled their ancestral lands in Oregon to escape persecution by the US Army (see p230). Today, the National Park Service recognizes formal affiliations with 25 modern Native American peoples.

For a historical chronicle of the park's original inhabitants, try *Indians in Yellowstone National Park*, a slim volume by Joel C Janetski.

Trappers, Traders & Tourists

The first Europeans to come in contact with Native Americans in Greater Yellowstone were French fur trappers from eastern Canada. They encountered the Crow and Sioux in the late 1700s while exploring the upper Missouri River tributaries in search of beaver. It was these lonesome French-speaking trappers who gave the Tetons their name for their highly tenuous resemblance to female breasts. (As one writer wryly noted, that's what happens when you let French fur trappers name mountains!)

The USA's Louisiana Purchase of present-day Montana, most of Wyoming, and eastern Colorado from the French in 1803 led President Thomas Jefferson to commission the famous Lewis and Clark Corps of Discovery in 1804–06. The Shoshone and Nez Percé told the expedition's leaders about a 'thundering volcano to the south' that made the earth tremble, though the expedition only made it as far south as the lower Gallatin Valley (which they named) and the area along the Yellowstone River, east of Livingston, Montana.

As knowledge of the American West grew, so did interest in its exploitable resources. Most sought after was the beaver, whose 'plews' (pelts) became known among the trappers as 'hairy dollars.' John Colter, a member of the Lewis and Clark expedition, returned to explore the Yellowstone area during the winter of 1807–08 to try his luck as a trapper. Colter headed south from the Bighorn River into the Absaroka Mountains, into Jackson Hole, over the Tetons (in winter!) and then north past Yellowstone Lake. His epic 500-mile loop hike made him the first white person to visit the Yellowstone region, though it's not thought that he saw any of the region's geysers.

Colter's most famous exploit was when he was captured by Blackfoot, stripped naked and forced to run for his life. He managed to elude the Blackfoot by hiding in a valley and he walked 300 miles back to civilization, living off berries and roots.

1807–08	1829	1834	1835–39
John Colter's winter journey into Greater Yellowstone makes him the first 'white man' to travel through the area. Colter's Hell, a series of thermal features along the Shoshone River, are named after him.	Bill Sublette names Jackson Hole ('hole' means valley) after fellow trapper David Jackson; trapper Joe Meek stumbles upon Norris Geyser Basin.	Warren Ferris is the first 'tourist' to Yellowstone and the first person to use the word 'geyser' to describe Yellowstone's thermal features.	Trapper Osborne Russell travels through Yellowstone three times, eventually penning his story in the classic autobiography *Journal of a Trapper*.

After the War of 1812, renewed demand for furs propelled another generation of trappers westward. Legendary 'mountain men' including Jedediah Smith, Jim Bridger, David Jackson (after whom Jackson Hole is named), William Sublette, Kit Carson, Jim Beckwourth (a free African American) and Thomas Fitzpatrick came to know the rugged Rockies' backcountry better than anyone except the Native Americans, with whom many of the men formed beneficial relationships, often learning the languages and taking Native American wives. Annual summer rendezvous – huge trading fairs attended by suppliers, Native Americans and even tourists – began in 1825 at the headwaters of Wyoming's Green River, only to peter out in 1840, as the fur trade hit the skids.

THE FLIGHT OF THE NEZ PERCÉ

The discovery of gold in 1877 spurred the US government (under army General Oliver Howard) to forcibly relocate the Nez Percé (Nimi'ipuu in their language) from Oregon's Wallowa Valley. After an initial skirmish, the Nez Percé (pronounced 'Nez Purse') set off on what would become an epic 1100-mile flight from the US Army. The route of their journey is now a national historic trail. For more information about this, see www.fs.fed.us/npnht.

By August 23, 1877, 700 of the Nez Percé (of whom only 250 were braves), led by Chief Joseph, crossed the Targhee Pass and entered Yellowstone Park along the Madison River, crossing the Firehole River at modern-day Nez Percé Creek. At that time only 25 tourists were visiting the park, and the Nez Percé somehow managed to bump into all of them, taking six hostage, killing one, and releasing the others near Mud Volcano. Just before reaching Pelican Creek, a band of braves diverted General Howard's men up into the Hayden and Lamar Valleys (at one point camping at Indian Pond) while the bulk of the tribe hurried up Pelican Creek and out of the park's northeast corner. You can visit the spot of two of the group's river crossings at Nez Percé Creek and the Nez Percé Ford.

In September they progressed through Crandall Creek into the Clarks Fork of the Yellowstone, with US forces pressing hard on their heels, and troops led by General Sturgis blocking routes ahead. Sturgis' son had been killed by Native Americans the year before at the Battle of Little Bighorn, and one can only imagine that he was itching for revenge. The Percé once again pulled off a brilliant escape. A group of braves diverted Sturgis' troops while the Nez Percé slipped through the net, passing out of the valley through a gorge thought impassable by the US Army.

Believing they were in Canada, the Nez Percé slowed down just 30 tragic miles before the border, where US troops under General Nelson Miles finally caught up with them at the Battle of Bear Paw. After a 1500-mile, 3½-month chase that included four battles, 87 men, 184 women and 47 children surrendered on October 5, 1877, with Chief Joseph's words: 'From where the sun now stands, I will fight no more forever.' It was the end of a fight they had not sought. Joseph was never allowed to return to his homeland and died in 1904, allegedly of a broken heart.

1869	1870	1871	1872
Folsom, Cook and Peterson's month-long expedition into what would later become Yellowstone National Park takes them as far south as Shoshone and Yellowstone Lakes.	Washburn-Langford-Doane expedition names Old Faithful, Tower Fall and Mt Washburn, and starts the legend of the founding of Yellowstone National Park.	Hayden expedition to Yellowstone, with photographer William Henry Jackson and artist Thomas Moran, whose images are instrumental in the creation of the park the following year.	President Ulysses S Grant signs the *Yellowstone National Park Act* on March 1; Nathaniel Langford claims to have climbed Grand Teton.

The romantic image of the mountain man is an exaggeration. Rather than rugged individualists selling their catch to the highest bidder, most of the trappers were salaried company men who were often advanced a year's supplies and ended the year in debt (many a mountain man blew his entire year's income on women and liquor during a two-week-long rendezvous binge). The lasting contribution of the mountain men was their local knowledge of the terrain and the opening up of the routes across the mountains, which paved the way for later immigrants and explorers. After the decline in the beaver trade, many mountain men became army scouts or tourist guides.

Official Explorations

The US defeat of Mexico in the 1846–48 Mexican War yielded a bounty of new western territory to explore. The US Corps of Topographical Engineers, guided by ex-trapper Jim Bridger, attempted to explore the Yellowstone Plateau from the south in 1860, but snow-covered mountain passes put the kibosh on their journey.

In the fall of 1869, the private three-member Folsom-Cook-Peterson expedition headed south from Bozeman, Montana, for a month to explore the divide between the Gallatin and Yellowstone Rivers. They made it past the Grand Canyon and Yellowstone Lake as far south as Shoshone Lake and returned in fine fettle to write a popular magazine article that refueled interest in exploration among the eastern establishment. Upon witnessing a 150ft eruption of Great Fountain Geyser in the Firehole Lake region, the team wrote: 'We could not contain our enthusiasm; with one accord we all took off our hats and yelled with all our might!'

With considerable foresight, Cook wrote 'We knew that as soon as the wonderful character of the country was generally known outside there would be plenty of people hurrying in to get possession, unless something was done.'

Folsom, Cook and Peterson gained enough notoriety to be invited along for the landmark 1870 Washburn-Langford-Doane expedition, bankrolled primarily by the Northern Pacific Railroad, which was seeking a route across the Montana Territory and publicity to attract investors and tourists. The 19-person party, led by former Montana tax collector Nathaniel Langford and Montana Surveyor-General Henry Washburn, was given a military escort by Lt Gustavus Doane from Fort Ellis (near present-day Bozeman). They successfully traced the route of the 1869 expedition, named many thermal features (including Old Faithful) and returned to the East Coast 40 days later. They received a hero's welcome from the national media, which finally began to take seriously their reports of a landscape 'so grand as to strain conception and stagger belief.' One of Langford's lectures about Yellowstone caught the attention

For insight into the mountain men, try *The Mountain Men*, by George Laycock, which provides individual portraits of John Colter, Jim Bridger, Jedediah Smith and others, and illuminates the craft of trapping.

HISTORY OFFICIAL EXPLORATIONS

1877	1883	1890	1902
Philetus W Norris becomes park superintendent and builds the first roads; the Nez Percé, led by Chief Joseph, flee the US Army through Yellowstone National Park.	Railroad spur line finished to Cinnabar, near north entrance of Yellowstone National Park; Great Plains bison pronounced extinct east of Continental Divide; first bicycle tour of the park.	First tourist guidebook to Yellowstone published; Wyoming becomes the 44th state of the USA, one week after Idaho becomes the 43rd state.	Only 25 bison remain in Yellowstone National Park, despite the passing of the *Lacey Act* eight years earlier, which prohibited hunting in the park.

of Dr Ferdinand Hayden, director of the newly formed US Geological Survey (USGS). Hayden soon persuaded Congress, with substantial lobbying muscle from Northern Pacific supporters, to appropriate $40,000 for the first federally funded scientific expedition to the Greater Yellowstone region.

In 1871 the 34-person Hayden expedition set out from Fort Ellis with a full cavalry escort. Hayden's scientific work was fairly pedestrian, but two members of his party, landscape painter Thomas Moran and photographer William Henry Jackson, produced works of art that offered proof of the region's amazing sights and ultimately led to the designation of Yellowstone as a national park in 1872.

The National Park Idea

Portrait artist George Catlin is credited with originally suggesting the idea of a 'national park' during an 1832 trip through the wild Dakota Territory. The US' first nationally protected area was created a few

MILLION-DOLLAR MICROBES

In 1966 microbiologist Dr Thomas Brock isolated a unique enzyme in a thermophilic micro-organism called *Thermus aquaticus*, or 'Taq,' which he extracted from the 158°F+ Mushroom Pool in Yellowstone's Lower Geyser Basin. Brock's discovery ultimately facilitated the replication of DNA for fingerprinting and genetic engineering, sparking an ongoing debate about 'bioprospecting' and the commercialization of public domain resources.

The National Park Service (NPS) continues to issue around 50 free research permits per year to scientists studying microbes. 'Extremeophiles' harvested for free have generated hundreds of millions of dollars of revenue for patent holders, including over $100 million a year for the Taq enzyme alone. Only recently has the NPS begun to gain financially from benefit-sharing agreements.

Not all research efforts are strictly commercial. NASA has studied the biogeochemical signature of cyanobacteria found around hot springs in an attempt to match this signature with a similar one on Mars, which would help to decide where to land on the red planet when attempting to confirm the existence of ancient volcanoes and hot springs.

Other startling discoveries include the DNA sequencing analysis of an organism found in a hot spring in the Hayden Valley. This revealed what is considered to be the living entity most closely related to the primordial origin of life.

Researchers estimate there are at least 18,000 active thermal features in Yellowstone National Park, and that as many as 99% of species present in Yellowstone's extreme environments have yet to be identified. And with more thermophiles estimated to live in one square inch of a hot spring than the number of people living on earth, there's plenty of room for research.

1903	1908	1915	1916–18
President Theodore Roosevelt dedicates Yellowstone National Park North Entrance Arch; Northern Pacific Railroad line reaches Gardiner; construction starts on Old Faithful Inn and Fort Yellowstone.	Union Pacific Railroad spur line arrives in West Yellowstone; first dude ranch opens in Jackson Hole; Teton National Forest established by Teddy Roosevelt.	The first car (a Model T Ford) is allowed into Yellowstone National Park; car entry fees cost the modern equivalent of $93 per vehicle.	In 1916 the National Park Service (NPS) is created under President Wilson. In 1918 the NPS assumes management of Yellowstone from the US Army, which has governed the park since 1886.

months later at Hot Springs, Arkansas. For decades the park service promoted the romanticized notion that the idea of a Yellowstone national park was born at Madison junction by the members of the Hayden expedition, though the reality was more complex.

In 1872 President Ulysses S Grant signed the landmark *Yellowstone National Park Act,* setting aside 'the tract of land in the Territories of Montana and Wyoming, lying near the headwaters of the Yellowstone River,' and 'all timber, mineral deposits, natural curiosities, or wonders... in their natural condition.' The proclamation put a box on the map around what was thought to be the extent of the region's thermal areas but neglected to appropriate any management funds. The park's first superintendent, one Nathaniel Langford (he of the 1870 expedition), was unpaid and only visited the park twice in his five-year tenure. This lack of funding led the park to seek private business partners, such as the railroads, to develop infrastructure and promote tourism; a problem that today's park administrators would recognize well.

The most important legacy of the National Park Service is much greater than simply preserving a unique ecosystem. That the national park and preservation idea has spread worldwide is a testament to the pioneering thinking of early US conservationists.

The US Army & Early Stewardship

A decade of rampant squatting, wildlife poaching, wanton vandalism of thermal features and general lawlessness in Yellowstone National Park preceded an 1882 visit by Civil War hero General Philip Sheridan. Sheridan persuaded Congress to appropriate $9000 to hire 10 protective assistants to aid the park's staff-less superintendent. But park regulations still didn't allow for any substantial punishments beyond expelling trespassers. The jurisdiction of Wyoming territorial law was extended into the park in 1884, but poaching remained rampant.

After a series of political scandals in the early 1880s involving landgrab attempts by a string of shady park superintendents (widely perceived to be in the pocket of railroad interests, who wanted a monopoly on lodging and transportation in the park), Congress flatly refused to fund the park's civilian administration in 1886. With no budget forthcoming, the secretary of the interior had little choice but to call in the US cavalry from nearby Fort Custer to provide protection.

In the absence of park rangers, the army patrolled the park from 1886 until the handover to the newly created National Park Service and first park superintendent Horace Albright in 1918. At first, troops were stationed in a makeshift fort at Mammoth Hot Springs called Camp Sheridan. Construction of nearby Fort Yellowstone (present-day park headquarters) began in 1891. By the early 1900s, mounted troops were

Jellystone's Yogi Bear, Ranger Smith and Boo-Boo were all inspired by Yellowstone National Park, with a little help from baseball star Yogi Berra.

HISTORY THE US ARMY & EARLY STEWARDSHIP

Learn more about early park history by taking one of the five daily historic tours of the Old Faithful Inn or a ranger-led historical walk around Fort Yellowstone at Mammoth.

1923	1926	1929	1943
A meeting is held at the cabin of Maude Noble to try to establish Grand Teton National Park; the last gray wolf den in Yellowstone National Park is destroyed by park rangers.	Rockefeller travels through the Yellowstone and Teton region, encouraged by the park superintendent, leading to the purchase of thousands of acres of land later donated to the nation.	Congress creates Grand Teton National Park; President Hoover extends the east and northwest extents of Yellowstone National Park, adding a further northern chunk three years later.	President Franklin Roosevelt creates the Jackson Hole National Monument, with Forest Service and Rockefeller's land.

ROCKEFELLER, ROOSEVELT & THE TETONS

Despite the precedent set by Yellowstone, transformation of the Tetons into a national park was no easy matter, as commercial ranching and hunting interests resisted attempts to transfer private and forestry service lands to the National Park Service. At its creation in 1929, Grand Teton National Park included only the main part of the Teton Range and the lakes immediately below. Distressed at Jackson Hole's commercial development, John D Rockefeller Jr surreptitiously purchased more than 55 sq miles of land to donate to the park (but retained rights to all park concessions), but political bickering prevented the philanthropist's tax write-off until President Franklin D Roosevelt interceded.

Rockefeller's 32,000-acre bequest finally came under NPS jurisdiction when Roosevelt declared Jackson Hole a national monument in 1943. With post-WWII tourism booming in 1950, legislation conferred national park status and expanded the boundaries to include most of Jackson Hole. A final piece of the puzzle slipped into place in 2008 when the Rockefellers' private retreat, the former JY Ranch, was handed over to the park service to become the Laurance S Rockefeller Preserve.

Today, the Rockefeller-founded Grand Teton Lodge Company remains the park's major concessionaire.

stationed year-round throughout the backcountry. Fighting fires, building roads, protecting desirable wildlife (bison and elk) from poaching and predators, entertaining visitors and preserving the park's natural features were the soldiers' primary duties. Predator control, such as poisoning coyotes, was common, but under the army's rule Yellowstone's environmental status quo was largely maintained. Of the 16 original soldier stations, three remain – at Norris (now a park ranger museum), Tower and Bechler.

You can see examples of Jackson and Moran's iconic artwork at Mammoth's Albright Visitor Center, alongside a copy of the 1872 act of Congress that created Yellowstone National Park.

Railroads, Automobiles & Mass Tourism

The Northern Pacific Railroad arrived in Livingston, Montana, in 1883, the same year Congress allocated funds to begin construction of the Grand Loop Rd in Yellowstone National Park. Park tourism and the railways were intimate bedfellows and it was the railways that ushered in the era of modern mass tourism in Greater Yellowstone.

Early park visitors rode the rails to West Yellowstone (via the Union Pacific Railroad), Livingston and later Cinnabar (Northern Pacific), Cody (Burlington) or Gallatin Gateway (Chicago, Milwaukee, St Paul & Pacific) and then transferred to stagecoaches for a six-day park tour that still mirrors today's overnight stops. The 'dudes' (tourists) would brave dust clouds and holdups to stay in classy hotels attended by 'savages'

1948	1959	1968–77	1970
Yellowstone National Park receives one million visitors in a single year for the first time, in a post-WWII tourist boom.	A huge 7.5-scale earthquake hits the Hebgen region, creating Earthquake Lake and causing the eruptions of several Yellowstone geysers.	Signing into law of the Wild & Scenic Rivers Act (1968), National Trails System Act (1968), National Environmental Policy Act (1969), Endangered Species Act (1973), Clean Water Act (1977) and Clean Air Act (1977).	New bear management plan; last of the bear-feeding garbage dumps closed, emphasizing the shift from recreational use to environmental protection.

(concession employees) and beanery girls, entertained at night by string quartets, while generally behaving badly during the day – throwing handkerchiefs into geysers, bathing in hot springs and (later) feeding the bears.

The railroad's grand plans to monopolize public access to the park even went as far as a plan to extend rail tracks through the park itself, though Congress put its foot down about this. Ultimately, it was the arrival of the automobile that would scuttle the railroad's bid for domination of concession and transportation interests. Whereas over 80% of Yellowstone's 52,000 visitors in 1915 arrived via railroad, by 1940 nearly all of Yellowstone's half million visitors entered the park in private automobiles.

In 1905 completion of the skeleton of what is known today as the Grand Loop Rd by the US Army Corps of Engineers established the blueprint of the standardized Yellowstone tourist experience. Lobbying by motoring clubs persuaded the NPS to admit automobiles in 1915. Constant clashes between cars and stagecoaches over right-of-way on the narrow one-way roads led to the banishment of horse-drawn wagons in 1916.

Establishment of the nation's first forestry reserve, the Yellowstone Timber Reserve (part of today's Shoshone and Bridger-Teton National Forest), in 1891, Jackson's National Elk Refuge in 1912 and Grand Teton National Park in 1929 opened up Greater Yellowstone's south flank to public visitation. East Coast philanthropist John D Rockefeller's 200,000-acre land grant in 1949 added the final pieces of Grand Teton National Park and marked the tipping point in Greater Yellowstone's transition from a resource-based region to a tourist-driven economy.

Modern intensive development of a small area (about 1%) of Yellowstone National Park for tourism, however, has not been without controversy. The park is now home to more than 2000 buildings, thousands of employees and tens of thousands of nightly tourists. Historian Richard White has argued that rather than being a vestige of wild America, Yellowstone is 'a petting zoo with a highway running through it.'

Herein lies possibly the biggest challenge facing Greater Yellowstone today – is it possible for swarms of wilderness- and wildlife-seekers to enjoy solitude and appreciate nature en masse?

Managing Natural Resources

During its formative years, the National Park Service in Yellowstone racked up a – shall we say – checkered history. It poisoned predators, shot wolves, stocked fisheries with nonendemic species, destroyed habitat in the name of development and arranged bear-feeding displays, all of which contributed to the development of an artificial and ultimately

To get a sense of the importance of the railways in the development of the park, visit West Yellowstone's Yellowstone Historic Center, the Depot Center in Livingston or Gallatin Gateway Inn – all former railway depots.

Get a radical retake on the Wild West in *The Empire of Shadows*, by George Black. It's about Yellowstone's creation via forces of exploration, the violent Indian Wars and the 'civilizing' frontier.

1972	1988	1994	1995
Yellowstone National Park turns 100 and welcomes its 50-millionth visitor – the next 50 million arrive by 1992. John D Rockefeller Jr Memorial Parkway is established, linking Yellowstone and Grand Teton.	Much-publicized wildfires sweep through the Greater Yellowstone region, burning one-third of the park; the entire park closes on August 20 for the first time in history.	Invasive lake trout in Yellowstone Lake decimate the native cutthroat trout population, affecting bear and osprey food sources. An aggressive eradication campaign spends $2 million annually.	Fourteen Canadian gray wolves are reintroduced to Yellowstone National Park; Yellowstone joins the list of World Heritage Sites in danger.

unsustainable ecology. Modern managers openly admit that many early park policies were misguided.

Beginning in 1959 with John and Frank Craighead's pioneering studies of Yellowstone's grizzly population, the NPS emphasized scientific study of its natural resources. The landmark Leopold Report, published in 1963, suggested that 'a national park should represent a vignette of primitive America.' The report concluded that a more passive 'natural regulation' regime should replace past policies biased toward hands-on resource manipulation.

A major test of that policy was the summer fire season of 1988, when one-third of the park went up in smoke as 25 fires raged through the park for 3½ months. More than 25,000 firefighters were drafted in to battle the flames at a cost of $120 million, and TV anchors proclaimed 'the death of Yellowstone National Park.' The event cast a critical spotlight on the park service's policy of letting natural fires burn. Twenty-five years on, a mosaic of meadows and new-growth forest has rejuvenated the park. Regardless of an instinctive desire to protect the park, fire is in fact essential to replenish the poor soils of the Yellowstone plateau, and Yellowstone is a healthier place for it.

Controversy has been no stranger to Yellowstone. One prominent 15-year battle over snowmobile access was resolved in 2013 when new government regulations were announced to allow 51 snowmobile groups per day in the park, with improved technology to curb noise and air pollution.

Between 2011 and 2012, grizzly bears were put on threatened status and wolves were delisted from threatened status, though these designations are contested and likely momentary. The only certainty is that the management of recovering grizzly, bison and wolf populations continues to provoke controversy, as park regulations are often at odds with those proposed by the three states that surround the park. The diverging interests of tourism, conservation and ranching have pitted neighbors against one another. Even among scientists, it can be difficult to achieve agreement on the best measures to keep this dynamic ecosystem in balance, particularly as climate change plays its own role in shaping the environment.

Given that contradictions are inherent in the park's mandate of both preservation and utilization, high-stakes negotiations will continue to be integral to the future of Yellowstone.

In Gardiner, the Yellowstone Heritage & Research Center houses precious park archives, with 90,000 photographic prints and negatives, 20,000 books and 35,000 archaeological artifacts. Behind-the-scenes tours take place every Tuesday morning.

The Battle for Yellowstone, by Justin Farrell, tells a gripping story of the park by examining the morality and struggles of its stakeholders.

2011	2013	2014	2014
Wolf delisted as an endangered species and control is given over to individual states. Wolf hunts are allowed in Montana, Wyoming and Idaho.	In October, a 16-day government shutdown causes a loss of over $9 million dollars to Yellowstone and its nearby communities.	On March 30, a 4.8-magnitude earthquake hits 5 miles from Norris Basin, the first significant quake since the early 1980s.	A federal judge restores protection for the gray wolf in Wyoming.

Geology

As a supervolcano sitting on one of the foremost hot spots on earth, Yellowstone hosts some of the premier geothermal features found anywhere on the planet. These geysers, hot springs and steam vents offer geologists and visitors a vivid peek into the center of our world. From acidic soils to waterlogged valleys, the environment on this superheated plateau shapes the lives of the plants and animals that call the park home, and has made it one of the leading wildlife destinations in North America.

The Yellowstone Hot Spot

Standing in the park, you are perched atop a thin piece of crust floating over a huge 125-mile-deep plume of molten rock known as a hot spot. This buoyant molten rock, heated by magma deep under the earth's crust, has risen through the upper mantle close to the earth's surface.

Glaciers in the Teton range were formed in the Little Ice Age, a cold period from roughly 1400 to 1850. Numbering around a dozen, they will likely disappear if climate change continues its current path.

Hot spots may be fixed, but as the earth's crust moves over them, it forms a line of progressively newer volcanoes. The North American plate moves southwest one inch per year. Its contact with the Yellowstone hot spot has burned a chain of volcanoes across the West from southeastern Oregon (where it was active 16 million years ago) to northern Wyoming (where it was last active 600,000 years ago). After a few million years, it will slide over to North Dakota.

The Yellowstone region has been sitting atop this hot spot for about two million years, with massive supervolcanic eruptions occurring roughly every 650,000 years. The last three have been centered on Island Park, Henry's Fork and Yellowstone.

What do these eruptions entail? The most recent explosion formed the 1000-sq-mile Yellowstone caldera at the center of the park 600,000 years ago. The explosion spat out magma and clouds of 1800°F liquid ash at supersonic speeds, vaporizing all in its path and suffocating the land in blisteringly hot ash flows. Billowing ash traveled thousands of square miles in minutes, landing as far away as the Gulf of Mexico. The crater roof and floor then imploded and dropped thousands of feet, creating a

---

PSYCHEDELIC SCIENCE

Given that Yellowstone, with its 10,000 geothermal features, is the world's foremost source of heated water, it comes as no surprise that heat-loving (thermophilic) micro-organisms were first discovered in the park's boiling waters.

A huge variety of microbes and bacteria thrive in these extreme waters, tolerating heat, extremely acidic or alkaline conditions and toxic minerals. One such species has yielded an important enzyme crucial to DNA fingerprinting tests. Other research is revealing important clues about the origins of life on earth and survival of life in outer space.

Much of this activity occurs on a microscopic scale, but visitors can still appreciate the brilliant colors these micro-organisms produce in bodies of water. Each species inhabits a highly specific temperature and chemical zone, so each layer produces the rings and patches of vibrant color that give Yellowstone's waters their psychedelic signature.

smoldering volcanic pit 48 miles by 27 miles wide. Ash circling the globe caused a volcanic winter by reducing the amount of solar heat reaching the earth.

Visitors may be surprised that Yellowstone is not more mountainous; the reason quite simply is that the mountains were either blown away by the explosion or sank into the caldera.

Since the explosion, at least 30 subsequent lava flows, dating from 150,000 to 70,000 years ago, have filled in and obscured the caldera, and forests have reclaimed the area, though you can still make out the caldera in numerous places. Turnouts on the road south of Dunraven Pass provide excellent views of its northern part, and much of the caldera's outline can be seen from the summit of Mt Washburn.

The Yellowstone Volcano Observatory, created in partnership with the United States Geological Survey (USGS), monitors volcanic and earthquake unrest in the park. See its work at http://volcanoes.usgs.gov/yvo.

Yellowstone's Thermal Features

Fueled by its underground furnace, Yellowstone is a bubbling cauldron of more than 10,000 geothermal features – more than all other geothermal areas on the planet combined. Maybe it isn't all that surprising. Magma, the earth's molten rock, is just 3 to 5 miles underground, closer to the surface here than anywhere else on earth. The average heat flow from the region is 40 times the global average.

But heat isn't everything. Essential to Yellowstone's thermal features is the addition of water, falling onto the park as rain or, more commonly, snow. This surface water may seep as deep as 2 miles over long periods of time before it drains through the side channels of geysers, hot springs and underground aquifers. The next time you watch a geyser, remember that the water spurting out may have fallen as snow or rain up to 500 years ago.

With Yellowstone's geothermal activity constantly in flux, what seem like permanent features are mere blips on the geologic timescale. Geysers suddenly erupt, or dry up; hot springs gradually appear, or explode so violently that they destroy themselves.

The plumbing beneath the supervolcano has long been mysterious. In 2015, University of Utah seismologists discovered and imaged an enormous lower magma chamber located 12 to 28 miles underground. Over four times the size of an upper chamber, its contents could fill the Grand Canyon more than 11 times. Documented in the journal *Science,* the discovery will help scientists predict potential seismic and volcanic activity.

Scientists are only beginning to fathom these complex underground systems, but it's clear that this is a threatened landscape – unless the

---

GEOLOGIC WONDERS

Grand Prismatic Spring (p112) The park's most beautiful geothermal feature.

Grand Teton (p189) Molten dikes, fault scarps and those peaks!

Hebgen Lake (p159) Ponder the awesome result of the 1959 earthquake.

Mammoth Hot Springs (p87) Graceful travertine terraces.

Mud pots Head to Mud Volcano (p97) south of Canyon; Artist Paint Pots (p104) south of Norris; or Fountain Paint Pot (p113) in the Lower Geyser Basin.

Norris Geyser Basin (p103) The region's hottest geothermal area, featuring Echinus Geyser, the park's largest acidic geyser.

Obsidian Cliff (p91) Dark volcanic glass from the interior of a cooled lava flow.

Petrified forests (p56) Hike up Specimen Ridge in Yellowstone or take the interpretive walk at Tom Miner Basin in Paradise Valley.

Calcite Springs (p93) Hexagonal basalt columns near Tower Falls.

Upper Geyser Basin (p105) Old Faithful, Morning Glory Pool and other gems.

broader region is safeguarded thoughtfully. Through conservation, Yellowstone protects about half of the world's geysers, but in areas like Iceland and New Zealand, where geothermal features have been developed as energy sources, geysers and geothermal activity may be altered or cease altogether.

Geysers

Only a handful of Yellowstone's thermal features are active geysers (from the Icelandic *geysir*, meaning 'to gush or rage'), but these still comprise about 50% of the global total, making the park a globally significant resource.

How do geysers form? First, snowmelt trickles into hot rock where it is superheated. The heated water begins to rise, creating convection currents. The earth acts like a giant pressure cooker, keeping the water liquid even though it reaches temperatures of over 400°F. As the water rises, it dissolves silica trapped in the surrounding rhyolite rock base. At the surface this silica is deposited as the mineral sinter (geyserite), creating the familiar ash-colored landscape of Yellowstone's thermal basins.

What gives geysers their 'oomph' is the sinter seal that junks up the escape valves in geyser chambers. This temporary blockage causes an intense buildup of gas until the seal breaks and releases the accumulated pressure. As the superheated water rushes toward the surface, water pressure drops and the water expands more than 1500 times in a violent chain reaction as it flashes into steam and explodes into the sky. Geysers require walls of hard rock such as rhyolite, which is part of the reason why Yellowstone's geysers are concentrated in the southwest of the park.

Geysers and hot springs are often connected in complex and delicate underground networks and affect each other in ways not yet fully understood.

Hot Springs

Hot springs occur with a gradual release of hot water. Springs may rage like oil in a deep fryer, churn like giant washing machines or remain completely still. Their crazy colors are a combination of mineral content, which affects the absorption and reflection of light, and water temperature, which supports a range of algae communities. Since algae and thermophiles are very temperature-specific, they may create beautiful concentric bands of colors. Blue pools are the hottest, absorbing all color except blue. Green pools result when the blue is mixed with small amounts of yellow sulfur.

Mud Pots

Imagine that the sulfuric acid in groundwater is potent enough to dissolve rock, creating a sort of hot spring of viscous bubbling mud. The mud is known as kaolinite, a form of clay. Mud pots form above the water table, where less water is available. Most derive their water directly from rain, snow and condensation, so their consistency depends on precipitation and the seasons. Are they really boiling? No, the bubbling is actually the release of steam and gas. Sulfur and iron content give rise to the nickname 'paint pots.'

Fumaroles

Essentially dry geysers, fumaroles' water boils away before reaching the surface, where they burst with heat. These steam vents also give off carbon dioxide and some hydrogen sulfide (that nice 'rotten egg' smell) with a hiss or roaring sound.

Roaring Mountain on the Mammoth–Norris Rd is a huge collection of fumaroles.

For a unique angle on thermal activity, check out the aerial photographs of Norris Geyser Basin at http://volcanoes.usgs.gov/volcanoes/yellowstone/yellowstone_gallery_2.html.

GEOLOGY YELLOWSTONE'S THERMAL FEATURES

Yellowstone's fascinating geology is laid bare in *Windows into the Earth,* by Robert B Smith and Lee J Siegel.

Travertine Terraces

The limestone rock of the Mammoth region contrasts with the silica-rich rhyolite found elsewhere in the park. Here, carbon dioxide in the hot water forms carbonic acid, which then dissolves the surrounding limestone (calcium carbonate). As this watery solution breaks the surface, some carbon dioxide escapes from the solution and limestone is deposited as travertine, forming beautiful terraces. They can grow up to an inch per day and are in constant flux.

Yellowstone Lake

One of the world's largest alpine lakes, Yellowstone Lake was formed by the collapse of the Yellowstone caldera and shaped by glacial erosion. Hydrothermal explosions have further shaped the shoreline, creating the inlets of West Thumb (a smaller caldera within the larger one), Mary Bay and nearby Indian Pond. Robotic cameras have revealed underwater geysers, 20ft-high cones, rows of thermal spires and more than 200 vents and craters, some the size of football fields, on the lake floor. Mary Bay and the lake floor canyon west of Stevenson Island are the hottest parts of the lake, due to numerous hot springs and vents.

Grasshopper Glacier, outside Cooke City, was named for millions of extinct grasshoppers entombed in its ice. However, most of the grasshoppers have decomposed as the glacier melts due to global warming.

Grand Canyon of the Yellowstone

This canyon is one of the park's premier attractions. It was formed as rising magma lifted the land and the Yellowstone River carved through rhyolite weakened by thermal activity. The fledgling canyon was temporarily blocked up to three times by glaciers (18,000 to 14,000 years ago), and the subsequent glacial flooding created a classic V-shaped, river-eroded canyon. It reached its present form only about 10,000 years ago.

Like many of Yellowstone's waterfalls, the Lower Falls of the Yellowstone tumble over the junction of hard lava bedrock and softer rock, in this case rhyolite and thermal areas. The spectacular colors of the canyon walls are created as hot waters percolate through the rhyolite, picking up iron oxides that stain the walls many different colors.

The Teton Fault

The Tetons are mere geologic toddlers. Surrounding ranges like the Gallatins and Beartooths were formed 55 to 80 million years ago by volcanic action, as part of the east end of the Basin and Range region that dominates western USA. At this time Jackson Hole was still a high plateau. The Tetons started to rise only 13 million years ago as the earth's crust stretched apart. At that time the current peaks of the Tetons were still some 6 miles underground.

The key to the Tetons' breathtaking profile is the 40-mile-long Teton Fault, which runs along the base of the range. The range was essentially created by a succession of several thousand major earthquakes and slippages. Land east of the fault has fallen, over millions of years, as the west block has hinged and angled upward. The east block has in fact dropped four times further than the peaks have risen. Several of these scarps are visible near Jenny Lake.

As tall as the Tetons appear, their height is actually only a third of the fault's total displacement. Gradual erosion of the peaks, combined with sedimentation in the Jackson Hole valley, has diminished their scale by up to two-thirds.

The very tops of the Tetons consist of limestone, deposited by an ancient sea 360 million years ago. Time has eroded these relatively soft sedimentary rocks, exposing the more resistant granite. To create today's impressive pinnacles, freezing ice wedged and shattered the rock along its weakest joints.

In 1959 a 7.5-scale earthquake occurred in the Hebgen Lake region just west of the park, causing 300 of Yellowstone's geysers to spontaneously erupt and creating Quake Lake.

You can note the Tetons' angled faulting by observing the westward tilt of the entire Jackson Hole valley. The west half of Jackson Lake is three times deeper than the east, due to both tilting and glacial scouring. Oddly, the land west of the Teton peaks is drained to the east, unlike the drainage systems in most other mountain ranges.

Glaciation

As if supervolcanic activity weren't enough, sheets of ice up to 4000ft thick periodically covered Yellowstone and the Tetons, leaving only the tips of the highest mountain peaks visible. The most recent ice sheet, known as the Pinedale Glaciation, covered about 90% of Yellowstone National Park and melted about 13,000 years ago.

Moving glacial ice worked its artistry, sharpening peaks, carving out glacial valleys, scouring walls, and creating ridges of debris (moraines) and lakes. Glaciers shaped the piedmont lakes at the base of the Tetons and the classic U-shaped Cascade Valley, a popular Teton trail. While the Snake River once flowed south out of Jackson Lake, glacial moraines diverted its flow east. South of Jackson Lake, huge blocks of melting glacial ice formed the depressions known as the Potholes.

In Yellowstone's Geyser Basin, ice melted so quickly that large mounds of glacial debris formed low ranges like the Porcupine Hills, while deposits of glacial debris beneath today's thermal features act as water reservoirs for the various geysers and hot springs.

Today's glaciers have largely retreated; their best example are the nearby Wind River Mountains, with the largest glaciers in the lower 48.

Yellowstone's Future

The Yellowstone region has been geologically stable for about 10,000 years now, but the land remains restless. Continued tension in the earth's crust and earthquakes make this one of the most seismically active areas in the USA, with 1000 to 3000 earthquakes occurring each year.

Although a 6.1-scale earthquake rocked the Norris Geyser Basin in 1975, geologists don't expect large earthquakes in Yellowstone National Park because underground heat softens the bedrock and makes it less likely to fracture.

Yellowstone is rising or falling as much as an inch a year, moving 65ft with each slow-motion 'breath,' particularly at Mallard Lake Dome just east of Old Faithful, and Sour Creek Dome, east of the Hayden Valley. These movements in the earth's crust are probably due to the withdrawal of molten rock from twin magma chambers on the rim of the Yellowstone caldera.

No one knows for sure what will happen if (or when) Yellowstone's slumbering giant awakens. The last major Yellowstone eruption dwarfed every other volcanic eruption on the earth's surface for the past several million years, and such an explosion remains beyond human experience. But don't bet on Armageddon just yet. According to the United States Geological Survey (USGS), a supereruption is not imminent. If there is an explosive event, it is likely to be hydrothermal, involving a rock-hurling geyser eruption or lava flow.

For now, we can enjoy the wondrous spectacle of Yellowstone's thermal features. When you gaze up at Old Faithful or down through a hot spring into the bowels of the earth, remember the awesome forces at work below the grandeur.

GEOLOGY GLACIATION

Oil, gas, and groundwater development near the park, and drilling in Island Park, Idaho, and Corwin Springs, Montana, all have the potential to alter the natural function of geothermal systems in the park.

The pink to gray rhyolitic lava that dominates park landscapes owes its hue to silica. The same substance is known to clog up narrow steam vents to create powerful geyser explosions.

Wildlife

The 2.5 million acres of Yellowstone and Grand Teton National Parks constitute the biological heart of the Greater Yellowstone Ecosystem – the earth's largest intact temperate ecosystem. Greater Yellowstone radiates from its untamed core into 18 million acres of surrounding federal lands and private property, forming a vast wilderness among the world's premier wildlife-viewing areas, especially for larger mammals.

Animals and plant communities within Yellowstone are shaped by the region's legacy as a geologic and geothermal 'hot spot.' Not only has uplift made the park a high-elevation landscape, but the leaching of rhyolite volcanic deposits has created acidic soils ideal for the lodgepole pine forests covering 60% of Yellowstone's main plateau. The elevation that led to extensive glaciation during the ice ages left behind impermeable deposits creating waterlogged landscapes in places like Hayden Valley.

Charismatic species living in Yellowstone include the lynx, bald eagle, grizzly bear, whooping crane and the reintroduced gray wolf.

Animals

Large Mammals

For a leg up on spotting wildlife carry a field guide such as *Watching Yellowstone & Grand Teton Wildlife*, by Todd Wilkinson.

Yellowstone National Park alone harbors 60 resident mammal species, including seven native species of ungulates (hoofed mammals). Much wildlife also ranges beyond the parks' boundaries into surrounding areas.

Bears

The black bear roams montane and subalpine forests throughout Greater Yellowstone, hibernating in a den over winter. It's an adaptable, primarily vegetarian forager that sporadically hunts smaller animals. Although they are generally more tolerant of humans and less aggressive than grizzlies, black bears should always be respected.

The grizzly bear once ranged across the western US but in 2009 it returned to the endangered species list. Today its population in the lower 48 has been reduced to fewer than 1200, with 600 grizzlies inhabiting the Greater Yellowstone region.

Male grizzlies reach up to 8ft in length (from nose to tail) and 3.5ft in height at the shoulder (when on all fours) and can weigh more than 700lb at maturity. If you find some bear tracks, you might notice that the toe pads of a black bear are widely spaced and form a strong arc, while grizzly bear tracks show closely spaced toes in a fairly straight line, along with impressions from their very long claws. About half of black bears are black in color; the anomalies are brown or cinnamon. Black bears are somewhat smaller than grizzlies and have more tapered muzzles, larger ears and smaller claws.

Omnivorous opportunists and notorious berry eaters, grizzlies have an amazing sense of smell – acute enough to detect food miles away. Their wide range of food sources varies seasonally. After bears emerge from hibernation between early March and late May, they feed mostly on roots and winter-killed carrion, turning to elk calves and then spawning cutthroat trout in late June. A feast of army cutworm moths lures bears to higher elevations in early September. Fall signals the buildup to hibernation, and consumption of whitebark nuts and the raiding of squirrels' pinecone stashes becomes an obsession. Before hibernation, bears can eat up to 100,000 berries in a single day. Scientists are concerned that falling levels of cutthroat trout in Yellowstone Lake and the spread of blister rust fungus, which kills whitebark pines, will have an increasingly detrimental effect on grizzly food supplies in the park.

Male grizzlies generally live alone, require over 800 sq miles of territory, and live for up to 30 years. Females have one to four cubs every three years and are fiercely protective of their young, which stay by their mother's side for two years.

Grizzlies are most active at dawn and dusk in open meadows and grasslands near whitebark and lodgepole pines. They can become extremely agitated and aggressive if approached or surprised, but otherwise they do not normally attack humans. However, they viciously defend carcasses and can outrun a horse when provoked; thus, trails are often closed when a grizzly is feeding nearby on a bison, elk or moose.

Learn more about wolves and advocacy at www.wolfwatcher.org. Kids can track the activities of individual wolves or wolf packs via www.yellowstonewolves.org.

Coyotes, Foxes & Wolves

The cagey coyote (locally pronounced 'kye-oat') is actually a small opportunistic wolf species that devours anything from carrion to berries and insects. Its slender, reddish-gray form and nocturnal yelps soon become familiar to hikers. Coyotes form small packs to hunt larger prey such as elk calves or livestock, for which ranchers detest them. While wide-scale coyote eradication programs have had no lasting impact, the reintroduction of wolves (which fill a similar ecological niche) is estimated to have reduced the region's coyote population by 50%.

The small, nimble red fox grows to 3.5ft, weighs up to 15lb and has a brilliant red coat. Foxes have catlike pupils, whereas wolves and coyotes have round pupils. Foxes favor meadows and forest edges and are primarily nocturnal. Although widely distributed, the red fox is not as abundant as the coyote, perhaps because the latter is such a strong competitor.

FINDING WILDLIFE

ANIMAL	HABITAT	WHEN & WHERE	PRECAUTIONS
black bear	forest and meadows	in summer at Tower and Mammoth areas	keep minimum distance of 100yd
grizzly bear	forest and meadows	at dawn and dusk; Hayden and Lamar Valleys; Fishing Bridge to East Entrance	keep distance of 100yd
bison	grasslands	year-round in Hayden and Lamar Valleys; in winter at hydrothermals around Madison River	responsible for more human injuries than bears; a lifted tail signals charge, keep a distance, drive slowly around herds
moose	marshes, lakeshores and rivers	at lower elevations in summer such as Willow Flats (Grand Teton National Park); migrate to subalpine and forests of Douglas fir in winter	don't corner or approach calves, adult may kick
pronghorn	sagebrush and grasslands	in summer at Lamar Valley near North Entrance; in winter between North Entrance and Reese Creek	keep distance of 25yd
wolf	forest and meadows	at dawn and dusk in Lamar and Hayden Valleys	don't feed, keep a respectable distance

WOLF POLITICS

Wolves flourished in the West until the late 19th century, when homesteaders' livestock replaced bison herds. Poaching and predator control greatly reduced wolf populations and by the 1920s they had become extinct in Yellowstone. Despite controversy, wolves were reintroduced to restore balance to the ecosystem in the Lamar Valley in 1995 and thrived. Today, the future of wolf populations remains uncertain. Wolves were initially delisted as an endangered species in 2008, and again in 2011 after initial directives were rescinded.

Wolf reintroduction has been contentious. Since 1995 thousands of sheep and cattle have reportedly been killed, and many ranchers compensated for their losses. At the same time 'wolf-watching' now brings in about $35 million a year to the local economy. Wolves have also proven key to keeping coyote populations under control and may have even assisted in the regrowth of key species such as aspen and willow, by limiting elk grazing.

The return of the wolves has been shown to be key to providing balance to native ecosystems, though their restoration to the West remains precarious. In 2015 there were around 104 wolves in Yellowstone and more than 400 in the Greater Yellowstone Ecosystem. Numbers are down from a peak of 275 over a decade earlier – and more than 1600 in the surrounding area. Part of the problem is that states have vastly different approaches to management.

Wolves remain protected in the national parks, but parks are unable to keep these populations from roaming outside the park boundaries into unprotected areas. Both Montana and Idaho now allow the licensed seasonal hunting of wolves. In 2014 a federal judge reinstated protection for wolves in Wyoming because, in this case, state management was providing inadequate protection.

Critics of state plans decry the fact that politicians, rather than wildlife biologists, are deciding on animal management issues. Regions where tourism is the primary focus, such as Teton County, Wyoming, are concerned about the huge impact these policies may have on visitation. For additional info you might consult Douglas Smith and Gary Ferguson's *Decade of the Wolf: Returning the Wild to Yellowstone* or Hank Fischer's *Wolf Wars*.

The gray wolf, aka timber wolf, was once the Rocky Mountains' main predator, but relentless persecution has reduced its territory to a narrow belt stretching from Canada to the northern Rockies. Its successful reintroduction continues to spark much controversy. Wolves roam in close-knit packs of five to eight animals ruled by a dominant male-and-female pair. This alpha pair are the only members of a pack to breed (normally in February), but the entire pack cares for the pups. Between four and six pups are born in April or May, and denning lasts into August.

Wolves eat meat only and, in Greater Yellowstone, tend to focus their predation on elk. Packs communicate via facial expressions, scent markings and long, mournful howls that can be heard from miles away.

Elk

Greater Yellowstone's most abundant large mammal, elk (aka wapiti, or red deer in Europe) can weigh 700lb and stand up to 5ft tall at the shoulder. Their summer coats are golden-brown, and the males (bulls) have a darker throat mane. Each spring bulls grow impressive multipoint antlers (up to 5ft long, weighing up to 30lb) for the fall rut (mating season), when they round up harems of up to 60 females (hinds) and unleash resonant, bugling calls to warn off other males. Although elk populations were decimated in the 19th century, their numbers have largely recovered – beyond sustainable levels, say some. Elk are cautious and elusive, and prized by trophy hunters who covet the massive rack of antlers that male elk briefly carry each fall.

Elk graze along forest edges; the largest herd in Yellowstone National Park beds down in the meadows west of Madison Campground. September to mid-October is the rutting season, and irresistibly cute calves appear in May to late June. An estimated 10,000 to 20,000 elk from seven to eight different herds summer in Yellowstone National Park, and a further 17,000 summer in Jackson Hole. In winter, large herds migrate south to the National Elk Refuge in Jackson. While winter counts of elk have plummeted since wolves were reintroduced, Yellowstone numbers grew in 2015, possibly because of the elimination of a late-season hunt outside the park.

Bison

The continent's largest land mammal, the American bison – commonly called 'buffalo' – once roamed the American West in vast numbers (60 million), often migrating to Greater Yellowstone's high plateaus during summer. It is a national symbol long revered by Native Americans, and Yellowstone's bison are some of the USA's last free-roaming herds. Today's herd is wild, descended from ancient bison that roamed the same territory in prehistoric times, unlike other bison in the West which are managed as livestock. Greater Yellowstone is the only region where wild bison have lived since primitive times.

By 1902 there were only 23 wild bison living in the Yellowstone region. The park's current population of 4900 was effectively bred back from the brink of extinction. Today, numerous herds exist throughout the Greater Yellowstone Ecosystem (an increasing number on private ranches), with three distinct herds ranging in Yellowstone National Park and another in Grand Teton National Park.

This is a truly majestic animal: full-grown male (bull) bison may stand over 6ft high at the shoulder, have a total length of 12ft and weigh 2000lb. Bison have a thick, shaggy, light-brown coat and a high, rounded back. Both sexes have short black horns that curve upward.

Despite their docile, hulking appearance and 'aloof' manner, bison are surprisingly agile. They become increasingly uneasy when approached. A raised tail indicates one of two subsequent events: a charge or discharge. Statistically speaking, bison are much more dangerous than bears. Every year several visitors are gored and seriously injured by these animals, and sometimes even killed.

Bison roam three main park areas: Lamar Valley, Pelican Valley at the north end of Yellowstone Lake, and along the Mary Mountain corridor between Hayden Valley and Lower Geyser Basin beside the Firehole River. August is rutting season – keep your distance to avoid becoming an unwilling rodeo clown.

The bacterial disease brucellosis is one of the ecosystem's hottest issues. Management plans call for intense monitoring of bison populations,

Wildlife-Watching Protocol

Animals have the right of way on roads

Never position yourself between an animal and its young

Resist feeding animals and never chase one for a photo

Stay 100yd from bears and wolves, 25yd from other animals, as per park regulations

If you cause an animal to move, you are too close

WILDLIFE ANIMALS

BISON & BRUCELLOSIS

Some of Yellowstone's 4900 bison are infected with brucellosis, a bacterium that causes domestic cows to abort their calves. Brucellosis spreads from the region's abundant elk population to the bison, who merely carry the bacteria while themselves remaining unaffected.

Bison are protected within the national park but their migration patterns bring them beyond its protective borders and, in 2000, a long-term management plan authorized the extermination of thousands of bison. Bison protectors point out that there are no documented cases of bison transmitting brucellosis to livestock. And advocates with the Buffalo Field Campaign maintain that the herd is headed toward extinction under these policies. Advocates for control counter that the absence of this evidence is due to these stringent actions.

The development of a vaccine has been somewhat impeded by the stringent controls around virus handling due to bio-terrorism concerns. After many lawsuits, public dissatisfaction and controversy, Yellowstone's bison management plan is facing revision, with new regulations set to be out by the fall of 2017. It is still uncertain whether a new plan will advocate for a larger herd.

with a goal of reducing the herd and maintaining Montana's 'brucellosis class-free' status.

Moose

The largest of the world's deer species, moose typically stand 5ft to 7ft at the shoulder, can reach 10ft in length and weigh as much as 1000lb. They have a brownish-black coat and a thick, black horselike muzzle. The male (bull) has massive, cupped antlers, each weighing up to 50lb, which are shed after the fall rut. Moose populations are facing decline, possibly due to a lack of food sources, and fires in the summer ranges of migrating moose.

An estimated 200 moose are found in Yellowstone National Park, favoring marshy meadows like Willow Valley, just south of Mammoth Springs, or on the east side of Lamar Valley. They are also found throughout the Tetons. Moose mainly browse aspen and willows, but also feed on aquatic plants. Superb swimmers, they can dive to depths of 20ft.

Moose may become aggressive if cornered or if defending calves and may strike out with powerful blows from their front hooves.

Pronghorn undertake the longest migration in the lower 48. Since 2007 both Yellowstone and Grand Teton National Parks have been part of a dedicated migratory pathway called Yellowstone to Yukon (www.y2y.net).

Bighorn Sheep & Mountain Goats

Bighorn sheep are arguably the animal that best symbolize the Rocky Mountains. They are robust, muscular beasts, colored grayish brown with a white muzzle tip, underbelly and rump patch. Males (rams) grow up to 6ft long, stand almost 4ft at the shoulder and weigh more than 300lb. Their ideal habitat is alpine meadows or subalpine forests fringed by rocky ridges, which allow them to easily escape predators. Rams have thick, curled horns (weighing up to 40lb), which they use during the fall rut (from mid-September to late October) in fierce head-butting bouts with rivals. Discreet hikers can often closely observe bighorn herds around ridges or alpine valleys; try looking for them on rocky crags between Mammoth and Gardiner.

Introduced to Montana for sports hunting, non-native mountain goats expanded their range into Yellowstone in 1990 and more recently to Cascade Canyon in the Tetons, raising concerns that they might impact the area's fragile mountain meadows and have an adverse effect on the native bighorn sheep population. Surefooted and confident in even the most precipitous terrain, the mountain goat is highly adapted to the harsh environment of the upper subalpine and alpine zones. It

WILDLIFE-WATCHING

The Lamar Valley is dubbed the 'Serengeti of North America' for its large herds of bison, elk and the occasional grizzly or coyote. It's the best place to spot wolves, particularly in spring. Wolf-watchers can get a copy of the park's wolf observation sheet, which differentiates the various packs and individual members. The best wolf-watching bases are posted at campgrounds at Pebble and Slough Creeks.

The central Hayden Valley is the other main wildlife-watching area, where spotters crowd the pullouts around dusk. It's a good place to view large predators such as wolves and grizzlies, especially in spring when thawing winter carcasses offer almost guaranteed sightings. Coyotes, elk and bison are all common.

In general, spring and fall are the best times to view wildlife, but different seasons each offer their own highlights. Spotted wapiti calves and baby bison are adorable in late spring, while the fall rut brings the call of bugling elk. In summer you need to head out around dawn and dusk because most animals withdraw to forests to avoid the midday heat.

The tree line is a good place to scan for wildlife. The more you know about animals' habitat and habits, the more likely you are to catch a glimpse of them.

It is worth having good binoculars or even renting a spotting scope. A good-quality telephoto camera lens can help the observation of wildlife at a safe distance.

has a shaggy, snow-white coat that includes a thin beard and narrow, almost straight, black horns. Mountain goats can reach 5ft, stand 4ft at the shoulder and weigh up to 300lb. Beware where you pee: goats crave salt and will gnaw down vegetation (and anything in their way) in order to satisfy their hankering.

Cats

The solitary, mostly nocturnal, bobcat is a handsome feline (a scaled-up version of the domestic tabby) with a brown-spotted, yellowish-tan coat and a cropped tail. It mainly eats birds and rodents, but when easier prey is scarce it may take small deer or pronghorn. Bobcats are thought to be widespread in the region, and it's not unusual to see one darting across a meadow or into a willow thicket.

Surveys in 2001 confirmed the presence of at least one lynx in Yellowstone. This threatened cat is similar in appearance to the bobcat, but can be recognized by its entirely black tail tip.

North America's largest cat, the mountain lion (aka cougar) prefers remote, forested areas of the park. With a size and shape similar to that of a smallish (African) lioness, the mountain lion may reach 7.5ft from nose to tail and can weigh up to 170lb. Even biologists who study it rarely encounter this solitary and highly elusive creature. It typically preys on mule deer, elk and small mammals, following their summer migrations to higher ground. While curious mountain lions are known to 'stalk' people without harmful intent, they occasionally attack humans.

Birds

Boasting 316 recorded winged species (of which 148 stay to nest), Greater Yellowstone offers a delightful bird-watching experience. The American Bird Conservancy recognizes Yellowstone National Park as a 'globally important bird area.' Noteworthy large birds include common ravens, resurgent peregrine falcons, reclusive sandhill cranes, honking Canadian geese and American white pelicans. Smaller birds including pesky black-billed magpies and yellow-headed blackbirds are common sights.

Birds of Prey

This group of birds (aka raptors) includes eagles, falcons, hawks and harriers. Sweeping across lakes, forests or plains in search of fish or small game, they are some of the most interesting and easily watched birds in the area.

The iconic bald eagle is a large raptor, with a wingspan up to 8ft, brown plumage and a distinctive 'bald' white head. Bald eagle pairs mate for life, building their nest close to water. Nests grow with each breeding season to become truly massive structures up to 12ft in diameter. The bald eagle takes fish (or harasses an osprey until it drops its catch), but also preys on other birds or smaller mammals. Nesting eagles are extremely sensitive to human disturbance.

The true 'King of the Rockies,' the gracious golden eagle is sometimes spotted riding thermals high above craggy ridges. Native Americans fashioned headdresses from its golden-brown plumage. Marginally smaller but heavier than the bald eagle, they typically nest on rocky cliff ledges and can easily spot potential prey and predators. They have a varied diet and will swoop on anything from fish and rodents to deer fawns.

The great horned owl is mottled gray-brown with prominent, 'horned' ear tufts, a white throat and a deep, resonant hoot. Its camouflage is so effective that few hikers even notice its presence. Asleep during the day, it preys on nocturnal rodents but also feasts on grouse and other birds.

The fish-eating osprey haunts larger lakes and rivers, nesting in shoreline treetops. Its upper wings and body are dark brown, and its underside is white and speckled on the outer wings. This well-adapted hunter

Catch up with cool research happening at the park at www. greateryellow stonescience.org, a portal that lays out the natural and cultural resources of both Yellowstone and Grand Teton.

WILDLIFE ANIMALS

A YELLOWSTONE FISH STORY

When lake trout were surreptitiously introduced some 20 years ago, no one knew the trouble they would cause. In 1994 an angler who reeled one in alerted authorities. By 2012, their numbers had grown to 800,000.

The effects have been devastating, particularly for native cutthroat trout. Aggressive predators, lake trout can grow to up to 35lb. Each lake trout can consume 41 cutthroat trout per year. Since cutthroat trout spawn in rivers, they provide an important food source for grizzlies. Around 40 other species, including bald eagles and river otters, also depend on the cutthroat trout for survival. But lake trout reproduce in the depths of Yellowstone Lake, making them inaccessible to predators.

To preserve the native species and restore the ecosystem, park authorities have had to be aggressive, spending $2 million per year to eradicate the lake trout, mostly through the means of gill netting. Finally, cutthroat numbers may be rebounding. Currently, there are around a million in the lake, only a quarter of a healthy population, but one that has recovered from the worst days of the lake trout invasion.

has efficient water-shedding feathers and clamplike feet with two pairs of opposing toes to better grasp slippery, wriggling fish.

Waterfowl

A vast number of waterfowl visit the many lakes, marshes and rivers of Greater Yellowstone; coots, cranes, gulls and some ducks stay to nest.

North America's largest wild fowl, the spectacular trumpeter swan, is hardy enough to winter here in the Henry's Fork and Red Rock Lakes region west of the park. In 1932 only 69 swans remained alive in the lower 48 states, all of them in Greater Yellowstone. Since then numbers have climbed to around 2500, but are declining again. It has proven difficult to wean them from winter feeding to find their own wild foods, and cantankerous Canadian trumpeter populations continue to crowd them out.

Long-legged great blue herons and red-capped sandhill cranes may be seen striding gracefully in wet meadows and along the edges of water, where they use their long bills to capture fish, snakes, frogs and rodents. In the fall and spring, cranes gather into large noisy flocks.

On larger bodies of water the common loon is prevalent, its beautiful mournful wail echoes across tranquil backcountry lakes. Up to 35in long, it has a black-green head with a speckled upper body and white underparts. Its dense body mass enables it to dive to 150ft but also necessitates a long runway for takeoff, which limits it to larger lakes.

Smaller Birds

The boisterous Clark's nutcracker, a member of the crow family, is light gray with black wings and a white tail. It patrols subalpine forests, feeding largely on conifer nuts, which it breaks open with its long, black beak.

The diminutive mountain chickadee is a playful and gregarious year-round resident of subalpine forests. It has a black cap and throat bib, and its onomatopoeic name describes its distinctive call, 'chick-a-dee-dee.'

The red-naped sapsucker is a woodpecker species with a black beak, white stripes above and below each eye, and a red chin and forehead. It bores into tree bark (preferably aspen or willow), discharging gooey sap that traps insects, devouring both. Ironically, the bird's activity helps control the even more destructive bark beetle and other noxious insects.

The striking blue Steller's jay has a black crest, head and nape. Its grating 'ack-ack-ack' is unmistakable. Although it consumes pine nuts, berries and insects, it's also an incorrigible scavenger and frequently raids camps for scraps.

Fish

Yellowstone Lake is at the heart of one of North America's most significant aquatic wildernesses, home to 21 gilled species, including non-natives such as rainbow trout, brown trout, brook trout, lake trout, lake chub and a cutthroat-rainbow trout hybrid. Fish provide critical foraging fodder for bears, waterfowl, otters and raptors throughout the ecosystem.

Yellowstone has more than 220 lakes and at least a thousand streams. Yet when it became a national park, 40% of its waters were fishless. The stocking of some 310 million fish drastically altered the aquatic environment. Current threats to Yellowstone's near-pristine aquatic ecosystem include the illegal introduction of predatory lake trout (the biggest culprits in the decline of endangered native cutthroat) into Yellowstone Lake, and the invasion of New Zealand mud snails, which have been found in densities of half a million snails per square yard and which crowd out native aquatic insects. Invasive mussel species are also a threat.

Today 40 of the park's lakes are fishable, with native sport fish being catch-and-release. It's worth watching cutthroat trout spawn in spring at the outlet of Yellowstone Lake at Fishing Bridge and LeHardy's Rapids.

Plants of Yellowstone and Grand Teton National Parks, by Richard J Shaw (Wheelwright Press, 2000), is a well-illustrated introduction to the region's rich vegetation.

Plants

Flora from the surrounding mountains, deserts, montane forests, arctic tundra and Great Plains all converge in Greater Yellowstone, where they are grouped into five distinct vegetation zones – riparian, foothills, montane, subalpine and alpine. Yellowstone National Park's herbarium has inventoried 1717 species, 7% of which are considered rare.

Trees

Harsh climatic conditions at higher elevations strongly favor hardy conifers. With the exception of aspen, eight conifers dominate these forests and make up 60% of the region's total vegetation.

Douglas firs, quaking aspens, shrubs and berry bushes blanket parts of the landscape from 6000ft to 7000ft. Lodgepole pine forests, which range from 7600ft to 8400ft, cover 60% of the park's broad plateaus. Above

---

WILDFLOWER PRIMER

Look for a breathtaking variety of wildflowers peaking throughout June and July.

Trumpet-like gentian A late-bloomer found above 10,000ft in moist arctic bogs, pretty arctic gentian has greenish-white flowers with purple stripes.

Columbine Found at the edges of small, shaded clearings up to 9000ft. Colorado columbine has blue-white flowers with delicate long spurs carrying nectar attracting butterflies and hummingbirds.

Fireweed A single-stem perennial that grows up to 6ft tall, crowned by clusters of pink, four-petaled flowers about an inch in diameter. It colonizes recent burn areas.

Succulent Indian hellebore (aka corn lily) On subalpine slopes, these 7ft stalks have large leathery leaves crowned by maize-like flower tassels. Native Americans used it as an insecticide.

Delicate, yellow glacier lily (aka dogtooth violet) Blankets entire tundra slopes. Bears eagerly extract their edible bulbs.

Beargrass A fragrant lily relative with white starlike flowers on 4ft stalks in well-drained montane and subalpine clearings. Its waxy, blade-like leaves are favored spring forage among grizzly bears.

Bright red Indian paintbrush Prolific in the Tetons and a favorite food source for hummingbirds.

8400ft, Engelmann spruce and subalpine fir predominate, interspersed with lodgepoles. Above the tree line (10,000ft), alpine tundra supports lichen, sedges, grasses and delicate wildflowers.

Aspen has radiant silver-white bark and rounded leaves that 'tremble' in the mountain breezes and turn gold in fall. A regeneration species, aspen tends to reproduce by sending out root runners rather than by seeding. A stand of aspen is mainly cloned from an original parent tree.

Not a true fir, Douglas fir is a tall, adaptable and extremely widespread tree that ranges from the foothills to the subalpine zone and from very dry to quite moist locations. It has flattened, irregularly arranged needles, 4in-long cones, and thick, corky bark that protects it from fire.

True firs resemble spruces, but have flat, blunt needles and cones pointing upward on upper branches. The most widespread is subalpine fir with silvery-gray bark bearing horizontal blister scars.

Many lodgepole pines are dependent on periodic forest fires to melt the resins that seal their cones shut, ensuring seed dispersal after fire has prepared a fertile bed of ash. Lodgepoles sport needles in bunches of two, and straight, narrow 'polelike' trunks that make for dense stands in recently regenerated forests.

Found in subalpine zones, the five-needled whitebark pine has small-ish, almost round cones that remain purple until maturity. Its seeds provide crucial autumnal forage for grizzly bears. Large individuals stand near Dunraven Pass in Yellowstone and South Cascade Canyon in Grand Teton National Park.

Dominating subalpine forests, Engelmann spruce is a towering, cold-tolerant conifer capable of withstanding winter temperatures of -50°F. Like other spruces, Engelmann has round, slightly pointed needles and pendant cones. Its resonant wood is used to make piano sounding boards.

Shrubs

These small woody plants may grow as heaths, form thickets or stand as single bushes on slopes and in meadows. For herbivores, they are one thing: the bulk food aisle. Know your shrubs and you are one step closer to finding the wildlife.

Shrubby cinquefoil grows in meadows from the foothills to the tundra, sometimes in association with sagebrush. All summer long this multi-branched bush (up to 4ft high) is covered in yellow, buttercup-like flowers with five petals. Deer and bighorn sheep browse the foliage, but only when no other food is available.

Several dozen species of small willows are found in Greater Yellowstone, with fluffy, silky flowers like small bottlebrushes. Shrub willows, including the common gray-leafed willow, form thickets along subalpine and alpine stream basins. Moose eat willow year-round.

The scrumptious blueberry genus includes species locally known as bilberry, cranberry, grouseberry, huckleberry and whortleberry. Almost all produce small, round fruits of bright red to deep purple that sustain bears and other wildlife throughout the Rockies. One of the most common is the fragrant dwarf blueberry, which typically grows among lodgepole pines.

Junipers are aromatic, cedar-like conifers that generally thrive in dry, well-drained areas. Rocky Mountain juniper can approach the size of a small tree, and older shrubs (which may reach 1500 years) are gnarled and knotted. Birds feed on juniper 'berries,' allowing the seed to sprout by removing its fleshy covering.

Strongly aromatic sagebrush thrives on foothills and drier montane meadows. Since grazing mammals shun the bitter foliage, overgrazing results in the spread of sagebrush.

Check out the *Yellowstone Journal*, with information on the park, as well as extensive listings useful for trip planning and travel within the Yellowstone region.

For Everything There Is a Season is a delightful account of wildlife through the seasons by one of Yellowstone's legendary naturalists, Frank C Craighead.

Conservation

A vast and complex wilderness, the Greater Yellowstone Ecosystem is home to a broad range of species, including humans. For the last century, humans' intervention and simple presence has branded an indelible mark on the natural habitat. How we both preserve and inhabit this region remains of critical importance, especially today.

The diverse issues that affect the national parks are continually evolving. Today's number-one issue is climate change, which is already producing big impacts on the ecosystem. Preserving native species and their habitats is a priority, in addition to the question of invasive species, which could look like anything from the New Zealand mud snail obstructing waterways to drones crashing into thermal pools. It takes a deep understanding of these issues and a dialogue among diverse stakeholders in order to begin to manage them.

The Bigger Picture

The Greater Yellowstone Ecosystem is among the largest intact temperate ecosystems in the world. We are only beginning to understand the intricate workings of this community, how individual species interact and how best to preserve this amazing environment.

This is only an introduction to some of today's key issues. For a better understanding, download the free *Yellowstone Issues and Resources* handbook (www.nps.gov/yell/learn/resources-and-issues.htm).

Get a taste of Yellowstone, see spurting geysers and spy wildlife up close by taking a virtual nature tour at www.nps. gov/yell/learn/ photosmulti media/index.htm.

Protecting Wildlife

Given Yellowstone's mandate to protect wildlife, it's not surprising that some of the fiercest battles are fought over questions of how to manage it. One question is how to protect top-level predators such as gray wolves when they leave the park and run into conflict with local ranchers. Contributing to the confusion is the fact that each state has different laws on these issues. The slaughter of disease-carrying bison that wander out of the park is another vexing topic.

In Greater Yellowstone waterways, invasive species such as whirling disease parasites, zebra mussels and New Zealand mud snails are threatening native species. Currently, the state of Wyoming requires boaters to purchase an invasive-species decal as part of an education campaign. In addition, visiting boats and fishing equipment must be scrubbed of mud and plants that may carry exotics.

The Greater Yellowstone Coalition (www. greateryellow stone.org) works on behalf of every major issue affecting the Yellowstone region, from environmental concerns to species survival.

Migration Corridors

Protecting migration corridors allows elk and other migratory animals to move from their summer to winter habitats. As population and road infrastructure increases, they become critical to ensure the survival of diverse species. The nonprofit initiative Yellowstone to Yukon (www.y2y. net) supports a dedicated migratory pathway through Grand Teton National Park all the way to Canada. Native pronghorn have been using this corridor for 6000 years to undertake the second-longest animal migration in North America. By modifying livestock fences and creating road crossings, conservationists can help this millennial process to continue.

Can Fire Be Good?

In 1998, 30% of the park blazed in a major inferno that only ceased with the first snows of September. Front-page news, the event was more a public-relations disaster than an environmental catastrophe. Today's scientific views on land stewardship are evolving. Fire sparked by lightning strikes is seen as a natural process that has been occurring for thousands of years. In Yellowstone the current policy is to allow natural fires to burn under strict guidelines, as they encourage new growth in plant communities, restore nutrients to the soil and burn off accumulated deadwood.

Climate Change is Local

Climate change may be everywhere, but it appears to be happening at an accelerated pace in the Greater Yellowstone Ecosystem. Its consequences are multiple and intricately related. Scientists are predicting major changes by the end of this century.

With average temperatures on the rise, scientists predicted in a special park report that Yellowstone will be dryer than it has been in 10,000 years. The Yellowstone River, a renowned trout-fishing stream, will become a warm-water fishery. Changing water levels affect both life in the park and downstream ranchers, farms and cities. Rising temperatures have also caused whitebark pines to die off at a rate of 85%, which in turn will impact grizzlies as they're an important food source. Researchers have also found much longer wildfire seasons, less snowpack and changing habitats. The specific impacts on wildlife are difficult to predict, but migration patterns are already changing. Grizzlies are denning later, foxes must start adapting to different winter hunting conditions and wolverines may lack enough snow for proper denning. Amphibians are threatened both here and on a global scale. While scientists study the issue, it's evident that reducing the stress we place on the environment is a clear step in maintaining it.

Sustainability

The Greening of Recreation

In recent years, snowmobile usage in both national parks has been drastically reduced, though proponents decry the regulations' impact on winter tourism. In Yellowstone, snowmobilers are now only allowed on professionally guided tours. In Grand Teton, use has been reduced to the frozen Jackson Lake. Both parks require quieter and more efficient BAT (best available technology) snow machines. In addition, the two-stroke engines of rental boats have been replaced with cleaner four-stroke versions. For purists, snowmobile emissions and their noise pollution remain an issue.

Park Innovation

To learn more about sustainable and ecofriendly options in the region, check out National Geographic's 'sustainable visit' map at http://yellowstone.natgeotourism.com.

When Yellowstone approached its 125th anniversary in 1997, the park began planning for the next 125 years. One result was Yellowstone Environmental Stewardship (YES!), an ambitious project aiming to reduce greenhouse gases by 30%, electricity consumption by 15%, fossil fuel consumption by 18%, water consumption by 15% and to divert all solid waste from landfills. Solar energy, composting and alternative fuels are a few ways the park has started meeting these goals. In 2011 alone, it was able to divert 72% of waste from landfills.

Concessions are an area of major improvement, with park concessionaire Xanterra employing corn-based biodegradables to help annually divert more than 280,000 plastic bottles from landfills. Gift shops sell greener souvenirs, and dining services pitch in by serving fair-trade coffee and naturally raised meats. In both Yellowstone and Grand Teton, park employees use some hybrid vehicles. LEED-certified park buildings also herald a new era – they include Xanterra employee housing and the new Old Faithful Visitor Center, as well as the new Laurance S Rockefeller Preserve Center in Grand Teton National Park.

Survival Guide

Clothing & Equipment

Knowing what gear is essential for a trip, and what will only weigh down an already brimming backpack, is an art. Those overnighting on the trail should be particularly ruthless when it comes to packing. Weigh the benefits of a freshly laundered shirt against the pain of an achy back and you'll see why most experienced backpackers choose to harmonize with the riper smells of nature.

CLOTHING

The Right Layers

Layering is the key to packing for Yellowstone. Locals will tell you there are only three seasons here – July, August and winter – so pack for changeable weather. Even on a cloudless summer day, it's smart to pack a shell jacket and a knit cap.

Synthetic, silk or wool base layers (not cotton) are the most effective. A waterproof but breathable rain jacket and an insulating fleece are musts. A down vest or light jacket is useful in spring and fall, when it can also be useful to have thermal underwear and wind/waterproof shell pants.

Winter travel brings its own specialised equipment demands.

Footwear & Socks

Light to medium hiking boots are recommended for day hikes, while sturdy boots with ankle support are better for demanding hikes or extended trips with a heavy pack. Most important, they should be well broken in with a non-slip (such as Vibram) sole.

Snow and boggy meadows in spring and early summer mean you should bring waterproof boots then. In midsummer, running or hiking shoes can work for easier hikes in dry conditions.

Buy boots in warm conditions and walk around while trying them on. Trekking sandals are useful if you need to ford rivers and for wearing around camp.

Synthetic and wool-blend hiking socks are the most practical option. They should be free of ridged seams in the toes and heels.

EQUIPMENT

Backpacks & Daypacks

For day hikes, daypacks (30L to 40L) will usually suffice, but multiday hikes require an internal frame pack (45L to 90L). Bring a waterproof pack cover if your pack doesn't have one built in.

A comfortable fit and padded waistband is essential. A waistband water-bottle holder is a nice extra; otherwise consider a CamelBak-style internal water bladder and hose.

Tents & Tarps

A three-season tent will suffice in most conditions. The floor and the fly should have taped or sealed seams and covered zips to stop leaks. Weight ranges from around 2lb for a stripped-down, low-profile tent to 6.5lb for a roomy four-season model.

Dome- and tunnel-shaped tents handle blustery conditions better than flat-sided tents. Bring a tarp and short lengths of rope to make a covered cook shelter in rain.

Sleeping Bags & Mats

Goose-down bags are warm, lightweight and compact, but expensive and useless if they get wet. Synthetic bags are cheaper and better when wet, but bulkier. Mummy-shaped designs prove best for weight and warmth. The rating (23°F, or -5°C, for instance) is the coldest temperature at which a person should feel comfortable in the bag. A three-season 68°F to 86°F (20°C to 30°C) bag should be fine for Yellowstone summer camping. For extra warmth and to keep your bag clean, a silk liner is invaluable.

CHECKLIST

The following is a general guideline. Know yourself and what special items you may need on the trail.

Things to Carry on Every Day Hike
➡ waterproof shell or jacket
➡ a day's worth of snack bars and trail mix; water bottle
➡ blister kit with moleskin
➡ map and compass
➡ cell phone
➡ ziplock bag of toilet paper; sunscreen and lip balm; mosquito spray; pocket knife
➡ sun hat; sunglasses
➡ whistle; bear spray

Clothing
➡ boots; camp shoes/sandals
➡ warm hat
➡ shorts and trousers; wicking T-shirt
➡ socks and underwear
➡ sweater or fleece jacket; thermal underwear

Overnight Hikes
➡ bear canister or 30ft of rope to hang food
➡ cooking, eating and drinking utensils; dishwashing items
➡ matches and lighter
➡ sewing/repair kit
➡ sleeping bag and liner; sleeping mat (and, if inflatable, patch kit)
➡ stove and fuel
➡ tent, pegs, poles and ropes
➡ travel-sized toiletries; mini-towel
➡ water filter, purification tablets or drops
➡ ziplock plastic bags
➡ first-aid kit
➡ headlamp and spare batteries

Optional Items
➡ altimeter
➡ bathing suit; gaiters; scarf and gloves; waterproof pants
➡ binoculars; camera and spare card/batteries
➡ candle
➡ emergency distress beacon
➡ GPS unit
➡ hiking poles
➡ mosquito net
➡ tarp
➡ notebook and pen
➡ duct tape and floss – together will fix almost anything

BEAR SPRAY

Most studies show that pepper spray is the most effective last line of defense against a charging or attacking bear. You should carry bear spray on any hike in Yellowstone. Remember that carrying pepper spray is not a substitute for vigilance or other safety precautions – we suggest keeping a distance of 300ft if you see a bear.

Airlines do not allow the transportation of bear spray, but outdoor gear shops in the gateway towns and general stores inside Yellowstone National Park sell spray (around $50). UDAP and Counter Assault are good brands.

You can also rent cans by the day or week from **Bear Aware** (Map p96; www.bearaware. com; bear spray rental per day/week $9.25/28; ⊙8am-5:30pm May–mid-Sep) at Canyon, which plans to expand operations into Grand Teton.

Spray Requirements

➡ Buy a minimum size of 7.9oz (225g).

➡ Concentration should be 1.4% to 1.8% capsaicin.

➡ Spray jet should reach 30ft.

Proper Use

➡ Carry within easy and immediate reach, preferably in a hip holster – not in your pack.

➡ Use when the bear is charging, within 30ft to 60ft.

➡ Aim at a 45-degree angle toward the ground and remember to disarm the safety cap.

➡ Make sure you are not downwind.

➡ And no, it doesn't work like mosquito repellent, so don't spray it all over your tent or body!

➡ After use recycle the can at any Yellowstone park visitor center or hotel.

Inflatable sleeping mats, such as those made by Therm-a-Rest, provide more comfort and better insulation from the cold than cheaper foam mats.

Stoves & Fuel

When buying a stove, think lightweight and easy to operate. Most outdoors stores sell and rent stoves. Butane stoves are the easiest to operate, though you are never quite sure how much gas is left and you have to dispose of the canisters properly. Multi-fuel stoves are versatile but need pumping, priming and lots of tender loving care.

In general, liquid fuels are efficient and cheap; look for high-performance, cleaner-burning fuel. Gas is more expensive, cleaner and a reasonable performer. Fuel can be found at outdoor gear shops, hardware stores (white gas) and some supermarkets.

Airlines prohibit flammable materials and may well reject empty liquid-fuel bottles or even the stoves themselves – check with the airline.

In terms of cookware, titanium pots are the lightest, toughest and most expensive option. A spork covers all the cutlery bases.

Water Purifiers & Tablets

Mountain streams may look crystal clear, but with the prevalence of bacteriological contamination, sipping from the source has the potential to quickly ruin a backcountry trip. Boiling water rapidly for 10 minutes is effective, but uses precious fuel.

When buying a filter, note that giardia requires a filter with a rating of 1.0 to 4.0 microns and E coli requires a microfilter rating of 0.2 to 1.0 microns. When filtering, go for clear water in the current of a stream instead of stagnant water. Avoid silty water. A SteriPEN (UV light-based purifier) is a convenient useful alternative.

If you don't plan to be in the backcountry often, chemical tablets are the most convenient and cost-effective solution. Some tablets purify water in 30 minutes, while others take up to four hours, so check when buying. Two-step tablets come with a neutralizing tablet that improves the taste, but you must add this only after the water has been purified.

Electronic Gear & Chargers

Many people take smartphones and tablets into the backcountry these days, either to view custom maps or guidebooks, or to use the GPS capabilities of their devices to map their route.

To keep devices charged, consider packing a spare battery pack or a solar charger. When shopping for a solar charger, look for one that sits conveniently on your backpack, works even in partial sunlight and charges multiple devices using a USB outlet. A charger that fits into the cigarette lighter or USB port of your car is essential.

Buying & Renting Locally

A hotbed for outdoor-gear innovation and consumption, the Rocky Mountain area offers high-quality products, though in-park selection is usually poor. The closer you get to the parks, the higher the rental rates.

All winter resorts have good rental shops with ski, snowboard and Nordic equipment, as well as mountain bikes in summer. Most have a program to 'demo' new equipment models.

Yellowstone National Park & Around

Kayak rentals are available in Cody, Jackson, Livingston and Gardiner. Ski and snowshoe rentals are available at ski centers and popular Nordic locations such as Big Sky and West Yellowstone. Fishing-gear rentals are available in West Yellowstone, Livingston and elsewhere.

Absaroka Bicycles (Map p140; ☑307-527-5566; 2201 17th St, Kmart Plaza; ⊙10am-6pm Mon-Thu, to 4pm Fri, to 2pm Sat) Mountain-bike rentals ($40 per day), repairs and tours, in Cody.

Bear Den Bike (Map p108; Old Faithful Snow Lodge gift shop; half/full day $25/35, kids' bikes $15/22.50) This small booth inside the Old Faithful Snow Lodge rents out kids' and adults' bikes during the summer, and snowshoes, skis and other equipment in the winter.

Bridge Bay Marina (☑307-242-3880, boat shuttle 307-242-3893; ⊙8am-8pm mid-Jun–early Sep) Rowboat ($10/45 per hour/day) and outboard ($50 per hour) rentals for Yellowstone Lake.

Free Heel & Wheel (Map p162; ☑406-646-7744; www.freeheelandwheel.com; 33 Yellowstone Ave; ⊙9am-6pm Mon-Sat, to 5pm Sun) West Yellowstone's center for cycling and skiing advice rents mountain bikes ($35 per day), Nordic skis and snowshoes ($20).

Northern Lights (☑866-586-2225; www.northernlights trading.com; 1716 W Babcock) Backpacking, kayak and winter rentals, including bear canisters, in Bozeman.

Sunlight Sports (Map p140; ☑307-587-9517; www.sunlightsports.com; 1131 Sheridan Ave) Cody's best gear shop offers full backpacking equipment rentals (tents, stoves, backpacks).

Grand Teton National Park & Around

Outside the park, Jackson Hole has a number of outdoor shops selling and renting gear.

Adventure Sports (Dornan's; ☑307-733-3307; www.dornans.com/adventures; Moose Village, WY; ⊙9am-7pm) Rents kayaks, canoes and paddle boards ($50 per day), plus mountain and road bikes ($40 to $55 per day), kids' bikes and racks, with discounted weekly rates. Winter rentals include Nordic skis, snowshoes and sleds. Part of Dornan's.

Colter Bay Marina (Map p195; ☑307-543-2811; ⊙8am-5pm) Rents motorboats ($35/175 per hour/day), rowboats and canoes ($15 to $17 per hour).

Signal Mountain Marina (Map p195; ☑307-543-2831; ⊙7am-7:30pm mid-May–early Sep) Rents canoes ($17/85 per hour/day), kayaks ($15/79), motorboats ($36/175) and pontoon cruisers ($80/480).

Skinny Skis (Map p212; ☑307-733-6094; 65 W Deloney Ave) One of the best backcountry ski shops in the US, with summer backpacking rentals and winter Nordic skis.

Teton Mountaineering (Map p212; ☑307-733-3595; 170 N Cache St) Rents mountaineering and backpacking equipment in summer, plus full ski and snowshoe rentals in winter.

Directory A–Z

Accommodations

It will come as no surprise that rates for accommodations are noticeably higher in the Yellowstone region than in the surrounding areas of Wyoming, Idaho and Montana, particularly in the mad high-season months of July and August. Still, you'll find a wide range of places to stay, from the excellent National Park Service (NPS) and US Forest Service (USFS) campgrounds to private RV parks, simple motels, B&Bs and five-star luxury hotels, as well as that uniquely Western institution, the guest or dude ranch (p260). You should be able to find something reasonably priced in most areas, especially off season.

Yellowstone itself remains the biggest headache, with noncamping accommodations limited to a handful of lodges or cabins, all of which get booked up months in advance, despite there being almost 2200 rooms in the park. The key here is to reserve well ahead.

Outside the parks the more popular hotels fill up a month or two in advance of high summer (July and August). You can normally find somewhere to stay if you just roll into town, but it's still a good idea to make a reservation at least a day or two in advance.

The good news is that you can score great discounts of up to 50% on lodging outside the parks in the shoulder season months of April, May and October through to mid-December, with winter discounts of at least 30% from January to March, depending on the destination.

Camping

Camping is the cheapest and, in many ways, the most enjoyable approach to a Yellowstone vacation. Toasting marshmallows over an open fire, stargazing in the crisp mountain air and taking in an evening ranger talk are essential parts of the national park family-bonding experience.

Around half of the campsites in Yellowstone, and all sites in Grand Teton, are on a first-come, first-served basis. In July and August campsites get snapped up quicker than you can find them on the map. Establish your campsite in the morning before you head off sightseeing (a 'site occupied' sign can be useful) and once you have a site that you like, hold onto it and use it as a base to visit neighboring sights.

If you have a tight itinerary and will be moving around a lot, try to plan at least a few overnight stays at Yellowstone's concession (Xanterra) campgrounds, where you can make site reservations in advance. Gamblers should remember that even if you manage to score a same-day site at a Xanterra campground, you may have to move out the next day if your spot is booked that night. Concessionaire campsites are a little pricier than the park-service sites.

If all else fails, you'll find some great USFS campsites outside the park, and these generally only fill up on summer or holiday weekends.

Fishing Bridge in Yellowstone, Colter Bay in Grand Teton and Flagg Ranch in the John D Rockefeller Jr Memorial Parkway are the only places with full hookups, though a couple of grounds have RV dumps. Generators are generally only allowed between 8am and 8pm, and no generators are allowed at any time at Yellowstone's Indian Creek, Lewis Lake, Pebble Creek, Slough Creek and Tower Fall sites.

CAMPGROUND RULES

Some rules to remember from the NPS and USFS:

➡ Camping in pullouts, trailheads, picnic areas or anywhere except designated campgrounds is illegal.

➡ Wash dishes, hair, teeth etc away from the spigot. Camp wastewater must be disposed of in waste sinks, restroom sinks (no grease) or the toilet, not chucked into your neighbor's site.

➜ Campfires must be in established grates. Never leave a fire unattended.

➜ Cutting trees or shrubs for firewood is prohibited.

➜ Don't build trenches around campsites.

➜ A maximum of six people and two cars are allowed at each site (some USFS sites charge extra for a second car).

➜ No food, ice chests, food containers, utensils or camp stoves may be left outside unattended. If you are tenting, store all food and containers in bear boxes. Don't dispose of food in the camp area; put it in a bag or container and dispose of it in the trash.

➜ Pets must be physically controlled at all times. Please pick up after your pet.

➜ Bear restrictions require that only hard-sided campers (no pop-ups) can occupy sites at Fishing Bridge in Yellowstone and certain USFS grounds outside Cooke City and in the upper Wapiti Valley.

XANTERRA CAMPGROUNDS

Yellowstone's concessionaire, **Xanterra** (☎866-439-7375, 307-344-7311; www.yellowstonenationalparklodges.com), runs five campgrounds. Reservations can be made over the phone, online or from other Xanterra campgrounds or facilities in the park.

Be careful to specify the type of site you want: tent or non-tent, reverse-in or pull-through, and even the length of the site. If your site requirements change,

BOOK YOUR STAY ONLINE

For more accommodations reviews by Lonely Planet authors, check out http://lonelyplanet.com/hotels/. You'll find independent reviews, as well as recommendations on the best places to stay. Best of all, you can book online.

you'll need to change the reservation. Some sites are designated tent-only – you don't *have* to put up a tent in these, but you can't roll up in a giant RV. Site fees are for up to six adults.

➜ When you make an online or phone booking, you must pay by credit card and then receive a booking reference number.

➜ You'll need to show that credit card when you turn up at the campground. Xanterra doesn't take checks.

➜ If you cancel your reservation you'll have to pay the first night of each individual reservation.

➜ If the campground office is closed when you arrive, look on the notice board for your name on an envelope, which will contain your site allocation.

➜ If you arrive late at night without a reservation, look on the notice board to see if any sites are vacant and pay the next morning before 11am.

NATIONAL PARK SERVICE CAMPGROUNDS

Yellowstone and Grand Teton campgrounds usually have flush toilets (cheaper sites have vault toilets), drinking water, garbage disposal, fire pits (or charcoal grills) and picnic benches. Most

hold some kind of nightly campfire talk. Days, times and topics are prominently posted and are listed in the park newspapers.

The process of picking a site varies with the campground, but generally involves picking up an envelope from a box at the entrance, driving around the various loops until you find an available site you like, marking the site with either the tab from the envelope, some camp furniture, or the most agreeable family member, and then filling out the envelope and depositing it with the correct fee back at the entrance. Don't dally trying to find the world's best campsite – by the time you get back, the earlier one you liked may well have been snapped up.

When choosing a site, discerning campers scrutinize its proximity to a bathroom, trash and water supply, whether the ground is level and, most importantly, the neighbors (a scattering of beer cans can be a bad sign). In general, back-in sites offer a little more privacy; parallel sites are little more than car parks by the side of the road. A campground's outer loops are usually the most private.

In larger campgrounds, such as Colter Bay in Teton and Mammoth in Yellowstone, you register and pay at the entrance and are computer-assigned a spot, so there's no need to mark your site.

➜ Some grounds ask you to keep the receipt tab displayed on your car windshield; others ask you to tag it to the campsite post.

➜ Rangers often come around at night to check receipts against vehicle number plates.

FREE PARK ADMISSION!

Admission to Yellowstone and Grand Teton National Parks is generally free on August 25, the anniversary of the founding of the National Park Service. There are over a half-dozen other free admission days, including on National Public Lands Day (September 26), but these change annually – see www.nps.gov/yell/planyourvisit/fees.htm.

➤ A 'site occupied' sign can be useful to mark your turf, and these are for sale in most campgrounds.

➤ NPS campgrounds generally do not accept checks or credit cards (with the exception of Signal Mountain in Grand Teton and Mammoth in Yellowstone) and are self-service, so make sure you bring plenty of $1 and $5 bills.

➤ Golden Age and Golden Access Passports give 50% reductions on most camping fees in national parks and national forests.

➤ Most campgrounds sell boxes of firewood ($7.85) and kindling.

➤ A few campsites are normally reserved for hikers and cyclists at a discounted price.

OUTSIDE THE PARKS

USFS campgrounds are generally less developed than NPS campgrounds – some don't have drinking water and require you to pack out all trash. A few of these sites are free. Many turn off the water supply about mid-September and then either close or run the site for a while at half-price. At any rate, it's always a good idea to bring a few gallons of water when camping. Checks are accepted at most USFS campgrounds.

Sites can be reserved in certain USFS campgrounds in the Gallatin Valley and in Targhee, Shoshone and Custer (around Red Lodge) National Forests through the **National Recreation Reservation Service** (☎877-444-6777; www.recreation.gov). There is a nonrefundable $9 reservation fee for most sites and a cancellation charge of $10. It's possible to select and reserve specific campsites online, or with the useful app. Sites need to be booked a minimum of three days and maximum of eight months in advance.

Free dispersed camping (meaning you can camp almost anywhere) is permitted in some public backcountry areas. Sometimes you can pull off a dirt road and into a small lay-by where you can camp. In other places, you must be 0.25 miles from a developed campground and often not within 0.5 miles of a major highway. Check with the local district ranger office.

Private campgrounds outside the park are mostly designed with RVs in mind.

Tenters can camp, but fees are double the public campgrounds and sites are normally crushed together to maximize profits. Facilities can include hot showers, coin laundry, swimming pool, full RV hookups with phone and satellite TV, games area, playground and a convenience store.

If you don't have kids, you'll find campgrounds to be much quieter outside school summer holidays.

Lodging

If you aren't camping, accommodations in Yellowstone and Grand Teton are limited to concession-run park lodges and cabins. Lodges are often grand reminders of a bygone era, but the rooms have usually been renovated and are generally quite comfortable. Not all rooms are equal, and there's often a vast range of different room permutations available.

Cabins are generally remnants from the 1950s, almost always jammed into a small area and resembling anything from an affluent suburb to a military barracks. The cheaper cabins are simple (sometimes without bathrooms), but contain a modicum of rustic charm.

DUDE RANCHES

Dude-ranch history dates back to the late 19th century, when visiting family and friends from eastern cities offered money to the informal accommodations supplied as a sideline by the region's ranches.

These days you can find anything from a working-ranch experience (5am wake-up calls included) to top-of-the-line resorts frequented by the rich and famous. Ironically, working cattle ranches are increasingly hard to find in the tourist-driven Yellowstone economy.

A few ranches offer nightly accommodations-only rates, but most offer all-inclusive rates and require a minimum stay of three days to a week. Typical weekly rates run $200 to $250 per person per day, which includes accommodations, meals, activities and equipment. Ranches are proud of the connections they form with their clients, many of whose families return to the same ranch generation after generation.

While the highlight of dude-ranch vacations is horseback riding, many ranches have expanded their activity lists to include fly-fishing, hiking, mountain biking and cross-country skiing. Accommodations range from rustic log cabins to cushy suites with Jacuzzis and cable TV. Meals range from steak and beans to four-course gourmet extravaganzas.

Yellowstone's dude ranches (increasingly called guest ranches) are concentrated in the Wapiti Valley near Cody, Jackson Hole and the Gallatin Valley northwest of Yellowstone. For more information contact the **Dude Ranchers' Association** (www.duderanch.org), the **Wyoming Dude Ranchers' Association** (www.wyomingdra.com) or **Montana Dude Ranchers' Association** (www.montanadra.com).

The pricier cabins have modern interiors but are pretty charmless.

In general, park accommodations are decent value, considering the premium real estate. Lodge accommodations start around $80 for a double without bath and $120 for a double with bath. Cabins start at $65 for a double without bath, and $100 with bath.

➤ There are no TVs or radios in park accommodations (don't panic!), so bring a book.

➤ Room rates listed are for two people and without tax.

➤ Children under 12 usually stay free.

➤ Check the Xanterra website for occasional internet specials, especially discounts of 20% for advance bookings in October and early winter (book before November 1 for mid-December).

➤ In winter you'll save money by signing up for a joint accommodations-and-activities package.

Xanterra Parks & Resorts (☎866-439-7375, 307-344-7311; www.yellowstonenationalparklodges.com) Runs Yellowstone accommodations and some campgrounds. Also known as Yellowstone National Park Lodges.

Grand Teton Lodge Company (☎307-543-2811; www.gtlc.com) Runs most of that park's private lodges, cabins and campgrounds.

OUTSIDE THE PARKS

Accommodations outside the parks offer much greater variety, from hostels to top-of-the-line dude ranches and fly-fishing lodges.

USFS cabins are a little-known option and are particularly fun in winter, when you can either snowshoe or snowmobile into a basic cabin equipped with a wood stove, cooking utensils and bunk beds. There are cabins in the vicinity of Hebgen Lake and the Paradise Valley. Book these at www.recreation.gov.

Houses or condos are available for rent in ski-

Climate

Mammoth, WY

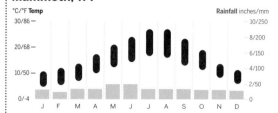

Teton Village, WY

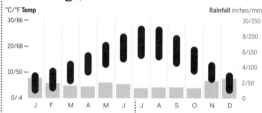

resort areas and can be good value for large groups or families, as they almost invariably include a kitchen and living room. Most hotels offer multi-room suites with a small kitchen that suit families.

There are several B&Bs scattered around the gateway corridors to the parks, ranging from Victorian houses to wolf sanctuaries. Some offer rooms in the owner's house, while others offer stand-alone accommodations.

Some useful websites:

B&Bs, Ranches & Inns of Wyoming (www.wyomingbnb-ranchrec.com)

Jackson Hole Bed & Breakfasts (www.jacksonholebnb.com)

Montana Bed & Breakfast Association (www.mtbba.com)

RESERVATIONS

If you find yourself without a reservation, any of the parks' accommodations can tell you exactly what's available parkwide on the spot and can make bookings for up to two days ahead. If you are desperate, keep heading back to check, as cancellations open up a limited number of accommodations every day.

Make sure to let the hotel know if you plan on a late arrival – many places will give your room away if you haven't arrived or called by 6pm. Cancellation policies vary; inquire when you book.

Most of the gateway towns surrounding the parks have agencies that will gladly book your entire vacation, from car rental to hotel rooms and excursions.

Jackson Hole Central Reservations (☎888-838-6306; www.jacksonholewy.com)

Yellowstone Tour and Travel (Map p162; ☎800-221-1151; www.yellowstone-travel.com; 211 Yellowstone Ave, West Yellowstone)

Yellowstone Vacations (Map p162; ☎800-426-7669; www.yellowstonevacations.com; 415 Yellowstone Ave, West Yellowstone)

Courses

Established in 1907, the nonprofit **Yellowstone Institute** (Map p92; ☎307-344-2293; www.yellowstoneassociation.org/institute) conducts an educational field program offering one- to five-day outdoor courses in everything from identifying mammal tracks and wild edible plants to wolf behavior and Yellowstone's colorful history. It also runs multiday backpacking and horse-pack trips, kayaking, fly-fishing for teens and women and backcountry trips, as well as courses on photography and wildlife-watching. 'Lodging and Learning Programs' are four- to five-day packages that include food and park accommodations. These are particularly popular in winter.

Most courses are conducted from late May to late September (plus some in January and February) at the historic Buffalo Ranch in Yellowstone's Lamar Valley, though some day courses meet at the Yellowstone Association building in Gardiner. Courses cost $100 to $150 per day, excluding food and accommodations. Accommodations are in the self-catering log-cabin bunkhouses of Buffalo Ranch and small groups can stay in the Yellowstone Overlook Field Campus cabins in Gardiner. View the course catalogs online.

The highly regarded **Teton Science School** (☑307-733-4765; www.tetonscience.org) in Kelly runs half- and full-day wildlife tours, plus week-long programs. It also houses the free Murie Natural History Museum; call for an appointment to visit.

If all of that sounds too much like school, try a fly-fishing course at the **Yellowstone Fly Fishing School** (☑406-220-5234; www.yellowstoneflyfishing school.com; 271 Old Clyde Park Rd, Livingston). Women-only courses, kids' courses, private lessons and four-hour clinics ($100 per person in a group of three) are available, some based at Chico Hot Springs.

Discount Cards

Always ask for some kind of discount, whether it be AAA, Good Sam, seniors, off-season, shoulder season, multiday or any other even half-credible reason you can imagine. Rates are notoriously flexible in the Yellowstone region. Student cards are of little use.

Electricity

Voltage in the USA is AC 110V. You'll need an AC adapter and probably a voltage converter to run most non-US electronics.

120V/60Hz

120V/60Hz

Food

Food in Yellowstone is generally more functional than fun, though you shouldn't have difficulty finding somewhere to eat, whatever your budget. The parks offer a multitude of fast-food outlets and sandwich bars, as well as the occasional need-to-eat-something-different gourmet restaurant.

The following price ranges are for a main course, not including tips or drinks:

$ under $15

$$ $15 to $25

$$$ over $25

Outside the tourist-driven eateries in the parks, local cuisine is a stick-to-your-ribs diet of biscuits and gravy, chicken-fried steaks, turkey loaf and mashed potatoes, plus half-pound burgers and bloody steaks. One local 'delicacy' that always gets foisted (with a grin) on tourists is Rocky Mountain oysters – deep-fried bison testicles, normally served in pairs.

If you plan on sticking to a strict vegetarian diet while traveling in Greater Yellowstone, you'll have to get used to two things: baked potatoes and grudging looks from local ranchers.

Given the lovely locations and abundant picnic areas, picnicking is a popular option. A cooler is invaluable, and ice is available at most park junctions. The majority of campers bring a dual-burner stove to speed along cookouts.

Insurance

Foreign visitors to the US should take out adequate travel insurance, purchased before departure. At a minimum, you need coverage for medical emergencies and treatment, including hospital stays and an emergency flight home if necessary. Medical treatment in the US is of the highest caliber, but the expense could kill you.

You should also consider coverage for luggage theft or loss, and trip-cancellation insurance.

Finally, if you're driving it's essential that you have liability insurance. Car-rental agencies offer insurance that covers damage to the rental vehicle and separate liability insurance (which covers damage to people and other vehicles).

Worldwide travel insurance is available at www.lonelyplanet.com/bookings. You can buy, extend and claim online anytime – even if you're already on the road.

Internet Access

In Yellowstone wi-fi is available only in the lobby of the Old Faithful Snow Lodge, at Lake Hotel, the lodges at Grant Village and at Mammoth and Canyon lounge bars, for a fee of $5/12/25 per 1/24/72 hours. Call ☑877-658-5597 for details. Only Lake Hotel has wired internet connection in some of the rooms and an internet-connected 24-hour business center.

In Grand Teton the Craig Thomas Discovery & Visitor Center offers wi-fi.

Most hotels, libraries, visitor centers, bookstores and cafes in the neighboring towns offer free wi-fi access.

Money

Yellowstone has 24-hour ATMs at almost all hotels and general stores.

In Grand Teton look for 24-hour ATMs at Dornan's and Jackson Lake Lodge and other ATMs at Colter Bay grocery store and Signal Mountain.

Bear in mind that tipping (around 15%) is generally expected on horse-packing and rafting trips and stays at dude ranches.

➡ Accommodations tax ranges from 4% to 8% and varies from county to county, even inside the parks.

➡ Sales tax is 4% in Wyoming (plus up to 2% county tax).

PARK PASSES

Several types of annual passes grant unlimited access to national parks. The passes admit a private vehicle and its passengers, or the pass holder, spouse and children. You'll need a photo ID to purchase and use the pass.

➡ **Annual Pass** Year-long access to Yellowstone and Grand Teton costs $60 per park.

➡ **Nationwide Annual Pass** Excellent-value Interagency Pass ($80) that gives access to any fee-paying site administered by the NPS, USFS, United States Fish & Wildlife Service (USFWS) or Bureau of Land Management (BLM).

➡ **Seniors Pass** A lifetime seniors pass covering the same areas costs a one-off fee of $10 and is a great bargain. It allows US residents 62 years and older (and accompanying passengers in a private vehicle) unlimited entry to all sites, with a further 50% discount on many camping and other fees (except Fishing Bridge RV Park).

➡ **Access Pass** This free pass offers the same benefits to US residents who are blind or permanently disabled (proof is required). If you have an old Golden Age or Golden Access pass, there's no need to replace it with the new passes.

You can buy the passes at all park entrances, or purchase one online at http://store.usgs.gov/pass. For more information see www.nps.gov/fees_passes.htm.

➡ There is no statewide sales tax in Montana, though a few places such as Red Lodge, Big Sky and Cooke City impose a local 'resort' tax of 3%.

Opening Hours

Opening hours for all facilities are very seasonal. Outside of the high season, from Memorial Day to Labor Day, you can expect opening hours to be shorter by an hour or two. The park newspapers detail exact opening hours and dates. The following are standard business hours:

Banks, post offices and government offices 9am to 5pm weekdays, half-day Saturday.

Park visitor centers Generally 8am to 7pm in summer.

Convenience stores Normally until 9:30pm within the parks.

Restaurants 7am to 10:30am, 11:30am to 2:30pm and 5pm to 9:30pm.

Shops 9:30am to 5:30pm.

Pets

National parks are a challenging place for pets. Strict restrictions limit pets to paved parking lots and picnic areas. If you want to go hiking with Fido you are better off sticking to the scenic national forests around the parks. In general, Red Lodge, Bozeman and Jackson are the most pet-friendly towns.

➡ In the national parks pets must be leashed at all times. They are not allowed on any boardwalks, geyser basins or backcountry trails, or more than 100ft from roads or paved paths.

➡ You are not allowed to tie your pet (aka bear bait) to objects or leave him/her unattended.

➡ Never let your pet get near thermal features – they won't know it's hot until it's too late.

➡ Pets are allowed in Yellowstone's cabins,

PARK SUPPORT

The following organizations do good work to ensure the parks' future:

➡ **Yellowstone Association** (www.yellowstoneassociation.org) Supports educational, historical and scientific programs through memberships, book sales and courses at the Yellowstone Institute.

➡ **Yellowstone Park Foundation** (www.ypf.org) Funds numerous park projects, from wolf monitoring to trail upkeep and raises funds through Yellowstone National Park credit cards and number plates.

➡ **Grand Teton National Park Foundation** (www.gtnpf.org) This organization's mission is to enhance, preserve and protect the park, using member donations to fund park projects.

➡ **Grand Teton Association** (www.grandtetonpark.org) Book sales and membership dues fund educational, interpretive and scientific programs in Grand Teton.

➡ **Greater Yellowstone Coalition** (www.greateryellowstone.org) Monitors environmental issues in areas around the park, from snowmobile use to mining concerns.

➡ **National Parks Conservation Association** (www.npca.org) This national organization strives to protect and enhance America's national parks. Members can subscribe to the magazine or sign up for an association credit card.

but not in its hotels. Most campgrounds allow dogs, but do not permit them to go loose.

➡ Our lodging reviews indicate when pets are allowed, usually for a fee ($10 to $35).

➡ Almost all the national forests in the area allow dogs on leashes. In Jedediah Smith Wilderness, dogs must be under voice control at all times.

➡ Service animals such as seeing-eye dogs are welcome in the parks. The following kennels for dogs and cats are in the gateway towns surrounding the parks. If you don't see one, ask for the local veterinary clinic.

Cody Country Bed & Biscuit (☑307-587-3379; www.woofyproducts.com; 134 E Cooper Lane, Cody)

Doggie Daycare & Motel (☑406-763-5585; www.doggiedaycareandmotel.com; 421 Garnet Mt Way, Gallatin Gateway, Bozeman)

Dogjax (☑307-733-3647; www.dogjax.com; 3590 Southpark Dr, Jackson)

Happy Tails Pet Resort (☑307-733-1606; www.springcreekanimalhospital.com; 1035 W Broadway, Jackson)

Kennels at the Smith Family Ranch (☑406-848-7477; www.paradisevalleyvacation.com; 1828 Old Yellowstone Trail South)

Querencia Kennels (☑406-333-4500; www.querencia.com; 55 Querencia Dr, Emigrant, Paradise Valley)

Trail Creek Pet Center (☑208-354-2571; www.trailcreekpet.com; 1778 S 1500 E, Driggs; ⊙8am-6pm)

Wagging Tails Retreat (☑406-823-9978; 5288 US Hwy 89 S, Livingston)

Post

The only year-round post office in Yellowstone is at Mammoth Hot Springs. Seasonal post offices are at Canyon, Lake and Grant Villages and Old Faithful.

In Grand Teton you'll find post offices at Colter Bay (summer only) and Kelly, Moose and Moran Junctions.

Public Holidays

On the following national public holidays, banks, schools and post offices are closed, and transportation, museums and other services operate on a Sunday

schedule. Park visitor centers and facilities are open on the public holidays that fall within their normal opening dates. Holidays falling on a weekend are usually observed the following Monday.

January 1 New Year's Day

Third Monday in January Martin Luther King Jr Day

Third Monday in February Presidents' Day

Last Monday in May Memorial Day

July 4 Independence Day

First Monday in September Labor Day

Second Monday in October Columbus Day

November 11 Veterans' Day

Fourth Thursday in November Thanksgiving

December 25 Christmas Day

Telephone

Cell phone coverage is good in Grand Teton (except for the canyons) and at Yellowstone's main junctions. Verizon has by far the best regional coverage. Bring your phone along, but don't rely on it for emergency communications.

There are pay phones at most junctions, but they can be expensive, especially for collect calls.

Tourist Information

Visitors to Yellowstone and Grand Teton are well supported with information from various organizations.

Yellowstone National Park

Albright Visitor Center (Map p88; ✆307-344-2263; ⏰8am-7pm)

Central backcountry office (✆307-344-2160; YELL_Backcountry_Office@nps.gov)

Fire information (✆307-344-2580)

Lost & found (✆307-344-2109, for items lost in Xanterra accommodations or restaurants 307-344-5387)

Old Faithful Visitor Center (Map p108; ✆307-545-2750; ♿)

Park road updates (✆307-344-2117)

Recorded campground & accommodations information (✆307-344-2114)

Xanterra (✆307-344-7311, 866-439-7375; www.yellowstonenationalparklodges.com)

Yellowstone National Park (✆307-344-7381, TDD 307-344-2386; www.nps.gov/yell)

Grand Teton National Park

Grand Teton Lodge Company (GTLC; ✆307-543-3100, 800-628-9988; www.gtlc.com)

Grand Teton National Park (✆307-739-3300; www.nps.gov/grte)

Jackson Hole & Greater Yellowstone Visitor Center (Map p212; ✆307-733-3316; www.jacksonholechamber.com; 532 N Cache Dr)

Recorded campground information (✆307-739-3603)

Recorded weather (✆317-739-3611)

Greater Yellowstone

Recreation.gov reservation service (✆1-877-444-6777; http://recreation.gov)

State road & weather conditions (✆Idaho 208-336-6600, Montana 800-226-7623, Wyoming 307-772-0824)

Travelers with Disabilities

Yellowstone has many accessible boardwalks and trails, and even several wheelchair-accessible backcountry campsites, including Goose Lake (OD5) south of Fountain Flats Dr in Geyser Country and Ice Lake (4D3) on the Norris–Canyon road, which is 0.5 miles from the trailhead and has a wheelchair-accessible vault toilet. The Madison River, in the west of the park, offers a wheelchair-accessible fishing platform.

The pamphlet *Visitor Guide to Accessible Features in Yellowstone National Park* lists accessible sights and facilities, and is available online at the 'Plan Your Visit' section of the park website. In Yellowstone there are wheelchair-accessible campsites at Bridge Bay, Canyon, Grant Village, Madison and Mammoth.

Deaf visitors can get information at ✆TDD 307-344-2386 (Yellowstone) or ✆TDD 307-739-3400 (Grand Teton). The park will provide sign-language interpreters for ranger-led programs if

---

VIRTUAL YELLOWSTONE

You can use a combination of MP3 players, smartphones and your car stereo to liven up the drive to the parks.

➡ You can download the free NPS video podcasts *Yellowstone in Depth, Visiting Yellowstone* or *Inside Yellowstone* from iTunes.

➡ Yellowstone and Grand Teton National Parks offer several free apps, including the Mobile Guides official app for Grand Teton. The free Yellowstone Geysers app gives upcoming eruption times and webcams for a half-dozen geysers around Old Faithful. A search will dig up other apps, from hiking guides to flora identification.

➡ The Gypsy Guides app (www.gypsyguides.com; $5) uses your phone's GPS to give automatic driving commentary through the park.

➡ Gaper Guide (www.gaperguide.com) is a stand-alone, GPS-enabled audioguide to the park. It's not cheap at $45 per day, but you can rent the unit in one gateway town and drop it at another.

➡ Go old school with an audio book. Tim Cahill's *Lost in My Own Backyard* is available on audio CD or MP3 and is read by the author.

➡ The park service operates webcams at Old Faithful and from the top of Mt Washburn, among others – see www.nps.gov/yell/learn/photosmultimedia/webcams.htm. Also check out the amazing 360-degree panoramas at www.360panos.com.

INTERNATIONAL VISITORS

Embassies & Consulates

British and Australian consulates are maintained in Denver, but they can't replace lost passports. For all other countries, the nearest options are in Washington, DC or San Francisco.

Entering the Country

If you have a non-US passport, you must complete an arrival/departure record (form I-94) before you reach the immigration desk. It's usually handed out on the plane, along with the customs declaration. On arrival most visitors will have their photo taken and electronic fingerprints made of each index finger; the process takes less than a minute.

No matter what your visa says, US immigration officers have absolute authority to refuse admission to the country or impose conditions on admission. They will ask about your plans and whether you have sufficient funds. It's a good idea to list an itinerary, produce an onward or round-trip ticket and have at least one major credit card.

If connecting on a domestic flight you will pick up your bag, go through customs and then place your bag back on a baggage belt before continuing to your domestic gate.

Money

Foreign-currency traveler's checks are a headache, so do yourself a favor and bring US-dollar checks, as many businesses will simply accept them as cash. The front desks of all park accommodations exchange foreign-currency cash 9am to 5pm weekdays.

Passports & Visas

Most visitors from Western Europe, Australia, New Zealand, Japan and Singapore can enter the US for stays of 90 days or less on a visa waiver program (VWP).

To qualify for this, your passport must meet one of the following conditions:

➡ It was issued before October 26, 2005, but is 'machine readable'.

➡ It was issued on or after October 26, 2005, and includes a digital photo as well as being machine readable.

➡ It was issued on or after October 26, 2006, and contains a digital photo and 'biometric data,' such as digital iris scans and fingerprints.

Citizens of the 27 countries in the VWP need to register with the government online **Electronic System for Travel Authorisation** (ESTA; https://esta.cbp.dhs.gov) before their visit. The registration is valid for two years and costs $14.

For more details see the **US State Department** website (www.travel.state.gov).

Telephone

To call interstate (long distance) dial ☎1 followed by the state code: Montana ☎406 or Wyoming ☎307. To call abroad dial the international code ☎011.

Time

The Yellowstone region operates on US Mountain Time, which is -7 hours GMT. The US subscribes to daylight savings time (DST): on the first Sunday in April clocks are set one hour ahead; on the last Sunday of October, clocks are turned back one hour.

Weights & Measures

The US uses the imperial system (miles, yards, pints and quarts). A US gallon is slightly larger than an imperial gallon and the US ton is slightly heavier than a metric tonne. Sadly, a US pint is 20% smaller than a British pint.

booked three weeks in advance – call ☏307-344-2251.

Wheelchair-accessible trails in Grand Teton include the 6-mile paved trail along String Lake. Accessible accommodations are available at several campsites and all lodging facilities. For more details view the *Accessibility* brochure on the park's website.

Blind and permanently disabled people can obtain a free lifetime access pass, good for all federal parks. Get one at park entrances.

Access Tours (☏208-787-2332; www.accesstours.org) runs tours in Grand Teton and Yellowstone for those with physical disabilities.

Volunteering

The NPS runs a Volunteer in Parks (VIP) program. See www.nps.gov/volunteer and www.nps.gov/yell/supportyourpark/volunteer.htm for details.

For information about Grand Teton's volunteer program, contact the **Park Volunteer Coordinators** (☏307-739-3657; www.nps.gov/grte/getinvolved/volunteer.htm).

The USFS accepts a wider range of volunteers, from trail maintenance workers to campground hosts, and normally supplies rooms and board with a subsistence wage. Visit www.fs.fed.us/working-with-us/volunteers or www.volunteer.gov.

The **Student Conservation Association** (www.thesca.org) places student volunteers in the parks.

Youth Conservation Corps (YCC; www.nps.gov/yell/parkmgmt/yccjobs.htm) offers month-long programs for teenagers (aged 15 to 18), who work in the park on jobs such as trail construction, often in the backcountry.

Other volunteering options in the region:

Community Foundation of Jackson Hole (☏303-739-1026; www.volunteerjacksonhole.

GETTING HITCHED

Thinking of getting married in the region? Weddings in the park require a $50 permit, but you won't have far to travel for your honeymoon! Consider the following:

➡ The lovely, classic English-style church at Mammoth (☏307-344-2003), for a $100 reservation fee.

➡ Church of the Transfiguration at Moose, a tiny chapel with huge Teton views.

org) Lists opportunities with dozens of local agencies, from therapeutic riding to art and wilderness organizations.

Continental Divide Trail Alliance (☏303-278-3177; www.continentaldividetrail.org) Volunteers help with trail construction, PR work or fundraising, with several hands-on maintenance projects in the Yellowstone region each summer.

Wilderness Volunteers (☏928-556-0038; www.wildernessvolunteers.org) Week-long trips helping maintain America's parks and wild lands.

Yellowstone Association (☏307-344-2293; www.yellowstoneassociation.org) Volunteers at the Buffalo Ranch center assist with courses for summer or winter seasons.

Work

Occasional seasonal jobs (for US citizens only) are available as rangers or laborers with the NPS, though competition for the jobs is fierce. Check for openings at www.nps.gov/personnel and www.usajobs.gov.

Your first stop should be **Coolworks** (www.coolworks.com), which is an excellent clearing house for jobs both in and around the parks. The page www.coolworks.com/yell.htm deals specifically with the Yellowstone region.

The main Yellowstone concessionaire, **Xanterra** (www.yellowstonejobs.com), employs 3000 people in summer and 300 in winter,

who do everything from making beds to making soup. Pay hovers around minimum wage and the work is fairly humdrum, though you won't have to go far to find a place to hike on your days off. Employee housing and food cost around $75 per week (a few RV sites are also available). Apply December to March for summer jobs and in August/September for winter positions. Staff are a mix of students, overseas workers (who need to arrange their own work visas) and retirees living in their RVs.

You may also find opportunities with **Delaware North** (www.visityellowstonepark.com/Jobs.aspx), which runs the Yellowstone General Stores and several hotels in West Yellowstone. It employs around 600 people a year.

The third Yellowstone concessionaire, **Yellowstone Parks Service Stations** (www.ypss.com), is based in Gardiner and has work for clerical as well as automotive technicians.

For job opportunities in Grand Teton, contact the following:

Dornan's (www.dornans.com/employment)

Flagg Ranch (www.gtlc.com/headwaters/about/employment.aspx)

Grand Teton Lodge Company (www.gtlc.com/employment/index.aspx)

Signal Mountain Lodge (www.coolworks.com/signalmt)

Transportation

GETTING THERE & AWAY

The main gateways (and airports) nearest to Yellowstone National Park are Jackson (56 miles), Cody (52 miles), Bozeman (65 miles), Billings (129 miles) and Idaho Falls (107 miles). Grand Teton National Park sits right outside Jackson (13 miles). Depending on your direction of travel, it may be cheaper to land in larger hubs such as Salt Lake City (390 miles) or Denver (563 miles) and rent a car there.

Flights, tours and rail tickets can be booked online at www.lonelyplanet.com/bookings.

Air

Airports

Private planes can land at Jackson Hole Airport and several small airstrips, including Driggs and Mission Field, east of Livingston, Montana.

Billings Logan International Airport (BIL;☑406-247-8609; www.flybillings.com) Service to Salt Lake City, Minneapolis, Denver, Chicago, Seattle, Portland, Phoenix, Los Angeles, Las Vegas, other Montana destinations.

Gallatin Field Airport (BZN;☑406-388-8321; www.bozemanairport.com) Located 8 miles northwest of downtown Bozeman.

Idaho Falls Regional Airport (IDA;☑206-612-8221; www.idahofallsidaho.gov/city/city-departments/idaho-falls-regional-airport.html) Service to Las Vegas, Oakland, Los Angeles and Phoenix. Also serves Salt Lake City and Denver.

Jackson Hole Airport (JAC; Map p198;☑307-733-7682; www.jacksonholeairport.com) Located 7 miles north of Jackson off US 26/89/189/191 within Grand Teton National Park. Daily flights serve Denver, Salt Lake City, LA, San Francisco, Chicago, Dallas and Houston.

Yellowstone Airport (WYS; ☑406-646-7631; www.yellowstoneairport.org; ⊙Jun-Sep) In West Yellowstone; the closest airport to Yellowstone National Park. Three daily summer flights (June through September) to and from Salt Lake City. Closes in winter.

Yellowstone Regional Airport (COD; www.flyyra.com) Located 1 mile east of Cody; runs daily flights to Chicago, Salt Lake City and Denver.

Flights from UK & Ireland

British Airways (www.britishairways.com) Has the most direct route to Denver, where US carriers connect to Jackson Hole (11 hours plus layover). Also consider American, United, Delta and Virgin Atlantic.

Flights from Australia & New Zealand

Route through Los Angeles or San Francisco before continuing to regional airports. Via the Pacific route, the first leg is 12 to 14 hours. Flying through Asia probably means spending a night or considerable layover time in a connecting city.

Land

Bus

Unfortunately, long-distance bus services are a slow, somewhat infrequent and highly inconvenient way to get to Yellowstone and Grand Teton National Parks. But they will get you to major cities, from where you could then rent a car or bicycle or book a local shuttle.

Companies may charge extra to transport skis or bicycles.

Alltrans Jackson Hole Express (Mountain States Express;☑307-733-1719, 800-443-6133; www.jacksonholebus.com; one-way $75) Daily service from Jackson to Salt Lake City (six hours).

Greyhound (☑800-231-2222; www.greyhound.com) The major long-distance bus company, with routes to Cody, Wyoming, and Bozeman, Montana.

Karst Stage (☑406-556-3540; www.karststage.com; West Yellowstone shuttle adult/child age 3-12 $155/78) Airport shuttle service from Bozeman's Gallatin Field to Big Sky and West Yellowstone.

Trailways (☑800-255-7655; www.trailways.com) Travels to Bozeman and Billings, Montana.

Salt Lake Express (☎800-356-9796; www.saltlakeexpress.com) Daily minibus service to Idaho Falls, Salt Lake City and Boise from West Yellowstone and Jackson.

Car & Motorcycle

Despite high fuel costs, this is the way to see the parks. Be aware that soft-shelled vehicles (such as Jeeps) do not provide safe storage for food in bear country, and that parks require vehicles to have proper bear-proof canisters to carry food, although a few sites provide storage boxes. Car and motorcycle drivers will need the vehicle's registration papers and liability insurance.

AUTOMOBILE ASSOCIATIONS

American Automobile Association (AAA; ☎800-874-7532; www.aaa.com) The main US auto club with 24-hour roadside assistance, free maps and trip planning help. It has reciprocal membership agreements with several international auto clubs (check with AAA and bring your membership card).

Better World Club (☎866-238-1137; www.betterworldclub.com) This small auto club with traveler services donates 1% of earnings to environmental cleanups and offers ecologically sensitive choices for services.

DRIVER'S LICENSE

Visitors to the USA must have a valid driver's license from their home country. Individual states, including Montana, may have additional requirements, such as an International Driving Permit (IDP). An IDP is especially helpful in all states if your home license doesn't have a photo or is in a foreign language. Your automobile association at home can issue an IDP, valid for one year, for a small fee. You must carry your home license together with the IDP.

To ride a motorcycle you need a US state motorcycle license or an IDP appropriate for motorcycles. Helmets are required in most states.

RENTAL

Car rental rates in the towns around Yellowstone vary considerably throughout the year, with summer weekends bringing the highest rates.

Jackson, Billings, Bozeman and Cody have the best selection of rental companies and, thus, slightly lower rates. All the airports have car rentals. The major companies are **Hertz** (www.hertz.com), **Avis** (www.avis.com), **Thrifty** (www.thrifty.com) and **National** (www.nationalcar.com).

While renting an RV can save money in accommodations and dining out, higher RV campsite fees and the cost of gas can quickly negate these savings. Between gas consumption (most RVs average between 5 and 10 miles per gallon) and electricity use at campsites, camper vans are a convenient smaller alternative.

Campervan North America (☎1-208-712-8100; www.campervannorthamerica.com) Camper van rentals with one-way options. Locations in Las Vegas and Bozeman.

Cruise America (☎800-671-8042; www.cruiseamerica.com) For a range of RVs, Cruise America rents through local dealers in Salt Lake City. Renters face a three-day minimum, not including mileage fees. Summer rentals should be reserved well in advance.

INSURANCE

Don't put the key in the ignition if you don't have auto insurance. In most states it's compulsory; moreover, you risk financial ruin if you have an accident without insurance. If you already have auto insurance, make sure it will cover your rental car. Rental companies provide limited insurance, usually charging extra for collision damage. Check to see if your credit card covers collision damage coverage for rental cars; most do and it saves a bundle of money.

ROAD RULES

Most US natives know that cars drive on the right side of the road, but bear this mind if you're from the UK, Australia, New Zealand or Japan. Seatbelts and child-safety seats are required in every state. On motorcycles, helmets are required for anyone under 17 years in Montana, Idaho and Wyoming.

Littering brings fines of up to $1000. Most states don't allow you to transport open containers of alcohol, and penalties for driving under the influence of drugs or alcohol (DUI) are severe.

CLIMATE CHANGE & TRAVEL

Every form of transport that relies on carbon-based fuel generates CO_2, the main cause of human-induced climate change. Modern travel is dependent on airplanes, which might use less fuel per mile per person than most cars but travel much greater distances. The altitude at which aircraft emit gases (including CO_2) and particles also contributes to their climate change impact. Many websites offer 'carbon calculators' that allow people to estimate the carbon emissions generated by their journey and, for those who wish to do so, to offset the impact of the greenhouse gases emitted with contributions to portfolios of climate-friendly initiatives throughout the world. Lonely Planet offsets the carbon footprint of all staff and author travel.

Limits vary by state but a blood alcohol limit of 0.08% or more is considered driving under the influence.

The speed limit is generally 65mph to 75mph on western highways, 25mph in cities and 15mph in school zones.

Speed limits in the park are generally 45mph, dropping to 25mph or less at popular pullouts or junctions. Hwy 191 in Grand Teton National Park has a limit of 55mph.

In the park, practice courteous driving etiquette. If you're driving a slow vehicle, use one of the numerous pullouts to let faster traffic pass. If you don't want your open driver's side door torn off by a passing bus, pull off the road fully when watching wildlife. Wildlife always has the right of way.

Train

In its heyday the *Union Pacific* pulled right into West Yellowstone and Gardiner; now this social event is preserved as a quaint memory by the local historical society. If you are not intimidated by the fact that the closest passenger trains to this region service destinations over 300 miles away (Denver and Salt Lake City), contact **Amtrak** (☑800-872-7245; www.amtrak.com) for more information.

GETTING AROUND

It's almost impossible to visit Yellowstone without your own vehicle. There's no public transportation of any kind inside the park and only minimal transportation in the gateway corridors. Despite a high volume of traffic trundling through the park, there appears to be little movement toward developing a mass transit system inside the park.

Bicycle

Touring by bicycle is popular, although cycling through Yellowstone National Park presents its own special challenges. Specifically, many riders report that it can be very unpleasant navigating narrow roads jammed with RVs – whose side mirrors and wide loads present a real danger to the little people.

Cyclists using national-park campgrounds usually pay the same fee as walk-ins, which can be considerably lower than the fee for a vehicle. Mountain biking in areas around the national parks is outstanding; however, bike travel on national-park trails is severely limited and wilderness areas may also have restrictions. Bike shops frequently have group rides and can provide information on local trails. **Better World Club** (☑866-238-1137; www.betterworldclub.com) offers a bicycle roadside assistance program.

Rental

Long-term bike rentals are easy to find. Rates run from $350 per week and up, and a credit-card authorization for several hundred dollars is usually necessary as a security deposit.

Buying a bike and reselling it before you leave may be a more economical option. Check out local yard sales or message boards in local coffee shops for used bikes, and be sure to tune up your ride before hitting the road.

Bus

Although some long-distance touring companies visit the parks, only Jackson has regular bus service.

Yellowstone National Park

Services should be reserved in advance.

Historic Yellow Bus Tours (☑866-439-7375; www.yellow stonenationalparklodges.com; morning wildlife tour adult/child age 3-11 $83/42; ☺Jun-Sep) Yellowstone reinstates these classic vintage vehicles for tours ranging from one hour to all day.

Xanterra (☑307-344-7311; www.travelyellowstone.com) Runs interpretive tours that leave from the visitor centers. The 'Yellowstone in a day' tour (adult/child aged three to 11 $105/53) starts in Mammoth, Old Faithful Inn or, for slightly more, in Gardiner.

Grand Teton National Park

Jackson has a free town shuttle that runs every 20 to 30 minutes and the Start Bus (www.startbus.com) public service to Teton Village.

Alltrans Park Shuttle (☑800-443-6133, 307-733-3135; www.alltransparkshuttle.com; daily pass $15; ☺7am-7pm Jun-Sep) Operates several buses a day in summer between Jackson, Moose, Jenny Lake Lodge, Signal Mountain Lodge, Jackson Lake Lodge and Colter Bay. Riders can pay with cash or credit cards. Rides are unlimited on the daily pass. The service is free for guests of GTLC properties.

Jackson Hole Express (☑307-733-3135, 800-443-6133; www.jacksonholebus.com) For regional shuttle service, Alltrans shuttles daily from Jackson to Idaho Falls (2½ hours), Salt Lake City (4½ hours) and points in between. Reservations are recommended. In winter, the Targhee Express operates between Jackson, Teton Village and Grand Targhee Resort in Idaho.

Car & Motorcycle

While drivers in this region tend to be lead-footed on the interstate, traffic in the park is exasperatingly slow, typified by lumbering RVs wheezing over the Continental Divide. At the slightest whiff of a bison or moose, traffic slams to a halt. For this reason, it pays to be extra attentive when driving.

Fuel & Spare Parts

Gas prices inside the park are slightly higher than elsewhere in Wyoming and Montana. Prices rise as you get closer to the park, peaking at Red Lodge and Cooke City. Most gateway towns have an auto-parts store (Napa or Checker) and bicycle shop. Yellowstone has a car-repair garage in Bridge Bay, next to the gas station, but if your car is struggling, it is best to take it to a shop outside the park.

Road Conditions

Harsh winter conditions create frost heaves and potholes that mar even recently repaved roads. Grand Teton National Park's roads are generally in better condition than Yellowstone's. At Yellowstone, there's usually one section of the Grand Loop under construction, causing delays of up to an hour. Sometimes sections of road are closed between certain hours; make sure you check the parks' newspapers or websites for current road conditions.

For road closures and conditions outside the parks, contact www.fhwa.dot.gov/traffic info/index.htm or the state agencies.

Idaho Transportation Department (☑1-888-432-7623; www.511.idaho.gov) Official state site with road closures and information.

Montana Travel Information (☑1-800-226-7623; www.mdt.mt.gov/travinfo) State travel resource.

Wyoming Road Conditions (☑888-996-7623; www.wyoroad.info) Up-to-date info on road conditions and closures.

Road Hazards

Every year hundreds of wild animals meet their fate on the grill of a car. Keep an eye out for crossing animals and drive with particular care at dawn and dusk.

Higher-risk areas have signs marked with a deer,

ROAD DISTANCES TO YELLOWSTONE (WEST ENTRANCE)

DEPARTURE POINT	MILES
Boston	2450
Chicago	1450
Denver	640
Los Angeles	1010
Miami	2600
New York	2300
Salt Lake City	325
San Francisco	950
Seattle	750
Washington, DC	2200

though all areas, even those outside the park, may have animals crossing. Bison should be passed very carefully – they are not nearly as passive as cattle.

Hitchhiking

Hitchhiking is potentially dangerous and not recommended. While it is prohibited on highways, you'll see more people hitchhiking (and stopping) on rural roads, especially near hiking trailheads.

If you are hiking a long loop, it's sometimes difficult to encounter a ride for those last few road miles, although more likely at the most popular trailheads.

You can check ride-share boards at ranger stations and in hostels.

Snowcoach Tours

In Yellowstone National Park only, converted vans on snow tracks provide transportation in and around the park in winter, also providing a useful service for skiers. Snowcoach tours depart daily from West Yellowstone, Flagg Ranch Resort, Wapiti Valley and Mammoth; most stop at Old Faithful and all stop for wildlife-watching opportunities.

Xanterra (www.travel yellowstone.com; adult/child age 3-11 snowcoach tour $94/47) operates park-based tours between Mammoth and Old Faithful.

Tours

Buffalo Bus Co (☑406-646-9353, 800-426-7669; http://yellowstonevacations.com; both loops adult/child 15yr and under $139/125) Northern or southern loops of Yellowstone from West Yellowstone; free pick-up from hotels or campgrounds.

Grand Teton Lodge Company (☑800-628-9988; www.gtlc.com; Grand Teton adult/child 3-12yr $65/30; Yellowstone) Half-day Grand Teton tours, full-day tours of Yellowstone or a combination of both parks.

Gray Line National Park Tours (☑800-443-6133, 307-733-3135; www.graylinejh.com; adult/child $100/50) Full-day park tours from Jackson.

Headwaters Lodge & Cabins (Flagg Ranch;☑800-443-2311; www.flaggranch.com; snowmobiling from $275) Visits Yellowstone.

Xanterra (☑307-344-7311; www.travelyellowstone.com) Yellowstone concessionaire offering coach tours, including the classic Old Yellow Bus, wildlife-viewing and photography, plus transport and accommodation packages.

Health & Safety

Keeping healthy depends on your predeparture preparations, your daily health care while traveling and how you handle any medical problems that develop. While the potential problems can seem daunting, in reality few visitors experience anything worse than a skinned knee. Read up in preparation.

BEFORE YOU GO

The best preparation for a hiking vacation is to embark on some regular, dedicated exercise at least three weeks prior to travel. To lessen the chances of getting sore shoulders, blisters and foot fatigue, wear in your boots thoroughly by undertaking long walks with a loaded pack. This also allows you to try different pack adjustments, socks and footwear.

Those coming from sea level should wait several days after arriving before undertaking any strenuous activity at altitude. Prepare your metabolism for acclimation to the higher elevations by drinking more water and laying off the alcohol.

EMERGENCIES
Dial 📟911 in any emergency. Emergency messages to friends or family can be posted at park entry stations and at visitor centers.

Medical Checklist

First-aid kits should include:

- ➤ acetaminophen (paracetamol) or aspirin
- ➤ adhesive or paper tape
- ➤ antibacterial ointment for cuts and abrasions
- ➤ antibiotics
- ➤ anti-diarrhea drugs (eg loperamide)
- ➤ anti-inflammatory drugs (eg ibuprofen)
- ➤ antihistamines (for hay fever and allergic reactions)
- ➤ bandages, gauze swabs, gauze rolls and safety pins
- ➤ insect repellent with DEET
- ➤ iodine tablets or water filter (for water purification)
- ➤ moleskin (to prevent chafing of blisters)
- ➤ non-adhesive dressing
- ➤ oral rehydration salts
- ➤ paper stitches
- ➤ pocket knife
- ➤ reverse syringe (for snakebites)
- ➤ scissors, safety pins, tweezers, thermometer
- ➤ sterile alcohol wipes
- ➤ steroid cream or cortizone (for allergic rashes)
- ➤ sticking plasters

Further Reading

If you're hiking in remote areas, consider the following detailed health guides.

➤ *NOLS Wilderness Medicine*, by Tod Schimelpfenig and Joan Safford, prepares hikers for outdoor medical emergencies.

➤ *Medicine for the Outdoors*, by Paul Auerbach, is a general reference with brief explanations of many medical problems and practical treatment options.

➤ *Wilderness 911*, by Eric A Weiss, is a step-by-step guide to first aid and advanced care in remote areas.

IN THE PARKS

Availability & Cost of Health Care

Health-care costs will vary widely depending on your insurance. Travel with your insurance card and know the co-payments and conditions of coverage before traveling.

Yellowstone National Park
Yellowstone operates three clinics:

Lake Hospital (📟307-242-7241; ⊗8:30am-8:30pm mid-May–mid-Sep) Summer-only, with 24-hour emergency service through 911.

Mammoth Clinic (📟307-344-7965; ⊗8:30am-5pm) The only year-round clinic.

Old Faithful Clinic (📟307-545-7325; ⊗7am-7pm mid-May–mid-Sep) Summer-only clinic.

COMMON AILMENTS

Fatigue Stay within your capabilities, take breaks and eat properly.

Blisters Wear broken-in boots and moisture-wicking socks, and carry special blister bandages.

Knee pain Use hiking poles and descend with shorter steps without twisting or hyperextending your foot.

Emergency medical services are provided by rangers on duty.

Grand Teton National Park

Grand Teton Medical Clinic (☎307-543-2514; ⏰9am-5pm mid-May–mid-Oct) Near Jackson Lake Lodge.

Infectious Diseases

Amoebic Dysentery

Fluid replacement is the mainstay of management for serious diarrhea. Weak black tea with a little sugar, soda water, or soft drink allowed to go flat and 50% diluted with water are all good. With severe diarrhea, a rehydrating solution is necessary to replace minerals and salts. Commercially available oral rehydration salts (ORS) are very useful. Stick to a bland diet as you recover.

Lyme Disease

A bacterial infection, in the Rocky Mountains Lyme disease is mainly transmitted by the deer (wood) tick. Although the number of cases reported in the US has skyrocketed during the last two decades, Lyme disease remains relatively uncommon over large parts of the Rockies. Early symptoms, which may take months to develop, are similar to influenza – headaches, stiff neck, tiredness and painful swelling of the joints. If left untreated, complications such as meningitis, facial palsy or heart abnormalities may occur, but fatalities are rare. A safe vaccination is not yet available, but Lyme disease responds well to antibiotics.

West Nile Disease

Unknown in the United States until a few years ago, this disease has now been reported in almost all 50 states. It's transmitted by culex mosquitoes, which are active in late summer and early fall, and generally bite after dusk. Most infections are mild or asymptomatic, but the virus may infect the central nervous system, leading to fever, headache, confusion, lethargy, coma and sometimes death. There is no treatment for West Nile virus. See affected areas at the US Geological Survey website (http://diseasemaps.usgs.gov/mapviewer).

Environmental Hazards

Altitude

In the thinner atmosphere of the Rockies, a lack of oxygen may cause headaches, nausea, nosebleeds, shortness of breath, physical weakness and other symptoms. These can lead to serious consequences, especially if combined with heat exhaustion, sunburn or hypothermia. Most people adjust to altitude within a few hours or days. Be careful (especially with children) when driving and overnighting on the Beartooth Plateau, where altitudes reach 10,000ft. In mild cases of altitude sickness, everyday painkillers such as aspirin may relieve discomfort. If symptoms persist, descend to lower elevations.

Bears

Bears live a sedentary life and will typically avoid contact if given sufficient warning of an approaching individual. Yet travelers need to be bear aware. The main causes of human-bear conflict include the animal's instinctual protection of its young, the presence of food and surprise encounters. In July 2011, a man was killed when he surprised a female with her cubs. In the same summer, a grizzly fatally attacked a lone hiker on an infrequently used trail for unknown reasons. In Greater Yellowstone history, 2011 was unique, since very high snowpack brought spring conditions (with high bear activity) in midsummer, which increased human encounters. In recent years,

SAFE WATER

Giardia

➡ This microscopic, waterborne parasite causes intestinal disorders.

➡ Symptoms – which can appear weeks after exposure – include chronic diarrhea, cramps, bloating and gas.

➡ See a doctor if you have symptoms. Treatment requires a course of antibiotics.

Prevention

➡ Don't drink any snowmelt, stream, lake or ground water without filtering it.

➡ Boiling water for 10 minutes is effective against most microbes *except* giardia.

➡ Use a filter at 0.5 microns or smaller, a Steripen or treat with water tablets.

the population of grizzly bears has increased in Grand Teton National Park, where they were previously rare. Hikers should follow all suggested precautions. But remember, there's a one-in-three-million chance of being attacked by a grizzly in Yellowstone.

BEARS & HIKING

When hiking in grizzly country, always stay alert and make plenty of noise on the trail. Never hike after dusk. While grizzlies have a highly acute sense of smell, they may not catch your scent if you approach from downwind. Some hikers wear 'bear bells' to announce their approach, but bears are better able to hear deeper sounds such as shouting or clapping. The human voice is effective: while some prefer show tunes, many shout, 'Hey, bear!' when approaching a blind corner.

If you encounter a bear at close range:

➡ Do not run – bears can easily outrun humans and will instinctively pursue a fleeing animal.

➡ Do not drop your pack as a decoy – this may teach the bear that threatening humans procures food.

➡ Back away slowly, talking soothingly to the bear while avoiding direct eye contact.

➡ Bears very often 'bluff charge' an intruder, veering away at the last instant.

Using a pepper spray (p256) may deter a charging bear. But if an attack ensues:

➡ Play dead.

➡ Lie down and pull your knees against your chest, and (if not wearing a large backpack) pull in your head and shield your neck with your hands.

➡ In most cases the bear will eventually leave the scene once assured that you present no danger.

➡ In extremely rare cases, grizzly bears with clear predatory intent have attacked humans. Such attacks tend to occur around campsites at dusk or during the night, and are the only time when you should fight back against an aggressive grizzly.

BEARS & FOOD

Bears are obsessed with food and rarely 'unlearn' knowledge acquired in finding it. In the past, Yellowstone's bears were regularly fed and given access to garbage dumps while tourists watched in grandstand seating. While this tradition has ceased, visitors are unnecessarily careless and the problem persists.

Conditioned to associate humans with food, large numbers of 'habituated' bears have harassed picnickers or aggressively raided camps. Nowadays, even mildly troublesome bears are usually destroyed. Don't let your carelessness result in the death of one of these magnificent creatures.

➡ Never leave food unattended, even in a backpack.

➡ Use the bear boxes at developed campgrounds or lock food in your car.

➡ Never store food or eat in your tent.

➡ Don't sleep in clothes worn while fishing or cooking.

➡ Don't camp downwind of your food stash.

In Yellowstone National Park, backcountry campers must hang food and scented items such as garbage, toothpaste, soap and sunscreen at least 10ft above the ground, 4ft from trunks and 200ft from their tents. Carry a robust stuff-sack attached to a 35ft length of rope. First weight the sack with a rock and throw it over a high, sturdy limb at least 4ft from the tree trunk. Gently lower the sack to the ground with the rope, stash everything with food smells and perfumes, and raise the sack back up close to the tree limb. Finally, tie off the end of the rope to another trunk or tree limb well out of the way. Backcountry campgrounds usually supply a food pole, which simplifies the process.

Grand Teton National Park requires backpackers to use approved bear-resistant canisters instead of hanging food. Backcountry permitting locations currently loan canisters for free.

Bison, Moose, Mountain Lions & Wolves

A too-common sight in Yellowstone involves watching enthusiastic visitors edge toward a seemingly tame, fuzzy bison for an exclusive photo op. Not a good idea. These 2-ton creatures can sprint at 30mph and have actually harmed more visitors

WHICH BEAR IS THAT?

TYPE	COLOR	BODY	FACE	TRACKS	AGILITY
Grizzly bears	blonde to black	larger with distinctive shoulder hump	dish-shaped face with short, rounded ears	long, straight front claws (2-4in)	can't climb trees well
Black bears	blonde to black	no shoulder hump	straight profile from nose to ears; tall, pointed ears	short, curved front claws (1-2in)	climb trees

than bears have. In the summer of 2015 alone there were four bison attacks in under two months. The message is clear: this is selfie suicide!

Moose usually flee intruding humans but if a moose feels cornered or otherwise threatened, it may suddenly charge. Moose cows with calves are especially dangerous, as they will aggressively defend their young. Moose can inflict severe injuries by striking out with their powerful front hoofs.

Your chances of encountering an aggressive mountain lion remain extremely small, but as humans encroach on their territory attacks appear to be on the increase. Avoid hiking alone in prime mountain-lion habitats. Keep children within view at all times. If you happen to encounter a mountain lion, raise your arms and back away slowly. Speak firmly or shout. If attacked, fight back fiercely.

There have been no reliable documented cases of fatal wolf attacks on humans for over a century. Attacks on humans by wild wolves are believed to be attributable to either rabies infection or habituation – when a wolf has lost its fear of people.

If you stay aware and keep a respectful distance from all wildlife, most encounters will be avoided.

Bites & Stings
LEECHES

Sometimes present in lakes, leeches attach themselves to your skin to suck your blood. Salt or a lit cigarette end will make them fall off. Do not pull them off, as the bite is then more likely to become infected. Clean and apply pressure if the point of attachment is bleeding.

MOSQUITOES

Mosquitoes can be a major irritant in early and mid-summer (until around mid-August), so remember to carry mosquito repellent. The most effective sprays contain DEET (the higher the per-

---

BEAR JAMS

For some reason, perfectly reasonable adults lose all their sense when sighting wildlife: it's happened to us and it will probably happen to you. Rubbernecking at wildlife doesn't just cause traffic jams; along with speeding, it's the main cause of more than 600 annual vehicular accidents in Yellowstone.

Trust us when we tell you, the bear, bison or moose you're stalking won't be the last one you see in the park. If you absolutely must get that rutting elk snapshot, pull completely off the road. If there's no room to park, just wait for a better opportunity. Also, vehicles dispatch about 100 animals a year in Yellowstone, so watch your speed and the road, especially at dusk.

---

centage of DEET, the more effective the spray). DEET is powerful stuff and should be kept away from plastics. Citronella is a kinder (to the skin at least) alternative.

SNAKES & SPIDERS

In the history of the park there have been only two recorded snakebites. The prairie rattlesnake is the only poisonous snake in the region, found in the driest and warmest river areas of Yellowstone. There are some spiders with dangerous bites but antivenins are usually available.

For snakebites, immediately apply a reverse syringe (Sawyer Extractor). Keep the victim calm and still, wrap the bitten limb tightly and immobilize with a splint. Get the victim to a doctor as soon as possible.

TICKS

Ticks may be present from mid-March through July. Always check all over your body if you have been walking through a potentially tick-infested area, as ticks can cause skin infections and other more serious diseases. Ticks are most active from spring to autumn, especially where there are plenty of sheep or deer. They usually lurk in overhanging vegetation, so avoid pushing through tall bushes if possible.

To remove, press down around the tick's head with tweezers, grab the head and gently pull upward; avoid

---

pulling the rear of the body. Smearing chemicals is not recommended.

Cold
HYPOTHERMIA

This occurs when the body loses heat faster than it can produce it and the core temperature of the body falls.

It is frighteningly easy to progress from being very cold to dangerously cold due to a combination of wind, wet clothing, fatigue and hunger, even if the air temperature is above freezing. If the weather deteriorates, put on extra layers: a wind and/or waterproof jacket, plus a wool or fleece hat and gloves are all essential. Have something energy-rich to eat and ensure that everyone in your group is fit, feeling well and alert.

Symptoms of hypothermia are exhaustion, numb skin (particularly toes and fingers), shivering, slurred speech, irrational or violent behavior, lethargy, stumbling, dizzy spells, muscle cramps and violent bursts of energy. Irrationality may take the form of sufferers claiming they are warm and trying to take off their clothes.

The early recognition and treatment of mild hypothermia is the only way to prevent severe hypothermia, which is a critical condition.

For mild hypothermia, get the person out of the elements, remove clothing if it's wet and replace it with dry, warm clothing. Give hot

GEOTHERMALS

You'll see plenty of signs warning you to stay on existing boardwalks and maintain a safe distance from all geothermal features. Thin crusts of earth can break, giving way to boiling water. Even warm springs can be dangerous; temperatures often fluctuate, sometimes dramatically, so what is safe one day may not be safe the next. About 20 people have died in Yellowstone's hot springs since the 1880s; some have backed into hot springs while taking photos, and more than one unknowing pet has jumped into a boiling pool.

The park service warns that spring waters can cause a rash and that thermophilic amoebas in the water can transmit amoebic meningitis (though there are no recorded cases). If you do swim in any of the parks, keep your head above the surface and don't take in any water.

liquids (not alcohol) and high-energy, easily digestible food. Allow the victim to slowly warm up – don't rub them.

FROSTBITE

This refers to the freezing of extremities, including fingers, toes and nose. Pain and swelling are inevitable. Signs of frostbite include a whitish or waxy cast to the skin, or even crystals on the surface, plus itching, numbness and pain.

For frostbite, warm affected areas by immersion in warm (not hot) water or warm with blankets or clothes (only until skin becomes flushed). Frostbitten parts should not be rubbed, and blisters should not be broken. Get medical attention right away.

Heat

DEHYDRATION & HEAT EXHAUSTION

Dehydration is a potentially dangerous and generally preventable condition caused by excessive fluid loss. Sweating combined with inadequate fluid intake is one of the most common causes of dehydration in trekkers, but other important causes are diarrhea, vomiting and high fever.

The first symptoms are weakness, thirst and passing small amounts of very concentrated urine. This may progress to drowsiness, dizziness or fainting on standing up, and, finally, coma.

It's easy to forget how much fluid you are losing via perspiration while you are trekking, particularly if a strong breeze is drying your skin quickly. You should always maintain a good fluid intake – a minimum of 3L a day is recommended.

Dehydration and salt deficiency can cause heat exhaustion. Salt deficiency is characterized by fatigue, lethargy, headaches, giddiness and muscle cramps. Salt tablets are overkill; just adding extra salt to your food is probably sufficient.

HEATSTROKE

This is a serious, occasionally fatal, condition that occurs if the body's heat-regulating mechanism breaks down and the body temperature rises to dangerous levels. Long, continuous periods of exposure to high temperatures and insufficient fluids can leave you vulnerable to heatstroke.

The symptoms include feeling unwell, not sweating very much (or at all) and a high body temperature (102°F to 106°F or 39°C to 41°C). Where sweating has ceased, the skin becomes flushed and red. Severe, throbbing headaches and lack of coordination will also occur, and the sufferer may be confused or aggressive. Eventually the victim will become delirious or convulse.

Hospitalization is essential but in the meantime get victims out of the sun, remove their clothing, cover them with a wet sheet or towel and then fan continually. Give fluids if they are conscious.

Snow Blindness

This is a temporary, painful condition resulting from sunburn of the surface of the eye (cornea). It usually occurs when someone walks on snow or in bright sunshine without sunglasses.

Treatment is to relieve the pain – cold cloths on closed eyelids may help. Antibiotic and anesthetic eye drops are not necessary. The condition usually resolves itself within a few days and there are no long-term consequences.

Sun

Protection against the sun should always be taken seriously. Sunburn occurs rapidly in the rarified air and deceptive coolness of the mountains. Slap on the sunscreen and a barrier cream for your nose and lips, wear a broad-brimmed hat and protect your eyes with good-quality sunglasses with UV lenses, particularly near water, sand or snow. If you get sunburned, calamine lotion, aloe vera or other commercial sunburn-relief preparations will soothe.

SAFE HIKING

Trail Safety Tips

➡ Allow plenty of time to accomplish a walk before dark, particularly when daylight hours are shorter.

➡ Study the route carefully before setting out, noting possible alternate routes and the point of no return (where it's quicker to continue than to turn back).

➡ It's wise not to walk alone. Always leave details of your intended route, the number of people in your group and the expected return time with someone responsible before you set off; later, announce your return.

➡ Before setting off, make sure you have a relevant map, compass and whistle, and that you know the weather forecast for the area for the next 24 hours.

➡ Be aware of whether the trail should be climbing or descending.

➡ Check the north-point arrow on the map and determine the general direction of the trail.

➡ Time your progress over a known distance to monitor further progress with reasonable accuracy.

➡ Watch the path – look for boot prints and other signs of previous passage.

Crossing Streams

Sudden downpours are common in the mountains and can speedily turn a gentle stream into a raging torrent. If you're in any doubt about the safety of a crossing, look for a safer passage upstream or wait. If the rain is short-lived, it should subside quickly. Late in the day, crossing may be essential.

➡ Look for a wide, shallower stretch (not a bend).

➡ Keep boots on to prevent injury.

➡ Store clothes and a towel in a plastic bag near the top of your pack.

➡ Unclip the chest strap and belt buckle of your pack (in case you have to swim).

➡ Use a hiking pole, grasped in both hands, on the upstream side as a third leg.

➡ With a companion, clasp at the wrist and cross side-on to the flow in short steps.

Fire

Fire danger in the Rockies varies from year to year, but is often extreme in July and August. Local park and USFS offices can advise hikers about forest fires, and fire warnings are usually posted at wilderness access points. For fire updates contact the park service, stop at a visitor center or check out official websites. Also contact the **National Interagency Fire Center** (☎208-387-5512; www.nifc.gov).

Lightning

Getting struck by lightning during a summer afternoon storm is a real possibility. Your best bet is to undertake long hikes early. Follow these tips during lightning storms:

➡ Avoid exposed ridges, open areas and lone trees.

➡ Move away from bodies of water or beaches.

➡ If camping, crouch on a sleeping pad with your arms around your knees.

Rockfall

Even a small falling rock could shatter your hand or crack your skull, so be alert to the danger of rockfall. Don't dally below cliffs or on trails fringed by large fields of raw talus. If you accidentally let a rock loose, loudly warn other hikers below. Mountain goats and bighorn sheep sometimes dislodge rocks, so be vigilant.

Rescue & Evacuation

Search-and-rescue operations are expensive and often require emergency personnel to risk their own welfare. Self-evacuation should be your first consideration.

For serious accidents or illness, seek help, but don't leave the injured party alone. If that's impossible, leave warm clothing, food and water. Leave a whistle and flashlight, and mark the position with something conspicuous.

SAFE CYCLING

Bicycles are subject to the same traffic rules as cars. While cycling is permitted on established public roads, parking areas and designated routes, it is prohibited on backcountry trails and boardwalks.

Yellowstone is not an easy place to bike. Road shoulders are slim and many a cyclist has been threatened by an encroaching RV mirror. Cyclists must be very aware. For this reason, it's best to bike early in the morning or after 6:30pm when traffic thins out. Drivers sometimes pass on hill crests, blind curves or in oncoming traffic. Wearing a helmet and high-visibility clothing, and using mirrors, is essential. Never use headphones while cycling.

Bison may be a hazard to cyclists. If you come upon some, dismount and walk far around them or wait for a vehicle to drive through (the bison will follow it).

Visitor centers will have additional information.

Road Conditions

Use extreme caution when cycling in the parks; roads are winding and narrow, and shoulders are either narrow or nonexistent. Vehicle traffic is heavy most of the time. There are no bicycle paths along roads. Road elevations range from 5300ft to 8860ft, and services and facilities are relatively far apart – typically 20 to 30 miles.

Cyclists should take advantage of shoulder seasons. A great time to bike is between October and mid-November, when there is little traffic and less wind. Springtime cyclists can enjoy some roads closed to motorized vehicles: cycling is permitted between the West Entrance and Mammoth Hot Springs from about mid-March (weather allowing) through to the third Thursday in April. Note that high snow banks from April to June can make travel more dangerous. August is typically the windiest month.

General road closures are posted at www.nps.gov/yell/planyourvisit/hours.htm.

Behind the Scenes

SEND US YOUR FEEDBACK

We love to hear from travelers – your comments keep us on our toes and help make our books better. Our well-traveled team reads every word on what you loved or loathed about this book. Although we cannot reply individually to postal submissions, we always guarantee that your feedback goes straight to the appropriate authors, in time for the next edition. Each person who sends us information is thanked in the next edition – the most useful submissions are rewarded with a selection of digital PDF chapters.

Visit **lonelyplanet.com/contact** to submit your updates and suggestions or to ask for help. Our award-winning website also features inspirational travel stories, news and discussions.

Note: We may edit, reproduce and incorporate your comments in Lonely Planet products such as guidebooks, websites and digital products, so let us know if you don't want your comments reproduced or your name acknowledged. For a copy of our privacy policy visit lonelyplanet.com/privacy.

OUR READERS

Many thanks to the travelers who used the last edition and wrote to us with helpful hints, useful advice and interesting anecdotes:

Shobhan Agarwal, Julio Balthazar, Neil Dunford, Angela McLean, Amanda Supple

AUTHOR THANKS

Bradley Mayhew

Thanks to the ever-professional Carolyn McCarthy for her assistance, and to my wife, Kelli, who has shared many hikes and trips with me across the Yellowstone region.

Carolyn McCarthy

Many thanks to those who helped support my trip and the writing process, especially co-author Bradley Mayhew. Kristen MacConnell,

Debbie and Kevan were stellar companions on the trail. Thanks once more to Drew for the canoe tour of Leigh Lake. My gratitude goes out to Jackie Skaggs, a parks service wonder, as well as Sue Muncaster and Christian Santelices. The Climbers' Ranch continues to be an incredible resource. For Tara Breed, who will always be in the mountains.

ACKNOWLEDGMENTS

Climate map data adapted from Peel MC, Finlayson BL & McMahon TA (2007) 'Updated World Map of the Köppen-Geiger Climate Classification', *Hydrology and Earth System Sciences,* 11, 163344.

Cover photograph: Bison, Grand Teton National Park, Drew Rush/Robert Harding.

THIS BOOK

This 4th edition of Lonely Planet's *Yellowstone & Grand Teton National Parks* guidebook was written and researched by Bradley Mayhew and Carolyn McCarthy. They also wrote the previous edition. This guidebook was produced by the following:

Destination Editor
Alexander Howard
Product Editors Carolyn Boicos, Martine Power
Senior Cartographer Alison Lyall
Book Designer Wendy Wright
Assisting Editors Andrew Bain, Anne Mulvaney, Charlotte Orr, Kirsten Rawlings

Cartographers Mark Griffiths, Gabe Lindquist
Cover Researcher Naomi Parker

Thanks to Joel Cotterell, Melanie Dankel, Grace Dobell, Andi Jones, Claire Naylor, Karyn Noble, Ellie Simpson, Victoria Smith, Luna Soo, Lauren Wellicome, Tony Wheeler, Clifton Wilkinson

Index

Map Legend

Sights
- Beach
- Bird Sanctuary
- Buddhist
- Castle/Palace
- Christian
- Confucian
- Hindu
- Islamic
- Jain
- Jewish
- Monument
- Museum/Gallery/Historic Building
- Ruin
- Shinto
- Sikh
- Taoist
- Winery/Vineyard
- Zoo/Wildlife Sanctuary
- Other Sight

Activities, Courses & Tours
- Bodysurfing
- Diving
- Canoeing/Kayaking
- Course/Tour
- Sento Hot Baths/Onsen
- Skiing
- Snorkeling
- Surfing
- Swimming/Pool
- Walking
- Windsurfing
- Other Activity

Sleeping
- Sleeping
- Camping

Eating
- Eating

Drinking & Nightlife
- Drinking & Nightlife
- Cafe

Entertainment
- Entertainment

Shopping
- Shopping

Information
- Bank
- Embassy/Consulate
- Hospital/Medical
- @ Internet
- Police
- Post Office
- Telephone
- Toilet
- Tourist Information
- • Other Information

Geographic
- Beach
- Gate
- Hut/Shelter
- Lighthouse
- Lookout
- Mountain/Volcano
- Oasis
- Park
- Pass
- Picnic Area
- Waterfall

Population
- Capital (National)
- Capital (State/Province)
- City/Large Town
- Town/Village

Transport
- Airport
- BART station
- Border crossing
- Boston T station
- Bus
- Cable car/Funicular
- Cycling
- Ferry
- Metro/Muni station
- Monorail
- Parking
- Petrol station
- Subway/SkyTrain station
- Taxi
- Train station/Railway
- Tram
- Underground station
- • Other Transport

Note: Not all symbols displayed above appear on the maps in this book

Routes
- Tollway
- Freeway
- Primary
- Secondary
- Tertiary
- Lane
- Unsealed road
- Road under construction
- Plaza/Mall
- Steps
- Tunnel
- Pedestrian overpass
- Walking Tour
- Walking Tour detour
- Path/Walking Trail

Boundaries
- International
- State/Province
- Disputed
- Regional/Suburb
- Marine Park
- Cliff
- Wall

Hydrography
- River, Creek
- Intermittent River
- Canal
- Water
- Dry/Salt/Intermittent Lake
- Reef

Areas
- Airport/Runway
- Beach/Desert
- Cemetery (Christian)
- Cemetery (Other)
- Glacier
- Mudflat
- Park/Forest
- Sight (Building)
- Sportsground
- Swamp/Mangrove

OUR STORY

A beat-up old car, a few dollars in the pocket and a sense of adventure. In 1972 that's all Tony and Maureen Wheeler needed for the trip of a lifetime – across Europe and Asia overland to Australia. It took several months, and at the end – broke but inspired – they sat at their kitchen table writing and stapling together their first travel guide, *Across Asia on the Cheap*. Within a week they'd sold 1500 copies. Lonely Planet was born.

Today, Lonely Planet has offices in Franklin, London, Melbourne, Oakland, Beijing and Delhi, with more than 600 staff and writers. We share Tony's belief that 'a great guidebook should do three things: inform, educate and amuse'.

OUR WRITERS

Bradley Mayhew

Yellowstone National Park, Around Yellowstone An expat Brit, Bradley currently calls Yellowstone County, Montana home and hikes the parks and nearby Beartooth Plateau every chance he gets. Half a lifetime of travel through Central Asia, Tibet and Mongolia has made him feel quite at home in Big Sky country. He was the coordinating author of the first three editions of this guide and is the coordinating author of many Lonely Planet guides, including *Tibet, Bhutan, Nepal, Trekking in the Nepal Himalaya* and *Central Asia*. See what he's currently up to at www.bradleymayhew.blogspot.com. Bradley also wrote the Plan section, and Clothing & Equipment and Directory A–Z chapters.

Read more about Bradley at:
http://auth.lonelyplanet.com/profiles/nepalibrad

Carolyn McCarthy

Grand Teton National Park, Around Grand Teton When not roaming the Tetons with an eye out for grizzly scat, Carolyn can be found in Patagonia. She has contributed to more than 30 titles for Lonely Planet, including *Trekking in the Patagonian Andes, Zion & Bryce Canyon National Parks, Chile, Argentina* and *Peru*. She has written for *National Geographic, Outside* and *Boston Globe*, among other publications. She also teaches travel writing at Grub Street in Boston. Follow her adventures on Instagram @masmerquen and Twitter @roamingMcC. Carolyn also wrote the Understand section, and Transportation and Health & Safety chapters.

Published by Lonely Planet Publications Pty Ltd
ABN 36 005 607 983
4th edition – Apr 2016
ISBN 978 1 74220 743 8
© Lonely Planet 2016   Photographs © as indicated 2016
10 9 8 7 6 5 4 3 2
Printed in China